WRITING AND LIFE

A Rhetoric for Nonfiction with Readings

WRITING AND LIFE

A Rhetoric for Nonfiction with Readings

Don Knefel

Loras College

HOLT, RINEHART AND WINSTON

New York   Chicago   San Francisco   Philadelphia
Montreal   Toronto   London   Sydney
Tokyo   Mexico City   Rio de Janeiro   Madrid

Library of Congress Cataloging in Publication Data

Knefel, Don.
  Writing and life.

  Includes index.
  1. English language—Rhetoric. 2. College readers.
I. Title.
PE1408.K688   1986   808'.0427   85-7602

ISBN 0-03-001503-0

CBS COLLEGE PUBLISHING
Holt, Rinehart and Winston
The Dryden Press
Saunders College Publishing

For Mary Anne and John

PREFACE:
TO INSTRUCTORS

Writing and Life: A Rhetoric for Nonfiction with Readings argues for a different view of composition. It redefines the traditional boundaries of college writing, placing it within the broad context of nonfiction and introducing students to aims and forms beyond those of the literary essay. While it keeps what is useful about traditional rhetoric, the book avoids exclusive attention to modes or patterns of discourse. Instead of concentrating on description, comparison, process analysis, and so on, as ends in themselves, *Writing and Life* assumes that the controlling influence in any writing task is its purpose, and that writers select forms and strategies, and engage processes, to suit the aims they have in mind.

The book isn't just a writing teacher's pet theory, however. It is based on experience, especially with students early in their writing education, for whom writing is often a vague, mysterious, and subjective thing, largely guesswork—trying to figure out what the teacher wants without a concrete, practical sense of context or meaning. *Writing and Life* tries to show that writing shares much with other ordinary activities, that it comes from the same real-world forces that shape any undertaking. The book is built from three such elements—*purpose*, *form*, and *process*—and each writing situation for study and practice expresses the meeting of these elements. Each task is a realistic example of commonplace nonfiction, of the real meeting of writing with life.

This is, above all, a writing book. It is designed to help students master the writing process—to become more able, intelligent, and commanding writers. The book has a second purpose, also, upon which the first rests: to let nonfiction enter the college curriculum, not just as personal and critical essays but as a range of genres—a literature—as much a part of life as short stories, novels, poems, and plays. As an introduction to the world of nonfiction, *Writing and Life* offers students a framework, a meaningful context, for their own college reading and writing.

Here is an overview:

Part One introduces students to the world every writer inhabits: the reasons people write, the writing process, the forms of nonfiction, and the standards writers use to assess their own and others' work. In addition, Part One starts students thinking, talking, and writing immediately through exercises and discussion/writing topics in preparation for the following chapters.

Part Two explains nonfiction's most basic purpose, conveying information, through three essentially different forms: *reports* (communicating facts), *essays* (making a point), and *narratives* (telling a story). Each of these is covered in a separate chapter, and each chapter contains a full discussion of how purpose, form, and process work together. Beginning with Part Two, as well, each chapter includes readings, in addition to exercises, discussion questions, and writing suggestions.

Part Three builds upon Part Two as it turns to a more complex purpose: writing to analyze or explain information. Here the focus is chiefly on the essay, starting with a presentation of rhetorical methods in the context of analytical thinking and writing. Part Three also includes a chapter on *combining* rhetorical strategies in a single essay, as well as a detailed illustration of the analytical writing process as it evolves from an initial problem or question. Part Three concludes with a chapter on using narrative form for an analytical aim.

Part Four addresses the purpose of changing readers' minds or actions, with chapters devoted to argumentative, critical, and persuasive essays. The discussions in Part Four continue to expand those of earlier chapters, too, showing how writing to convince depends on sound information and analysis.

Part Five considers the personal or expressive aim in nonfiction, with chapters on the essay and narrative forms, as well as a final one on writing to entertain. Instructors who wish to begin with personal essays and stories will find it easy to use this section early in their courses.

Part Six treats the research paper as a multi-purposed, extended essay with an analytical or argumentative emphasis. It includes discussion of the research-writing process, using sources, and documentation, and it contains two student papers (a short, critical essay and a longer, analytical term paper) as models.

Writing and Life has a number of features that should add to its appeal. Its 17 chapters comprise a program for English composition that provides a year's work. For advanced or one-semester courses, the book offers an even greater freedom for instructors to select and emphasize certain features as they desire. Moreover, this text is fully suited to upper-level courses in creative nonfiction writing, now becoming increasingly popular on college campuses.

The book contains two separate but related tracks of study: the *essay* track, with nine writing units, each a distinct application of the essay form (Chapters 6, 8, 9, 11, 12, 13, 14, 16, and 17); the *narrative* track, with four writing units for story application (Chapters 7, 10, 15, and 16). The report-writing unit (Chapter 5) discusses fact-gathering methods also useful in the subsequent chapters.

In addition, *Writing and Life* places much emphasis on *process* and gives clear instructions to students on how to get started, develop ideas and plans, shape structures, read critically, and make revision vital to all of one's writing. Likewise, attention to *audience* throughout the text shows revision to be practical, a matter of content and structure as well as style.

To encourage students to write actively, I have included nearly 200 exercises and writing suggestions (with many more specific topics) that often call for interviewing and observation to gather material. The assignments in this book are designed to challenge students to write about life in ways that stretch their minds, that depart from established routines and give them new writing experiences. And because their work always occurs in a context of purpose, form, and audience, students have specific limits within which to discover and build pieces of nonfiction. Such limits are the kind professional writers face all the time, and they help channel students' energies toward greater concreteness and control.

Last, I have tried to select readings that are clear examples, easily imitated, and enjoyable, lively, thoughtful nonfiction in their own right. Because I intend the book as a writing text and introduction to a form of literature, I've included works of representative nonfiction writers from a variety of disciplines, as well as a number of contemporary classics. Also, several excellent student authors appear in these pages.

I hope this book is a commonsense alternative for teachers, one that will help us convince students that writing really matters, that it is more than a technical process or an academic requirement: that it can be the most important and lasting foundation of one's education, and a valued part of one's life. Most of all, I hope it will give students better reason to enjoy writing—to see beyond its difficulties to its enduring rewards.

Acknowledgments

I would like to thank the many who helped this book come to be.

From the beginning, the following writing teachers offered much useful criticism and support. I am grateful to Kathleen Bell, University of Miami; Roger Bresnahan, Michigan State University; Charles Dodson, University of North Carolina, Wilmington; Dorothy Guinn, Arizona State University; Richard Halstead, Terra Technical College; Nevin Laib, Texas Tech University; and Eileen Lundy, University of Texas at San Antonio.

For help with biographical research, thanks to Mary Faino Timmer, Loras College. For her contribution to Part Six, thanks to Mary Anne Knefel, University of Dubuque.

I am especially indebted to the staff of Holt, Rinehart and Winston. Working with Maruta Mitchell (project editor), Kate Morgan (developmental editor), and Charlyce Jones Owen (English editor) is a great pleasure. All have been wonderfully kind and supportive. To Charlyce Owen, an extra vote of thanks for her willingness to take a chance, and for her confidence.

The following students generously allowed their work to appear here, and, with too many others to name, have made teaching a delight: Joan Hall, Sharon Hayden, Janet Kiefer, Kathleen Kilnoski, Mike Miller, Eric Schwister, Randy Wakitsch.

I would also like to express my gratitude to my teachers at the University of Iowa and at Knox College, especially Robin Metz and the Knox English faculty, who made all the difference.

Finally, thanks to my friends and family for their support, and to my wife, Mary Anne, for everything.

CONTENTS

9 ANALYTICAL ESSAYS   188

12 CRITICISM   269

13 PERSUASION   292

THEMATIC TABLE OF CONTENTS

Personal Experience

Family Life

People

Behavior

Culture and the Arts

Language and Writing

Nature

Places

Current Issues and Events

Business and Commerce

Ethics

Science and Technology

WRITING AND LIFE

A Rhetoric for Nonfiction
with Readings

PART ONE

The Writer's World

1

REASONS FOR WRITING

WRITING IN LIFE AND IN COLLEGE

For as long as people have sent their children to school, they have faced a dilemma: Should the aims of education be practical or liberal? Should school emphasize training for specific fields and professions, or should it emphasize more general abilities—thinking, making critical judgments, solving problems, understanding the past?

Two different kinds of educational institutions have arisen in response. Vocational, technical, and professional schools emphasize the practical; liberal arts colleges emphasize the liberal. (Universities often contain both types in a single institution, but the distinctions between them remain.) Depending upon personal goals, students eventually choose one kind of school or the other.

According to the conventional wisdom, students who receive a practical education, and who graduate with degrees in business, engineering, nursing, and so on, have specific but narrow knowledge. They may be able to accomplish practical tasks, but may have little or no experience in the arts and humanities. Liberal arts graduates, by contrast, are said to have lots of general knowledge but few practical skills.

Does such a division of educational values make sense? Is it impossible for us to have both kinds of knowledge?

A student forced to make a choice between the practical and the liberal view is like a son or daughter asked to decide which parent he or she loves more. To deny either one divides the child's loyalties and unfairly separates him or her from a vital source of life.

There is a similar conflict of philosophy in the way we regard writing. From one perspective, writing is a practical skill. We master it through practice and the study of rules, and we learn how to execute certain forms— personal essays, research papers, critical arguments. The opposing school of thought sees writing more as a creative art. We become better writers by allowing the writing process itself to be a means of discovery, and the object of writing is less the mastery of forms than increased personal expressiveness.

But, again, is such a choice really necessary? Isn't writing both practical and creative? Isn't it both a skill and an art?

When we look at the real world of writing—what people produce every day in the course of ordinary experience—we find a huge assortment of forms: news stories, sales reports, instructions, letters, memos, poems, magazine articles, newspaper columns, book reviews, novels and short stories, professional studies, complaints, analyses, editorials, research reports, applications, planning proposals, humorous essays, autobiographies, biographies and histories, advertising copy, speeches. There is no end to the list. Some writing is purely practical (an interoffice memo, for example); some is purely creative or expressive (poetry, novels, and short stories). Most, however, fall between these two extremes.

In the real world of writing, we see an answer to the dilemma with which we began. By its very nature, writing is a blend of the practical and the creative. We always write with a purpose in mind, but work toward that aim through a creative process. By becoming better writers, we build a bridge between practical skill and creative thought and expression, and we help to unify the contending goals of our own education.

If it is true that we live in an environment of language—a "web of words"—how are we to make sense of this increasingly complex world of writing? By not losing sight of the human uses people make of language, of the reasons they speak and write to one another.

Language evolved because it was necessary; we needed it to make our way in the world. And the place of language in human life has not changed since the earliest moments of our attempts to speak. Language arises from the most basic, concrete features of our experience: the need *to convey information*, the need *to discover meaning*, the need *to influence the opinions of others*, the need *to give expression* to our own thoughts and feelings.

Whenever we speak or write, we do so in a real world of needs and purposes. But too often, when we study speaking and writing in the classroom, we can forget the human context in which they always take place. In this book, instead of viewing methods as if these were the goals of writing, we will look at methods as techniques or tools, not goals. For example, one common technique writers use is description—writing so that the reader receives a vivid impression of something. Description may be used in any number of ways: to evoke a sense of a place, a person or an object; to enhance the telling of a story; to create a mood; or to let the reader see the writer's feelings. Yet description, as an object of classroom study, is typically removed from its uses and made a goal unto itself. Students wind up writing descriptive essays about their tennis shoes, their dorm rooms, or other subjects for which there may be no real audience—not even themselves.

One of the guiding principles of *Writing and Life* is that writers—whether students or not—do not sit at their desks with the goal of practicing a method. Rather, they begin with a purpose or combination of purposes in mind, and they employ the methods available to them in order to achieve those purposes.

There is a problem, however. We cannot escape the fact that, in school, writing is a *course,* a program of academic study. And although writing is very much more than that, college composition courses can all too easily encourage students to think of writing as little more than a bureaucratic requirement. Composition class becomes something to be endured with the least possible degree of pain—and then fled.

The goal of *Writing and Life* is to encourage you to embrace writing, not merely endure it. Because writing is so basic, it is the most potentially useful, far-reaching element in anyone's education. When we willingly accept writing—its demands and its gifts—we unlock our own inherent capacities for growth.

When we write, we come to know ourselves, each other, and the world. We write to communicate an ever-increasing volume of information. We write to discover significance, to explain things to ourselves and others, to analyze and evaluate our products, our goals, our lives, our beliefs. We write to effect change in the world, to convince others of the rightness of our point of view, to move others to actions we believe to be correct. And we write to express our sense of humor, our hopes, our dreads, and our dreams.

DISCOVERY, PROCESS, AND PURPOSE

In recent years, many writing teachers have realized that writing must be taught not only as something toward which the writer works—a finished product—but also as a creative process of discovery. When we write, we reveal what we may not have known we thought or felt before we began to write. Composition scholars have broken the writing process into various stages in order to analyze and describe it. There is no question that writing unfolds through a process and that the process has distinct parts or stages. What is often left out in the teaching of the process, however, is the impulse behind it. What gets us started? What drives us to make the leap into the unknown of the blank page?

In fiction or drama, where characters act in situations, the audience almost always asks that characters have motives for their actions, and that these motives be understandable, logical, realistic. Characters who act without apparent motive are usually less interesting to us. The randomness of their behavior keeps us at a distance, keeps us from entering their point of view so that we can understand them.

Similarly, writing that has no apparent motive or purpose also seems random to us, pointless, needless. As readers, if we don't know what a piece of writing sets out to do, we are much less likely to devote our time to it. And as writers, working without a sound reason becomes an exercise in futility.

We might make an analogy between writing and the world of sport. Games are processes, too, often quite like writing, with advances, retreats, rallies, miserable setbacks. Few games are without a goal, however, and play is driven by the existence of the goal.

Norman Mailer, the novelist and nonfiction writer, likens writing to the sport of boxing, a warlike, combative process. He emphasizes the aspects of struggle in his use of the boxing metaphor. Whether struggle or play—writing is often both at once—the writing process proceeds toward an end. Without it, there can be little reason to begin.

FOUR PURPOSES

Almost all of the writing we do in the course of our daily lives fulfills one or more of four general aims or purposes. These are to inform, to analyze or explain, to convince, and to express. (This book considers only nonfiction, but fiction, poetry, and drama also fit the model as examples of expressive writing.)

1. To Inform

To communicate information clearly, accurately, simply, and directly is the most basic purpose of most nonfiction. News stories, business reports, the minutes of meetings, laboratory reports, case studies, newsletters, magazine articles, informative essays, technical descriptions—all serve this most fundamental purpose. When we write to inform, our goal is to convey our message to our audience efficiently, precisely, completely: from reporter to public, from organization to member, from employee to supervisor, from scholar to student, from friend to friend. Our world rests on a foundation of informative writing.

2. To Analyze or Explain

A second and closely related purpose of nonfiction builds upon the first: the need to discover meaning. Facts are neutral until we seek to understand them. When we analyze information, we do something to it or with it; we try to answer questions and to solve problems. When we analyze, we try to evaluate or explain the facts before us. Analytical writing addresses the questions "Why?" and "How?" in addition to the "What?" of informative prose. Examples of explanatory writing are common in the media, business, the sciences, and the professions as news analysis, employee evaluations, interpretations of data, product comparisons, analytical essays. Although the need to analyze or interpret information is a clear purpose of much nonfiction, analysis can also help achieve a third, more complex purpose.

3. To Convince

Conveying information clearly and accurately, and explaining or evaluating the significance of that information, prepare writers for another central goal of nonfiction: to convince readers, to influence them to change their opinions or actions. The prose we find in newspaper editorials, speeches, journals of opinion, argumentative essays, critical reviews, proposals, advertising, and propaganda aims to move us to a position different from the one we held before we started to read.

Writing that tries to affect the beliefs or behavior of its audience is usually classified either as argument or persuasion. In this book, we define *argument* as writing that uses logic and evidence to convince us. It may give information or analysis, but it takes a stand; it attempts to show us why we should agree or change our minds. Writing that considers the merits or flaws of literary works, films, plays, musical performances, architectural projects or other creations, ideas and values is called criticism, and it is a form of argument. By the term *persuasion,* we mean writing that may use methods other than logic, such as appeals to the reader's emotions or sense of right and wrong.

Informative, analytical, and argumentative writing form the bulk of most college prose. These three purposes often work together, as in library research papers, yet each remains distinct.

4. To Express

There is a fourth basic aim of nonfiction, a purpose somewhat less practical than the first three, and one that has much in common with the genres of imaginative writing—fiction, poetry, and drama. When we write because we feel compelled to say something, we are writing expressively. Much informal nonfiction, from personal essays, autobiographical memoirs, human interest stories, to "thought" pieces, columns, humorous essays and entertainments, can be called writing for its own sake. It expresses the writer's feelings, thoughts, experiences; or it amuses or delights us, makes us laugh or cry.

Expressive nonfiction is probably the most difficult to do well, but it may also be the most satisfying. It may be the most freeing to our creative energies, but it also asks the most of our honesty, intelligence, and sensitivity. To write expressively, we must be willing to encounter ourselves, sometimes in ways that may disturb us. We may come face-to-face with parts of ourselves that we tend to ignore, or we may dredge up memories that we may have worked hard to bury. When we write to express our-selves, however, we experience our nature in a unique way: We become conscious of ourselves—our thoughts, our feelings, our lives. We discover that writing is a process of education, but that we are our own teachers.

With these four clear, basic purposes in mind, college writers can open themselves to the writing process—its accidents and mysteries—while at the same time having a means of channeling their ideas, discoveries, and plans.

THE ASSUMPTIONS OF THIS BOOK

Writing and Life is based on the belief that most of the writing people do, whether in business, the sciences, the professions, the media, or the aca-demic world, begins with the need to achieve a specific goal. We assume that writers write to fulfill one or more of the basic purposes outlined above, and that the strategies and methods writers use are not ends in themselves but tools for serving their objectives.

We assume, also, that the writing process is open-ended, that it tosses up all sorts of surprises as it unfolds, but that writers decide what they will keep—which accidents they can use and which they should ignore—as a function of their intention. The purpose of a piece of writing determines much about it, limits its possibilities, but thereby helps the writer keep control of its growth and final form.

Last, we assume that learning to write good, clear, precise, effective prose—prose that sets out to do something and then does it—is an essen-tial part of one's education. The mastery of writing opens doors, no matter what the field, whether in the workplace, at school, at home, or at large. By becoming better writers we can become more thoughtful and creative, more expressive and intelligent, and better able to achieve the goals we set for ourselves.

FOR DISCUSSION OR WRITING

1. Of the kinds of writing you've done, which give you the most pleasure? Do you keep a diary or journal of your private life? If so, what does writing for yourself alone provide you? (It may be that such writing is freer—that no one supervises or judges it.) Does private writing help you to work through problems? Does it help you find out what you think or feel about something? Similarly, if you enjoy writing letters to friends or family, what makes *writing* special—different, say, from talking on the

telephone? (One student answered this question by saying he liked to get mail back.) Do you write short stories, poems, songs, satirical pieces? What seems to be the motive behind these attempts?

2. What is the most satisfying single piece of writing you have ever produced? Was it written for class, on the job, for private use, for publication in a student or other type of paper or magazine? What was it about the writing situation—your purpose, the audience or reader you wrote for, and what you ended up saying—that made the project pleasing to you? How much of the pleasure was a result of your own engagement in the work of writing, and how much due to your readers' responses?

3. Can you name an instance (or several) when writing about a subject helped you better to learn it? Can you describe the effect writing had on the learning process? On the other hand, have there been times when writing only seemed to get in the way of learning? If so, why do you think writing may have complicated the situation? Could the writing have been made to be more useful as a self-teaching tool?

4. What do you think are the main obstacles to your becoming a better, or more fluent or relaxed writer? Do these apparent stumbling blocks seem vague or easy to identify? What is the worst thing, for you, about writing? What is the best?

EXERCISES

1. From what you know (either directly or indirectly) about the following occupations, what kinds of writing tasks are associated with each?

Secretary	Congresswoman
Engineer	Corporate middle manager
Store owner	Accountant
Teacher	Doctor
Lawyer	Salesman
Nurse	Public relations person

2. In the following examples of writing from "the real world," what do you think is the main purpose of each?

Job application letter	A book or movie review
Instructions for assembling and using a home computer	A magazine article recounting a year of travel in Europe
Report of recent sales figures	Advertising copy
The President's State of the Union address	A humorous newspaper column
	Complaint letter
A biography of a popular sports personality	An article in an historical journal about the causes of
News story	the arms race
An interoffice memo announcing vacation schedules	A product evaluation

3.   Can you name other school- or job-related writing situations with which you are familiar? Why is writing necessary to accomplish the task?

4.   Examine a copy of your daily newspaper or favorite magazine. Which pieces of writing seek chiefly to inform? Which to analyze or explain? Which to influence your opinion or behavior? Which to express or entertain? Are the differences among the purposes of the articles fairly clear? Do some pieces seem to have a combined purpose—such as giving information and analyzing it as well?

5.   On a subject of interest to you, try to find examples of writing that attempt to fulfill each of the four basic purposes, such as an informative essay or report, an analytical article, an editorial, and an expressive personal narrative. For example, say your subject is "the high-tech society." You might be able to find (a) a report on a new consumer electronics show, (b) a newspaper column about the problem of computer literacy in colleges, (c) an editorial in favor of expanding present cable TV service, and (d) an autobiographical or humorous essay about a frustrating encounter with gadgetry.

2

THE WRITING PROCESS

SOME USEFUL METAPHORS

Each of us has a story to tell about the time we tried to write something and had such a frustrating, maddening experience that we decided, once and for all, that writing was something we could never enjoy, much less do well. We may think of writing as a kind of occult ritual, a mysterious, even alien, practice, mastered only by an egg-headed elite. Or we may view writing ability as a gift, something we are either born with—or not.

Certainly some writers are gifted. Most of us learn to write, however, even if we aren't particularly talented, and most of us can be much better than we are without feeling we must attain the rank of genius. How can we become better writers? By allowing ourselves to engage actively in the writing process, by taking it a step at a time, by letting the nature of the process take its course.

But what, exactly, is this process? How is it that someone can start with a blank sheet of paper and in time produce prose that is useful, effective, even memorable?

People who write for a living know that a written work evolves over time. It grows, develops, expands, contracts, and it eventually reaches maturity or fails to. Although some writers can work very fast and do little revising, most writing does not spring full-blown from the author's mind. Rather, it emerges.

Writing emerges through a process of gesture and revision. We make a creative gesture on paper—write a word, phrase, sentence, paragraph—and ask ourselves if it's what we want. Our initial gesture is the first vision of what we're trying to say. Asking if it's what we *want* is the *re*-vision of what we have written. The writing process moves us back and forth between these two positions, and it means always being open to the need for another look. In all the writing we do, we gesture and revise, and each revision becomes a new gesture that may call for further revising. The willingness to view writing as an open-ended process is the key to becoming a better, more successful writer—and the focus of much of this book. In the discussion that follows, we will look at writing and revising in terms of three other basic processes.

We can think of writing as a planned, directed process, like painting by numbers or assembling a kit; or we can think of it as a more spontaneous, uncontrolled one, like making up a ghost story off the top of your head. In fact, writing is both of these—directed yet at times uncontrolled, planned yet at times spontaneous. Writing is complicated enough so that no one metaphor completely describes it.

The metaphor of organic growth, the process of development from seed to mature life, is attractive as a way of understanding how writing works; sometimes a piece of writing does seem to take off, growing almost automatically. Still, any metaphor that helps us better understand writing must include the person doing the work. Three such metaphors—three among many—can give us a sense of how the writing process is grounded in, and very similar to, certain simple human activities.

Our three metaphors are:

1. Writing is exploring.
2. Writing is playing.
3. Writing is building.

Writing Is Exploring

It would be hard to imagine an impulse more basic to human life than the need to explore the world. As soon as a baby is able to focus its eyes, it uses them to search. After it learns to crawl, attempts at discovery multiply. Childhood is almost completely given over to exploration, and it forms the basis of all the learning we will do thereafter.

Adults, too, spend great amounts of time exploring. Men and women in all walks of life devote entire careers to seeking out new information, new technologies, new ideas, new products, new experiences.

Writing is exploration *because we don't know where it will take us.* (How many of us, when we start a sentence, always know how it will end?) The beginning of writing is like the beginning of a journey; we may have a specific idea where we want to go, but we rarely know ahead of time what will happen along the way. Writing is an attempt to map new territory, to launch an expedition that will lead us where we have never been before.

Say that you are visiting a strange city and that you have the afternoon free. Everywhere you walk is new to you. At first, your direction may be aimless, and you may even find yourself lost. But you keep walking, and before long you begin to sense the dimensions of the place. As you walk, you begin to feel less a stranger. You notice details, landmarks, a pattern. Soon enough you're confident that on your next visit you'll be able to discover even more, because you have begun to learn your way around.

Because writing is exploring, it is a process of learning about something new. Each sentence you start is a turn onto a new and unfamiliar street. Once in a while it will lead to a dead end; more often, it will take you down a path of thought to a new sentence, a new street. Soon enough, you will have started to become familiar with that new territory.

No effort at exploration is ever wasted. Even an afternoon of dead ends can be productive. At least you'll know not to go down those streets again.

The message? Write as if you are exploring—not with fear and uncertainty, but with openness, curiosity, excitement.

Writing Is Playing

The essence of play is imagination. For children, play is make-believe, a game of "what if?" This kind of play is creative; the players make up the game as they go along. It is play as experimentation—just about anything can happen.

As play grows more sophisticated, it becomes organized. Rules evolve and control the game. There still is room for invention, but only within established boundaries. Unfettered creativity turns to skill.

Play can also be a contest, however, a battle of strategies and good fortune, and a matter of performing well or poorly.

All of these elements of play are found in writing. Often, when we start to write, even when we have a clear purpose, we have no clear idea of what we want to say. Exploration should give us a few things to play with, but they may be of little use to us until we ask "what if?" What if I say this instead of that? What if I start this sentence a different way? What if I follow this line of thought a little farther? What if I junk this whole paragraph? What if I move these ideas to a new spot? What if I combine these other things? What if I ask the teacher if I can have an extension?

A second element of play, sticking to the rules, also happens in writing. Once we have begun, certain internal limits emerge from the actions we have already taken. Once embarked on a train of thought, we must try to stay on the track. Every piece of writing has its own logic, and our task as writers is to discover that logic or internal shape, and be true to it. Our playfulness and creativity then resembles the work of the sculptor, trying to find the best form for our material.

Writing is playing because it forces us to experiment, to not settle for the first thing that occurs to us. And, in a sense, this means that we are in a contest (remember Mailer's idea that writing is like entering the boxing ring?). If it is a contest, then, who is our opponent? It may be the very act of writing itself, or it may be our own resistance to the demands of the process. Perhaps a more positive way to view writing is as the contest of an athlete competing against his or her own best record. All efforts are aimed at bettering what the athlete already knows he or she can do. As with all competition, the object is not only to win but to play as well as we possibly can—to play seriously, carefully, and hard.

Writing Is Building

Not only do people explore the world and experiment with it, they produce from it the objects they need or want. The world we live in, and the one we take most for granted, is the one we build.

It would be an endless task to inventory all the objects made by human beings in our daily life. From the eraser at the tip of your pencil to the satellites in the sky, our world has been constructed, built from scratch. Think of your neighborhood, its houses and everything in them, its streets and sidewalks, its streetlights, telephone poles, and buried cables. Imagine Manhattan Island before the arrival of the Europeans, and now.

The impulse to build is true not only of engineers and architects. Writers have the same goal. Every piece of finished prose is a construction, an object assembled from the raw material of language and experience. It is *put together*. The writer, like any good artisan, should want to make something useful, sturdy, and attractive—something he or she hopes will last.

The process of building takes time, and it occurs in stages. If we trace these steps, we will see that the process of writing is similar.

First, we must determine our purpose. What do we intend to build, and why? We can't just start hammering boards together in the hope that a solid, well-made house will emerge. We must know, at least in a general way, what we want to accomplish.

Next, we make some preliminary sketches. What sort of house do we want? We may not know, exactly. First, we make a sketch, then another, and another. We may combine the drawings, keeping the features we like, dropping those we don't. How many rooms do we need? How large should they be? At this stage, we are trying to discover what we wish to build.

Once we have enough preliminary material, we can draft a tentative blueprint, trying to give a more formal shape to our early ideas. In the drafting of this more detailed picture, we continue to discover the nature of our project. Problems may arise; we forgot to put windows in the living room, or we made the kitchen too small. And on second thought, maybe we don't need three baths.

Equally important is our need, at times, to take a break from our work. When we return, refreshed, we are in a better position to evaluate what we've done so far. Distance has given us more objectivity. As we continue to shape our material, adding here, deleting there, we eventually come to a decision: We are satisfied, ready to execute our design.

Now we can enjoy the coming-to-be of our efforts. The work still demands care and concentration, more than ever, but now at least we know what we are doing. We can see it taking shape before our eyes. When we are finished, we can step back and inspect our work with pride.

Metaphors are metaphors; they are not literal descriptions. The writing process has a great deal in common with other creative activities, and these three metaphors do not give us the last word on how people write. But they do suggest three of the most basic elements in the process. Keeping them in mind can help remind us that writing is not something beyond our normal talents or abilities, but a process grounded in the ordinary, and one, therefore, that we can master.

THE PROCESS IN GENERAL

The writing process is a sequence of actions aimed at fulfilling a specific purpose. Whether we wish to inform, explain something, convince the reader to change his or her mind, or express ourselves, the writing we do will usually evolve as follows . . . unless we try to short-circuit the process through impatience, trying to finish before we've really started, thinking that the first draft might as well be the last. We begin with a goal in mind, and perhaps only a vague idea of how to achieve it. By opening ourselves to a process of thinking through writing, and writing as we think, however, we gradually emerge from the fog.

Our first writing may be fragmented and chaotic—random thoughts, notes, lists, words, phrases. A sentence or two might form but lead nowhere, and there may be more than one moment when we think nothing at all will emerge. We shouldn't worry. Beginnings can be very disorganized and yet quite productive. Our work is almost purely exploratory at this point, and we should not hold back from plunging headlong into the tangle of our own confusion. This isn't the time to worry about quality, organization, editing—all that comes later. For now, we should write whatever occurs to us and follow where it leads, digging up all we can before we step back to see what we've unearthed.

No one ever said the writing process was simple, and it soon grows more complex as we amass material. Before long, we will find ourselves evaluating what we've written, playing with some of its possibilities. Which of our ideas seem most promising? What would happen if we chose one and kept pushing it? What if we combined two or three? Gradually, our fragmented notes begin to lead us toward a tentative focus, a strong possibility. In a paragraph or two, we start to play it out, seeing where it might go. Is it worth staying with? Can it work? In the spirit of play, if we get stuck we try another approach, remembering that we're still early in the process, still discovering what we want to say, still playing with possibility.

As we write, exploring for material and experimenting with it, we build a structure of words. Slowly, one or more potential designs begin to take shape, and we see that in some mysterious way our random thoughts and fragments have (or at least have started to) become ordered, focused. We are on our way to a first draft.

It is important to note that the writing process is not as neat as any of our descriptions. We do not finish one stage and graduate to the next; if anything, we keep moving back and forth between stages—digging more here, fiddling there, dismantling designs and rearranging parts—until finally we come to some sense of completeness. We explore, play, and build all through the process—writing, revising, writing, revising. Unfortunately there's no perfect answer to the question "How do I know when I'm finished?" Some parts of our work may be complete and polished after only two drafts; others may require many rewrites before we feel satisfied.

As we move back and forth from writing to revising, we move between the roles of creator and critic. As we do, we find our ideas growing clearer, our language growing more precise, our design growing more logical and coherent. We find ourselves moving toward greater control, subtlety, complexity in our writing.

Finishing the process, as in any craft or art, requires us to make our work presentable. Editing, proofreading, polishing—checking spelling, grammar, punctuation—good writing cannot be complete without this final step. It is our parting gesture to our work, and our opening one to our reader. When we treat our work with respect, we treat our reader with it, too.

MASTERING THE PROCESS

Some professional writers tell us that they don't compose their works so much as record them, that writing for them is like listening to a voice. Writers who have these experiences tell us that once they become engaged in the creative process, they lose consciousness of themselves, that the process carries them along as if it has a mind of its own.

This feeling of being caught up, of being an observer or the instrument through which the process unfolds, is often described by writers—and by professional athletes, concert pianists, actors, scientists—as *flowing*. It is the feeling of one who has mastered the process through practice and study, of one who has learned how to be open to the possibilities that engagement in the process brings forth.

Yet how do we achieve such a sense of mastery? First of all, we have to *want* to achieve it. Is there anything else we can do?

We can let ourselves write.

This may seem a self-evident, even silly remark. Of course we have to let ourselves write. Easy to say, and no one would argue with it. Still, the greatest single obstacle to our improvement as writers is our avoidance of writing. If we can overcome this obstacle, we will clear our way to become more comfortable with, and more in control of, the writing process.

Is there any practical advice that can help us embrace writing and make the most of our encounter with it? Let's look again at our three metaphors and what they imply.

Curiosity and Courage

If explorers have one thing in common, it is a powerful curiosity, a real hunger for new experience. Along with curiosity, however, explorers must have courage, a willingness to take chances.

Curiosity impels us to ask questions, sometimes dumb ones, and to seek answers. We cannot be satisfied with what we know; we must want to know more.

We can use our natural curiosity as a way to help us write. Instead of starting a writing task with a sense of dread ("How am I ever going to do this?"), ask yourself: What is the most interesting feature of this assignment? How can I use it to teach myself something I didn't know before? Is there a way I can slant the problem toward my best creative potential?

Moreover, tell yourself that you are simply not going to worry about what happens in the early stages of writing. Have faith in your own intelligence and ability to discover; know that if you engage in the process freely, you will come up with something you can use. Believe that an honest and healthy curiosity will be a friend to you as you write.

Courage is also important. It is a strong word, and we don't typically think of writing as a brave or heroic undertaking. Yet trying to write anything worthwhile takes a certain amount of nerve—especially when we know we could be in for frustration and disappointment. It takes courage to leap if you know you might hit a stone wall.

Writing need not by nature be a painful process, but certainly it can have its painful moments. It may show us, first of all, that we have a long way to go before we finish. It can also reveal to us things we'd prefer not to know: An idea of ours might be half-baked, our facts might be incomplete, our logic might be flawed. We need a certain strength of character to face the truth about our own work.

On the other hand, we can never hope to grow and mature as writers without being willing to take risks. Writing seriously asks much of us, asks that we not shrink from its challenges.

Playfulness

All right, you say. Curiosity I can accept. Courage, too. But playfulness? Writing fun? *Impossible.*

True enough for many of us. Writing can never be fun if we're intimidated by it, in awe of it. We have been taught all these years that it is such grueling work, that it is so easy to make mistakes or to look foolish in a piece of writing.

Why aren't we as intimidated by other skills, such as learning to play tennis or the guitar? Those also take practice and hard work. Yet this hasn't stopped millions of people from making the effort. One reason must be that such activities do not frighten us off. Rather, they seem attractive to us and within our grasp.

By adopting a playful attitude toward writing, by letting ourselves enjoy it, we can shrug off our feelings of intimidation. Just as we don't expect our first attempts to serve a tennis ball or strum a song on the guitar to be perfect, so we shouldn't panic if our writing skills could use some work. *Relax.* Allow yourself the freedom to experiment. Encourage yourself to be inventive, even daring. And try to write at the limits, and beyond, of what you already know you can do. Don't settle for repeating yourself or trying to please the teacher. Please yourself first. Write what you think is right, and be prepared to support it. Become your own best audience. Push yourself, as you would in sport, to excel.

If you allow the spirit of play to enter the writing process, you may find that what was once pure drudgery is now exciting, enjoyable, rewarding. Freed of our feelings of anxiety, we can dive into the flow.

The Pleasure of Making Something

Finally, our willingness to be curious and to take risks, but to have fun while we're doing it, will bring us to the part of the process that can provide the real and lasting satisfaction of writing: a sense of accomplishment.

The building we do in writing can be a great source of pride and self-esteem. When we are engaged in the process of discovering, developing, and executing a piece of writing, when we struggle with the problems of content, form, style—and when we finally finish, having addressed these problems as best we can—we experience a very complex form of pleasure. Nothing else we do in life gives us this same feeling. It touches some vital part of our makeup. It is the pleasure of the artist, the composer, the artisan, the architect, and the engineer; and it is also the pleasure of the backyard gardener, the weaver, the model railroader, the amateur songwriter, the struggling poet.

By taking pride in our accomplishments in writing, we make it easier for ourselves to improve. Each well-made piece of prose we produce adds to our sense of mastery. Becoming a better writer takes patience, and it happens sometimes almost imperceptibly.

But it happens.

FOR DISCUSSION OR WRITING

1. What are some other ordinary activities that might be described through the metaphors of exploring, playing, and building? (*Some examples:* staging a play, preparing a sports team for an important tournament or play-off game, learning a new language, starting a business, making a friend.) Consider the similarities and differences in the way the creative process unfolds in these activities, and in the activity of writing. Try giving a detailed account of the creative process in one of your choices, and pay particular attention to the moments when useful surprises seem to come from nowhere.

2. Are there other metaphors or analogies you can think of to describe the creative (or writing) process? (*Example:* getting struck by lightning.) What do these figurative comparisons suggest about the way the process may work?

3. Think of some major accomplishment in your experience, such as working to win an award, mastering a skill or art (a musical instrument, for instance), or even overcoming a particular fear or doubt. What were the steps that led you to the finish line? Do you remember how you felt at the very start of the undertaking? (Did you even know you were at the start when you were?) Were there times in the process when you wanted more than anything to give it up—to chuck the whole thing for something else? What made you stick with it? How much of what you did was planned, and how much seemed to emerge from unplanned action? How did you feel when your persistence finally achieved results? Did you come to some final end to the process, or is it still going on?

4. Can you recall an instance when an overwhelming curiosity got the best of you? What was it that drew you forward to find out more? What was the experience like? What is the hardest thing about forcing yourself to act when you're not curious? Are there times when you can summon that feeling of wonder or thirst for knowledge even when you are not overwhelmed?

5. Can you name a time when you experienced the sensation of "flowing"? What activity were you engaged in? Was it a mental activity (such as playing chess), a physical activity (chopping wood), or a blend of both (playing a sport)? What seems to produce the feeling of the flow? Can you make it happen, or do you have to wait for it to arrive on its own? Are there more ordinary instances in everyday life when the experience of flowing takes place? (A smooth and spontaneous conversation might be one example.)

6. Have you ever made something of which you were especially proud? What was it? Did you enjoy the process of making it, or only the finished product? Do you think it is possible to transfer your sense of artistry from one activity, such as painting, to another, such as writing?

EXERCISES

1.   Writers use a variety of techniques for exploring their subjects. Among these are making lists, "brainstorming" (talking or writing in a stream-of-consciousness style, and writing down whatever occurs to you), outlining, and asking questions (especially the journalist's "who, what, when, where, why, and how"). All share the same goal: to get the writer writing.

As a whole-class exercise, choose a topic of current interest, such as the nuclear freeze movement, the debate over the quality of American public education, and so on; then divide up into small work groups. Your purpose in this exercise will be to explore the topic in an attempt to discover all you know (or wish to know) about it so that you can write an informative essay defining the central issue and its major points.

Select a member of each group to record, in brief, the ideas that will emerge from the discussion. Then, as a group, brainstorm for five to 10 minutes, talking freely and with curiosity about the topic, trying to unearth as much raw material as possible. (*Elapsed time:* 15 minutes.)

Now, try exploring individually for a while. First, the secretary of each group should read the list of points, with each member (including the secretary) selecting one to develop in writing. Then, for 10 minutes, each student should draft one or more paragraphs on the subtopic he or she has chosen. Try to get down as much as you can quickly. Concentrate on what you know or need to know to develop the point fully. (15 minutes.)

For the next 10 minutes, share your paragraphs and experiment with various ways of arranging them. Is there one or more that might serve as an effective or striking introduction? Which of the paragraphs seem to develop or support any single point or central idea? Is there one that might serve as a draft for a conclusion or wrap-up?

For the last few minutes of class, a member of each group (not the secretary this time) should read aloud the rough draft his or her team developed. (Admittedly, these may be *extremely* rough, perhaps confused and disorganized. However, take pains to note what you have discovered. Only a few minutes ago, the topic was just a vague, undefined phrase. How much closer have you come to a clearer understanding of the issue?) What similarities do you find between these drafts? What ideas seem to occur more frequently than others? Is there one draft that stands out as clearer or more comprehensive than the rest?

How difficult would it be, now that you have a first draft, to continue building toward a more detailed and polished final version?

2.   As another process exercise, each student should choose a topic and work alone this time. For 10 minutes, write whatever you can think of, whatever comes to you, without worrying if it will be useful. Then, for 15 minutes, select three of the best or most promising points you've jotted down, and spend five to seven minutes drafting a paragraph or more about each. After writing for a half-hour or so, stop and evaluate what you've got. Ask yourself which of your three tentative directions seems to be giving you the most potential—which seems to be open to development into a full, short essay? Choose your best bet and continue revising and expanding for another 10 or 15 minutes. At the end of class, compare your present working draft to your brainstorming notes.

3

FORMS OF NONFICTION

WHAT IS NONFICTION?

So far, we have talked about *why* people write (the four basic purposes) and *how* they write (the writing process). We now turn our attention to *what* they write.

Because the focus of this book is nonfiction, we will not consider the literary genres of fiction, poetry, and drama. These specialized forms have their own rules, different from those of nonfiction.

Just what, exactly, is nonfiction?

By its very name, nonfiction is a grab-bag. It is writing that is not imaginary or fictional. It can include everything from cookbooks and articles about boating to the essays of George Orwell and the works of Freud. The world of nonfiction contains writing in history, biography, economics, social and literary criticism, the natural and social sciences, as well as business and technical prose.

We define *nonfiction* as writing that aims to deal factually with the world, with people and places, events and ideas. Whether its purpose is informative, analytical, persuasive, or expressive, nonfiction addresses human experience directly. It attempts to shed light upon the actual world rather than to create an imaginary one.

THREE BASIC FORMS

Despite the great variety of subjects and approaches in nonfiction writing, three fundamental forms (each with many different applications) underlie most of the nonfiction we write in our daily lives. These forms are:

1. Report
2. Essay
3. Narrative

We will first consider the nature of each form, then the purposes to which each is best suited.

Reports: Communicating Facts

Reports collect, organize, and present information. They are objective, impartial, sometimes even anonymous. Whether as news stories, research summaries, survey results, case studies, reports occur in every walk of life: in science, industry, law, medicine, and, of course, school. Much of the information we receive through the media or on the job is in the form of reports.

When we write reports, we face several problems: What information are we to collect? How are we to collect it? What is the best way to organize it for our reader?

The answers to these questions can vary, depending on the specific requirements of reports in different fields. Generally, however, most reports follow these guidelines:

The natural boundaries of the subject determine which information pertains and which does not. For example, if the subject is this morning's chemistry-lab experiment, the report will be limited to a description of its materials, methods, and results. Similarly, if you are taking the minutes of your school's student senate meeting, only the formal deliberations of the session (not every, last, off-hand remark of the participants) belong in the report. No matter what the subject, the writer's job is to collect as much pertinent information as possible and then to select from this body of data the material deemed most important.

The methods writers use to gather facts can also vary. Depending on the scope and nature of the report, facts can be collected in one or more of four basic ways: research (studying the published or unpublished findings of others), interviewing (asking questions), direct observation, or experiment. (Each of these methods will be described in more detail in Chapter Five, "Reports.")

Determining the best way to present the information you have assembled is often a matter of selecting from among conventional or traditional formats. Standard structures (the news story is a familiar example) have evolved to avoid confusion and to help keep reporting objective and uniform. Sometimes, however, there is no predetermined format. Whether a report takes a conventional form or one geared to a unique situation, its organization must ensure that the facts be presented clearly, completely, and that the most important facts be given greatest emphasis. (More on this in Chapter Five.)

The audience for reports can be divided into two broad categories: general and specialized. Most of us are members of a general audience of readers. We read reports in newspapers and magazines, we view them on television, and we listen to them on radio. The subjects of reports addressed to a general audience are assumed to interest large numbers of people. Such reports, on everything from gardening to international rela-

tions, are presented in ordinary, nontechnical language. Specialized reports, on the other hand, are addressed to much smaller audiences—the
members of a club or organization, fellow scientists or researchers, business colleagues, and so on. These official or professional reports frequently
employ a language heavy in jargon, specialized terminology often incomprehensible to the general reader.

Most specialized reports, such as those found in business or the physical
sciences (including student lab-reports), are beyond the scope of this book.
The specialized *content* and *form* of these reports require study within specific disciplines beyond English or writing. The general audience report,
however, is well within the grasp of most writing students, so we begin
our discussion of informative writing with it (see Part Two, "Writing to
Inform").

Essays: Making a Point

As useful as reports are, they cannot accomplish what essays do best. This
separate form of nonfiction is better suited to certain of our purposes.

The term *essay* usually refers, as a noun, to the literary form: a piece of
writing with specific characteristics. The word *essay* is also a verb, however, meaning to put to a test or to make an experimental effort. This latter
definition tells us much about what essays are. An essay is a writer's attempt to discover significance, *to make a point.*

An essay, by nature, is an individual writer's encounter with a subject. It
is always personal—whether written from a first *or* third person point of
view—in the sense that we read the author's mind as he or she addresses
a subject.

It is possible, for example, for dozens of people to contribute to a report,
as in those issued by commissions and agencies. It would be impossible for
as many people to compose an essay, however. An essay reveals not just
the subject, as in reports, but the writer's attitudes toward the subject as
well.

The essay is a powerful form, or at least potentially so. Some of the most
influential documents in the Western tradition are essays. The Declaration
of Independence is a superb example, a few hundred English words with a
point that changed the course of history.

The essay is also the workhorse of college writing. It has applications in
every field of knowledge, and it is an ideal, natural form for analyzing
information and ideas compactly. The essay isn't only academic, however.
We see essays every day in newspapers and magazines, as columns, editorials, analyses, reviews, letters to the editor, arguments, personal commentary, and in books of essays such as those by Annie Dillard and Lewis
Thomas, which are sometimes bestsellers.

The essay is one of the oldest, most popular, and most useful forms of nonfiction. Whether it is as short as 500 words or as long as a book, the essay is as necessary to our writing about the world as is the report.

Although the essay is a very flexible form, it does have certain characteristics. Essays can be divided into two groups: formal and informal. Formal essays tend to follow more rigid structures, while informal essays may experiment with form in an attempt to shape themselves according to the unique demands of their subject.

Formal Essays

Every essay, whether formal or informal, has a central point, controlling idea, or *thesis*. In formal essays, this focus usually appears early, after an introductory passage that seeks to draw the reader in, to capture his or her interest. Some kinds of formal essays, however, reverse this structure, introducing the piece but leaving the thesis unstated. This technique creates a certain tension in the essay; the writer maintains suspense and encourages the reader to continue reading. At the conclusion of the essay, the controlling idea emerges and receives emphasis as the last thing the reader sees.

The advantage of placing the thesis early, on the other hand, is that the reader knows clearly what the essay will attempt to do. You can follow its development while keeping the thesis in mind as a sort of map. Complex or difficult subjects often demand this structure. Maintaining suspense for too long may only encourage the reader to stop reading.

Regardless of the placement of the thesis, the body of the essay supports, defends, or develops the main point. It gives a detailed elaboration, explaining the implications of the thesis, why it is true, what it means. It may give illustrations or examples in support of the main idea; it may show how the thesis is derived from detailed evidence. No matter what the body's means of development, its content must correspond directly to the content of the thesis statement.

Formal essays usually conclude with a paragraph or section clearly separate from the body. This final part typically sums up the writer's presentation, offers a prediction or recommendation, gives a final illustration, closes with a question—or in some way leaves the reader with an emphatic, unexpected, or memorable sense of the essay's thrust.

Informal Essays

Essays that are less "practical"—less informational, analytical or persuasive—but more personal, expressive, or experimental, sometimes abandon the strict conventions of the formal essay. They are more likely to blur the edges of the form, to abbreviate or omit introductions or conclusions, or to incorporate the techniques of storytelling, for example. Accomplished essayists may feel constrained by the traditional formalities and experiment openly with them, allowing for a more spontaneous or freer development. Humorous essays (such as Woody Allen's, in Chapter 16) are good examples of this kind of creative informality.

Most of the essays students write in college are more formal than not, and they are usually classified as either exposition, or argument and persuasion.

Exposition

In exposition, we seek to shed light on a subject so that both writer and reader can know it better, in greater depth, in finer focus. Exposition can range from informative essays on technical subjects (the nature of inflation, say) to analysis of general subjects (the effect of television viewing on children). When we write exposition, we seek to give a subject careful, detailed consideration.

Argument and Persuasion

The methods of argument and persuasion are aimed at influencing readers' opinions or actions, convincing them to change their minds.

In argument, the writer relies on logic and evidence to make a case. Attempting to keep the language reasonable and objective, the writer anticipates the likely counterarguments of the reader, and constructs what appears to be a flawless line of thought leading to an unarguable conclusion. The argumentative essay seeks to win the reader's agreement, or, short of that, at least the reader's acceptance that a valid point has been made.

As writing moves from the logical use of evidence, sound reasoning, and objective language to less logical, less rational, and less objective prose, it moves from argument to persuasion.

The techniques of persuasion appeal to our other side, our emotions, our subjectivity, our (at times) irrationality. This is not to say that persuasion is by definition dangerous or evil. It can appeal to our highest motives and qualities: sympathy for others, selflessness, generosity. It can also appeal, however, to the less noble in us, our weaknesses and our fears.

Most of the prose that attempts to affect our opinions is not purely either argument or persuasion, but a blend. Critics, for example, often find it hard to avoid colorful, subjective language in their reviews. Appeals to our emotions or sense of right and wrong also may have rational underpinnings.

Narratives: Telling a Story

Reports focus on information. Essays show us a subject and the writer's attitude toward it. Narratives give us a picture of human experience in the form of a story.

Each of these forms of nonfiction is a different way to capture or organize reality, and each corresponds to different features of our experience. Reports are necessary because we need to distill life into discrete units or bits of information. Essays are necessary because we need to make sense of the world. Narratives are necessary because they reflect and embody our direct experience of life.

The story is quite likely the oldest form of human expression. We understand the world through stories—the sacred texts of our religions, our history, our myths, and legends. The creation of the world is a story, and each of our own lives is one. People tell stories to each other in countless ways: across a campfire, on television, in the theater, in the newspaper, in short stories and novels, in films. Some of the stories we tell are true; some we make up. And some, as they are passed along over the years, seem to be both at once.

Narratives are concrete. They show us people in action, the details of life, the texture of experience. Whereas essays may approach abstractions directly, narratives approach ideas indirectly, in the context of events. Narrative puts the story first, and although it may include analysis and interpretation (history and biography, for example), the story is the foundation. While the essay usually makes a single point, narratives may embody a number of different themes or ideas.

Sometimes, however, writers combine the two forms to produce a hybrid: the narrative essay. Is the narrative essay mostly narrative or mostly essay? It depends. More often than not, one form or the other will dominate. It seems to make more sense, then, to regard each form as distinct, with its own techniques. Narratives may incorporate essaylike elements or passages while keeping their overall shape as a story with a beginning, middle, and end. Essays may incorporate narrative elements, such as scenes and dialogue, while still remaining essentially in the essay form.

Examples of narrative nonfiction abound: newspaper and magazine features such as human interest stories, travel pieces, memoirs; books of autobiography, biography, and history; and much general nonfiction about contemporary life.

We can divide narrative nonfiction into two broad categories according to the narrator's point of view: objective and subjective.

Writing in the Third Person

When we tell a story in the third person, we take the objective point of view, usually by writing as an impartial observer and leaving ourselves out of the action (even if we were present when it took place). As always, there are exceptions to this convention; it is possible to write about yourself in the third person. Generally, however, the objective point of view assumes that the narrator is not part of the story itself. Rather, he or she is the window through which the reader sees the story unfold.

Now we might ask, why must we detach ourselves—especially from events in which we were directly involved—and adopt this somewhat artificial attitude? It depends on the purpose we wish to fulfill. The truth of a story may be greater than our individual perception or experience of it. It may not be possible to tell a story fully or accurately from a personal point of view. In biography or history, for example, the writer tries to give a complete account of a person's life or a period of time. Unless the writer intends to produce a personal or subjective version, the demands of the informative purpose compel as much objectivity as possible.

One can argue that complete objectivity does not exist. Human beings are subjective by nature; they cannot escape their personal point of view. In absolute terms, this argument may be impossible to refute. Nevertheless, objectivity is a goal toward which we can move. We *must* move toward it in certain writing tasks, or we will place drastic, crippling limitations on our ability to use writing as a means of discovery and communication.

Writing in the First Person

When we write in the first person, telling a story as an "I" narrator, we openly acknowledge our subjectivity. We say to the reader: I am telling you this story as I know it and understand it; it may not be the only version, but it is mine. Take it for what you will.

First-person narration includes as part of the story the writer, who may or may not be the story's subject. We can write about others from a subjective point of view, or we can write about ourselves. A first-person narrative does not need to dwell on its being subjective; whichever point of view seems most appropriate, the story remains the focus of narrative.

Telling a story in the first person does not release the writer from the responsibility to be accurate, precise, and careful. The personal or subjective voice, the speaking "I," however, does allow for more informality. First-person narratives often use slang, colloquial language, the rhythms of ordinary speech to create a sense of oral storytelling. The very voice of a first-person narrator can give us a strong feeling for his or her character, and the voice itself may be an important part of the story.

(*Another exception:* It is possible to write in the third person with the same informality. This technique calls for a good deal of skill and self-assurance, as well as experience in the more traditional methods of narration.)

Whether told from an objective point of view or a subjective one, narratives give us life not as a compilation of information, nor as a specific analytical, argumentative, or expressive point, but directly, as it is lived.

APPLYING FORMS TO PURPOSES

These three forms—report, essay, narrative—are the three legs of the triangle of nonfiction. Each supports the others, yet each is distinct.

How are these forms suited to nonfiction's four general purposes? Parts Two through Five are devoted to a detailed answer: writing to inform, analyze, convince, and express through one or more of the forms.

For now, here is an overview:

All three forms can be used to convey information, although each form is best suited for certain kinds. When the information is technical or statistical, for example, the report form is usually most useful. Essays may also carry a good deal of hard information, however, in the service of the essay's thesis. Narratives, as they focus on the details of life, as they tell us what happened, also serve an informative purpose.

Although some kinds of reports contain sections devoted to analysis, especially on technical subjects, the essay is perfectly suited to the general purpose of analyzing, evaluating, or explaining information. Since the point of an essay is to discover significance, it is an ideal form for addressing problems or questions. Narratives, too, can serve an analytical purpose as writers interpret the subjects of their stories.

For argument, criticism, and persuasion—usually essays serve best, although narratives and reports, by the weight of their detail, can be powerful, if indirect, arguments. Certainly formal argument and criticism, however, require the essay form. Narrative can be an effective means of persuasion, too, by appealing to our concrete sense of life.

Expressive writing rarely employs the report form—except to parody it. When our purpose is to give expression to our feelings and experiences, or when it is to amuse or entertain our reader, we rely on essays and narratives for their flexibility and openness to the personal voice.

Most college writing is divided between reports and essays for the purposes of informing, analyzing, and arguing. The library research project, which combines these three practical purposes, usually in the form of an extended essay, is explained in Part Six.

A final word: It is a common experience for entering college students to be given a great deal of experience in writing personal or expressive short essays. When they leave their composition classes, however, it is unlikely that they will be asked to produce such prose for their courses in science, history, engineering, economics, psychology, or philosophy.

There are two results: Students are often poorly prepared for the practical demands of writing to communicate information effectively, analyze or address problems logically and clearly, and marshal evidence in a soundly reasoned and convincing argument. Moreover, they are often denied the opportunity to continue writing in a way that helps them to discover themselves, their values, and their hopes.

In this book we try to strike a balance between the practical, systematic goals of nonfiction and the opposite, the expressive and experimental. We hope that young writers will be encouraged, and will encourage themselves, to develop such a balance in the writing they do in school and on their own.

FOR DISCUSSION OR WRITING

1. What is the best or worst piece of nonfiction you've ever read? Why did you especially like or dislike it? What was its main purpose—to convey information, to analyze a problem or question, to change your mind, to express the author's thoughts, feelings, or experiences? Did the piece combine any of these purposes?

2. When you read nonfiction for pleasure, what's your first choice—news stories, columns, feature stories, how-to articles, biographies, editorials, personal essays, autobiographies? What is the purpose of most of your leisure-time reading?

EXERCISES

1. In the following writing situations, which form of nonfiction is best suited to each? Give your reasons.

- As a reporter on the student paper, you've been assigned to interview a guest lecturer and write up a short, informative article about the speaker's accomplishments, interests, current projects, publications, and so on.
- You are applying for a scholarship to your college's financial aid office. The competition is fierce, and you must make a strong case for your financial need and your desire to remain in school.
- In your volunteer work for a local or student politician, you need to produce campaign material that will help get your candidate elected. During a staff brainstorming session, it is suggested that someone write a sketch of your person's history as a civic or student leader and emphasize a record of increasing responsibilities.
- Your organization plans to take a poll of its members in the form of a questionnaire by asking their opinions on certain issues. It's your job to tabulate the results and write a summary of the findings.
- A recent case of student vandalism has provoked harsh measures by the administration. You believe the response is unfair, and you write a letter of complaint to the editor of the student newspaper.

2. Say that your purpose is to help convince an audience of your peers to act on some issue of social importance, such as child abuse, drunk driving, income-tax cheating, voter apathy, and so on. What kind of potential does each

of the three forms of nonfiction offer to serve your purpose? How might a report on the problem differ from an argument or personal essay? How might an essay differ from a narrative?

3.   Using examples from your own reading and job or school experience, list by purpose some of the types of nonfiction you're familiar with. What form does each take? Are the forms combined or mixed? (*Examples:* A play or novel summary would inform as a report. The written response in a history exam would analyze as an essay.)

Purpose	*Form*	*Example*
To inform	Report	_____
		_____
	Essay	_____
		_____
	Narrative	_____
		_____
To analyze or explain	Report	_____
		_____
	Essay	_____
		_____
	Narrative	_____
		_____
To convince	Essay	_____
		_____
	Narrative	_____
		_____
To express or entertain	Essay	_____
		_____
	Narrative	_____
		_____

4

GOOD WRITING

THE PROBLEM OF RULES AND STANDARDS

Here is an excerpt from a recent magazine ad for AT&T Communications (formerly known as the telephone company):

AT&T is in Antiques.
Who'd ever think of that?
The people of AT&T Communications.
   People who know business.
   We can help antique dealers use our AT&T Long Distance Network so that they can hold an auction with different customers in up to 58 different locations.
   Anywhere in the United States.
   Simultaneously.
   So they can find out immediately what the trade is willing to pay for a rare antique bowl.
   And any other items in the catalog mailed out beforehand. So their business, in effect, is national.
   And they can compete as efficiently as businesses many times their size and sales force.

Is this good writing? Before you answer, what guidelines will you use to decide? If we apply to this passage the conventional standards of written English, it's bound to come up short. What about all those sentence fragments and undeveloped paragraphs? And the redundancy! (Could the dealers hold an auction with the *same* customers in 58 locations simultaneously?) And what does the phrase "people who know business" mean? Don't we take it for granted that the people at AT&T, a business, know business?

Like beauty, good writing often is in the eye of the beholder. The upbeat, fragmentary, boastful copy of an advertising writer may sink the heart of an English teacher but please the agency executives and accomplish the ad's goal of arresting the reader's attention long enough to make a dent in it.

Here's another example, this one quoted by Richard A. Lanham in his *Revising Business Prose:*

The purpose of this project is to develop the capability for institutions of higher learning and community agencies and organizations to coalesce for the development of community services that would maximize the available resources from a number of institutions and provide communication and priority needs and the responses of the educational needs of a given community.

Good writing? Clearly, someone must think so. Perhaps the passage, with its labored, abstract wordiness, lifts the bureaucrat's spirits—but it should give the rest of us blurred vision and a headache. What does the sentence mean? What is its purpose? Who is meant to read it? What reaction is the author trying to elicit?

These two examples illustrate what might be called the extremes of public, workaday writing: oversimplicity on the one hand, and overcomplexity on the other. We find both types just about everywhere, and both exert a heavy influence on us as readers, listeners, and writers. Does either of these passages seem to have been written by a living, breathing person? If we read them aloud, do we hear a human voice?

By contrast, here is the opening paragraph of the late playwright Lillian Hellman's memoir *Scoundrel Time,* which tells of her encounter with the House Committee on Un-American Activities in the early 1950s:

> I have tried twice before to write about what has come to be known as the McCarthy period but I didn't much like what I wrote. My reasons for not being able to write about my part in this sad, comic, miserable time of our history were simple to me, although some people thought I had avoided it for mysterious reasons. There was no mystery. I had strange hangups and they are always hard to explain. Now I tell myself that if I face them, maybe I can manage.

Perhaps the one unshakable quality of good writing is its humanness, its genuine human voice. But beyond that, is there a set of standards against which we can evaluate our work? Or is the merit of a piece of writing just a matter of opinion?

Certainly language, as an expression of life, changes as life changes. What was correct and appropriate yesterday may seem ridiculous today. In addition, the problem of rules and standards may be magnified in modern life. Our language, so much a product of ethnic, cultural, and racial diversity, resists efforts to make it unified or systematic. It may be impossible ever to arrive at a static description of what is eternally proper, acceptable, desirable.

Moreover, we may hope that American English never will be without its loose ends, its mélange of voices and styles. When "Let's get married" becomes "It seems that a marriage ceremony should be scheduled with respect to our prior discussion and agreed-to future plans," it will be time to sell our typewriters and head for the hills.

Loose ends are one thing, utter chaos another. Aren't there some principles we can say will guide us in our efforts to become good writers?

There are, and they can be derived from concrete experience—from ordinary life.

SOME REASONABLE EXPECTATIONS

We have said that writing is an ordinary activity, rooted in experience, and so it makes sense for us to expect from writing no less a sense of quality or excellence than we would from some other common undertaking at which we wished to do well. For example, what do we expect from an amateur athlete or sports team? We expect seriousness, skill, energy, concentration, respect for rules and the code of sportsmanship. We expect players to meet the demands that sports and games place on them. If a sport, such as baseball, demands that players be able to throw, catch, and hit the ball, then we expect this without question; we wouldn't think *not* to expect it. We are outraged when athletes make more than their share of mistakes (everyone is allowed his or her share), because the nature of the game demands that mistakes be the exception, not the rule. If players play badly too often we say they don't belong in the game, and we even may stop thinking of them as players at all.

In any aspect of life, our expectations about the quality of our performance are based on the demands of the situation. Cooks aren't supposed to burn the food; plumbers aren't supposed to leave leaky pipes, or electricians hot wires or short circuits. But what are writers, even amateur ones, supposed to do? What characteristics should we expect to find in a piece of writing produced by a person who wants to do well at making nonfiction?

Because nonfiction is communication from writer to reader in order to achieve specific purposes, the demands it places on us as writers are just as specific. Four fundamental elements are always present in nonfiction, and each has concrete requirements based upon the practical, everyday necessities of human discourse. These four elements are: *content*—what a piece of writing contains; *organization*—the arrangement of the content, the design of a piece of writing; *style*—how a work says what it says, its language; *execution*—the physical or mechanical proficiency of a piece of writing, its grammar, spelling, punctuation, and so on.

Content

If we order something from the store, we expect all of it to be in the package when it arrives. With writing, similarly, we have a right to expect *completeness*—that everything necessary to accomplish the writer's purpose is included. This means meeting your reader more than halfway, asking yourself what he or she needs to know to fully understand what you have to say. It means trying to see your own work from the reader's point of view and completing it for this person, not only for yourself. When your reader finishes, he or she should not be left wanting—wondering if perhaps you've omitted something vital. A sense of wholeness about what you've written should remain with the reader, that the work now stands fully realized, on its own.

As well as wanting completeness, we should further expect that there be no unnecessary or unrelated parts present, no loose ends. This is the principle of *unity*. Writing works best when it creates a single, consistent effect in the reader's mind. Extraneous sentences and paragraphs distract us; they shift our attention away from the matter at hand. Unity demands that everything in a piece of writing have a reason for being there, that it justify its part in the composition. Again, unity, like completeness, is an ordinary expectation. We want it not only in writing, but in music, painting, architecture, dance, film, and many other created things.

Last, we should expect the content of a piece of writing to have *significance*. By this we do not mean that everything we write must set the world on fire. Good writing can be grand, and it can be small. At least we should want it to say something worthwhile to us, however—to tell us something we didn't know, to help us understand something better, to shake us out of our unquestioning acceptance of things, to delight and surprise us. Good writing doesn't insult our intelligence or our character, it doesn't belabor the obvious, it doesn't put on airs. Significant work is honest work, and the more truthful writers are with themselves and their readers, the more significant their work is likely to be.

Organization

It is difficult to view the organization of a piece of writing as something separate from its content. Yet writing may be complete but poorly or ineffectively designed. Usually, we expect good writing to be coherent, logical, and emphatic.

When all the parts of a piece of writing are not only necessary but fit together in an appropriate pattern, we say the work has *coherence*. Coherent organization allows the reader to absorb the full impact of what you are stating. It prepares the reader for major points, ties related ideas or facts together, makes smooth connections between parts. The rhetorical devices of thesis statement, transitional words and phrases, topic sentences, headings and subheadings, and others help writers show their readers how the work is put together. Well-organized writing is transparently mapped so that readers always know where they are, where they have been, and where they are likely to go next.

Writers achieve coherence of design through common sense and *logic*. (We will talk more about logic in Chapter 11 "Argument.") For example, common sense forces us to expect conclusions to be supported by assumptions and evidence. Writing that assumes the conclusion it seeks to prove or that asserts conclusions without support will seem illogical to us, and if the work doesn't make sense, it's unlikely its purpose can be fulfilled. Since most nonfiction prose is a linear means of communication (the reader begins with the first word of the first sentence and proceeds along a line to the last word of the last sentence), your audience will expect ideas to be introduced, developed, and concluded in this linear order (although some kinds of impressionistic nonfiction, especially narratives, experiment with the linear form of prose). As we shall see, certain basic structures for works of writing have evolved from the demands of logic.

Coherence and common sense in design go hand in hand with *emphasis*, placing what we want to stress where it will receive the most attention. As a rule, words and phrases at the end of sentences, and sentences at the end of paragraphs, receive the greatest stress. Emphasis, clearly placed, completes the coherence and logic of the design. It gives focus and weight to the shape of your plan of organization, and it gives the reader a firm place to stand in the structure you have built.

Style

The three passages at the opening of this chapter illustrate very different prose styles. The conversational style of the ad copy, typical for advertising and other kinds of promotional writing, is meant to convey a sense of friendliness, even intimacy, in order to draw the reader into the embrace of the ad's message. The highly formal and official-sounding style of the second passage is meant to do just the opposite, to make it seem that the writer is an expert in command of extremely complex knowledge that only he or she fully understands. The third selection is written in a direct, informal, even blunt style that expresses the author's personal voice and way of looking at the world.

Style in nonfiction prose ranges from the colloquial or conversational language of everyday speech (often including slang, profanity, exaggeration) to the formal language and diction of science, the law, and business and technical writing (with its frequent reliance on jargon). Most of the nonfiction we read and write, however, whether in college or not, employs a style that seeks a middle ground between these two extremes. This informal or plain style uses ordinary language in a simple, straightforward and precise way. It usually avoids both slang (which may be expressive but imprecise) and jargon (which may not be understood by the ordinary reader). The plain style is the one we find in newspaper and magazine articles, books of history, biography, autobiography and general nonfiction, personal essays, textbooks, and many other common forms of writing. It is the style best suited to most nonfiction purposes in most situations, and it has certain distinct features:

Clarity

First, the plain style is clear. Since our purpose is to communicate, our first obligation is to make sure the reader knows exactly what's being said, without confusion, ambiguity, or vagueness. Writers achieve clarity in their prose by using concrete language (words and phrases that point to specific things, not generalities) whenever possible. However, we cannot always, nor should we always try to, avoid abstract language; when writing about ideas, especially, a certain amount of abstraction or generality is necessary. Relying on a general word when a more specific one is appropriate, however, undermines clarity.

Economy

In addition to being clear, the plain style is economical. That is, it uses the fewest words necessary to say something clearly and completely. It avoids clutter. Writers who want to master the plain style go after their prose with a knife, cutting anything unneeded: padding, redundancy, repetition not necessary for emphasis. The plain style is a clean, even elegant, style, where (as with the parts of the whole composition) every word is justified, with work to do.

Directness

The plain style avoids the roundabout, evasive manner of much "official" prose. Rather than using passive verbs and long, noun-choked phrases ("It has been determined that, due to unforeseen fiscal revenue-enhancement policies, certain remedial corrective adjustments must be implemented . . ."), the plain style employs concise, active verbs, brisk rather than plodding sentence rhythms, and precise, concrete nouns ("Because of poor planning, the government must raise taxes."). Directness is saying what you mean, and meaning what you say.

Variety

Finally, the plain style avoids uniform sentence patterns, which tend to be monotonous, in favor of variety. The structure of a sentence should embody its content—short sentences for simple ideas and emphasis, longer sentences for more complex ideas or facts. The plain style is one easily adaptable to the human voice and to the rhythms of human speech. When we write well in the plain style, our prose should be able to be read aloud easily, naturally. (Reading your work aloud may be the best test for effective style, and it is always a good practice before you decide you are finished with the writing.)

The plain style is not plain in the sense of being dull, boring, unexciting. On the contrary, it is the style best suited to the energy, precision, and expressiveness of English.

Execution

The word *execution* has a fatal connotation, and for many of us—whether we write for a living or regularly at school or on the job—it can be the element of good writing most difficult to master. The word may conjure up the stereotypical image of the brooding and ruthless English teacher swatting our knuckles for each comma fault and dangling participle. Certainly the dread of grammatical or mechanical incorrectness has been firmly instilled in most of us. We may, in fact, forget that good writing is more than just good spelling and punctuation.

The first definitions of the verb *execute* are "to carry out fully" and "to put completely into effect." The word also means "to make or produce . . . especially by carrying out a design" and "to perform what is required to give validity to." A useful synonym might be the word *finish*, as in "to bring to an end" or "the quality or state of being perfected." All of these definitions point toward the idea of craftwork—of making sure that what we write is in suitable shape to be presented to our audience.

Good execution in a piece of writing hinges on the writer's acceptance of basic *conventions,* and here we must again consult the dictionary. The word *convention* means first "agreement, contract" as in "a general agreement about basic principles." It is no coincidence that convention also means "an assembly of persons met for a common purpose." The conventions of written English are the basic "rules of conduct or behavior" that have evolved over time through use and practice. They are the practical guidelines that ensure that our writing will be understood by the community of readers. They are much like the laws that regulate the flow of traffic over streets and highways.

It is beyond the scope of this book to present the complete code of conventions of written English. (Every writer, whether amateur or seasoned professional, needs a comprehensive English handbook for study and reference.) In broad outline, however, these practical guidelines fall into three categories: usage, grammar, and mechanics.

Usage is a set of conventions (rules) that evolves in any community of language users. Such accepted uses help keep meanings clear, consistent, and generally uniform. (Language can frustrate our desire for perfectly fixed meaning, however. Slang enters language when words are used in new, unexpected, unconventional ways.) Generally, unless their point is to bend language into new shapes, good writers take pains to obey the conventions of usage. Since words are signs that carry meaning (not unlike traffic signs), we should use them as they are accustomed to being used. Otherwise, we risk giving our readers signals they will not be able to follow.

Just as the rules of usage govern how we use words (and other signs, such as punctuation marks), the conventions of grammar give us meaningful structures or patterns for language. Of these basic patterns, sentences are the most ordinary yet flexible units of meaning. The grammar of English leads us to expect that sentences should be distinct and self-contained (not jammed together in comma splices or cut up into fragments), and that within each sentence the various parts be clearly related and connected to each other. (Punctuation, the nemesis of many a good writer, is just a set of signs for keeping sentence meaning and structure clear.)

The conventions of mechanics, such as using a capital letter to begin a sentence, similarly provide guidelines for the use of an assortment of items: numbers, titles, abbreviations, foreign words, and so on. Mechanical consistency in writing is as important as it is in musical notation, for example. Readers of both depend on uniform mechanics for meaning.

Taken together, then, the conventional or widely accepted standards of usage, grammar, and mechanics give our written language boundaries and a sense of direction. Without these standards, we write in a void—never knowing whether what we say, or how we say it, meets any of our reader's expectations. By respecting the common conventions of English prose, we respect not only the community of readers to whom our work is addressed, but we respect ourselves as fellow members of that community.

In summary, we can reasonably expect good nonfiction writing to have complete, unified, and significant content; to be organized coherently, with sound logic and appropriate emphasis; to be written clearly and economically, with directness and variety; and to be carefully executed according to the conventions of usage, grammar, and mechanics. If we can make our work embody our respect for these standards, we will have come a long way toward being able writers.

COMMITMENT

The qualities of good writing we've outlined so far are those we must master before we can go on to bigger and better things. Good writing is even more than good control of these four elements, however. There's something missing from our definition.

That missing element takes us back to the title of this book. A piece of writing may be perfectly adequate in its content, design, style, and craftwork, and yet be relatively lifeless. We may read it and think, "Well done—but who cares?" We may think, "Where's the *life* in this?"

Granted, some of the work we do is doomed to fall short of a grand purpose. A report on a budget meeting is by nature unlikely to move us to tears or revolt (although it's been known to happen). More often than we might guess, however, ordinary nonfiction has the potential to be very fine, even great, writing.

Here are some brief examples. In your mind, what characteristics do these passages illustrate?

> There was a map of Vietnam on the wall of my apartment in Saigon and some nights, coming back late to the city, I'd lie out on my bed and look at it, too tired to do anything more than just get my boots off. That map was a marvel, especially now that it wasn't real anymore. For one thing, it was very old. It had been left there years before by another tenant, probably a Frenchman, since the map had been made in Paris. The paper had buckled in its frame after years in the wet Saigon heat, laying a kind of veil over the countries it depicted. Vietnam was divided into its older territories of Tonkin, Annam and Cochin China, and to the west past Laos and Cambodge sat Siam, a kingdom. That's old, I'd tell visitors, that's a really old map.
>
> If dead ground could come back and haunt you the way dead people do, they'd have been able to mark my map *current* and burn the ones they'd been using since '64, but count on it, nothing like that was going to happen. It was late '67 now, even the most detailed maps didn't reveal much anymore; reading them was like trying to read the faces of the Vietnamese, and that was like trying to read the wind. We knew that the uses of most information were flexible, different pieces of ground told different stories to different people. We also knew that for years now there had been no country here but the war.

These opening paragraphs of Michael Herr's *Dispatches* introduce us to one of the dominant features of his book and of much memorable nonfiction: prose *voice*. Although the purpose of *Dispatches* is to inform, to let us know what the Vietnam war was like for those who fought it and covered it, Herr made a decision to write the book in an intensely expressive way. He abandoned the convention of reportorial distance and wrote instead from his own point of view. While keeping to factual accuracy, he allows subjective feeling to play a role in carrying out the informative purpose. He lets his language express experience directly. And it is his voice—an indefinable quality of a writer's prose, part personal style but more than style alone—that lends these words, and all of *Dispatches*, such power.

Here is another example of voice, this one from a writer whose prose is almost instantly recognizable:

All writers know that on some golden mornings they are touched by the wand; they are on intimate terms with poetry and cosmic truth. I have experienced those moments myself. Their lesson is simple; they are a total illusion. And the danger in the illusion is that you will wait for them. Such is the horror of having to face the typewriter that you will spend all your time waiting. I am persuaded that, hangovers apart, most writers, like most other artisans, are about as good one day as the next . . . . The seeming difference is the result of euphoria, alcohol or imagination. All this means that one had better go to his or her typewriter every morning and stay there regardless of the results. It will be much the same.

In this excerpt from "Writing and Typing," noted economist and writer John Kenneth Galbraith explains why regular working habits are vital—an unpleasant message. Although Galbraith in his long career has written on a variety of subjects, most of his books and articles address the complex, difficult subject of economics. Yet, he has been a best-selling author. Why do his books have wide appeal? Galbraith believes that no subject is too complex to be explained in plain English, and he maintains a ready wit and wry humor in his prose. Economics has been called "the dismal science," but Galbraith, in his love for the subject and concern for his readers, renders it accessible, and even at times entertaining. He demystifies it, removing it from the sole proprietorship of experts.

A third example follows. The writer's purpose here should be obvious:

Two paths lie before us. One leads to death, the other to life. If we choose the first path—if we numbly refuse the nearness of extinction, all the while increasing our preparations to bring it about—then we in effect become the allies of death, and in everything we do our attachment to life will weaken: our vision, blinded to the abyss that has opened at our feet, will dim and grow confused; our will, discouraged by the thought of trying to build on such a precarious foundation anything that is meant to last, will slacken; and we will sink into stupefaction, as though we were gradually weaning ourselves from life in preparation for the end. On the other hand, if we reject our doom, and bend our efforts toward survival—if we arouse ourselves to the peril and act to forestall it, making ourselves the allies of life—then the anesthetic fog will lift: our vision, no longer straining not to see the obvious, will sharpen; our will, finding secure ground to build on, will be restored; and we will take full and clear possession of life again. One day—and it is hard to believe that it will not be soon—we will make our choice. Either we will sink into the final coma and end it all or, as I trust and believe, we will awaken to the truth of our peril, a truth as great as life itself, and, like a person who has swallowed a lethal poison but shakes off his stupor at the last moment and vomits the poison up, we will break through the layers of our denials, put aside our faint-hearted excuses, and rise up to cleanse the earth of nuclear weapons.

This is the resounding final paragraph of Jonathan Schell's *The Fate of the Earth*, a book which first appeared as a series of three articles in *The New*

Yorker and was published in 1982 amid much controversy. Whatever one's opinion of Schell's argument for banning nuclear weapons, it is hard to deny that these words and sentences are stirring in their force and depth of feeling (especially coming after Schell's excruciating list of nuclear horrors). Despite its faults, Schell's book is shocking, memorable, and convincing. Because his purpose is to awaken us to awareness and action, the author must persuade us that the issue is deadly serious and that his commitment to changing our minds is total. He must put his heart and soul into his language.

Finally, here is a passage from a writer whose chief purpose is to express a sense of wonder about nature's beauty:

> In autumn the winding passage of ravens from the north heralds the great fall migration of caribou. The shaggy-necked birds spread their wing tips to the skin of convection currents rising, and hie them south. The great deer meet herd on herd in arctic and subarctic valleys, milling and massing and gathering force like a waterfall, till they pour across the barren grounds wide as a tidal wave. Their coats are new and fine. Their thin spring coats—which had been scraped off in great hunks by the southern forests and were riddled with black-fly and gadfly stings, warble and botfly maggots—are gone, and a lustrous new pelage has appeared, a luxurious brown fur backed by a plush layer of hollow hairs that insulate and waterproof. Four inches of creamy fat cover even their backs. A loose cartilage in their fetlocks makes their huge strides click, mile upon mile over the tundra south to the shelter of trees, and you can hear them before they've come and after they've gone, rumbling like rivers, ticking like clocks.

Annie Dillard's *Pilgrim at Tinker Creek* records a year spent observing nature at close range. Although prose from start to finish, the book is richly poetic in its language and sensibility. Dillard's mysticism is not vague or sloppy; she writes with great care about what she sees and thinks. Her work embodies a complex balance of humility toward her subject and a robust confidence in her ability to write well about it. She is not afraid to stretch herself, to push her prose to its full creative potential, yet she never lets creative exuberance get the best of her, never inflicts herself upon her subject or stands between it and her readers. One might say, even, that Annie Dillard—like all superb writers—writes as an act of faith. Her work reveals an attitude of reverence, of belief that the world and the act of writing about it are supremely important.

What do these examples tell us? Readers will notice a number of qualities in any writer's work. Here is one interpretation:

Interest in one's subject.   It's probably safe to say that no fine or lasting work can emerge without the writer's compelling interest in what he or she is writing about. Whenever possible, then, try to find some vital center of interest—your own honest interest—in your subject.

Concern for one's audience.   Likewise, really good writing extends itself to the reader, draws the audience in toward it. Writers' concern for their audience, like their interest in their subject, is a subtle quality, but almost impossible to fake.

Seriousness.   By this word we do not mean gravity or solemnity. Humorists are serious writers. Rather, we mean an attitude of devotedness, of faithfulness (if you will) to the importance of writing and to the importance of one's own work.

Creativity.   Although some people are gifted with an unusual or remarkable creative imagination, all of us can be creative to the extent of our powers; it's just that we let the powers languish much of the time. All writing is creative to some degree—we bring something new into being. But how can we allow the full creative impulse to enter our work? Creativity is less a mystery when we can foster it ourselves, as do all people in the creative arts. We can answer by observing what creative people do.

- They develop the discipline to stay with the creative process through its roughest moments, knowing that sooner or later persistence will be rewarded.
- They cultivate a speculative, venturesome imagination, one that plays with fancy for its own sake, just to see what new things it might come up with (though not all will be of equal value).
- They ask questions, sometimes quite unconventional ones. The creative thinker must question closely held assumptions, traditional ways of belief and behavior, "obvious" truths, received wisdom, established values. The question does not itself imply rejection of these things; it may lead to greater acceptance of them. The creative person, however, asks the question simply because he or she is curious to know the answer.

When we adopt the attitude of creative people, we help develop a greater openness to possibility, to the unforeseen.

All of this brings us to the edge of the mystery of writing as a human enterprise—why we do it at all, why we put ourselves through the hard work of it, why we seem to have a hunger for good writing. Finally, all we really know is that people do it, and have done it for thousands of years. We also know that they write, many of them, as though their work will be read thousands of years hence.

If there is one idea that can complete our definition of good writing, perhaps it is commitment. Certainly in the work of Herr, Galbraith, Schell, and Dillard, and, as we shall see, many others, we feel an abiding love for the enterprise. These writers tell us that writing is much more than the sum of its purposes, forms, and methods: It is a way of life.

FOR DISCUSSION OR WRITING

1. Of the four elements of good writing (content, organization, style, execution) detailed above, which tends to give you the most trouble? Which do you feel most at ease with? Does your sense of control over each element vary from one writing task to another, or do you have fairly consistent strengths and weaknesses?

2. When you read nonfiction, how aware are you of the presence and interplay of content, organization, and style? (By the time something is published, its execution usually isn't an issue.) When you read published prose, do you automatically assume it is well written, or do you try to evaluate it and judge its effectiveness for yourself? Do you tend to read only for content and to ignore other elements? What effect might this reading habit have on your writing?

3. How much does revising help you gain control of your work? Does rewriting usually enrich its *content*, or does it have little effect? Similarly, as you revise do you find the *organization* of your work improving? How is your *style* affected by redrafting? Do you find yourself cutting needless words and phrases, combining sentences, inserting specific nouns and active verbs? Last, does revising have any effect on the way you *execute* your final draft? For instance, does revising help improve your punctuation?

4. Are there writers you particularly admire? If so, who are they, and why do you like or respect them? What do they write? What distinctive qualities would you attribute to them and their work?

5. What are your views on what makes for good writing? To what extent do you agree or disagree with the one presented above? Which qualities would your definition omit or add?

EXERCISES

1. Evaluate each of the paragraphs to follow for content, organization, and style. Use the following questions for your analysis, and try to answer each as precisely as possible; quote from the examples to support your views.

   A. *Questions on content*
       1. What does the paragraph say?
       2. Does it seem complete and self-contained?
       3. Is it unified by a controlling point or idea?
       4. Does it say something significant?
   B. *Questions on organization*
       5. Do the sentences in the paragraph fit together in a clear pattern?
       6. Does the paragraph make sense?
       7. Is it clear what's being emphasized?

C. *Questions on style*
   8. Are the sentences clear and understandable?
   9. Is the style economical, without padding?
  10. Are the sentences direct, straight to the point?
  11. Does the writer vary sentence structures according to their content and meaning?
D. *A final question*
  12. Does the paragraph make you want to keep reading?

Example 1
It is desirable that voting decisions be studied in, among others, a consumption behavior perspective, for they cannot be deemed outside the larger context of the household's investment–consumption process. The decision to vote or not, and for whom, has some bearing on the election of representatives who have an important public "purchasing agent" role. In that role, elected representatives influence the choice, quantity, and price of publicly supplied goods and services that are indispensable to the household in its production of final output (or utility) over a time horizon that may extend for several years. The decision to vote for or against a particular public good in a referendum has, of course, a more immediate relevance to the household's utility and production process.

Journal of Consumer Research, March 1983

Example 2
Every religion requires faith and a set of believers in something. The believers put their faith in ideas which sometimes seem farfetched, contradictory, or illogical even to the most determined. Moments of crisis are usually the great "litmus paper" of faith. If the believer remains faithful, then the faith was strong; if not, it was not ready for such a test. One reason is that the religion if often used only for support, to sort of ward off bad times like garlic necklaces repel vampires. When the system does not work it is abandoned for its faultiness. That is more of a bad side-effect of religion and by no means the point of it. Religion is a way of expressing faith in something higher than oneself. It is a philosophy for understanding tragedies (and good things), not eliminating them.

Student writer

Example 3
As the twentieth century approaches its end, the conviction grows that many other things are ending too. Storm warnings, portents, hints of catastrophe haunt our times. The "sense of an ending," which has given shape to so much of twentieth-century literature, now pervades the popular imagination as well. The Nazi holocaust, the threat of nuclear annihilation, the depletion of natural resources, well-founded predictions of ecological disaster have fulfilled poetic prophecy, giving

concrete historical substance to the nightmare, or death wish, that avant-garde artists were the first to express. The question of whether the world will end in fire or in ice, with a bang or a whimper, no longer interests artists alone. Impending disaster has become an everyday concern, so commonplace and familiar that nobody any longer gives much thought to how disaster might be averted. People busy themselves instead with survival strategies, measures designed to prolong their own lives, or programs guaranteed to ensure good health and peace of mind.

Christopher Lasch, *The Culture of Narcissism*

2.   In a recent newspaper or magazine, find what you consider a well-written prose passage (length comparable to those above). Using the questions in Exercise 1 as your guide, write a brief analysis explaining your view. (As above, use the quotation for support.)

3.   Select a passage from your own recent writing—one that you know needs improvement. Using the questions in Exercise 1, evaluate it carefully and objectively in writing (as above); then revise the passage, using your evaluation as your guide.

PART TWO

Writing to Inform

INFORMATIVE WRITING

Pick up a copy of almost any popular magazine and you will likely find a cover story or major article devoted to "the information age." The latest developments in satellite technology, interactive cable television systems, databases for home computer owners, the shift from an industrial to a service economy—all are signs that the world is changing under our feet.

Although the pace of change has quickened in recent decades, our entry into the information age has been going on for a long time. It started when people invented writing and began keeping records. Certainly in our own day the volume of information has become so vast that it is usually impossible for one person to know everything about a subject. The information world we have built, and now rely on, is so complicated that it dwarfs our ability to comprehend it. Still, much of our daily life is devoted to the attempt—through study at school, pursuit of our interests in reading and independent learning, hands-on experience, conversation, attention to the media. We seek to know more, to learn more, even as the goal of perfect knowledge recedes from us two steps for every one we take.

But we are more than just consumers of this glut of information. We are producers, too. As students, employees, citizens, we may be generators, developers, messengers, and interpreters of new knowledge. In the course of our schooling, careers, and private lives, our ability to create, understand, and communicate information will determine a great deal about the quality of our experience in this kind of world.

Still, one might ask: Why writing? We have television, radio, the telephone system, growing numbers of computer networks. Who needs language when you have a minicam?

For the simple reason that there is no field—business, law, medicine, science, the arts, entertainment, government, the media—that does not depend on the medium of the written word. An enormous amount of the information we rely on is recorded and transmitted in the form of writing.

5

REPORTS

WHAT REPORTS DO

The report is perhaps the most clearly practical form of nonfiction. Reports meet demands. They are based on the assumption that the information they contain is necessary—that someone needs it. For example, in a free society we assume that the public must have the information it needs to govern itself, so we establish a free press. In the sciences, we assume that the results of research must be communicated to other scientists in order to advance both the pure and applied forms of knowledge. In business, reports can be the basis of important, expensive decisions, and we assume that such decisions cannot be made without a study of available data.

Reports tell us what we need or want to know. Usually they do not try to influence our judgments about what we should think or do about the information they contain. Reports, in fact, cease to be trustworthy if we do not believe they are objective. We assume that information exists independent of our opinions about it. A good report is true to its subject. Otherwise, it is useless.

BASIC TYPES OF REPORTS

There are a great many different kinds of reports, from the one-line "filler" in your local newspaper to the massive tomes issued by government agencies. A catalog of everything in between would itself be a massive report, but it's hard to know who would want to read it. What we can say is that all reports are derived from certain basic types, each one tied to a way of gathering information. (More about this shortly.) As reports become more complex, they combine these basic types into various specialized forms for business, industry, science, law, and so on.

Reports Based on Research

One of the most basic report types, research-based reports range from summaries and abstracts to full-length papers, articles, and books. Such reports rely primarily (although not always exclusively) on information

49

gathered from published sources—newspapers, magazines, professional journals, speeches, books, often other reports. The typical newspaper or magazine feature article, for example, usually has a research base, although it may include other kinds of information as well.

Reports Based on Interviews

The interview is both a way of gathering information and a form for presenting it. Some interviews are presented *as* interviews, in a question-and-answer format, especially when the person being questioned is the subject of the report. Just as often, the facts and statements produced by an interview are integrated in a report that may include other kinds of information. The interview report is one of the mainstays of journalism, or any information-gathering process (such as poll taking) that relies on the statements of individuals.

Reports Based on Observation

Another basic report type comes from first-hand experience, either spontaneous or structured. When a reporter covers a protest march, for instance, he or she observes the action and distills the essence of what occurred. When social scientists conduct case studies, on the other hand, they observe behavior according to selected characteristics or actions. Some common observation-based reports include the minutes of meetings; studies of behavior in psychology, sociology, and political science; studies of efficiency in business and industry (office or factory operations, for example).

Reports Based on Experiment

Although largely beyond the bounds of this book, a fourth basic report type presents information gathered or created during controlled experiments, which couple observation with a highly limited, artificial situation. Such experiments, as conducted in the physical and social sciences, and in technological fields such as engineering, are governed by the methods and materials specific to each area of study. These are among the most complex report forms, and because they require knowledge outside the subject of English, we will confine our attention to the first three basic types.

Whether in the form of memos, announcements, press releases, newsletters, and so on, reports communicate facts. Reports are vehicles; they carry information from one place to another, and the way they are made is usually an expression of what they contain.

Why study report-writing? In the words of writer and teacher S. I. Hayakawa, "reports are verifiable." Their accuracy can be tested, and often is by those who dispute it. The reporting process thus plays an essential part in the larger process of writing nonfiction.

THE REPORT-WRITING PROCESS

The process of writing reports, although it may be difficult or time-consuming, can be more straightforward than the process of writing essays and narratives. Because reports usually follow well-defined patterns, and because of the fairly strict demands placed on reports, the writer is left with less room for invention or experimentation. Reports tend to be less "creative" than essays and narratives because the writer's uniqueness, his or her personal voice or perspective, remains outside of the report's content. The readers of the report are not interested in the writer's self-discovery or expressiveness; they are interested in the facts.

If we assume that the function of a report is to collect, organize, and communicate necessary useful or interesting information to a specific audience (even if this audience is the general public), then report writing presents us with several tasks. In order to get a better view of each of these, we can divide the report-writing process into the following stages:

1. Determining the report's purpose and audience
2. Gathering information
3. Selecting what is important and necessary
4. Organizing the material for presentation
5. Composing (drafting) the report
6. Revising and editing for a final draft

Let us describe each of these steps in greater detail.

Determining the Report's Audience and Purpose

By the term *purpose* here, we do not mean merely the general one of informing; that much we already know. Rather, what is the specific purpose of the report? Is it to summarize and condense research? Is it to present the methods and results of a laboratory experiment? Is it to disseminate news, coordinate activity, provide the data needed for a business or committee undertaking? The specific purpose of the report will help determine much of what the writer will do in the successive stages.

Who will read the report? Is the audience knowledgeable about the subject, or must the writer assume that additional background information should be included? Depending on the reader's familiarity with the subject, the language of the report may be specialized or technical in employing the jargon of the field, or it may be very simple, especially if the subject is both difficult and new for the reader.

Often, the audience for a report is large and hard to define. In such cases, writers usually assume their "general" audience to be of normal intelligence with at least some broad knowledge of the subject. The style of news reporting, for example, does not seek to oversimplify its language, but at the same time it avoids specialized or technical terms in favor of plain English. (The problem of writing for the general audience will turn up again when we discuss essays and narratives.)

The closer writers come to a specific purpose for a specific reader, the more closely they can tailor their reports to the individual needs of a unique situation. The less clear the purpose and audience, the less effective is the report likely to be.

Gathering Information

Once the writer has determined the report's purpose and audience, he or she must collect the facts, data, observed detail, statements, or other material that will form the basis of the report. Depending on the subject, this stage of the process may take only a few minutes or as long as several weeks or months to complete. Moreover, the writer may need to gather information in a number of ways, through research and interviewing, for example, or through observation and experiment. Each of these methods is a process unto itself:

Research

When we do research, we try to find out as much about a subject as we can by reading what has already been written on it. Chapter 17 discusses the process of researching and writing in detail; for now, however, we will focus only on the general outline of research as a means for collecting information.

Research begins with an assessment of potential sources. Where are we the most likely to find the information we need? The public library? The files of our organization? The county courthouse?

The next step is to determine which types of sources have the most potential value. Should we look for books, periodicals (magazines and newspapers), or reference books? Do we need specialized or technical information? (See "Types of Sources," Chapter 17.)

Having tracked down some preliminary sources, we next begin reading, taking notes, and keeping a record of useful material in a working bibliography. As research continues, we should stay alert for gaps in our information, additional sources, and questions that might be raised by the reader. Sometimes research may be necessary only for background information;

sometimes it may be the entire focus of the report. In either case, writers must keep their audience and purpose clearly in mind. Otherwise, the report might suffer from thin or inadequate research, or extraneous information—material not pertinent to the requirements of the report.

In the process of research we should stop now and then to assess what we have gathered. It is important that we maintain a grasp of the project as a whole, that we not become distracted by one or more of its parts. This leads us to the next step: building a working outline. As research progresses, we need to organize the material under major and minor headings or categories. Then, when it comes time to structure the report for presentation, we will be able to select from blocks of information rather than isolated facts. Apart from the quality of the research itself, how well we organize it will greatly affect the success of the final report.

As you move into the next stages of assembling a report—selecting the most important information, organizing it, and composing a first draft— you may discover that the research still is not complete. The research process does not end when we want it to. It ends when our honest and objective evaluation of the material tells us we have enough. More often than not, only the composing of a draft will reveal this to us.

Interviewing

If the focus of research is the written word, the focus of interviewing is the spoken word. When we interview someone, we seek information through his or her eyes, through a personal point of view. We may interview someone to learn beliefs, opinions, ideas, or experiences. Or, we may interview a number of people to determine widespread opinions, fears, desires.

The interview is common to many fields as a way to gather information. Businesses use it when hiring new employees. Journalists use it to collect eyewitness accounts, to produce material for sketches and profiles, and to press public figures to explain or justify their actions. Social scientists use it to gain a clearer understanding of individual or group behavior.

As in research, the interview is usually pointed toward a specific purpose, whether it is to find out about a person's background, views on a particular subject, or experience on a certain occasion. In order to conduct an effective session, therefore, interviewers must prepare ahead of time. First, they must learn enough about the subject (the person to be interviewed) so that their questions will be precise, intelligent, and likely to elicit the desired information. Second, they must form these questions, at least broadly, and keep them in mind (or written down) so that the interview does not stray too far afield.

Learning about an interviewee usually requires research—reading published works, excerpts, or news accounts of the subject's activities, and assembling a biographical sketch of his or her life and accomplishments.

Framing the controlling questions for the interview requires that you couple your knowledge of the person with the kind of information you seek. In other words, what do you want to know that the subject is uniquely qualified to tell you? Make a list of the major points you wish to cover during the course of the interview. (You may have to reduce the list if the time allowed you with the subject is limited.) Draft a number of questions for each point—as many as you think you may need to be comprehensive—and then ask yourself if the questions can be combined, shortened, or otherwise revised to make them clear, economical, and, most of all, specific. Vague or ill-informed questions will severely undermine your credibility with the subject and damage your ability to get good, hard information.

Although your set of questions should provide the general structure for the interview, don't adhere to these so rigidly that you miss opportunities to insert questions you hadn't anticipated asking. A good interviewer encourages the subject to give full answers; you may need to ask additional questions in order to pursue an answer to completion. While you want comprehensive information, you don't want your subject to take the lead away from you. If the interviewee wants to change the direction of the interview or to avoid answering a particular question, you must try to direct the subject back to the point.

You can record the subject's comments in writing or on tape. If you write down the responses, do so briefly and quickly. Do not attempt to capture every word. Note the major points of the answers, and pay close attention. As soon as you can, after finishing the interview, go over your notes and reconstruct the conversation in detail, recalling especially those remarks you wish to quote verbatim (word for word). If the interview will be published, the subject may wish to check the final copy to verify quotation accuracy.

Longer interviews, particularly those for publication, are usually tape-recorded and then transcribed (typed in manuscript). Few people object to being recorded—as long as they know it is happening. Don't presume, however; ask the subject's permission before you turn on the machine.

Observation

In both research and interviewing, the focus is information as expressed in language. Not all useful data come in this form, however. Sometimes the information we seek is in the form of behavior, actions rather than words. We then must translate the information from one form to another.

When we gather facts through observation, we attempt to do something akin to recording actions with a film or video camera. In our role as observer, we try to achieve a literally "clear-eyed" objectivity, to see without bias or preset expectations. We adopt what some have termed an "anthropological perspective"—that is, the point of view of a scientist studying a foreign culture.

Shedding our subjectivity is not easy. One way we can do so, however, is to avoid using language that expresses emotion or judgment. Instead, we should strive to record what we see in words that are descriptive but neutral.

For example, say that you are studying the behavior of commuters. You spend several hours riding the subway, watching the body language of people in crowded or cramped conditions. Your first impulse might be to write something like this: "These people act like zombies. They are in their own little shells, hidden behind their newspapers, looking as if they haven't a friend in the world. Everybody acts like everybody else is carrying a deadly disease."

Now this might even be an apt description—if our purpose were to express the way we thought the commuters behaved—but it could never pass for an objective or neutral picture. Rather, we would need to say something more along these lines: "Most of the men and women in the car do not look at or talk with their fellow riders. Of the 23 commuters, 19 were reading; 12 read newspapers, seven magazines or paperback books. The other four sat in various positions, their eyes fixed either on the floor of the car or on a spot above the heads of the people sitting across from them."

When setting out to gather information through observation, writers must know what they hope to do with the data; for what purpose are they collecting it? Then they must decide the limits of their investigation. That is, what will be the focus of their observation, and what will they disregard?

Having set the boundaries for the study, you now have two choices: to write down what is seen under a predetermined set of categories, or to observe the behavior as it takes place and categorize the data afterward. In practice, you will probably do both. Certainly you must have a clear sense of what you are watching for; you can't hope to absorb everything. On the other hand, since human behavior is fairly unpredictable, a careful and sensitive observer will note occurrences for which a ready slot does not exist. As a rule, it is always better to take down more than you need rather than less. You can always eliminate what you can't use, but it's much harder, and usually impossible, to go back for what you forgot.

Experiment

The methods for gathering data in the sciences and social sciences vary according to discipline and are beyond the scope of this book. We should say a word, however, about the scientific method in general, whether it is employed in the service of physics or psychology.

The essence of the scientific method is testing: seeing if our ideas about how the world works are borne out by observed phenomena. We conceive an idea, an hypothesis, in response to a problem; it is meant to answer a question we have about nature. We then design an experiment, or series of them, the results of which should either verify or call into question our original assumption. By repeated experiments under varied conditions, we can determine the likelihood that the hypothesis is valid.

The scientific method need not be confined to the laboratory. It can have broad application outside pure science—as a general way of thinking.

Any time we try to gather information, by whatever means, it pays to remember the lesson science teaches: that there may be nothing quite so valuable to the process of learning, or the process of information gathering, as an honest question. The advance of science is driven by the curiosity of the scientist. This curiosity is tempered by doubt, however; scientists want to know, but they also want to make sure that what they know is correct. So should it be for the rest of us.

When we collect facts, we should keep a questioning mind. We should test our assumptions against what we have read, heard, or observed. We should be skeptical of information that lacks support or can't be verified.

Like the scientist, we should ask ourselves if we have asked all the necessary questions—and the right ones—in our search.

We should also remind ourselves that the information-gathering process is never really finished, that our knowledge is provisional and subject to change without notice.

Holding to an experimental point of view when collecting facts—seeking to test and verify information before believing it—these are good habits for anyone, scientist or not.

Selecting What Is Important and Necessary

Having assembled a body of information, the writer must now decide which data are vital to the presentation and which may be omitted. As in everything else in report writing, purpose and audience provide the limits. Although there can be no final rule as to how to make such a determination (the writer's judgment must come into play in every report), these guidelines should make the selection part of the process more manageable:

First, read over your information and try to get a sense of it as a whole rather than as a collection of individual fragments. Review your working outline or list of categories. Is all the information accounted for in the outline? If not, there may be gaps in your data calling for further research.

If it appears that you have sufficient material from which to compile the report, the next step is to *rank* the data. Given the purpose of the project, which information is absolutely necessary? Which bears most closely on the subject of the report? Which, if left out, would change or distort the impact of the report?

Once you have determined the essential information, go through the data again for *background* or supporting material—whatever may be necessary to "set up" the main thrust of the report, provide a context for it, or make it more understandable to your reader. If the audience already knows the subject well, little or no supporting data may be needed. Likewise, an audience unfamiliar with the material in the report will require a greater degree of background information.

It should now be fairly clear which of the data meet neither of these two tests. Evaluate your body of facts one last time. Have you omitted anything important? Of the material remaining, which of it can reasonably be left out? Which merely repeats other information? Which is irrelevant?

Organizing the Material for Presentation

A report's format or pattern of organization usually depends on the field for which it is written. Yet few reports do not conform to a basic organization plan they share with essays, research papers, magazine articles, and other kinds of nonfiction. It is the introduction–body–conclusion structure.

In this standard pattern, writers first set the stage for the report, give background information, and state the topic or problem the report addresses. In the body, they present whatever information they have finally deemed significant. They conclude with a closing comment, often a synthesis of the information or a recommendation.

Within this basic structure, the report writer still must decide how to arrange the body, the bulk of what the report will say. Here are four of the most common patterns:

Decreasing order of importance.   As in the typical news story, this organizational pattern puts the essential information first and follows it with elaboration and detail. Because we are familiar with this method, readers understand that the first item in a news story is the most important, the story's focus.

Increasing order of importance.   The reverse of the journalistic approach, this pattern begins with preliminary or background information and builds toward an emphatic conclusion by leaving the most important material for the end.

Sequential order.   Here, the report follows a step-by-step or chronological pattern, beginning with the first part of a sequence and following it through to the end. Directions or instructions (how to make spaghetti sauce, for instance) and descriptions of technical processes are common examples of this method.

Spatial order.   When we report on the physical nature of something (the layout of a new park, the features of a new automobile) we use the spatial method, an attempt to give the reader a mental picture of the object about which we are writing.

Our choice of pattern shouldn't be arbitrary, like pulling a number out of a hat. The best pattern is the one indicated by the material itself. A few basic questions should help with the decision:

First, what must the reader know before the rest of the report will make sense? Second, given the nature of the material, what is the clearest, most logical way to present it? Third, what items should be given greatest emphasis?

For example, if the report describes an office hiring procedure, the step-by-step pattern would be most appropriate. If your dean of students wants a report about the goals of your organization, you might select the increasing-order-of-importance pattern, starting with minor goals and building to the ones you want to get the most emphasis. If your subject is complex or difficult, you might need to begin with general information and move toward more specific or technical points later.

Reports can be flexible enough to vary from situation to situation. Whether you organize the data according to a preset format or to the specific needs of a unique project, try to pattern the report for its readers. What is the most effective way to present the information to them?

Drafting the Report

In writing a draft of your report, your task is to take the raw information and from it construct a clear, accurate, and readable presentation. Report writing demands that the writer adhere to the most basic qualities of good nonfiction prose (see Chapter 4, "Good Writing"): complete, unified, and significant content; coherent, logical, and emphatic organization; a clear, economical, and direct prose style; standard usage, and correct grammar, punctuation, and mechanics in execution.

In composing a first draft, then, you should keep at least the first three sets of guidelines in mind. Try to write carefully and precisely. At this stage, you are not writing to discover *what* you want to say; the information provides the bulk of your content. Rather, you are trying to translate the facts at hand into writing.

Divide the information into manageable units corresponding to the various sections of the report. You may want to outline each section, too, especially if it is to contain more than a single paragraph. Then, when you have a general sense of the shape of each part, start with the introductory portion of the report and begin your draft.

Take it a section, and a paragraph, at a time. Focus your attention on the content and purpose of each paragraph as a building block for the larger part of the report that contains it. Try to keep each paragraph unified by a single topic, typically stated in the opening sentence. If you find your paragraphs getting long and out of focus, chances are you have introduced a new topic or have left the initial one behind.

And try to make your sentences *active* (with definite persons or things performing definite actions), *concrete* (using particular names rather than general or abstract categories), and *direct* and *economical* (saying only what you need to say in the fewest words). The language of a report should be invisible, in a way. It should direct us to the facts and place no obstacles in our path.

Revising and Editing

The guidelines for a final version of any successful piece of prose were detailed in Chapter 4. All are important, but several have special bearing on reports.

Accuracy: Since the purpose of a report is to communicate information, accuracy is paramount. Without it, the report has no value.

Objectivity: The reader must know that the information has not been tampered with, that it is reliable, that the writer has not tried to manipulate it in a self-serving way.

Clarity: The language of a report cannot contain vagueness or ambiguity (multiple meanings). It must be literal, denoting specific objects and facts, rather than figurative (interpretative language using devices such as simile and metaphor).

Completeness: A report that does not cover its subject thoroughly is as useless as one that is inaccurate, biased, or murky.

The qualities of good report writing are common to all effective communication. Mastering these fundamentals will give you a solid footing for the more difficult job of writing essays and narratives.

QUESTIONS

1.   What do reports do?
2.   What are four basic types of reports and their associated methods of gathering information?
3.   What are the stages of the report-writing process?

EXERCISES

1. *Determining purpose and audience*
A.   In many report-writing situations, either the report's purpose, its audience, or both, may be provided: for example, news stories, office memos, and so forth. In the following situations, however, one or the other (or both) of these elements is vague. What questions can you ask that might help you achieve a clearer sense of the specific purpose and audience in each?

- The leader of your church group wants you to produce a one-page handout for new church members to describe the group's activities, goals, and accomplishments.
- Your first task as a newly hired trainee in a local bank's trust department is to research investment newsletters and then write summaries for your boss.
- Your sociology professor has assigned a case study paper: to report on weeknight social life on your dorm floor.
- For a collaborative project in your science class, you and some fellow students have been asked to translate the results of a group of successful but highly technical experiments for a report to be published by the department. Audience: the nonscientific community of the college and the town.

B.   Examine the news-reporting sections of several national and local magazines or newspapers. (Some examples: *The New York Times, The Wall Street Journal, The Chicago Tribune, USA Today, Time Magazine, BusinessWeek,* and numerous local and regional publications.) How do the reporting purposes of these periodicals differ? What sort of audience does each address? Is there any relationship between the audiences of these newspapers and magazines and the reporting purposes they serve? Which publications seem to you to be the most objective or unbiased?

2. *Gathering information*
In the following reporting situations, your purpose and audience are specified. Which information-gathering techniques are most appropriate to the task?

- You've been hired as an assistant manager at a large supermarket, and your supervisor wants an informal report of how customers respond to the new computerized checkout system.
- As part of your summer job for the city newspaper, you've been assigned a project: to determine which subscribers should receive a special advertising mailing from "upscale" (expensive) stores and to present your findings to the advertising manager.
- Students on your campus are divided over a plan to reinstate the ROTC (Reserve Officers Training Corps). You wish to gather a sample of student opinion on the issue as raw material for a paper in your ethics class.

- You and some friends have been hired temporarily by a soft drink company to determine whether students on your campus like a new noncola beverage. The company has provided samples of the drink and wants a report of student preferences as soon as possible.

3. *Selecting what is important and necessary*
For a research project in your business class, you have collected data on several national companies. Your audience is prospective investors, and your purpose is to determine which companies have the best growth records. Which data, under the following headings, should pertain *most directly* to such a report?

Annual sales	Support of the arts
Profits	Book value
Year founded	Earnings growth rate
Number of employees	Stock performance (past 10 years)
Cooperative agreements with	Advertising budget
other companies	Research and development budget
Type of product(s) or service(s)	Industry forecasts
Public reputation	

Which data would apply if your purpose were to determine which companies had the best prospects for future growth?

4. *Organizing your presentation*
As part of your job for a local contractor, you've been asked to produce a pamphlet on home energy-saving tips. The contractor wants the information to be accurate and impartial, but plans to use the brochure to advertise the company. You have a large general audience of people who live in your town, people with widely different incomes. How might you organize the information to appeal to this large audience? You have data in the following categories:

Average heating costs	Types of fireplaces and wood-
Types of insulation	burning stoves
An explanation of R-values	Costs of passive solar
Cost and advantages of weather-	remodeling
stripping and caulking	Types of attached greenhouses
Cost and advantages of storm	Types of programmable
doors and windows	thermostats
Types of furnaces, various	Insulated window coverings
prices and efficiency ratings	

Readings

The ASSOCIATED PRESS was founded by six New York publishers in 1848 and is one of the pre-eminent news organizations in the world. The AP gathers news worldwide and disseminates it to thousands of newspapers and radio and television stations in the United States and abroad. Headquartered in New York City, the AP is a nonprofit organization. In the following news story, an AP writer distills the essential information of a private think-tank study about the likelihood of a reinstatement of the draft.

Draft May Be Back
by '90s: Study

WASHINGTON [AP]—Plans by the Reagan administration to expand the armed forces and deploy more highly sophisticated weapons could necessitate resumption of a peacetime draft by the 1990s, according to a Brookings Institution study released Sunday.

Despite optimism voiced by top Pentagon officials, the report said all-volunteer military services in coming years are likely to be pinched by a declining pool of qualified recruits and greater demand for highly skilled personnel.

Unless the American people can be counted on to support peacetime conscription, the study concluded, "it would be risky either to expand the size of the armed forces or to develop increasingly complicated weapon systems."

If either course is considered vital to U.S. security, "the nation's leadership should make these purposes clear and should prepare the American people for the reinstitution of compulsory service."

"Otherwise, the United States could end up fielding military forces in the 1990s whose effectiveness would depend on a military draft, only to find a citizenry unwilling to support it," it said.

The study was prepared by Martin Binkin, a Brookings specialist on defense manpower policy. The Brookings Institution is a nonprofit Washington public policy research center whose views often are considered liberal.

Defense Secretary Caspar Weinberger has hailed the success of the all-volunteer military, proclaiming that the volunteer force no longer was experimental.

More recently, however, defense manpower officials have tempered such optimism with cautionary remarks.

Assistant Defense Secretary Lawrence Korb warned on June 12 that "recruiting in the current improved economic environment has become more difficult." He predicted that the services would face "an increased challenge" in recruiting next year.

A report issued by Korb said that in the six months ending March 31, the armed forces had met or topped their recruitment goals.

In the Brookings study, Binkin pointed to the "demographic depression" in military-age youth that has resulted from ending of the post-World War II baby boom.

MEANING

1. As in any hard news report, the headline provides the essential information: "Draft May Be Back by '90s: Study." Does this report include other important points? What are they?
2. According to the Brookings Institution study, why will the peacetime draft be resumed? Does the study mention more than one reason?

METHOD

1. How is this report organized? Does it have an introduction and a conclusion?
2. Does the anonymous Associated Press reporter include background information in this news story? If so, where is it?
3. Which information-gathering method has been used for this report? How do you know?

AUDIENCE

1. At whom is this report aimed? What groups of people are likely to be interested in this piece? Who is likely to ignore it? Why?
2. What is your reaction to this report?

WRITING SUGGESTIONS

1. The author of this AP wire story summarizes the finding of the Brookings study. Summaries and abstracts, in which we distill from a piece of writing its essential points, are among our most useful tools for collecting and retaining information. Practicing writing summaries and abstracts is an excellent way to learn about the general nature of reports.

To write a summary, first carefully study the piece you're abstracting; become familiar with its overall content and outline. Then divide the passage into its clear parts and list the key words and phrases of each. Next, using these key terms, write a single sentence version of each part. Then group the sentences into a paragraph. (For longer works, you may have to expand the summary.) Now check the summary against the original; is it a brief but accurate translation?

Now try your hand at writing two or three short summaries. Choose articles from newspapers and magazines, chapters from textbooks, and so on. Include a photocopy of the original with this assignment.

2. Compile a short research report on a subject you know well, and one that should be interesting to your fellow students, from materials close at hand (books, local and national newspapers, favorite magazines). Summarize your findings, include background information, and choose a suitable pattern of organization. Some possible topics: romance novels, sports magazines, product ads, entertainment coverage.

USA TODAY began publishing in September 1982 and since has become one of the most widely circulated daily newspapers in the United States. Billing itself "The Nation's Newspaper," USA Today attempts to appeal to a broad audience of travelers and readers whose local papers lack national coverage. The paper's design and heavy reliance on graphics and color make it attractive to consumers who tend to get their news from television, and its journalistic point of view keeps stories brief and ideologically neutral. Although USA Today has its critics—some have dubbed it "McPaper"—its circulation has increased steadily, and its publishers, Gannett Co., are optimistic about its future. In the following article from the paper's editorial section, staffer Mark Lewyn interviews entrepreneur Steven Jobs, young co-founder and Chairman of Apple Computer.

Topic: High-Tech Wars

Steven Jobs, 29, co-founded Apple Computer Inc. in 1976 after he and Stephen Wozniak built the first Apple computer in his garage. Jobs is chairman of the board of Apple Computer Inc. and has been credited, more than any other individual, with sparking the personal computer revolution. Jobs was interviewed by USA TO-DAY's *computer writer, Mark Lewyn.*

USA TODAY: What's next in computer technology?
JOBS: Computers are very good at responding to what we ask them to do. Fundamentally, they're still servants. The next step is to make computers that anticipate what we want, that guide the users.

USA TODAY: How?

JOBS: Computer as servant will mature to computer as "agent" or guide. A little guide in the computer will anticipate what you might want, suggest things you might do, or watch your patterns and say, "You normally do it this way so I'll just assume you want to do it that way unless you ask me otherwise." That's coming in the next 24 to 36 months.

USA TODAY: How has the industry changed since you made one of the first personal computers in 1976?

JOBS: It has become a very, very high-stakes business. Apple and IBM will spend about $100 million in research and development for personal computers and $100 million or more on media advertising. If those investments are made wisely by Apple and IBM, it will be very difficult for companies that do not make those investments to play in the game.

USA TODAY: Why haven't others made those investments?

JOBS: They do not have the personal computer business to generate the revenues to make those investments from. To invest $50 million, $100 million or $200 million this year, they have to take cash from their company coffers and risk it. And they're not doing it. We've felt all along that it's going to come down to a two-horse race. Apple—a very young company in many ways—is one of the two key players in a $10 billion industry. It's a lot of fun.

USA TODAY: Does that mean the day of the garage-type startup is over?

JOBS: Certainly in the mainstream hardware, that is true. The investment required is too high. On the contrary, the environment has never been better to start a software company.

USA TODAY: IBM is expected to release its Popcorn personal computer soon. Can consumers expect anything new from Apple?

JOBS: Our primary objective right now is to simply be able to manufacture enough computers. While we're making more computers than ever before, the demand is even higher than that. Our challenge is just to increase our manufacturing capacity to keep up with demand.

USA TODAY: What's the most critical decision Apple has made?

JOBS: The decision we made a few years ago—and reconfirmed last year—to not be IBM-compatible, not live under IBM's umbrella. Everyone else seems to have run for the safe harbor of IBM compatibility. Living under IBM's umbrella might have been a very short-sighted decision. IBM may choose to fold that umbrella at any moment. They have already started to do so with the recent price cuts. We believe they will continue to close the umbrella over the next 12 months by adding proprietary features to their products, which the compatible vendors cannot match.

USA TODAY: What's Apple's strategy?

JOBS: IBM is trying to focus the marketplace on its strengths—service, support, and what we call "motherhood." IBM is very good at those things. But when you want to sell a million or 10 million computers a year, even IBM doesn't have enough mothers to send one with every computer. So we have to build the motherhood into the products. That's what Macintosh is all about. That is why we chose not to be IBM-compatible, because there was no way to do that using that old technology. Our goal is not to react to IBM. To the contrary, I think they are reacting to us.

USA TODAY: How has IBM reacted to Apple?

JOBS: I think the PCjr was an attempt by IBM to really go after the educational market, much more than the home market. But the PCjr's main strength was also its main weakness. Its strength was to allow it to run some of the IBM PC software. The weakness was that the IBM PC had no educational software. So the PCjr has really failed to even carve out a small niche of that market.

USA TODAY: Is the PCjr a flop, then?

JOBS: If IBM were smart, they'd run a big advertisement that said: "Please feel free to send back your PCjr for a full refund. We're really sorry we ever came out with this thing, and we're going to take the millions of them we have in the warehouses, and all of the ones you send back to us, and throw them in the Hudson River, and we're going to forget that this thing ever happened.

USA TODAY: And—

JOBS: Their business is in the office, in the big corporations. Their goal should be to keep Apples out of the Fortune 500. When they see an Apple computer on a Fortune 500 desk, it means they failed. The PCjr has communicated to the world that even IBM is fallible.

USA TODAY: What will be the fate of companies that sell IBM-compatible machines?

JOBS: One characteristic we've discovered about IBM is that they want it all. That characteristic will affect the clones in the next 12 months in a very big way.

USA TODAY: Has Apple made mistakes?

JOBS: Yes. The strength of Apple is to risk, potentially make mistakes and, when it does, admit them as fast as possible, pick up and move on. The largest mistakes we've made are when we've gotten our egos too involved in trying to make a bad decision successful just to save face.

USA TODAY: Have you ever been concerned about the company's survival?

JOBS: There was a time in the latter part of '83 when everyone was writing us off. We knew Macintosh was coming. We knew the Apple IIc was coming. To us inside, things had not looked better in a long time. But it got very hard because the world was saying we were going to be blown off the map by IBM and that technical innovation didn't matter anymore.

USA TODAY: Do you expect the Japanese will aggressively challenge the USA computer market soon?

JOBS: The Japanese will finally figure out how to make a decent personal computer in three to five years. It is essential that by that time we know how to manufacture as well as they do.

USA TODAY: Is there a danger the industry could become less creative as larger players become increasingly content to compete on price rather than technology?

JOBS: Sure. I think if IBM could have its way computers would enter sort of a Dark Ages for about 20 years. There would be very little innovation and it would be really sad.

USA TODAY: Where do you see American business by 2001?

JOBS: Look back 10 years. The personal computer industry didn't exist. Now it's a $10 billion industry. Apple didn't exist, not even in the garage. This year, we'll do probably $1.5 billion in revenue. 2001 is 17 years from now. Who knows?

USA TODAY: Do you see any trends?

JOBS: More than half of the gross national product today is generated not by industrial industries employing labor, but by information industries employing knowledge workers. What's very interesting about those industries is that power—the way you obtain influence over those organizations—is not based on traditional notions of seniority or position in the organization. It's based on what you know. The model of what a Fortune 500 company in the early 1990s will be is very different from what it was in the early '70s.

USA TODAY: How do you want Apple to be different from other companies?

JOBS: As companies grow, lots of layers of management get between the people who have the visions at the top, and the people who do the work, who have the visions, at the bottom. The layers of management in between generally aren't people who have visions. They don't really care about the products as much. We don't want to run a company that's based on management. We want to run a company based on leadership, vision; you get people to buy into your vision. When you're dealing with really bright people, they don't need to be managed. They're self-managing. They need to have a common vision, and that's the job of senior executives in our view of a great corporation.

USA TODAY: What lessons would you like other companies to learn from Apple?

JOBS: When we started, we had some very idealistic notions about the way a company should be run: You should share the success of the company with the people who make it happen—so we gave stock options to every professional who worked at Apple. We were the first company ever to do that. We believe very strongly in quality, that having great quality would make it cheaper in the long run, and doing it right the first time would be the best way to go. We stuck to these ideals and it turns out that most of them were right.

MEANING

1. Interviews may or may not be easily summarized in a headline. Does this interview convey a single, overriding fact or idea? If so, what is it? Does the interview have a specific purpose?
2. According to Jobs, what are some of Apple Computer's chief characteristics?
3. What crucial decisions has the company made in its short history? What has been the effect of these decisions?

METHOD

1. This interview is presented as a dialogue between Jobs and the interviewer, Mark Lewyn. Which of Lewyn's questions are likely to have been prepared ahead of time, and which arose spontaneously during the conversation? How do you know?

AUDIENCE

1. Must a reader love computers to be drawn to this interview? What appeal might it have for people *not* interested in computers?
2. Any extended interview will give us some sense of the subject's personality, values, goals, and so on. Based on what he says, how would you characterize Steven Jobs? Does this report increase your interest in him or his company? Does it make you more likely to buy an Apple computer?

WRITING SUGGESTIONS

1. Summarize the Jobs interview as a report, converting it from the dialog format to that of a news story. Feel free to quote liberally from the interview, especially those remarks which seem most important. (Try to find key phrases and sentences rather than quoting entire answers.)
2. Interview a teacher, fellow student, or member of the community on a topic about which he or she is especially qualified to speak. Find out as much as you can about your subject before the interview (in fact, you may need to ask him some preliminary questions before the real interview starts). Based on what you discover, and what you hope to learn, prepare at least 10 questions, and as many more as you can think of. If you tape the session, be sure to ask the subject's permission. Then, using summary and quotation of key remarks, present the interview as a report.

BARRY McLAUGHLIN was born in Newark, New Jersey, in 1937 and was educated at St. Louis University and Harvard, where he earned a PhD in social psychology. Mc-Laughlin has taught at Harvard, and currently he is an associate professor at the University of California, Santa Cruz. He has been a National Science Foundation Fellow and is a member of the American Psychological Association. In the following article, the author reports on the findings of research and on his own observation experiments about a tendency fathers exhibit when talking to their young children.

How Fathers Talk to Babies

by Barry McLaughlin

Much of what we know about the way children learn language comes from studies in which researchers observe mothers with their babies. . . . When mothers speak to their young children, their speech becomes slower, shorter, less complex, more repetitious, uses fewer pronouns. In fact, this way of talking is often called motherese.

Little is known about how fathers talk to babies, but one study indicates they do not say much. Every two weeks during the first three months of 10 babies' lives, Freda Rebelsky and Cheryl Hanks recorded everything fathers said to their infants in a 24-hour period. The fathers spoke to them an average of merely 38 seconds.

One of the few studies concerned with fathers' speech to young children was conducted by William Corsaro of Indiana University, who found that fathers asked more questions than did mothers during interactions with their two-year-olds. Nearly half of the fathers' utterances were leading questions: What is this? (no response). Is this a camel? (no response). Can you say that, camel? (no response). Camel?

Placed in the same situation, the children's mothers devoted only 18 percent of their utterances to questions of this sort. Such questions are one of the safest routes adults can take in conversation with small children. By asking leading questions, the adult feels comfortable with the child and controls the conversation.

The fathers' tendency to use a controlling language style with young children has been borne out by recent research I conducted with Caleb Schutz and David White. We found that fathers used significantly more imperatives with their five-year-old children than mothers did in the same situation.

In our experiment we recorded the conversations of 24 parents and their children while they were playing a table game called Capture the Hat. The game was new to the children, and the parents had to teach them the rules. What struck us immediately was the difference in teaching styles between the mothers and fathers. Mothers were involved with the children, they were careful about making rules clear, and they corrected mistakes and rule infractions. Fathers, on the other hand, were less involved; they often failed to cover the rules and tended to gloss over the children's mistakes or infractions. Although there were exceptions, fathers seemed uncomfortable and intent on getting the game over with. In fact, we found it difficult to find fathers who would participate in the study.

When playing the game, fathers appeared uncertain as to how to talk to their children. They often talked down to them, saying, "All right, say you roll five. How would you move? Show me how many you would move. You would go like this: One, two, three, four, five." In contrast, mothers tended to say the same thing more succinctly and less condescendingly: "Now, whatever number comes on the die, you get to move one of your hats that many places." Mothers did not count aloud because they knew the children could count spaces on a game board.

Although some fathers used speech that was too simple, underestimating what their children understood, others used language that was too advanced. In such cases the children did not understand the game, but their fathers' concern was not to explain it; they wanted to get it over with. These fathers glanced around uncomfortably, allowed rules to be broken, and seemed generally uninterested in the task.

Indirect information on the way fathers talk to young children comes from a study by Elaine Andersen at Stanford University, who had children aged between three and six play the role of parents. When the children pretended to be the father, their speech became shorter, their intonation changed (it became deeper, with less range in pitch), and they used more imperatives and fewer terms of endearment than when they played the mother.

> *Experimenter* (taking the child's role): Tell me a story.
> *Child* (in father's role): Mommy will.
> *Experimenter:* No, I want you to.
> *Child:* I'm going to sleep.
> *Experimenter:* Please tell me a story.
> *Child:* Ask your mother.
> *Experimenter:* Please, please.
> *Child:* All right. Sit down. Once upon a time. The end.

Other research suggests that the language of fathers to their children is less attuned to the child's needs than is the speech of mothers. Fathers neither repeat nor expand the speech of young children who are learning to talk to the same extent that mothers do. Fathers are generally less skilled in motherese, although there has been so little research on fathers' speech to young children that we do not know, for example, whether this is true of fathers who are equally involved with the mother in the child's upbringing. It appears that as long as most fathers leave the business of bringing up children to the mother, the language to which infants are exposed will continue to be principally the "mother tongue."

MEANING

1. According to this report, what is the main difference in the way fathers and mothers talk to babies?
2. Does the report draw any conclusions about why fathers talk differently? If so, what are these?
3. What style of speech do fathers use when speaking to infants? What are some of its characteristics?

METHOD

1. Is this report based primarily on one form of information gathering? If so, what is it? If not, what other methods does McLaughlin use?
2. How important is the background provided in this report? Where is it placed in the organization?
3. What pattern does the author use to structure his report?

AUDIENCE

1. Who is this report aimed at? Is any group of readers likely to respond in a strongly favorable or unfavorable way?
2. Does the information presented here jibe with your own experience and observation? Do these facts ("fathers spoke to them an average of merely 38 seconds") seem farfetched?

WRITING SUGGESTION

Choose a behavior you find interesting or unusual and observe it carefully, keeping your language as objective as possible. Using McLaughlin's piece as a model, present your findings in a two-to-three page report. Some sample topics: teacher–student dialog in the classroom, cafeteria etiquette, dormitory leisure, library study habits. Do some preliminary thinking and writing *before* you begin observing; what specific things do you plan to study? What do you already know about your subject? What kinds of obvious behavior can you likely ignore?

CONSUMER REPORTS is the United States' leading consumer magazine. Founded in 1936, it is published by Consumers Union, a Washington, D.C.-based nonprofit organization. Consumer Reports rates products by brand name after extensive testing and expert evaluation. Because the magazine accepts no advertising, its readers trust the impartiality of its judgments. In the following article, the editors of CR compile first-hand evaluations of popular fast-food restaurants and their menus, presenting an objective report of what the testers discovered.

Fast Foods

People who fear that fast foods are taking over America are worrying too late—it has already happened. Fast-food outlets account for about 45 percent of all eating places. Americans spend some $38-billion a year eating fast food.

Clearly, fast food suits American tastes. . . . But how well does the stuff feed you? And what about its taste?

To find out, we sampled the menus of 10 top chains: McDonald's, Burger King, and Wendy's, the three big burger chains; Jack in the Box, a West Coast burger chain; Roy Rogers, Arby's, and Hardee's, which sell hot sandwiches as well as burgers; and Kentucky Fried Chicken, Taco Bell, and Long John Silver's Sea Food Shoppes, the leading chains for their respective types of food. All these places meet the definition of classic "fast feeders": a limited menu, no table service, an atmosphere designed for serving lots of people as quickly as possible.

Obviously, we couldn't test every item on the menus. Where possible, we tried to test comparable things. We were able to order the archetypal fast-food meal of burger, chocolate shake, and fries from seven of the chains. In each chain, we chose the "name" burger (Big Mac, Whopper) or something close to it in content and in price. We sought out chicken, fish, and roast-beef entrées, and sampled other foods that were featured items on some menus. Since the fast-food breakfast is not yet an established meal—McDonald's aside—we didn't test any breakfast items.

Where's the beef?

We couldn't resist trying to answer Clara Peller's query. So we dissected samples of seven chains' burgers and weighed the components. Removing the sauce from the burgers was difficult and messy, but we did our best. Separating the melted cheese from the meat was next to impossible, so we weighed cheese and meat together.

From one sample to another, we often found a fairly wide variation in the weight of a chain's burger or bun. Perhaps the sauce had soaked into one bun more than another, or one meat patty had been cooked slightly longer than another (note that burgers listed as "quarter-pounders" on the menu are weighed raw, and they shrink considerably during cooking). But since a basic premise of fast foods is sameness from outlet to outlet, we think our measurements of a few samples from each chain are reasonable grounds for evaluation of Wendy's ad.

By our measure, Hardee's, in fact, has the beef. The meat and cheese in its Big Deluxe burger weighed, on average, about 3¾ ounces. Wendy's Single burger had the second most meat and cheese, just over 3½ ounces, on average. (Wendy's Single burger might *look* extra-large, however, since it's served on the smallest bun.) Roy Rogers' cheeseburger and Burger King's Whopper had slightly less than 3½ ounces of meat and cheese; the other burgers we tested weighed in at 3 ounces or less.

This comparison, of course, doesn't take into account the various burgers we didn't test. Wendy's Single is its smallest burger, with its Double and Triple burgers containing even more meat. McDonald's burgers range from a small hamburger to its Quarter-Pounder; Burger King sells Junior Whoppers and Double Whoppers. Other chains that specialize in burgers sell various sizes, too.

If Clara Peller had asked as a follow-up question, "Where are the potatoes?," the answer would be at Wendy's—and Kentucky Fried Chicken and Long John Silver's. Each sold a 3½-ounce portion of fries for 58 to 72 cents. McDonald's and Roy Rogers served a 3-ounce portion for about 60 cents. Those five chains offered the best value on fries, averaging 17 to 21 cents an ounce. Burger King, with a tiny 1¾-ounce serving for 59 cents, had the most expensive fries, averaging 34 cents an ounce. (This comparison is based on a small order of fries; except for Wendy's and Hardee's, the chains that sell fries also offer a large size that often costs less per ounce.)

Roy Rogers served the largest shake, at least when measured by weight. (Because shakes quickly lose the air whipped into them, we couldn't fairly compare them by volume.)

Where's the fish and the chicken? Breading can make it hard to tell, so we carefully picked the fish and chicken clean. Long John Silver's sandwich turned out to have the most fish, about 2½ ounces; Hardee's sandwich had slightly less. McDonald's Filet-O-Fish and Burger King's Whaler had only about an ounce of fish under all the breading.

Of the chicken items we tested, Jack in the Box's chicken sandwich had the most meat, nearly four ounces, with Kentucky Fried Chicken's two-piece dinner portion close behind. But the Colonel's chicken fillet sandwich provided only two ounces of meat, as did Wendy's chicken sandwich. The other chicken items, including Chicken McNuggets, were between those extremes. . . .

Where's the taste?

Since it was only fair to taste the fast foods fast, we sent our expert tasters out into the field. . . .

Overall, our experts thought the best-tasting food was at Kentucky Fried Chicken, Roy Rogers, and Wendy's. The chicken at all three places—and at Jack in the Box, too—was quite good. Its crisp, pleasantly spicy coating contrasted nicely with juicy, tender meat. Roy Rogers and Wendy's had the best burgers, Roy Rogers the best roast beef.

McDonald's, however, served the best fries as well as the best chocolate shake. The best fish sandwich came from the fish specialist, Long John Silver's.

A common criticism from the experts was that the food was too bland. That's not surprising, since many chains cater to children (who don't eat much, but whose parents do), and children tend to like bland, homogeneous food. A good example of the difference between adults' and children's perceptions is the opinion on Wendy's chili. Our experts thought the chili uninteresting because it was barely one-alarm. But their children, who came along for all the tastings, considered it too spicy.

When entrées—burgers, sandwiches, tacos—didn't taste good, the reason was generally some problem with the meat or fish. The meat in Arby's cheeseburger, for instance, had a distinct gamy flavor and was chewy and full of gristle. Arby's roast beef was made up of gray, pressed short strands that tasted more like ham than beef. The fish in Hardee's Big Fish sandwich was chewy, dry, and fibrous, with a noticeably fishy flavor.

A common criticism of the french fries was that they tasted too much like frozen potatoes—a taste our experts describe as reminiscent of cardboard. In the less-than-best fries, such a taste was often aggravated by cooking that left the fries too greasy or tough instead of crispy. But less can go wrong with fries than with more complicated menu items; every place that sold them produced fries that tasted pretty good.

Shakes present a difficult problem for the chains, since a basic premise of fast-food cookery is making the food ahead of the customer's request. A classic milk shake made only with ice cream, milk, and syrup would quickly melt away if left sitting. Consequently, fast-food shakes are apt to contain various additives that help them stay thick.

Unfortunately, shakes designed to sit around without melting often don't melt in your mouth, either. Our tasters found that many turned into foam instead of melting, as good ice cream would. Worse, some shakes left the mouth coated with an unpleasant, sometimes chalky film. In addition, the worst-tasting shakes had hardly any chocolate or cocoa flavor. Only McDonald's, Wendy's, and Roy Rogers made a shake that tasted even good, and none of those would beat a good soda-fountain creation.

Our expert tasters have had years of training and experience in carefully measuring differences in flavor and texture. How do their evaluations compare with those of ordinary people? For some items, we were able to tell from the survey we did last winter of subscribers.

Enough people polled had eaten at McDonald's, Burger King, and Wendy's so we could see how our readers rated those chains' burgers and fries. Wendy's burgers were tops for our readers, as they were for the experts. But readers rated burgers from Burger King second, while the experts thought the Big Mac a bit better than the Whopper. Readers and experts agreed that McDonald's served the best fries.

Where's the nutrition?

If junk food is food that contributes nothing but calories to the diet, fast foods aren't junk. Nutritionally, fast food is not very different from the typical American diet. The general criticisms of fast food are those often heard of the American diet: too much protein, fat, calories, sodium; not enough complex carbohydrates and fiber.

For example, take the cheeseburger–shake–fries combination that's often ordered as a fast-food meal. By our analysis, averaging samples from seven chains, here's how that meal compares with the dietary goals established by the Senate Select Committee on Nutrition and Human Needs. The table shows proportions of a day's calorie intake supplied by various nutrients:

Calories from	Fast-food meal	Dietary goal
Protein	14%	12%
Fat	43	30
Complex carbohydrates	23	43
Simple sugars	20	15

That meal would supply 70 to 90 percent of the daily protein requirement for most people, whereas a person eating three meals a day needs only a third of his or her protein from one meal. Extra protein eaten in a day just means extra calories for the body to use—or to store.

And fast food offers no shortage of calories. The average meal of burger, shake, and fries would supply about 1150 calories. That's about 40 percent of the number needed to maintain the weight of a 165-pound man, 60 percent of that needed by a 128-pound woman. For someone on a diet, 1150 calories is virtually an entire day's allowance. The main reason for all those calories? Fat.

About half of a cheeseburger's calories come from fat, because of the fat found in beef, cheese, and mayonnaise-type sauces. Chicken and fish normally have a low fat content and relatively few calories, but not when they are breaded and fried. For the most part, the chicken and fish items we tested were as fatty and as caloric as the burgers. Frying has the same effect on potatoes—they get almost none of their calories from fat when raw, but about half of them from fat when french fried.

Fat contributed a slightly smaller percentage of calories in the average roast beef or ham-and-cheese sandwiches. But tacos, which look as if they are a good part lettuce, get more than half their calories from fat, presumably from the meat, the cheese, and the fried tortilla.

Shakes get most of their 350 or so calories from sugars. An exception was Wendy's Frosty, which had less sugar and more fat than the others, but about the same number of calories.

Now that salads are available at many fast-food outlets, it's possible to choose a fairly well-balanced, even low-calorie meal. A salad adds the complex carbohydrates and fiber that are missing from most fast foods, and if you go easy on the dressing, a salad has very little fat or sugar. A salad, a diet soda, and a plain hamburger, without cheese or oily sauce, can make a meal that's fairly low in calories.

A salad, especially if you choose carrots, tomatoes, and dark green vegetables, can provide some of the vitamins—A, C, E, and folic acid—missing from ordinary fast-food fare. Shakes supply calcium (as does milk, of course). Beef-containing items are usually rich in B vitamins such as thiamin, niacin, riboflavin, and B-12, and are fairly good sources of the minerals iron and zinc. Entrées containing chicken and fish generally supply those nutrients, too, though to a lesser extent.

A salad might be one of the few things people who have to restrict their sodium intake could choose at the typical fast-food outlet. . . . [M]any of the items we tested contained more than 500 milligrams of sodium, some more than 1000.

Generally, fries had less sodium than any other food, even shakes. The potatoes may taste salty, but saltiness is not necessarily a good measure of sodium content. Many food additives other than salt contain sodium, some of which probably account for the sodium content of the shakes.

Recommendations

If you are choosing among the top three burger chains, we suggest trying Wendy's. Our expert tasters thought Wendy's Single burger better than a Big Mac or a Whopper; our readers thought Wendy's burgers best, too. The chicken sandwich at Wendy's was one of the best items our experts tasted, and Wendy's Frosty was one of the best shakes. Wendy's usually has a salad bar, too.

If you're in the mood for chicken, the Colonel does his well. Our experts considered both the two-piece chicken dinner and the fillet sandwich among the best items tasted.

For those who aren't quite sure what they want to eat, Roy Rogers does a lot of different foods well, from burgers to chicken to sandwiches. It too offers a salad bar. Everything our experts tasted there was better than average, except for the shake. There are also tasty items to be found at other chains—notably McDonald's french fries and shake and Jack in the Box's chicken sandwich.

Fast foods are far from being nutritionally worthless. For most people, an occasional meal at a fast-food chain in no way compromises a well-balanced diet. People who eat fast foods regularly, however, should choose what they eat with more care.

For most people, the greatest nutritional problem with typical fast food is the number of calories it contains. A lunch that consists of a burger, fries, and a shake can easily contain more calories than a home-cooked dinner. Teenage boys, perhaps, can consume such high-calorie meals without concern, but the rest of the population, by and large, can't afford to squander so much of the day's calorie allotment on one meal.

MEANING

1. This report presents a great deal of information. If you were to summarize it in a headline, what would it be?
2. Does this piece give an unbiased, objective view of its subject? What evidence can you cite to defend your opinion?

METHOD

1. How is this report organized? Does the pattern help you digest all the facts? Why?
2. What methods of information gathering were used for this report? Do they seem appropriate and reliable? Why?

AUDIENCE

1. Do you agree with the findings this report presents? Why or why not?
2. Is such a report likely to affect your fast-food eating habits or preferences? What audience of readers is most likely to disregard these findings, and which one likely to follow the report's recommendations?

WRITING SUGGESTIONS

1. If time (and money) allow, conduct your own similar survey. Following the *Consumer Reports* model, assemble a small group of testers and then sample the fare and some local cafes, fast-food joints, bistros. Be consistent in your choices, and try to keep your work serious and careful. Based

on your findings, draft a report for an audience of your fellow students in which you rank your samples and conclude with a recommendation. (Again, you are an objective researcher, not a booster for your favorite hangout.)

2. Using whatever methods are appropriate or useful, gather information on one of the following topics and write a report for a local audience of interested adults.
    - The three best places in town to get your car fixed
    - Little-known or inexpensive recreation sites
    - Where to find the best clothing values
    - Free services for visitors and people new to town
    - Where to find help for personal or family problems

ADDITIONAL WRITING SUGGESTIONS

1. Compose a questionnaire on a controversial topic among your fellow students, and poll them. Keep the questions objective, and avoid asking leading questions (ones that imply an answer). Do a profile of your sample (how many men, women, English majors, etc.). Present the profile and poll results in a report of your own design.
2. If you belong to an organization, compile a report on the group's goals, major activities, philosophy, and so on, as an informative brochure for the general public and prospective members.
3. Choose a city or town you know well and compose a descriptive brochure for new residents. What are the town's most important features? What is it known for? What would the newcomer be likely to want to know?
4. If you are knowledgeable about computer hardware or software, electronic gear, automobiles, and so on, compose a report for people *unfamiliar* with the subject in which you provide some basic information (for example: user-friendly home computers, digital audio components, high-performance sports cars).

6

INFORMATIVE ESSAYS

HOW ESSAYS DIFFER FROM REPORTS

Reports aren't the only useful way to convey information. Essays, too, are a popular, and more personal, form for this purpose.

Although reports and essays are different in many respects, the chief distinguishing characteristic of the essay is this personal dimension. Reports, as we have defined them, are objective and usually impersonal. They do not concern themselves with the writer's biases. When reading a report, we don't look for a sense of the writer's self—of personality, sensitivities, individuality. The report's first allegiance is to its subject.

With the essay, however, we have something quite different. The essay form has evolved as an expression of a writer's engagement with a subject. We are meant to see not only the bringing-to-light of the subject but that writer's special way of doing so. Even if the essay is a formal, third-person argument, for example, it will reveal the uniqueness of the author as he or she attempts to make the subject meaningful—to make a point.

Here we have the second major difference between reports and essays. A report may address a problem, issue a set of findings, even suggest recommendations; in this sense, reports may also have points to make. (A commission's study of automobile safety may find that airbags provide the greatest passenger protection, and it may recommend that laws be passed to require all new cars to include these devices.) The point of a report, however, is the thrust of its information. It is not the point of an individual writer. (I may think airbags a waste of money, but as the person charged with writing the report, I should have no difficulty putting my private view aside.) The meaningful point of an essay is one that only *that* writer can make in quite *that* way. An essay is like a fingerprint; the writer should be able to be identified by it.

For example, in a well-known essay, journalist Gay Talese paints an informative portrait of New York City. As he exhaustively catalogs the city's "things unnoticed"—the "tired trumpet players and homeward-bound bartenders," the "gas-station attendant sleeping next to Sloppy Louie's with the radio on," the "kids coming out of the Astor Hotel in white dinner jackets," the thousands of cabdrivers, bus drivers, bootblacks and subway riders, the chestnut vendors, mediums, tattooists, midget wrestlers, stray cats, pigeons—Talese gives us much more than a report of the city's diversity. Rather, through his choice of detail, tone of voice, attitude toward his subject, we learn not only of New York's "offbeat wonders" but of Talese's sense of awe, respect, and humility before such a spectacle. We are left not merely with a list of facts but with a picture of a man deeply engaged in trying to capture the essence of a great American city.

Another writer's portrait of New York, which might include many similar details, could be drastically different—showing us a city that is insanely overcrowded, filthy, teeming with mindless activity, criminally expensive, dangerous, an enormous machine intent on grinding people to dust.

When we write essays in order to inform, our purpose is identical to that of an informative report, but the way we go about fulfilling this purpose is different. An informative essay still presents facts and ideas to the reader. The content of the essay, however, more closely reflects the writer's point of view.

Here is another example: Suppose your college held a competition for the essay that best captured the essence of the school for prospective students. A report that listed the many features of the school (number of buildings and classrooms, athletic facilities, percentage of faculty holding PhDs, and so on) would be hard to individualize; the facts speak for themselves. If 100 students entered the essay competition, however, chances are the judges would find 100 different versions of the college's uniqueness. Certainly many of the essays would refer to many of the same qualities, but the tone, choice of language, details—the originality—of each would reflect each writer's special feeling about his or her subject. One student might focus on the school's superb faculty; another might look at the college's tradition of famous alumni; another might emphasize the link between the school and the community. More likely than not, no two essays would be the same overall, even if they addressed the same concerns. Each would have its unique point to make, and each would make it in its own way.

The essay form, therefore, lends itself well to the informative purpose, especially when there is no reason to keep the writer separate from the information or when the facts are directly tied to the writer's experience or knowledge. The purpose remains paramount, but the writer steps forward and openly acknowledges his or her role as messenger.

THE ESSAY-WRITING PROCESS

Whether your purpose is to inform your reader, analyze a subject, convince your audience, or express yourself, the process of writing an essay poses a set of problems different from those discussed in the previous chapter. Because essays reflect the writer's individuality, they are more directed toward discovery, creativity and inventiveness than are most reports. When we write an essay, we explore what we think about a topic, and we discover what we think, often, by writing. We attempt to find a suitable design for our thoughts, and we build a finished response.

In what follows, we will consider the overall process of writing essays, with our focus on the informative purpose. (In Chapters 8 and 9 we will look at the process again, but with greater emphasis on the purpose of analysis. Chapters 11 through 13 look at essays aimed at changing minds. Chapter 14 investigates the essays we write for their own sake, to express ourselves.) We can divide this process into the following general stages:

1. Determining the essay's purpose and audience
2. Preliminary writing
3. Drafting
4. Waiting
5. Revising
6. Editing

Let's look at each of these.

Determining the Essay's Purpose and Audience

Much of what we said about purpose and audience in report writing applies as well to essays. What are you trying to accomplish, and for whom?

Just as reports may speak to general or specialized audiences, so, too, may essays. As with reports, the essays useful for college study typically also address the interests of the general reader. While it's true that any writer should try to define his or her audience as precisely as possible, the essay writer may not know exactly who will read the work. (Again, consider the parallel to the journalist who writes for a mass audience.) Much of what we read and write is aimed at anyone who has an interest and can read standard English. The general audience exists, and there is no reason not to write for it if this is appropriate for your purpose.

Preliminary Writing

The beginning of the writing process, we've seen, does not require either your ideas or your language to be perfect or finished. All you should care about at this stage is achieving action. Simply start writing, even if your first words are nonsense. Remember that you are out to explore, to dig; you may make a rather large mess before you find what you are looking for.

The preliminary, or pre-writing, stage is different for each person. Depending on how you write, you may begin by making notes, lists, or rough or tentative outlines. You might jot down a number of questions that your prospective essay seeks to answer. If your essay is to contain documented information (and assuming you've begun your research), pre-writing might involve summarizing some or all of this material in order to get an overview. Sometimes writers just take a running jump into an introductory paragraph and hope that a clear direction will emerge. Whatever you do, try to discover the technique that best frees you to begin putting words down on paper. You might even talk to yourself aloud first, or discuss the writing task with a friend. Some people write more easily with a typewriter (you can keep up with your own train of thought if you can type fast), and some need to use a special sort of pen or paper. Writing is an intensely personal act, so don't be afraid to personalize it. Do whatever works.

While preliminary writing works best if it is spontaneous and free-flowing, that does not mean pre-writing will automatically give you all that you need. Do not lose sight of your purpose. Pre-writing may take you off on a tangent (or two, or three); you have to keep your concentration on the job at hand and follow those ideas that can be useful to your purpose. Abandon those which, although interesting, are not likely to survive the context of purpose and audience.

Just as you should avoid being drawn away from your goal, dogged persistence in the face of an obstacle to it may only exhaust you. If you get stuck, don't let the block take charge. Move aside. Switch to another path and worry about the problem later.

In writing an essay whose purpose is primarily informative, pre-writing might be devoted to mapping the boundaries of the subject and making a rough sketch of what falls within them. Say, for example, that you have entered the aforementioned essay contest. Your job is to capture for prospective students the essential character of your college. You might start by making a list of all the most obvious features you can think of: the beautiful campus, the friendly faculty, the intramural sports program, the high tuition, the huge number of business majors, and so on. Then you might try to think of some less obvious characteristics. Perhaps the teachers form lifelong friendships with some of their students. Perhaps a significant number of graduates have stayed on to work at the college. Or perhaps the institution has recently undergone a change from its past character, expanding its program, say, or redesigning its curriculum.

You then might write a bit on the reasons supporting any of these features as essential to the school's personality. Which of these would be likely to interest a prospective freshman? (Don't forget your audience.) You might ask yourself the question: What is the most important quality for *any* college to have? Is there only one? To what extent does my school meet this objective?

Eventually, one or more potential essays will begin to take shape in your mind and on paper. When it seems that you have enough material to provide the basis for a first draft (or perhaps a number of different ones), it is time to move to the next phase of the process.

Drafting

Writing the first draft is analogous to extemporaneous speaking. When we give directions, answer questions, speak "off the cuff," we do it unconsciously, for the most part. We don't first ask ourselves, "What am I going to say?" We just say it.

A first draft might rest upon a plan (an outline or list of parts), but the draft itself is largely extemporaneous. As in the pre-writing stage, your chief concern here is to get something out and on the paper. It may be extremely rough, but don't worry about it. The first draft is not called the *first* draft for nothing.

Write the draft as if you were speaking directly to your reader. Speak carefully, but not so much so that you slow to a dead stop. Try to use precise language, and be as clear as you can be without laboring over particular words and phrases. Your goal in the rough draft stage should be to achieve a general sense of the essay's content, organization, and main point.

Since the essay form has certain basic parts, you should draft your work according to these. That is, draft the introductory or lead section of the essay first, then the body, then the conclusion. (Some writers skip the introduction by drafting the body first. The problem with this method is that the body may lack focus or ramble more than necessary even for a rough draft. In the introduction, you should state or imply your controlling idea. This should help you keep the body unified and on track.) Try to maintain a sense of each of these major parts. Viewing the essay as a structure consisting of smaller building blocks will make it easier for you to stay in control of the whole.

When drafting the introduction, keep in mind that you must first capture your reader's interest before you can tell him your main point. As a rule of thumb, it makes sense to angle the topic specifically toward the common ground between reader and subject. What aspect of your subject is likely to interest the reader most? What about the subject affects him or her? What speaks directly to the reader's concerns or needs?

Writers use a variety of introductory techniques. Some of the most common of these are: opening with a question, a startling fact, an anecdote (a brief story), a flat or blunt statement, a quotation, or a definition. Or, you may combine two or more devices for an extended introduction. Whatever you do, however, remember that the introduction is a gesture. With it, you are offering an invitation into your essay, and you are encouraging the reader to stay awhile.

Once you've got the reader, you should tell him or her what to expect. In most cases, a direct statement of your thesis or main point should conclude your introduction. Why? First, the reader is likely to wonder what the introduction is leading to. Second, placing the thesis at the end of the introductory paragraph or section lends it particular emphasis. Unless there's a good reason, you don't want your readers to have to guess what they're reading.

Sometimes, writers leave the thesis of the essay implied. That is, they say enough in the introduction to lead the reader to infer the main point, a direct statement of which occurs at the conclusion of the essay. Because leading readers to infer what you mean is more difficult than telling them outright, it is wise to become proficient first with the straightforward method. Once you have mastered the technique of stating your ideas directly and developing an essay to support them, you will be ready to try your hand at other, more sophisticated approaches.

Finally, when drafting your tentative thesis statement, remember that this sentence is the key to the rest of the essay. It should tell the reader what to expect from the essay (its content and direction), and it should set forth a single, unified train of thought. The words we use to describe this key sentence are revealing: We speak of the essay's "thrust," its "point." The thesis is the essay reduced to one arrowlike statement. Eventually, if not in the first draft, the writer must shape the thesis to be strong and sharp—strong in its solid content, sharp in its precise language.

With a draft of the introduction out of the way, we can proceed to draft the body of the essay and to follow the direction of the thesis.

The body of any essay is an elaboration, a detailed development, of the work's central idea. In Gay Talese's piece on New York, for example, his main point is that the city is full of "things unnoticed." Throughout the rest of the essay, Talese notices things in elaborate and specific detail, and all his remarks are tied directly to this point.

Once the writer has achieved at least a rough idea of his thesis (or one thesis among a number of possibilities), he or she faces the problem of developing a solid body of support. During the pre-writing stage, the writer should have produced enough raw material to direct the overall approach to the essay. Drafting the body then becomes a matter of selecting and organizing this material according to the thesis, and expanding it in detail as we write.

In Chapter 8, we will look at a number of methods for organizing essays that explain or analyze information. In the present chapter, the chief purpose of the essay is to convey information without manipulating it. Two methods commonly used for the informative purpose are listing, and illustration or example.

Sometimes the simplest and most appropriate way to present the bulk of your information is to list it. Say, for example, that you wished to write an informative essay on the subject of exercise. Your thesis might be something like this: "Keeping in shape is easy if you perform the following exercises three or four times each week." The body of the essay supporting this thesis might list the exercises and the corresponding benefits of each one. Presenting information as a list of facts can be an effective, straightforward way to organize the body of your essay.

Another way to convey information is through illustration or example. If you wanted to inform high school students about the nature of drug addiction, you would be likely to cite specific instances of it. Concrete examples support your informative purpose with facts. The more specific your illustrations, the more informative your essay. (When you read the essays at the end of this chapter, study the authors' use of listing and example.)

Apart from the method(s) of development you use, there are several general guidelines for the drafting of the body paragraphs of your essay.

First, keep the paragraphs unified by a single topic. Second, make the first sentence of the paragraph the key, or topic, sentence (leading each paragraph with a controlling idea). Third, develop the paragraph with detailed support. It is especially important in a first draft to let your paragraphs unfold—to give them room. The more detail you can put down the first time around, the more you'll have to work with during revision. Finally, keep the readers' attention in mind and give them transitional markers, words and phrases, that connect the larger parts (the paragraphs) as well as the smaller ones (the sentences) together.

In general, when drafting the body of the essay, try to give a full, detailed and organized treatment to your subject. Remain flexible, however. The draft is a working paper, not a finished product.

The only part of an essay harder to write than the introduction is the conclusion. Conclusions may employ a number of the techniques used in introductions (questions, anecdotes, quotations, for instance), or they can send the reader off with a forecast or prediction, a final summary statement, or a memorable turn of phrase. Some essays have ringing conclusions, and for others the last word falls with a loud thud.

Two points to remember: Your conclusion is your last chance to have an effect on your audience, so give it careful thought. Draft a number of alternative conclusions if you are having trouble. (This is, likewise, a good suggestion for introductions.) Try to listen to the essay's own impulse. Does it seem to want to end in a special way? Is there a "natural" way to end it?

And think of your conclusion as your signature. Make your conclusion honest and forthright. This is your work, after all. Your name is attached to it. Try to speak so that your reader will remember you and your essay, and so that you yourself will remember it.

Waiting

A watched kettle never boils, or so the saying goes. Periodically, put your work aside and refresh yourself. Do something physical. (Sitting still may be one of writing's heaviest demands.) Chances are that when you return to the job, after a few hours or a day off, the glaze over your eyes will be gone, you'll be able to see the work more objectively (for both good and ill), and you will be able to resume work with a renewed sense of energy and enthusiasm. You will be ready to start:

Revising

In a way, revising is a part of the writing process that never stops until you type the last period of the last sentence of your final manuscript. Every gesture the writer makes—whether a word, sentence, paragraph, or section—is subject to revision, rethinking, rewriting. This means that revision occurs, *must* occur, on all these levels. We revise not only to correct word choice or sentence construction, but we reshape whole paragraphs and sections of our work, and thereby whole essays.

It helps, then, to keep these categories of revision separate. We will discuss each in turn.

First revision: The whole piece.   Once you have a first draft shaped (and have left it alone for a while), your first revision should address the whole essay. Are you satisfied with the overall presentation, the general outlines of the work? Does the introduction seem appropriate and effective in its content? Does it make an effort to speak directly to the reader's interest in the subject? Is the controlling idea of the essay more or less what you intend?

Reread the body of the essay. Does its overall shape and content seem satisfactory, or are there obvious places where you need to do more work? Are there any pieces missing from your design? Will a reader unfamiliar with this work be able to follow it? Does the body, in fact, support and develop the thesis? Are the sections of the body themselves adequately developed and supported?

If the introduction and body of the essay appear to hold together and meet your expectations, you may wish to worry about the conclusion later. If these first two essential parts need more basic work—greater use of detail, clearer development, the addition of whole new paragraphs and sentences to the draft—then you are not yet ready to begin the second revision. Continue fleshing out the working draft until all the major parts of the essay are in rough form. Only then will it make sense to attempt a closer revision of the individual sections and paragraphs.

Second revision: The major parts.   Now it is time to drop down a level and take a good look at the individual sections of the essay. Satisfied with the whole, you can begin to sharpen the focus, knowing that you are unlikely to change the overall piece. Evaluate each part—introduction, body paragraphs, conclusion—for its individual effectiveness. The introductory paragraph may be generally okay, but could it be improved in content or organization? Does the introductory prose lead directly to the thesis statement? Similarly with the body paragraphs, evaluate each in terms of its specific shape and content. Does the topic sentence give clear and specific direction? Is each paragraph unified around and in detailed support of the topic?

In this second revision, which may be your first full rewrite of the essay, it is very important that you actually *redraft* these parts. *Start at the beginning and rewrite the entire essay, paragraph by paragraph.* It is not enough to make some marginal notes and scratch-outs. By putting yourself, and the essay, through the drafting process a second time, you will open the work to all the possibilities that the writing process in general makes available. You may find, for instance, that although your first paragraph sounded pretty good, by redrafting it you've been able to say what you wanted in a much clearer, sharper, and more economical way. The reason for this is that the first draft provides you with a definite content and direction; you know what you are talking about. By trying to say it again and yet again, however, you say it better.

When you have completed a second revision or first redraft, check the whole essay again as you did for the first revision. If you are still happy (you should be happier than you were before), it is time for the third revision.

Third revision: Sentences, phrases, and words.   At this point you should be ready to take a close look at your style, the words and sentences themselves. Are your sentences clear? Will the reader know exactly what you mean? Are the sentences economical? Can you eliminate any unnecessary, repetitive, or trite words and phrases? Are the sentences active and direct, showing people and things performing specific actions? Are your words concrete and precise? Do the sentences flow one into the next, with good transitional links and directional signals? Are the sentences organized so that important information receives emphasis at the end?

After the third revision, your essay should be in fairly good shape. It is possible to overrevise (although most young writers tend to avoid this problem). Stand back from your work and inspect it. More likely than not, you are ready for a final read-through, a session of editing, polishing and proofreading.

Editing

Editing—polishing and proofreading—this is the last operation to be performed. It is technical: checking grammar, spelling, punctuation, mechanics—preparing for typing the final draft. Few of us are perfect, and few final manuscripts are without a minor error here and there. Perfection should be your goal, however. You want your copy to be clean, sharp, and letter-perfect—or as close, with a good English handbook by your side, as you can make it.

Learning to compose clear, solidly developed informative essays provides a base for the more complex tasks of writing to analyze information or to change the reader's mind—tasks for later chapters.

QUESTIONS

1. What is the chief difference between reports and essays? Are there other significant differences? If so, what?
2. Do you see any similarity in the report-writing and essay-writing processes? What would you say is the key difference?
3. What's the role of the thesis statement in an essay? Why is it important?
4. Why are introductions important in essays? What are some useful introductory devices?
5. What means of development are common in informative essays?
6. Why are conclusions important, and what does a good conclusion do?

EXERCISES

1.   How essays differ from reports
In newspapers or newsmagazines, find examples of essays—editorials, columns, news analysis pieces—that have been written in response to subjects covered by news reports. (*Example:* a report about a political debate and an analysis of whose side made the best showing.) Compare the essays with the news reports. Is the purpose of each clear? What seem to you to be the greatest differences between the reports and the essays? Do you see any similarities? Pay particular attention to the way the pieces are organized, and to the degree each does or doesn't reflect the writer's point of view. Can you find examples of essays that are primarily informative?

2.   Determining the essay's purpose and audience
A.   When analyzing the audience for a given essay-writing situation, you want to understand the values, attitudes, biases, and other concerns the reader may bring to the essay. It's not that the writer's job is to cater totally to the demands of his or her audience (although in some situations this is almost

unavoidable), but the writer should know something about the reader—or else communication takes place in a void. Say, for example, that you need to write a job application letter in answer to a newspaper ad. Chances are you would find out as much as you could about the company, you'd pay close attention to any specific requirements mentioned in the ad, you'd include all necessary information about your qualifications and experience, and you'd address your prospective employer in the manner he or she expected, according to the conventions of business letter writing.

In the following examples, your purpose is clear. Consider your reader: What should you be aware of as you undertake the essay-writing task?

- You have been asked to write a guest column for the local paper in which you give tips and advice on organic gardening. (Other subjects for this exercise: model railroading, furniture making or restoring, wine making, etc.)
- It is your job to write a letter to electric utility customers in which you inform them of new, sharply higher rates.
- You have evidence that proves you have been falsely accused of plagiarizing research material for a term paper; you must submit a written statement of the facts to your school's honor board.
- A doctor friend of yours has asked you to write an informative essay for children in which you give the patient's view of being in a hospital.

B.   Often, especially in the classroom, the essays we write address a general audience, that is, a potentially large and diverse group of people. The audience for a research paper on the subject of values in the media, for example, might include students, teachers, working people of the town, parents, and so on. Much of the writing that we read is addressed to this general mass. What do you think are the major characteristics of writing that seeks to address a broad readership? Is such writing watered-down or pitched to the lowest common level? First, name some sources of general-audience writing, and then try to describe its main features.

3.   *Preliminary writing*
Choose one of the topics below for an informative essay to an audience of your fellow students. Try your hand at list making, brainstorming, and so on, and write nonstop for 10 or 15 minutes. Evaluate what you've written, choose three or four of your best ideas, and continue writing freely in an attempt to develop some first draft material.

Topic: Things to remember when . . .

Planning a camping trip	Baking Christmas cookies
Choosing a college or university	Breaking up
Going on a blind date	Visiting New York City
Raising children	(or anywhere else)
Interviewing for a job	Getting fired
Asking your parents for money	Buying your first used car
Reading a book	Investing in the stock market

4.   Drafting

Using the material you developed for the previous exercise as the body of your essay, draft an introductory paragraph according to the guidelines just discussed. Angle your introduction directly toward your readers: Why would they be interested in your topic? (In this exercise, you might try structuring your introductory paragraph as an inverted pyramid—beginning with a general statement and narrowing to a specific, controlling idea: "When visiting _____, you should always remember to . . .") Place the main point of the essay, the thesis, at the end of the introductory paragraph, where it will receive the greatest emphasis.

Next, after reading your drafted introduction and body paragraphs, try your hand at a concluding paragraph. Does reading the rough draft through from start to finish seem to point toward a particular conclusion? If not, experiment (just as you have with your other paragraphs); you might review the list of opening and closing techniques discussed earlier.

When you have a complete rough draft for your essay, put it aside and do something else.

5.   Revising

A.   First revision: The whole piece. Return to the first draft of the essay you have begun to develop in the earlier exercises. Read it through and keep in mind the points we have discussed. Does the overall thrust of the essay meet your informative purpose? Does the essay speak directly to its audience? Do the body paragraphs clearly support your main point? If the essay seems weakly developed, incomplete, split in different directions, then you need to continue working on this rough draft. If you're satisfied that you have put together a workable base, go on to the next exercise.

B.   Second revision: The major parts. Write a fresh draft of the whole essay, part by part, according to our discussion. (*Remember:* Recomposing the paragraphs from scratch—even if you retain certain phrases and sentences—will reopen the creative process so that the next layer of your language should be more complete, more precise, more full-bodied than the first.) Check this draft against the same criteria you used for the first. Has the essay gained in clearness of focus, richness of detailed support, directness of purpose and emphasis?

C.   Third revision: Sentences, phrases, and words. Again, follow the guidelines we've discussed, but this time pay close attention to your language and style.

Readings

LOUISE B. YOUNG is a midwestern scientist, environmentalist, and writer born in 1919 in Springfield, Ohio. She attended Vassar College, and has been a research associate in the Radiation Laboratory at the Massachusetts Institute of Technology. From 1962 to 1973 she served as science editor for the American Foundation for Continuing Education, at Syracuse University. She directed the Lake Michigan Federation, in Chicago, from 1974 to 1980, and has worked for both Citizens for a Better Environment and the Open Lands Project. Young was a member of the Environmental Advisory Committee of the U.S. Department of Energy from 1974 to 1980. Among her books: Exploring the Universe *(editor; 1963 and 1971),* The Mystery of Matter *(1965),* Power over People *(1973), and* The Blue Planet *(1983). In the following excerpt from* Earth's Aura, *published in 1977, Young introduces us to the fundamental nature of our atmosphere in a way that makes the facts take on added significance.*

The View from Space

by Louise B. Young

The earth is now passing by my window. It's about as big as the end of my thumb.

—Astronaut in Apollo 8

A traveler coming in from outer space to visit the earth would be struck first by one of the most unusual features of this little planet—the soft blue glow that makes it look like a luminous raindrop set against the blackness of space. The light from most heavenly bodies is diamond bright or, where they shine by reflected light as in the case of our moon, the light is less intense but still sharply defined. Only the planets that hold an appreciable atmosphere return the light that they reflect, altered—softened and colored by its passage through the various layers of vapor. Venus is pale yellow, Jupiter a glowing gold and red. Saturn is set in iridescent rings of ice, and the earth is wrapped in a swirl of ethereal blue and white.

This is our sky—our blue heavens—seen inside out. It is the earth's aura. Not just a collection of gases and vapor, as we sometimes think of the atmosphere, it is a complex medium suffused with color and energy and possessing qualities distinctive of the body from which it emanates.

As the traveler from outer space comes closer to the earth, he can see the profile of the aura, outlined between the curving surface of the planet and the black void beyond. He discovers how slender is this fragile layer of atmosphere that forms the nourishing and protecting medium for all earth's living things. It shelters them from the fierce heat and cold of space. It filters out the damaging rays of sunlight and burns up several million billion meteors each day to harmless cinders before they reach the earth's surface. From the oceans and lakes it draws up the essential life ingredient, water, distills it and purifies it and distributes it again across the planet's surface. Mobile and impressionable, it is a medium constantly on the move, creating the infinite variety of conditions on earth, from winds that can uproot trees and tear clothes from a man's back to the gentlest of summer breezes, from paralyzing cold that would freeze an unprotected man in less than ten minutes to heat that can turn pools of water into steam.

The earth's aura makes our seasons and our sunsets. It adds glowing color where there would otherwise be blinding white light, too harsh to look upon. It holds and scatters the light long after the sun has set, making that lovely transition time, twilight. Unlike the sharp-edged light and darkness of space, we have hours that are neither day nor night—dusk and dawn. And the edges of things like the edges of time are softened by the air that envelops them, making their shapes and colors flow one into another.

Not only does the atmosphere alter the conditions on earth and make life possible, it is also formed and changed by them. Air is the hot breath of the earth itself poured forth from fiery volcanoes. It is the cumulative breath of all the living plants and animals on earth. Even the tiny bacteria who live in darkness under the earth's surface make their contribution to the composition of the earth's atmosphere. Man also, with his furnaces and his agriculture, changes earth's aura just as surely as the important conditions of his life are created by it.

And yet we who are born on the earth's surface and spend all our hours deeply immersed in the atmosphere take it so much for granted that we are almost unconscious of its existence. We use the words "thin air" synonymously with "emptiness." And we speak of the "limitless blue sky" as though it were space. We hardly notice the impact of the air on our senses. We are conscious only of the changes caused by its movement and the variations in its composition. We feel the wind and see the clouds and hear the waves breaking on the shore. Actually, the image of everything we see is affected by the air which diffuses the light. All the smells of the earth— the fragrance of flowers and the acrid smoke from industrial stacks—are nothing but chemicals carried in the atmosphere. And were it not for the air, there would be no sound at all, for sound is caused by waves of compression in the air. Although we think we cannot feel it, the atmosphere presses down on every square inch of our bodies with the weight of almost

15 pounds. This medium in which we live is so all-pervasive that it is the norm and, therefore, the nothingness.

A fish at the bottom of the sea must have the same impression of water. It does not really notice the water itself as much as the changes in it—the eddies that stir the sand on the ocean floor, the backwash of the waves that break over the rocks and swirl past the coral reef, the current of warm water that rushes northward from the tropical seas. The fish is not conscious of the way the water buoys up its body, counteracting the force of gravity (which indeed it has never experienced). So water would be nothingness to a fish just as air is to a man or a bird or a flower. Only a flying fish that breaks free of its medium, sailing in a long arc over the surface, can look down at the water's shining ruffled surface, see the deep indigo color, and feel the thick slipperiness of the liquid flow about its body again when it dives back in.

So man had to break free of his own medium and see it from outside before he could truly grasp its quality and significance.

"What beauty," exclaimed Yuri Gagarin, the first man to look back on the planet from space. "I saw clouds and their light shadows on the distant dear earth. . . . The water surface looked like darkish, slightly gleaming spots. . . . When I watched the horizon, I saw the abrupt, contrasting transition from the earth's light-colored surface to the absolutely black sky. I enjoyed the rich color spectrum of the earth. It is surrounded by a light blue aureole that gradually darkens, becomes turquoise, dark blue, violet, and finally coal black."

The Space Age has given us this new perspective. In a few short decades we have gained much new knowledge. Some mysteries have been solved and some have only deepened. The picture that has emerged is rich in variety and complexity. We have discovered that the atmosphere is moved by dynamic processes that were never suspected before man went into space. We have photographed the ghostly green glow of the ionosphere shining by its own light at night and have measured the current of solar wind that girdles the globe. Hundreds of miles above the veil of clouds where the atmosphere appears to fade away into infinity are regions where the earth's aura is still charged with power and energy, responding, in ways still just dimly understood, to the unexplained forces that flow in upon it from the farthest reaches of the universe.

MEANING

1. Louise B. Young's "The View from Space" is as factually informative as a report. What are some of the facts she includes?
2. Does the information in Young's essay support a single controlling point or thesis? If so, what is it?

3. What is Young's attitude toward her subject? How can you tell? Point out phrases and sentences that reveal Young's personal voice (an example: "the soft blue glow that makes it look like a luminous raindrop" [paragraph 1]).
4. Although Young does not state it directly, her essay may imply a meaning beyond its literal content. Can you say what this implied meaning might be? What evidence in the essay makes you think so?
5. Does Young's essay contain any scientific terms? How would you describe her language? Look up any words you don't understand. (Some examples: iridescent, ethereal [par. 1]; suffused, emanates [par. 2].)

METHOD

1. Young uses a fictional device in her introduction. What is this device, and what effect does it have in drawing in the reader?
2. Does this essay have a clear pattern of organization? What is it?
3. Toward the end of her essay, Young compares humanity to another of earth's creatures. What is the point of this comparison, and how effective is it?

AUDIENCE

1. What is your first impression of Young's essay? Do you think it succeeds in what it sets out to do?
2. Who is Young writing for? Would you put yourself in her intended audience?
3. Do you think the "new perspective" of the Space Age [par. 10] has had a significant impact on people's attitude toward the planet?

WRITING SUGGESTIONS

1. Based on what you already know about an aspect of nature, characterize its importance, function, beauty; your purpose is to give your readers information they don't have or don't usually consider (possible topics: wild animals, insects, winter, water, plant life, the constellations).
2. As in the suggestion above, characterize an important but perhaps ignored aspect of everyday life (not limited to nature). Some topics: the mood of your campus, the expectations of one's family or community, the values that guide our behavior even though we don't think about them.

FRANK CONROY was born in 1936 in New York and graduated from Haverford College in 1958. In 1967, Conroy published an autobiographical narrative called Stop-Time, *a book that went on to become one of the most widely read and admired works of the 1960s. Conroy has since contributed to many magazines, including* Esquire, The

New Yorker, Harper's, and The New York Times Magazine. *In this* Esquire
*essay, Conroy writes with honesty and sensitivity about his generation in an attempt to
let others know what the young men and women of the 1950s experienced, thought, and
felt.*

America in a Trance

by Frank Conroy

I remember asking, as a very young child, what was in the newspapers
when there wasn't a war going on. That was the Second World War, the
war to eradicate evil from the face of the earth, the war in which all Americans believed. Victory gardens, V-Mail, Gold Star Mothers, ration books
and air-raid drills were the order of the day. People talked lustfully of
three-inch-thick steaks, automobile tires and real butter. My father carried
in his vest pocket his own personal sugar dispenser for coffee and my
mother could be reduced to tears by a run in her stockings. The rationing of
food, the enemy without, common hardship, common purpose and the
almost godlike presence of Franklin Delano Roosevelt served to unify the
country as it had perhaps never been unified before. If the First World War,
however bloody, had been a bit of a lark, the Second was quite clearly a
war of survival. Americans did not expect to lose, yet they knew they'd
have to fight like hell to win. The discovery of the death camps of Central
Europe resolved all questions as to what the war had been about. The
forces of light against the forces of darkness, that was what we believed,
and no American thirty-two years old today can be untouched by that
memory.

We hated the evil Germans and the treacherous Japs, scorned the weak
Italians, loved the stalwart Russians, the plucky English and the wise Chinese. The double-fuselage P-38 was the fastest plane we knew about, the
B-25 our image of power. It was, to use Fitzgerald's phrase, "bracing to be
an American." Then came the atomic bomb and it was no longer quite so
bracing.

It goes without saying that the effects of the bomb on the American mind
were profound. We who were children at the time, with our childlike sensitivity to mystery, magic, and the unknown, with our social antennae fully
extended to pull in all sorts of information, regardless of its usefulness (the
ravenous hunger of children's minds, storing everything away undigested,
stockpiling the recognizable, the unrecognizable and the ephemeral
against a future time), were perhaps most deeply affected. We felt exhilaration at the indisputable proof that America was the strongest power on

earth, apprehension because the power was mysterious, and most significantly we felt guilt, secret guilt that verged on the traitorous, guilt we could not possibly talk about. Our political apathy later, as college students in the Eisenhower years, seems to me to trace directly to our inability to reorganize those simple, propagandistic concepts of democracy and political morality which had been our wartime heritage, and which the bomb had rendered untenable.

The war ended, the United Nations was born at Dumbarton Oaks, and America moved into a new phase. We grew toward adolescence during the postwar boom, a period of expansion and prosperity unparalleled in the history of man, a time of busy optimism during which America seemed to concern herself entirely with adult matters. The kids, and there were not many of us in those days, were more or less left out of things. We inhabited a shadow area within the culture—nothing was important about us except the fact that eventually we'd grow up. We were embarrassed at our minority and most of us kept quiet, attempting not to call attention to ourselves.

We were the last generation to grow up without television. The radio was our thing—*The Lone Ranger, The Green Hornet, Mr. and Mrs. North,* etc. When television arrived we greeted it in a state of tremendous excitement. Movies at home! Free! It was too good to be true. And of course it was. It disappointed, was oddly dull after the initial novelty had worn off, unsettlingly hypnogenetic, vaguely inducive of claustrophobia. TV was technically crude in those days, inferior in every way to the marvelously cathartic medium of films, so we kept on paying quarters to get into the children's sections of our neighborhood theatres. And we got a lot for our money. The programs changed every three or four days, with newsreel, cartoon, short, trailers and a double feature. I used to go to Loew's Orpheum, see the show, and then sneak into the balcony to wait for vaudeville at eight o'clock. Movies were a way of life.

We became teen-agers when to be a teen-ager was nothing, the lowest of the low. Our heroes were not of our own age group. For the most part they were athletes—Jackie Robinson, Joe DiMaggio, Sugar Ray Robinson. Our music was Dixieland jazz (a revival was going on at the time), pop music, and, for some of us, bebop. (When I met my wife's aged grandmother years later she turned to me, fixed me with her steel-blue New England eyes and said: "Ah, Mr. Conroy, I understand you are interested in music. Please tell me about bobeep.") At the age of fifteen I saw Charlie Parker on the stage of Carnegie Hall. Our clothing, manners and life-styles were unoriginal—scaled-down versions of what we saw in the adults. We had no sense of group identity, perhaps not much less than the teen-age generations that had preceded us, but unquestionably less than the generation that was to follow ten years later. We were mysteriously disenfranchised—the best-looking girls at high school would ignore the boys of their own age and prefer to go out with older men.

In college we were named. The Silent Generation. The Apathetic Generation. There was no doubt about it. The sleepy Eisenhower years. America
in a trance, drifting leisurely through a long golf game while the clouds
gathered. Among students it was hard to find a rebel, virtually impossible
to find a Marxist, a mystic, a reformer, or indeed, anyone who felt very
strongly about anything. When my roommate and I discovered secret fra-
ternities in our college, a college which advertised itself probably to be
fraternity-free, and exposed them in the newspaper, there was a bit of talk
but not much more. Most students thought it was a ploy from the psychology department. One can imagine what would happen now.

We believed in civil rights but did nothing active about it. Picketing was
unheard of, protest vaguely uncool. It was enough to send a few bucks to
the N.A.A.C.P., an organization we believed to be utterly safe, no more
and perhaps even less militant than the Parent-Teachers Association. We
were not afraid of Negroes and so made no attempt, as the students do
today, to identify ourselves with their power.

Our sexual mores were conservative in the extreme. It was the time of
going steady. Fiercely monogamous, we frowned on playing the field and
lived as if we were already married. Virginity in girls was not expected, but
faithfulness most certainly was. Promiscuity, which we interpreted as
going out with more than one person at a time, was a grievous sin. Our key
words were discretion, privacy and propriety. Needless to say, we lived
and breathed hypocrisy.

No one knew anything about drugs in those days. Marijuana, which was
to sweep through all levels of American society during the next decade,
was smoked, as far as I know, by only two students in my college of five
hundred. Heroin and cocaine were thought to be extremely dangerous (as
they doubtless are) and no one would have dreamed of experimenting
with them. LSD, Methedrine, and amyl nitrite were unknown. Mind-ex-
pansion was not a meaningless term, however. We read Blake, Zen, science fiction, the Christian mystics, and various studies on E.S.P. and psychic phenomena. We blew our minds without drugs. I remember lying, at
the age of nineteen, in the enclosed garden of the Bryn Mawr library,
under the cherry tree, watching the stars for hour after hour, aware that
light from unimaginable distances was collecting in my eye, getting high
on the universe. College was a straight scene for us. We didn't come across
pot until many years later.

Our literary heroes were more likely to be figures from the past than
from our own time. Most of us felt closer to the sixteenth, eighteenth, and
nineteenth centuries than to the seventeenth or the twentieth. James Joyce,
whom rightly or wrongly we thought of as a nineteenth-century writer, the
penultimate romantic, was a god. We took apart his difficult prose without
the least sense of resentment, dissecting clues as eagerly as Talmudic schol-

ars. *Portrait of the Artist* and *Ulysses* were books we knew well. The difficulties of *Finnegans Wake* were thought by us to be the inevitable result of the depth of Joyce's art rather than any failure of Joyce's mind. It would have been sacrilegious to suggest psychosis, and we scorned Stanislaus for having done so. Beckett was respected as much for having been Joyce's secretary as for his writings.

Closer to our own time, we admired Faulkner, Hemingway, Fitzgerald, early Steinbeck, and hated Wolfe, Dos Passos, Sinclair Lewis and James T. Farrell. Among young writers we liked Mailer, Capote, Styron and Salinger (who turned out not to live up to our expectations). There was a flurry about Françoise Sagan, mainly because she was nineteen, but on the whole we recognized her as a creation of the advertising age. The Beats were just beginning, Kerouac, et al., and we greeted them with a certain amount of suspicion, convinced that art was not that easy. Our standards were rather high, I think. The New Critics had filled us with an almost religious awe of language. We read Leavis, Edmund Wilson and Eliot as well, taking it all very seriously, worrying over every little point as if Truth and Beauty hung in the balance. The conservatism that colored so much of our experience did not evaporate when we dealt with literature. We defended literary art as if it were a castle under siege, in imminent danger of being destroyed by the vulgarians. In every college or university I knew anything about the most hated course was Social Science, as much a result of the incredibly rotten prose of the texts as it was of our disinterest in things social. We winced at bad prose, all of us, even the mathematicians and physicists who were presumably more interested in symbols than in language. We were neat, very neat, and sloppiness of any kind irritated us.

Fitzgerald calls a generation that reaction against the fathers which seems to occur about three times a century. There is the possibility that time has collapsed since he wrote those words, that life has accelerated to the point where changeovers occur much more rapidly, but nevertheless it is clear that those of us now in our early thirties were not a generation in any self-conscious sense. We had no leaders, no program, no sense of our own power, and no culture exclusively our own. Rather than saying, "Don't trust anyone over thirty," we would have been much more likely to say, "Don't trust anyone *under* thirty," or perhaps just, "Don't trust anyone." It is hard to believe that little more than ten years has gone by. Imagining, for the moment, American society as a huge mind, the students today can be thought of as representing the unconscious—they are pure emotion, they act first and figure it out later, they are the route through which revolutionary power is expressed—but most importantly they feel themselves to be a part of the social organism, they are the unconscious sensing the dimensions of the whole mind and their role within it. We felt nothing remotely like that. We were much more suspicious of society, without faith in its ability to respond to our minority voice. We were filled with precocious cynicism. We were stoics in our youth.

Now, as we come into power, we are aware of the paucity of our history. We have generation envy. How colorless were our times! Fitzgerald's people believed in their world—it really mattered who won the Princeton-Harvard game, it really meant something to appear at the theatre or the opera—and because they believed in their world they owned it. Until the Depression destroyed them they must have had a marvelous time. Styron's people had the war, a real war, a long, elaborate educational event plunging them directly into life. They had to learn to swim after they were in the water and, however sad their time, it was not dull. Brackman's people have faith. In a nonreligious age they have rediscovered faith. They are experimenters, revolutionaries and free-thinkers, possessed by their own creative force. They have their own particular kinds of sillinesses, of course, but they believe they can change the world, and recent evidence suggests they are correct in that assumption. It is no accident that they follow us, they are most immediately in revolt against the banality of those who immediately preceded them. We have already learned a great deal from them, and will learn more. We will never be like them, nor do we want to be, but we perhaps stand to gain more from their example than anyone else. We are still young, after all, relatively late bloomers, but still young. Our strength lies in our fluency in all languages now spoken in America, the old and the new. In tremendously exciting times, we stand at the exact center of American culture, ready for anything.

MEANING

1. What is the main point of Conroy's essay? Can it be found in a single statement?
2. Although Conroy's purpose is informative, he also conveys an attitude or impression about the 1950s. How would you describe this attitude? (Think about Conroy's tone and style.)
3. According to Conroy, what were the chief characteristics of his generation? Is he proud of his generation? Cynical about it? Nostalgic for the old days? What does he imply about those who grew up in the 1960s?
4. Does Conroy seem generally objective about his subject? Why do you or do you not think so?

METHOD

1. How does Conroy organize this essay? How does his choice help or hinder your understanding of the material?
2. Reread this essay and list as many topic sentences as you can find. Where

does Conroy tend to place his controlling ideas in his paragraphs? How are most of the paragraphs organized?

3. Conroy fills his essay with a variety of concrete detail, but some of his allusions (references) may be unfamiliar to you (Victory gardens, Gold Star Mothers, *The Green Hornet*, for instance). How important is it that the reader be able to recognize and understand these details? Can Conroy drop all these names without elaborate explanation and still be effective? Besides supporting his informative purpose, what other effect do these details have?

AUDIENCE

1. What's your reaction to Conroy's portrait of his generation?
2. Conroy says his was "not a generation in any self-conscious sense. We had no leaders, no program, no sense of our own power, and no culture exclusively our own." Does this statement apply to your generation? Why or why not?
3. What are the main differences you sense between your generation and the one Conroy describes? Do you find any similarities?

WRITING SUGGESTIONS

1. Using Conroy's essay as a model, characterize your own generation—its sense of identity, beliefs, values, fads, interests, heroes, and so on. If you write for your peers, try to inform them beyond what they already know; if you write for a different audience (say, parents), you may have to look closely at the things you yourself take for granted but which your audience may not know exist.
2. As above, characterize a generation *not* your own, such as that of an older or younger sibling, a parent, or an older relative. Again, depending on your audience, select the information your readers are least likely to know already but most likely to find interesting or revealing.

W[illiam] J[oseph] RORABAUGH is a native of Louisville, Kentucky, and was born in 1945. He received his AB from Stanford University in 1968, and earned a PhD in history from the University of California in 1976. He has been a teacher at San Jose State University and is currently a member of the History Department at the University of Washington, Seattle. Rorabaugh has been a Fellow at both the Newberry and Huntington Libraries and the recipient of a National Endowment for the Humanities grant. In the essay below, excerpted from the opening chapter of The Alcoholic Republic: An American Tradition, *Rorabaugh compiles some fascinating information about the drinking habits of early Americans.*

A Nation of Drunkards

by W.J. Rorabaugh

The thing has arrived to such a height, that we are actually threatened with, becoming a nation of drunkards.

Greene and Delaware Moral Society
1815

Was early nineteenth-century America really a nation of drunkards? Certainly the clergymen who were crusading for temperance thought so, as excerpts from their sermons and addresses attest. These self-appointed moral guardians, convinced that a hearty indulgence in alcohol was commonplace, increasing, and unprecedented, were filled with apprehension, their sermons filled with despair. Intemperance, they warned, was widespread, "too obvious not to be noticed;" "so common, as scarcely to be thought criminal;" "the fashionable vice of the day." They noted, too, that the United States was among the most addicted of nations, that in this respect it had outstripped all Europe, and that "no other people ever indulged, so universally." Even more alarming in their eyes was the fact that this intemperance was spreading "wider and wider;" "like the plague;" "throughout our country;" "with the rapidity and power of a tempest." Not only did they see excessive use as the crying sin of the nation, but they believed it to be "a *growing* evil;" "*still increasing;*" until America "was fast becoming a nation of drunkards."

A similar alarm was voiced by the nation's most prominent statesmen. It was not so much the use of alcohol that worried them—they all drank to some extent—as its excessive use. George Washington, a whiskey distiller himself, thought that distilled spirits were "the ruin of half the workmen in this Country. . . ." John Adams, whose daily breakfast included a tankard of hard cider, asked, ". . . is it not mortifying . . . that we, Americans, should exceed all other . . . people in the world in this degrading, beastly vice of intemperance?" And Thomas Jefferson, inventor of the presidential cocktail party, feared that the use of cheap, raw whiskey was "spreading through the mass of our citizens." In 1821 George Ticknor, a wealthy Boston scholar, warned Jefferson, "If the consumption of spirituous liquors should increase for thirty years to come at the rate it has for thirty years back we should be hardly better than a nation of sots." The Founding

Fathers, fearful that the American republic would be destroyed in a flood of alcohol, were anguished and perplexed.

Other observers, more dispassionate but no less articulate, found American drinking habits deplorable. Foreign travellers, for instance, were surprised and shocked at the amount of alcohol they saw consumed. A Swedish visitor, Carl D. Arfwedson, reported a "general addiction to hard drinking," while a visitor from England, Isaac Holmes, noted that intoxication pervaded all social classes. It was not surprising that Basil Hall, a retired Royal Navy Captain hostile to the new nation's democratic ideals, should be "perfectly astonished at the extent of intemperance." But even the sympathetic English reformer, William Cobbett, deplored American tippling. "I almost wished," he wrote, "that there were Boroughmongers here to *tax* these drinkers."

The more discerning visitors observed that while heavy drinking was widespread, public drunkenness was not common. This fact led William Dalton to suggest that Americans better deserved the appellation of tipplers than of drunkards. Infrequency of conspicuous drunkenness, however, was not inconsistent with an extensive overuse of alcohol. As a shrewd Scot by the name of Peter Neilson pointed out, the nation's citizens were "in a certain degree *seasoned*, and consequently it [was] by no means common to see an American *very* much intoxicated." In other words, as a result of habitual heavy drinking Americans had developed a high degree of tolerance for alcohol. Even so, in the opinion of Isaac Candler, Americans were "certainly not so sober as the French or Germans, but perhaps," he guessed, "about on a level with the Irish."

American travellers expressed similar views. They found "a great want of economy in the use of spirituous liquors," noted that drunkenness was "everywhere prevalent," and pronounced the quantity of alcohol consumed to be "scandalous." The well-travelled Anne Royall, who spent much of her life crisscrossing the country in stage coaches, wrote, "When I was in Virginia, it was too much whiskey—in Ohio, too much whiskey—in Tennessee, it is too, too much whiskey!"

It was the consensus, then, among a wide variety of observers that Americans drank great quantities of alcohol. The beverages they drank were for the most part distilled liquors, commonly known as spirits—whiskey, rum, gin, and brandy. On the average those liquors were 45 percent alcohol, or, in the language of distillers, 90 proof. It was the unrestrained consumption of liquors of such potency that amazed travellers and alarmed so many Americans. And there was cause for alarm. During the first third of the nineteenth century the typical American annually drank more distilled liquor than at any other time in our history. . . .

So the typical American was drinking heartily, but not all Americans drank their share. It is impossible to obtain an exact accounting, but the American Temperance Society estimated that during each year of the late

1820s nine million women and children drank 12 million gallons of distilled spirits; three million men, 60 million gallons. At this high point the average adult male was imbibing nearly a half pint a day. Few, however, were average. It was calculated that half the men drank 2 ounces a day; one-quarter ("habitual temperate drinkers"), 6 ounces; one-eighth ("regular topers, and occasional drunkards"), 12 ounces; and another eighth ("confirmed drunkards"), 24 ounces. Thus, half the adult males—one-eighth of the total population—were drinking two-thirds of all the distilled spirits consumed.

While men were the heartiest topers, women were not faint-hearted abstainers. Little, however, can be learned about either the reputed 100,000 female drunkards or the more numerous women who consumed from one-eighth to one-quarter of the nation's spirituous liquor. The subject received scant attention because it was "too delicate" to be discussed. The ideal of femininity did discourage tippling, for a woman was supposed to show restraint consistent with virtue, prudence consonant with delicacy, and a preference for beverages agreeable to a fragile constitution. The public was not tolerant of women drinking at taverns or groceries, unless they were travellers recovering from a day's arduous journey. Then the ladies might be permitted watered and highly sugared spirituous cordials.

The concept of feminine delicacy led women to drink alcohol-based medicines for their health; many who regarded spirits as "vulgar" happily downed a highly alcoholic "cordial or stomachic elixir." Furthermore, there were some social occasions when it was proper for women to imbibe freely and openly. For example, eastern ladies drank in mixed company at society dinners, suppers, and evening parties; and at pioneer dances the "whiskey bottle was . . . passed pretty briskly from mouth to mouth, exempting neither age nor sex." A surprised Frances Kemble learned that New York ladies who visited the public baths were "pretty often" supplied with mint juleps. Still, because a woman had to conform, at least outwardly, to the social precepts of the day, she was most likely to drink in the privacy of her own home. There she could suit herself. The usual roles of male and female were reversed when temperance reformer Edward Delavan called upon Dolly Madison. After the teetotaling Delavan declined a drink, the flustered hostess declared that "such an example was worthy of imitation" and proceeded to mix herself a toddy. . . .

White males were taught to drink as children, even as babies. "I have frequently seen Fathers," wrote one traveller, "wake their Child of a year old from a sound sleap to make it drink Rum, or Brandy." As soon as a toddler was old enough to drink from a cup, he was coaxed to consume the sugary residue at the bottom of an adult's nearly empty glass of spirits. Many parents intended this early exposure to alcohol to accustom their offspring to the taste of liquor, to encourage them to accept the idea of drinking small amounts, and thus to protect them from becoming drunkards. Children grew up imitating their elders' drinking customs. Boys who played 'militia' expected the game to end, like their fathers' musters, with a round of drinks. Adolescents perceived drinking at a public house to be a mark of manhood. Sometimes the swaggering young male made a ridiculous picture. "It is no uncommon thing," wrote one man, "to see a boy of twelve or fourteen years old . . . walk into a tavern in the forenoon to take a glass of brandy and bitters. . . ." Men encouraged this youthful drinking. Many a proud father glowed when his son became old enough to accompany him to the tavern where they could drink as equals from the same glass.

The male drinking cult pervaded all social and occupational groups. A western husbandman tarried at the tavern until drunk; an eastern harvest laborer received daily a half pint or pint of rum; a southern planter was considered temperate enough to belong to the Methodist Church if he restricted his daily intake of alcohol to a quart of peach brandy. A city mechanic went directly from work to the public house where he stayed late and spent his day's wages. Alcohol was such an accepted part of American life that in 1829 the secretary of war estimated that three-quarters of the nation's laborers drank daily at least 4 ounces of distilled spirits. Liquor was so popular that the army dared not bar the recruitment or reenlistment of habitual drunkards. If such a policy were adopted, warned the surgeon general, the army might have to be disbanded. The middle classes were scarcely more sober. Attorneys disputed with physicians as to which profession was the more besotted. Even more shocking was the indulgence of clergymen. One minister who considered himself temperate systematically downed 4 glasses of spirits to help him endure the fatigues of Sunday. At Andover Seminary, one of the most important centers of temperance activity, students regularly drank brandy toddies at the local tavern. Perhaps this practice was necessary to prepare would-be ministers for keeping up with their future congregations. . . .

Americans drank on all occasions. Every social event demanded a drink. When southerners served barbecue, they roasted hogs and provided "plenty of whiskey." Guests at urban dances and balls were often intoxicated; so were spectators at frontier horse races. Western newlyweds were customarily presented with a bottle of whiskey to be drunk before bedding down for the night. Liquor also entered into money-making and business affairs. When a bargain was negotiated or a contract signed, it was sealed with a drink; auctioneers passed a whiskey bottle to those who made bids. After the harvest, farmers held agricultural fairs that ended with dinners laced with dozens of toasts. Whiskey accompanied traditional communal activities such as house-raisings, huskings, land clearings, and reaping. It was even served when women gathered to sew, quilt, or pick the seeds out of cotton.

Liquor also flowed at such public events as militia musters, elections, and the quarterly sessions of the courts. Militiamen elected their officers with the expectation that the elected officers would treat. One newly elevated colonel pledged, "I can't make a speech, but what I lack in brains I will try and make up in rum." Voters demanded and received spirits in exchange for their ballots. Electoral success, explained one Kentucky politico, depended upon understanding that "the way to men's hearts, is, *down their throats*." At trials the bottle was passed among spectators, attorneys, clients—and to the judge. If the foreman of a jury became mellow in his cups, the defendant stood an excellent chance for acquittal.

Alcohol was pervasive in American society; it crossed regional, sexual, racial, and class lines. Americans drank at home and abroad, alone and together, at work and at play, in fun and in earnest. They drank from the crack of dawn to the crack of dawn. At nights taverns were filled with boisterous, mirth-making tipplers. Americans drank before meals, with meals, and after meals. They drank while working in the fields and while travelling across half a continent. They drank in their youth, and, if they lived long enough, in their old age. They drank at formal events, such as weddings, ministerial ordinations, and wakes, and on no occasion—by the fireside of an evening, on a hot afternoon, when the mood called. From sophisticated Andover to frontier Illinois, from Ohio to Georgia, in lumber-camps and on satin settees, in log taverns and at fashionable New York hotels, the American greeting was, "Come, Sir, take a dram first." Seldom was it refused.

Early nineteenth-century America may not have been 'a nation of drunkards,' but Americans were certainly enjoying a spectacular binge.

MEANING

1. What is the point or thesis of this essay? Is it contained in the title? Is the title in any way misleading?
2. What is Rorabaugh's attitude toward his subject? Solemn? Whimsical? What words and phrases can you find to support your view? Is his attitude appropriate to the subject?
3. Is there anything in the author's tone or language that indicates bias or opinion? Does he pass judgment on early nineteenth-century drinkers?

METHOD

1. What form of information gathering was used for this essay? What about the essay distinguishes it from a factual report?
2. How does Rorabaugh organize this piece? What introductory device does he use, and how does he carry it through the entire essay?
3. Each of Rorabaugh's paragraphs is controlled by a clear topic sentence.

What is the relationship between the topic sentences and the information that follows?

4.   What effect does the author's use of quoted remarks have on this essay?

AUDIENCE

1.   Are you surprised by the content of this essay? How do you react to Rorabaugh's descriptive catalog of early American drinking habits?
2.   Who is likely to be interested in such an essay? Who do you think the author is aiming at?

WRITING SUGGESTIONS

1.   Using observation and interviewing to gather facts, write an informative essay in which you characterize a national custom or social behavior. As you work up the essay, consider your attitude toward your subject. To what extent does it influence your choice of detail and language? Will you reveal any of this attitude in your finished draft? Try to maintain an objective stance toward the facts, but allow your attitude to enter the paper in a subtle, indirect way. Some topics: eating habits, courtship rites, TV-viewing patterns, leisure activities.
2.   Carefully reread Rorabaugh's essay and note his most important points. Then, using research and your own knowledge of the subject, write an informative essay describing late twentieth-century drinking habits according to these points. For instance, Rorabaugh says "Americans drank on all occasions"; is this still true, and if so, what occasions specific to this time in history? (Avoid obvious ones.)

ADDITIONAL WRITING SUGGESTIONS

1.   Write an informative essay for school-age children about the potential dangers of alcohol or drug use.
2.   A friend of yours is thinking about transferring to your school. She wants you to write her a letter in which you give an objective, informative appraisal of the school's bad points (she already knows the good ones). Write the letter as an essay.
3.   Your parents don't understand your interest in a certain kind of music, game, or other pastime. In an informative essay, focus your attention on the subject and try to make it interesting for your parents.
4.   Your coach has asked you to write a short informative essay for prospective college athletes. The subject: what it takes to be a successful gymnast, swimmer, diver, long-distance runner, tennis player, wrestler, basketball player, and so on. (Choose one.)
5.   A group of college administrators is planning a visit to your school. As

president of the student senate, you must write a short talk in which you welcome the visitors and inform them of the concerns of today's students.

6. Write an informative essay in which you introduce new employees to the company where you work. Assume that they have some general knowledge of the firm, and concentrate on information likely to be new to them. Some examples: employee benefits, company history, profit-sharing plans, educational reimbursement, or other features of the company that make it distinctive.

7. Characterize a place you know well—your home town or city, for instance—and try to capture its essential qualities with specific examples, details, statistics. Try to take a fresh look at your subject while concentrating on features that aren't obvious. Your audience is prospective visitors or residents.

8. If you've ever visited a place that seemed particularly odd, awesome, or memorable in any way, try to capture its essence as in the suggestion above. *Remember:* you're not expressing an opinion about the place, but trying to render it objectively for an audience of readers unfamiliar with it.

7

INFORMATIVE NARRATIVES

NARRATIVE

At the end of Chapter 3, we defined narrative in some detail. Here we will consider its similarities to both reports and essays, as well as how it may be used for the informative purpose.

Although narrative is a form of nonfiction separate from the report and the essay, it has one important characteristic in common with each of them. First, when we tell a nonfiction story in writing, we must know the story before we write it. Whether we know it through personal experience or have gathered the information through research, interviewing, or observation, a story is a set of specific facts. Like report writing, then, narration starts with a number of givens: certain people, certain events.

However, the story is one thing, the way of telling it something else. As in essay writing, we must create or discover the most effective form for the material. A story, in other words, may be told in a variety of ways. We saw in Chapter 3 that narrative employs two basic points of view: first person and third person. (A story may be told in the second person, addressed directly to the reader as "you," but as a rule this is a very limited technique.) As well as point of view, the structure or order of the narrative is open to the writer's choice. Not all narrative, for example, follows a strict chronology. It may be much more effective to open the story with a startling incident and then return to the chronological beginning.

Unlike reports and essays, which tend to be static, narratives are dynamic; in their focus on people and events, they move the reader forward through a series of actions. Narratives give us people doing things. When we write narrative, we attempt to capture the disorder and spontaneity of human experience. Because they tell us what we want or need to know about our lives and the lives of others, narratives also speak directly to the informative purpose.

THE NARRATIVE-WRITING PROCESS

Because narrative writing shares the factual basis of reports and the discovery element of essays, the process of putting a narrative together is a hybrid of the two other processes. To avoid repetition, we will look just at the unique challenges of this form:

1. Determining purpose and audience
2. Getting the story
3. Assembling a chronology
4. Organizing for interest
5. Using description, dialog, and scenes
6. Revising and editing

Again, let us consider each of these as it relates to the general process of composing effective narrative.

Determining Purpose and Audience

As usual, these matters are primary. When writing an informative narrative, you will want to give more attention to the facts of the story, less to your own interpretation of those facts. In narrative that seeks to explain events, the writer engages with the subject more personally. Especially in autobiographical narrative, the writer's chief purpose is personal expression. For the informative purpose, however, the writer's role is closer to that of the reporter—an objective observer or camera. This means that even if the writer adopts a first-person point of view, his or her focus is the story, not feelings about it.

Your audience may be small (an extended family's interest in its genealogy, for example) or large. It is likely, however, that the story will be told best in the ordinary language you'd use with a general audience, language appropriate to ordinary experience.

Getting the Story

The first job for the writer of narrative is to gather the facts of the story. If you already know what happened because it happened to you or to someone you know, the collecting stage will be a matter of calling the story to mind in all its detail. If the story demands that you dig it out, however, three information-gathering methods common to report writing will be of great use.

When the story you wish to tell is separated from you in time, *research* can be invaluable. (Assembling a family genealogy, for example, illustrates the importance of research as a tool.)

When the events you will narrate have been witnessed by others, even if you yourself were present, *interviewing* will provide you with a fuller, more detailed picture. Interviewing should confirm the facts of the story, although it may also yield a self-contradictory or conflicting body of data. In such cases, if you have pursued all possible leads, you may discover that the real story is that there is no single or uniform version.

Finally, first-hand *observation* of people and events allows you to write directly from experience. Unless you were the only person present, however, it may be a mistake to rely completely on your own perspective. You may have missed something, or you may have misunderstood what you thought you saw or heard.

Getting the story means using every available means to produce the most complete picture possible. Only when you have a sense of the whole will you be able to shape your narrative effectively to inform your reader.

Assembling a Chronology

In the process of getting the story you may already have arranged the events in chronological order. A check at this point would not be a bad idea, regardless. With more complicated stories, perhaps with several different narrative threads to be woven together, mapping out a chronology, a time line, will help you stay organized and in control. (How often, in telling a story to a friend, have we stopped cold when it suddenly dawned on us that we left something out?) Setting up a chronology will help you spot gaps, places where you need more information. The time line, as well, remains our most basic structure for understanding the flow of events; it is an essential tool of narrative.

One thing a chronology will not do is give us an automatic understanding of why events occurred or what they may mean. (Narrative whose purpose is informative may not concern itself with meaning at all.) In order to determine meaning, we must analyze events in seeking to understand them. (More on this in Chapter 10.)

Organizing for Interest

Say that as a project for your American History class you and some fellow students have researched the origins of the town where you attend school. You know all the facts, and you are ready to draft your narrative. How do you begin? Here is one possibility: "The town of Clancyville was founded in 1830 by Orville Clancy, a fur trapper. He set up a trading post, and soon a thriving village had formed."

Does this appeal to readers' interest? Does it attract their attention? Does it invite them in?

Telling a story, even a true story, is a kind of art. Good story-tellers never forget their audience, and they shape the telling of the story to hold their listener's interest. Among the organizational options available to narrative writers are the lead, reordered chronology, and the flashback.

The lead.   As we see from our example, telling the story from the chronological beginning is not always the best choice. However true the first facts may be, they may not be the most interesting ones. The essayist's techniques of opening with a startling statement, a question, or a quotation, for instance, are equally valid for the narrative writer. Ask yourself what interests you most about the story. Is there some odd bit of information that might provide a lively lead? (Perhaps Orville Clancy is on record somewhere as having said he'd rather die than stay in Clancyville, or perhaps the town was once a haven for runaway slaves or the center of a bootleg operation.) Whatever your story has to tell, leading it with a powerful, dramatic, amusing, or frightening detail will tell readers that it should be worth their time to read on.

Reordered chronology.   Because writers know the time line of the story, they are able to select from the chronology to suit their purposes. In a story with tragic consequences, for example, it might be most effective to begin at the end—with the tragic conclusion—and then to backtrack. Such a technique enforces the inevitable quality of the events and adds tension as the audience watches fate unfold. (Many novels and films have employed this structure.) Likewise, a story with a happy ending might be begun at the point where things look their bleakest; then the writer could show how events led to the impasse and how they were subsequently resolved.

Each story, like each essay, has a uniquely appropriate shape. Drafting a number of alternatives may be required before you find the best one.

Flashback.   A common technique in fiction writing, the flashback interrupts the storyline and drops the action from present time to past time. Typically, writers use it to fill in background information, to give the reader a feeling for a person's biography without including every detail of it, or to explain or at least shed light on someone's present behavior. Although a very useful device, it should not be overused, especially in nonfiction, since it may distract the reader from the essential thrust of the story.

Telling a story well is very much a matter of common sense. When organizing your narratives, as with all other forms of writing, put yourself in the readers' place. Tell them the story the way you would best tell it to yourself.

Using Description, Dialog, and Scenes

In addition to these organizational methods, narrative can benefit from several other basic storytelling devices.

Description.   Good description appeals to our senses; we see, hear, smell, taste, or touch what has been well described. Using description in narrative means integrating precise, vivid details of the people, places, and events of a story. It means paying close attention to the texture of things— facial expressions, the weather, the special look or feel of a place, the way people move. It means noticing the difference between a bungalow and a brownstone and not just calling it a house. Description provides another kind of information to the reader: the subtle, "unnoticed" facts that make a story come alive. (For more on description, see p. 139.)

Dialog.   Another of the fiction writer's tools, dialog has become more and more a staple of nonfiction. By dialog we don't mean merely a person's quoted remark. Rather, dialog is conversation between the actors in a story. You cannot invent it (although some professional nonfiction writers have been known to skirt the edges of fiction), and you should use it only if it serves a purpose: to reveal character or advance the story. Including small talk or idle chatter rarely helps a piece of nonfiction seem more realistic. Good dialog is difficult to write, and unless you have specific remarks on record you should use it *sparingly*. If you have the words of the people in the story, however, either through interviewing or observation, and these words will help in the telling of the story, then use them. In any case, try to keep your dialog economical and useful.

Scenes.   Allied with dialog are scenes, usually key moments or situations depicted in detail. Instead of telling the story always from a narrator's point of view, writers often drop back and allow the people of the story to be seen directly, as if on a stage or screen. Few narratives are composed entirely of separate scenes, as in a play, but breaking the narrative with scenes now and then, especially scenes that are particularly dramatic or revealing, can lend the story strength and a sense of immediacy.
Such techniques as these demand a degree of skill. The best way to learn how to use them is to first observe their use in narrative nonfiction (see, for example, the readings in this chapter). Then, try to put them into your own narratives. All of these methods, including those having to do with organizing stories, are natural to us in the oral stories we tell each other. We play with the order of events, we speak for the people involved in them, we construct scenes for emphasis. Learning to incorporate these same devices in our writing will help to make it compelling, vivid, and lifelike.

The guidelines for drafting, revising, and editing essays apply as well to narratives. Maintain the three levels of revision—the whole piece, the parts, and the individual words and sentences. As with essays, redrafting from start to finish is the only effective way to revise.

There will be one major difference. With the essay form, your attention should be directed to the controlling idea and its support. With narratives, on the other hand, there is no thesis or controlling point; there is only the story. You don't support a story, you tell it. During the revising and editing part of the narrative-writing process, evaluate your use of the lead, story order, description, dialog, and scenes. Speak to your readers, and tell them the story with imagination and intensity.

QUESTIONS

1. What principal characteristic does narrative writing share with report writing? What feature does it share with essay writing?
2. How are narratives different from either reports or essays?
3. Which of reporting's fact-gathering methods apply as well to getting the story?
4. Why is assembling a chronology a useful step when writing narrative?
5. What are some techniques narrative writers use to grab and hold audience interest?
6. Why are description, dialog, and scenes effective storytelling devices?
7. Have you read any narrative nonfiction recently? Which books or articles are particularly memorable? What sort of nonfiction stories tend to interest you most? Sports biographies and profiles? Popular histories? Biographies of rock stars? Travel books? Is narrative more, or less, appealing to you than other forms of nonfiction? Why?

EXERCISES

The narrative-writing process
Like the exercises in the previous chapter, the following are meant to take you through the writing process, this time the process of putting a nonfiction story together. Your purpose will be to compose a short, informative narrative of an important event in the life of one of your classmates. (The school plans to publish a collection of these profiles in a brochure for prospective freshmen.) Follow the steps in the process outlined in our discussion.

1. Getting the story. The instructor should divide the class into pairs (or, in the case of an odd number of students, pairs and one trio) so that each student is both a subject of a narrative and a writer of someone else's. For half of the class period, writers should interview their subjects; for the second half, the two should switch roles. Some hints for interviews: "What is the most exciting, scary, important, etc., thing that ever happened to you? How old were you at the time? Did you know it was going to happen, or was it a surprise? Can you describe your fellings before, during, and afterward? Were you alone or with someone? What effect did the event have on your life?"

2. *Assembling a chronology.* Outside of class, now, go over your interview material and construct a timeline of the event, placing all the major details in chronological order. Do you have a complete picture of the sequence, or are facts missing?

3. *Organizing for interest.* Next, review your information for a potentially striking lead item—a statement, detail, fact that would have immediate appeal to your readers. How should you tell the body of the story? Will a straight chronological pattern be best, or might a reordered chronology work better? Can the technique of flashback help in the telling of the story?

4. *Using description, dialog, and scenes.* Now try writing a draft of your lead paragraph. In your language, appeal vividly to the reader's senses—sight, sound, smell, taste, touch (not all, necessarily, but the appropriate ones). If description doesn't seem the best way to begin, try drafting a lead in which you report an exchange of dialog in the context of a constructed scene. In the dialog, attempt to capture the essence of a brief conversation; avoid small talk, filler, and so on. In your scenic construction, pay attention to the setting and any visual or other descriptive details that will allow the reader to "see" the scene.

As you continue to write, drafting the body of the narrative, employ description, dialog, and scenic construction for emphasis. It's easy to go too far with descriptions of movements, gestures, facial expressions, qualities of voice, so be careful. Sometimes it's better to say "she said" than "she exclaimed, tossing her head wildly." And remember, this profile is to be fairly brief, so two to three short scenes are probably all you'll have room for. Keep your language concise and concrete; you're writing about specific events, specific people, not vague generalities.

Readings

JOE McGINNISS, *born in New York in 1942, received his BS degree from Holy Cross College in 1964. He began his newspaper career on the* Port Chester Daily Item, *Port Chester, New York, and later worked for papers in Worcester, Massachusetts, and Philadelphia. He was a columnist for the* Philadelphia Inquirer *from 1967 to 1968, when he left to pursue full-time freelancing. His first book,* The Selling of the President, 1968, *was widely popular, and made McGinniss's reputation. In it, he recounts the story of the promoting of candidate Richard Nixon through television advertising. McGinniss is also the author of* The Dream Team *(1972),* Heroes *(1976), and* Fatal Vision *(1983). McGinniss has been a contributor to a number of magazines, including* Sports Illustrated *and* Harper's. *In the following chapter from his book* Going to Extremes *(1980), McGinniss narrates a portion of his first visit to Alaska.*

The First Day North

by Joe McGinniss

The alarm went off at five-thirty. I dressed quickly but carefully, trying to remember every layer. Long underwear first, top and bottom. Cotton socks, then heavy woolen socks. Then I went to the bathroom and brushed my teeth. Too early to shave. Too cold and too dark. I didn't want to get wet, didn't want to be any more awake than I had to be. Back to the bedroom. Jeans on over the thermal underwear. Then a flannel shirt, and a woolen shirt over that. My Pendleton wool shirt from Eddie Bauer. Check for mittens, notebooks, sharpened pencils. Not pens. In Fairbanks, in December, ball-point pens had a tendency to freeze.

I stepped into my Snowpacks and went out into the dark to start the Travel-All. There were a couple of inches of fresh snow on the ground, squeaking against the soles of the boots.

The Travel-All was parked on the street, fifty feet in front of Tom and Marnie's house. There was an electric heater attached to the engine block. A short cord that led from the heater was connected to a long extension cord that ran from the basement of the house to the curb. The Travel-All had been plugged in overnight, in order that it might start in the morning. This arrangement was quite common in Anchorage.

The engine started easily. There was heavy frost on the windshield. I put the defroster on and went back inside to drink some juice. In the bedroom I laced the Snowpacks up tight, and slipped into my Eddie Bauer maximum-strength, ultimate, super-warm Arctic parka. It had a hood with fur around the edge. When the parka was zipped tight and the hood was pulled forward all the way, there was created, for three or four inches in front of the nose, a little tunnel that warmed the air before you breathed it. Not necessary, or even desirable, at zero or 5 below, but in Fairbanks, in December, who could tell?

The Travel-All defroster was not working well. I scraped the windshield. At 6 A.M. in December there were no other headlights to be seen; no other house lights yet lit. It was still a clear and starry night. I put the Travel-All in gear. The tires made fresh tracks through the snow. The temperature was 3 below.

Out through Spenard. Not much traffic, even on Spenard Road, at 6 A.M. Spenard was the most raucous section of the city. The rowdiest bars. The highest concentration of massage parlors per square mile. The bars had been closed for an hour. The massage parlors had not. They were open twenty-four hours a day.

I reached the airport at six-twenty, parked and locked the Travel-All. The terminal was modern, brightly lit. There were glass cases containing stuffed moose, wolves, and bears. The lobby was almost empty: just one large, ragged cluster of men, mostly bearded, mostly overweight, and mostly dressed in flannel or woolen shirts. They were bunched around the gate from which the seven o'clock Wien Air Alaska flight to Fairbanks would depart. There were only two or three people in suits and ties. Only two or three women. Not exactly the Washington shuttle from La Guardia.

Wien Air Alaska was one of the two major airlines in the state, the other being Alaska Airlines, which flew mostly to southeastern Alaska and which, in fact, was based in Seattle. Wien did not fly to southeastern Alaska but went to almost all other parts of the state. It was the airline founded by the Wien brothers, immigrants from Minnesota, who were among the first people to fly airplanes in Alaska. It had been Noel Wien, in fact, who made the first flight ever from Anchorage to Fairbanks, in 1924, as aviation brought the concept of relativity to Alaska: space and time suddenly being perceived as less than absolute.

There was a rumor that the plane might not go. The weather in Fairbanks had been very cold, and ice fog had set in. No flights at all had made it yesterday. Only two or three the day before. Ice fog was produced when pollution in the air—particularly exhaust from motor vehicles—began to freeze and turned solid. This happened in Fairbanks when the temperature reached 35 or 40 below.

The plane did take off, half an hour late. A Boeing 727, with every seat filled. Some people had been trying to reach Fairbanks for several days.

It would have been possible to drive, of course: an all-day trip, over an icy, snowy, two-lane road, with only about four hours of daylight. Or it would have been possible to take the train. But in winter the train ran only two days a week and took twelve hours to get from Anchorage to Fairbanks—without problems. And in winter there were very few trips without problems. An avalanche, perhaps, or maybe a moose on the tracks. Moose liked the railroad tracks because they were kept plowed and it was easier for the animals to move along them than through the deep snow in the woods.

I wound up in a middle seat between two bearded men who reeked of alcohol. Immediately, they went to sleep. We flew north in the dark past Mount McKinley.

After forty-five minutes, the pilot came on the intercom. He said he was going to begin circling Fairbanks. If a break came in the fog, he would land. There was enough fuel to permit ninety minutes of circling. If he was not able to land in that time, we would return to Anchorage.

A first, faint gray light now appeared. My seatmate stirred and glanced out the window. The engines droned as the plane banked and turned once again.

"What do you think?"

" . . . I don't know. I don't even care, man. Either way, as long as we walk off this baby. I don't care if it's Fairbanks or Anchorage, or . . . Paris, France." He shut his eyes and went back to sleep.

Circling and circling and the pilot back on the intercom, saying twenty more minutes and we'll have to turn back, and the gray light stronger now, and seeing low hills, pine-covered, snow-covered, no signs of an actual city, and then a flat, impenetrable gray cloud beneath us: Fairbanks, the airport, the ice fog.

The No Smoking sign flashes on. There is a change in the pitch of the engines. The plane plunges into the fog. No visibility now, just the feeling of going down fast. High-pitched scream of the engines, a little tipping motion back and forth, seats into the full upright position, the gum chewers chewing a little faster, the arm-rest grippers gripping a little tighter, a sudden swirling gray outside the window, land right there, snow, pine trees, fog again, see nothing, then ground below, only ten feet below, five feet, inches, a bump, a roar, and the plane is down, fog all around, can't even see the terminal building, the pilot leaning on the reverse thrust to slow us on the bumpy, icy runway, blue lights flickering past, we're in Fairbanks.

A cheer goes up.

The pilot comes back on the intercom. Announces that the temperature in Fairbanks is 49 below.

At first, the cold was less of a shock than expected. With no wind, the fog, initially, asserted itself more. It was gritty, metallic: not so much an odor as a taste. A fog made not of moisture, but of microscopic particles of foulness; a blanket of frozen filth.

There was, at first, a sense of numbness rather than a feeling of being cold. With parka zipped tight, hood forward, and no wind, there was little direct contact with the cold. The difference from Anchorage—the difference between minus 3 and minus 49—seemed not so much physical, at first, as metaphysical. A deep chill in the marrow of the soul. A sense of not belonging; an awareness that this was not a part of the world—of the universe—that man was intended to inhabit.

I took a cab downtown. There was snow piled high on both sides of the road, much more than in Anchorage. If Anchorage had been the edge, then this seemed the capital, the heart, of the bleak and foreign world that lay beyond. The icy, fogbound essence of Alaska.

Neon glowed, then vanished in the fog. The cab inched toward downtown at no more than fifteen miles an hour. Already, my eyes stung from the poisonous fog and from the cold. Forty-nine below. At 9:30 A.M. It would not be light yet in Fairbanks even if there had not been any fog.

"Forty-nine below," the cab driver said. "That don't sound too bad if you say it fast enough."

Then he laughed. In Fairbanks, they made jokes about the cold. They were proud of it. It was their greatest natural resource.

The driver said he had kept the engine of his taxi running all night, parked outside his house.

"What does it cost me? Five bucks in gas? I'll make that back on this trip." A lot of the taxis in Fairbanks had not started this morning. At 49 below, even plugging in was not enough.

The thought occurred that this was, in a sense, nature fighting back. The cold was, after all, in Alaska, the strongest weapon nature had. With Fairbanks—with all of Alaska—under brutal technological assault, here, for the first time, was evidence that it would not succumb without a fight.

In this sort of cold you did not think of normal things—upset stomach, fatigue, financial problems, whether there was life after death. You were able to think only of the cold: it monopolized every facet of your being; like first love, or news of a death in the family. Actually, the first time, it was a marvelous novelty. For the visitor, the Arctic dilettante, the cold was fun.

The cab reached downtown. At least the driver said it was downtown. In the ice fog there was no way to be sure. There was a sense of multi-story buildings nearby, but you could not actually see them through the fog. There were supposed to be four hours and twenty-seven minutes of daylight in Fairbanks on this date, but with the ice fog there would not be any daylight at all.

Out of the cab, it was as if I were no longer on earth, but on a distant, foreign planet; a planet that was much farther from the sun.

The pipeline public relations office was one flight up, in a shabby old building across the street from the Chena Bar. That was the one sign I could read through the ice fog. A neon sign. Chena Bar. With only the R—the last letter—lit. CHENA BaR. ENTERTAINMENT NIGHTLY. GIRLS GIRLS GIRLS.

In the office, there was classical music on an FM radio station, the University of Alaska campus station. They were playing Rachmaninoff. At 49 below, with the R of CHENA BaR flashing pink. In Fairbanks, in winter, they played a lot of music by Russian composers.

A pipeline public relations man was going to drive me to Pump Station Eight, so I could see how the pipeline would work. This was something I had arranged in Anchorage the week before. The public relations man was not happy. He was sick of Pump Station Eight, sick of the pipeline, sick of leading writers and photographers around by the nose. Besides, he was tired and cold: he had been up most of the night with his girlfriend in

Anchorage, flying back to Fairbanks on the plane which I took; having to come back only because I was coming. Before the pipeline, he had worked for the Fairbanks newspaper. The pipeline was getting them all: the newsmen, the policemen, the short-order cooks. The trap was, first you fell in love with Alaska; then you had to work for the enemy—for the pipeline, for the oil companies, for the forces that were destroying what you loved— just to be able to remain.

For the PR man, all this would be over in a year. Then he would be able to move to London and to live for a year without even having to work. Just living off the money he was making now. But that would be next year. This was now. Forty-nine below. Heavy ice fog. And he had to drive, once again, out to Pump Station Eight, instead of remaining in his office with Rachmaninoff.

We rode for ten minutes, then went up a slight grade toward what turned out to be the edge of town. Suddenly it was a brilliant, clear day. A beautiful day. Soft, rolling hills, studded with evergreens, through the snow. The sky so bright it was painful. The sun, in late morning, low on the horizon to the south. Open land, uninhabited, rolling free, toward the sky, in all directions. From ice fog to no ice fog instantaneously. As if someone had pushed a projector button and changed a slide.

Pump Station Eight was thirty miles out of town, and still under construction. There were 170 men there working twelve hours a day, seven days a week, eight weeks at a stretch, then two weeks off. Earning up to $2,500 a week.

The pipeline was going to run almost 800 miles, from Prudhoe Bay, in the Arctic, to Valdez. There were going to be twelve pump stations along the way. The oil would flow in, get pumped, flow out. Something like that. To tell the truth, it was the cold I was interested in, more than the pipeline.

It was 35 below at Pump Station Eight. The sun was shining. We ate lunch, Polish sausage and rice, in a bright plastic cafeteria. Lots of pastry and pie for dessert. Liquor and drugs were supposedly prohibited in pipeline camps, and the workers were fed sweets instead.

After lunch, I climbed some winding metal stairs to the top of an oil-storage tank. It was the highest point for miles around. Thirty-five below, a slight wind starting to rise, and, from the top of the tank, I could see the distant, flat sun setting over far-away mountains. There was a bright orange glare, then the onset of twilight, and a quick blue darkening of the pine trees and the snow. Then cold and stillness everywhere. Except for the machinery in the foreground. Except for the pipeline.

My feet got cold, even in the Snowpacks. I went back inside to the pump station manager's office. He was eating a cream-filled chocolate-covered doughnut. And why not? It had been almost an hour since his lunch. He smiled at me, at my red nose and at the frost on my hair. He offered a doughnut. I declined. He took another. The buttons of his flannel shirt were stretched tight across a stomach that had not been there, in such dimension, a few months earlier. He had a good job. As part of management, he did not have to live in the barracks. He drove back and forth to Fairbanks every day, one of the more exotic commuting routes in North America. He explained to me how the pipeline was a miracle of modern technology. He was quite sincere, quite proud of the work he was doing. I had met army officers like him in Vietnam. The pipeline, he told me, would be able to withstand an earthquake that registered eight on the Richter scale; it would be 99 percent operable even if hit by an earthquake that registered nine. Every valve on every pump could be remote-controlled from Valdez. He went into great detail about the purpose and function and virtual perfection of Pump Station Eight. Quite clearly, he had long ago convinced himself. Now he just about convinced me. What the hell, for eight billion dollars it should work.

But eighteen months later, when the first oil would finally flow toward Valdez, it would be here, at Pump Station Eight, that the most serious mishap would occur. Someone would forget to throw a switch, and the mechanical backup system would fail, too, and a spark would ignite oil and the whole place would blow sky high. The whole pump station. One man would be killed, a dozen would be injured, and thousands of gallons of oil would spill out, across the tundra.

It was dark now, and colder. The manager had work to get back to. My tour guide was eager to leave. We returned to Fairbanks at high speed. Through clear, brilliant night air; then, suddenly, back into the fog; swirling, stinking, bitter fog. I would be tasting it in the back of my throat for a week.

We parked behind the pipeline office, across from the Chena Bar, which, by now, was filled with drinkers. Fairbanks was a sub-Arctic blue-collar town. A town—even more so than Anchorage—of Teamsters and drunkards and pimps. And a lot of people getting rich quick. The population had gone from 12,000 to 60,000 in three years. Two-bedroom apartments were renting for $700 a month. There was virtually no police force left in the city. The cops had all quit to work pipeline security, at four and five times their previous wage. There were drugs and whores and trailer camps, and disputes among residents were less likely to be settled in small-claims court than by small-caliber—or large-caliber—pistol. Compared to Fairbanks, Anchorage seemed like San Francisco.

The pipeline man drove me to the airport, slowly, carefully, through the fog. It had warmed up to 46 below. No telling if the plane would get in.

The airport was a madhouse. People trapped by the ice fog had been trying to get out for days. And discovering that trying to get out of Fairbanks could drive you much crazier than simply not being able to get in.

My luck held. My plane came in, and I got my seat. A middle seat again, but I did not complain. There were people at the gate offering two hundred dollars for boarding passes. For a seat which cost forty-six dollars.

I was back in Anchorage by dinnertime, feeling like I had just returned to earth. It was only 5 below at the airport and the air was clear and I walked to the Travel-All with my parka unzipped.

MEANING

1. McGinniss includes a good deal of information in this first-person narrative. Are the facts in this piece organized around a single informative focus, or are they merely colorful but random bits of information?
2. How can you tell, from the content of this narrative, that the author's chief purpose is to inform his audience about contemporary Alaska as objectively as possible?

METHOD

1. If McGinniss's purpose is informative, why does he choose to write in the first person? Does his presence as the narrator detract in any way from the informative thrust of this piece? Why or why not?
2. Point out places where McGinniss uses description, dialog, or scenes as narrative devices. Which passages strike you as most vivid or effective? Why? Are there other spots in this story where more description or dialog would have been helpful?
3. How would you describe the author's prose style? What is the effect of such a style?

AUDIENCE

1. Have you ever wanted to visit Alaska? Does McGinniss's narrative heighten or lessen this desire? What does he do to make the subject appealing, or unappealing, to you? Cite specific passages.

WRITING SUGGESTION

Using McGinniss as a model, construct a narrative in which you visit a place about which you think your audience would like to know more. Don't just give a static description, however; take the reader on a journey, even if a brief one, *through* the place, pointing up important features as you go along. Also, like McGinniss, you may need to integrate certain background information into your story. Include description, dialog, and scenes to enhance your informative purpose. Try to keep your attention focused on the most important or revealing details about the place, so that your reader will come away with a unified impression.

Born in 1963 in Chicago, Illinois, SHARON HAYDEN grew up in her home town and attended St. Francis de Sales High School. At Loras College, she studied writing and biology, and published poetry, criticism, and nonfiction in the college literary magazine, the Outlet. *Hayden left the midwest to study animal biology at Colorado State University, Fort Collins, where she worked summers as head wrangler at Trojan Ranch Summer Camp, belonged to the Collegiate Horseman's Association, worked as a lifeguard and swimming teacher for the Parks and Recreation Department in Fort Collins, and made the dean's list regularly. She is a 1985 honors graduate of Colorado State and plans to pursue graduate study in equine nutrition and breeding, with the hope of someday owning a ranch. In the piece below, Hayden tells the story of a Chicago friend's violent encounter with street crime.*

Nightmare on the El

by Sharon Hayden

Chicago calls itself a "city of neighborhoods." On a chilling night last April, a young Mexican man found himself in the wrong one.

Twenty-three-year-old Francisco Mendoza is a night watchman at Chicago's Field Museum of Natural History. Nearly every evening for six months he had ridden the Dan Ryan El to work, through twenty miles of the worst ghettos in the city.

On these trips north to downtown Chicago, he would stare through grime-speckled windows at the seemingly endless lights that surrounded him. Their effect kept it from ever being truly dark, and in the eerie orange night he could distinguish the looming shapes of the Robert Taylor housing project, miles of high-rise tenements squeezed onto the land along the tracks.

Francisco boarded the train at 95th Street, south. It was about nine-thirty, and he was one of the few passengers on this nighttime run. He knocked a Burger King cup from one of the seats and sat down.

Several stops later, four more people boarded the train. Two men and their girlfriends walked to the back of the car. The four joked loudly with each other, and Francisco thought he recognized a faint smell of alcohol.

The ride progressed uneventfully for five or ten minutes. Then, for no apparent reason, one of the men moved to the seat ahead of Francisco. The man turned to question him.

"Where you from, man?"

"South Chicago."

"What're you doin' in this neighborhood?"

"Just goin' to work."

Francisco had spent his whole life in South Chicago, and he knew that something was going to happen. It was only a matter of time.

The second man, encouraged that the two girls were enjoying the entertainment on what should have been a dull train ride, moved to the seat behind Francisco and took over the interrogation.

"What's in the bag, man?" He pointed to Francisco's gym bag, which held his guard's uniform.

"Just some clothes."

"Oh, yeah? Let me see."

As the second man reached for the gym bag, Francisco grabbed it and stood up, heading for the door. He had taken only a few steps when the first man took hold of the bag and tried to tear it from his grasp.

The assailants didn't know their target was a security guard who belonged to the Park District Amateur Boxing League.

Francisco punched the first man hard in the face. He fell to the floor, but was on his feet again a second later. This time he held a knife. He lunged at Francisco's head. Francisco ducked, but not fast enough. The blade caught his ear, slicing into it. Blood ran down his cheek and onto his shirt. Francisco punched wildly. The man's legs gave way, and he fell to the floor of the subway car. But now the second man had leaped to his feet, a gun in his hand.

Francisco thought: "I'm dead. But I'm not going to make it easy for him."

Francisco had worked his way to the door. Suddenly, the train screeched to a halt, and the doors opened. Francisco started running. He heard the man fire the gun.

The man continued shooting as he chased Francisco through the empty train station and onto a nearly deserted street. Only one other person was out at this time of night—and he was an off-duty policeman. When he saw what was happening, he went after the gunman and tackled him. Officer Grizzard arrested the attacker. His accomplice was caught soon after.

Although the muggers were captured, Francisco's nightmare wasn't over. Each night for over a week he awoke, screaming and sweating, reliving the experience in his dreams. Finally, Francisco found a way to release his pent-up emotion. He created an abstract sculpture of a terrified man covered with blood from a wound on his ear.

Francisco is an artist, and he has studied at the Art Institute of Chicago and the University of Barcelona, Spain. He worked as a security guard because emerging artists do not make much money.

Francisco is a painter, not a sculptor. His "Self-Portrait" was the first piece of sculpture he had ever produced. In May, he entered it, along with some of his paintings, in the Loop College State Street Mall Exhibition. The "Self-Portrait" took first place.

Francisco says he is glad something good came out of the experience, and he is encouraged about his future work in sculpture. But he hopes that the inspiration for other works will be "a little less dangerous."

MEANING

1. In this tale of an unsuccessful mugging and its unexpected reward, Hayden gives us a glimpse of two sides of city life. What are these? In what sense is the battle between Francisco and his attackers an instance of a larger urban conflict?
2. Does the author have a particular point to make with this story, or is she content to let it stand on its own as a "slice of life"? How do you know?

METHOD

1. Hayden maintains an objective point of view throughout. What is the effect of this objectivity? Why do you think she chose to keep herself out of the story?
2. From time to time, Hayden gets inside Francisco's head ("Francisco thought: 'I'm dead. But I'm not going to make it easy for him.'"). How does she know what her subject was thinking? What does such information add to the narrative?
3. Assess the author's use of description, dialog, and constructed scenes. How much, and how well, does she employ these narrative techniques? Could they be further used in an expanded draft of the story? How so?

AUDIENCE

Are you at all familiar with the kind of scene Hayden evokes in this story? Does it ring true to you? If this material is far removed from your experience, does Hayden convince you that it's authentic? Why or why not?

WRITING SUGGESTIONS

1. Following Hayden's lead, compose a chronological narrative about a significant event well known to you. Keep your focus on the story itself—when it happened, who was involved, how it happened. Use description, dialog, and scenes where appropriate to enhance your telling of the story. Interview the participants if necessary to obtain specific information. Some topics: a divorce, the loss of a job, an accident and its aftermath, a series of misunderstandings, a happy incident that was unforeseen or had pleasant or important consequences.
2. Write a narrative in which you recount an event of local significance. Interview the participants or witnesses, and include as much specific information as you can.

BOB WOODWARD is probably best known for his role (with co-author Carl Bernstein) in helping to expose the Watergate coverup in the early 1970s. Born in 1943 in Geneva, Illinois, he is a graduate of Yale University, from which he earned a BA in 1965. After college, Woodward served on active duty in the U.S. Naval Reserve, where he attained the rank of lieutenant. In 1970 he joined the Montgomery County Sentinel, *in Rockville, Maryland, and moved to the* Washington Post *in 1971. Woodward had been a* Post *reporter for only eight months when he was assigned to cover a police beat story that eventually led to a series of articles that exposed White House involvement in the Watergate break-in. Several presidential aides were convicted and jailed, and Nixon became the first president in U.S. history to resign. Woodward and Bernstein are the authors of* All the President's Men *(1974), and* The Final Days *(1976), both about Watergate. With co-author Scott Armstrong, Woodward published an investigative analysis of the United States Supreme Court,* The Brethren *(1979). Woodward's most recent book,* Wired *(1984), from which this excerpt is abridged, recounts the life of actor/comedian John Belushi, who, like Woodward, grew up in the Chicago suburb of Wheaton, Illinois. In this selection, Woodward follows Belushi during the days just before his drug overdose and death in 1982.*

Belushi's Last Hit

by Bob Woodward

Catherine Evelyn Smith, 35, had cut her heroin habit to about $25 a day, down considerably from the good times when she had been dealing. But she had close friends in the drug trade, and for that $25 she could get "half a tenth"—one-twentieth of a gram of heroin, 70 percent pure. It kept her going.

On Monday morning, March 1, 1982, Smith and John Ponse, 47, a waiter at the Polo Lounge in the Beverly Hills Hotel and her roommate of three years, began the day at Jerry's Family Coffee Shop near downtown Los Angeles. Ponse had breakfast. Smith had a double vodka with orange juice. Drinking made her heroin habit almost bearable.

Smith's life had been rough. She was born in a small town in Ontario, Canada, in 1947 and was put up for adoption by her parents. She became pregnant at 17 and gave up her baby, a great trauma given her own adoption.

She started dating a drummer for Bob Dylan's back-up group, later famous as the Band, then worked in a steel company for a while, and was briefly married. She lived with singer-songwriter Gordon Lightfoot from 1972 to 1975, then drove the tour bus for country singer Hoyt Axton and in 1977 ended up in California.

Once there, Smith and Sandra Turkis, a friend from Canada, rented a house in Bel Air and became deeply involved in the drug scene, hanging out with rock bands and going to parties. Turkis introduced Smith to the Rolling Stones, and she quickly latched onto the group, jet-setting with them to Paradise Island, Paris, New York, the Colorado ski slopes.

During this period Smith started using heroin, and by 1978 she had a secret habit. The next year Smith met a young drug dealer who operated under 13 aliases. He was helping wealthy, prominent people leave Iran after the fall of the Shah.

Some of these people had access to large amounts of pure heroin, and he arranged for the delivery of about 42 pounds of Persian brown to Smith's apartment on Sunset Boulevard. The street value was about $13 million. Smith sold the heroin, and a dealer came by and picked up the money each day. Smith's share of the profit was paid in heroin, which she kept in tin boxes in her closet.

After eight months the heroin was gone. Smith turned down other chances to deal large amounts, frightened of being caught. By early 1982 she was playing the horses or relying on Ponse for the money to get her daily $25 fix.

Smith was at home watching television on the evening of March 1 when the telephone rang. It was April Milstead, a young woman who had been helping John Belushi get cocaine.

"John Belushi is in town and is looking for some stuff," Milstead told Smith. "Can you get some?"

"I'll have to check and call you back," Smith replied. She made a connection through an old friend, Janet Alli, and brought the heroin to Milstead's apartment. Milstead took John aside and warned him that Smith was bad news—she lived off other people's money and drugs. At that moment, Smith was shooting about three-quarters of one of the tenths into her own vein.

Milstead did not like to shoot herself up, so she asked Smith to do it for her. John watched intently.

"You think you could do that for me?" he asked.

"Shoot me up," John said.

Smith expressed mild surprise that he did heroin.

John said he'd taken it before, back in New York, but didn't like people to know. He said he wanted a "speedball"—a mixture of cocaine and heroin. He'd heard that the high of the coke and the dulling effect of the heroin could create a wonderful sensation.

Smith used a small amount of coke and even less heroin—$10 to $20 worth of each. She tied off John's arm with a web belt to make the veins come to the surface, then quickly, deftly, jabbed in the needle.

John turned to Milstead. "Hey, I like it. It feels great," he said.

"You're 33 years old," Milstead replied. "So you know how you feel."

Around midnight the party moved to Belushi's bungalow at the Chateau

Marmont on Sunset Boulevard. As they stepped inside, John grabbed Smith's arm.

"Let's go in this bathroom," he said. "I want to do another hit."

The next morning, when all the drugs were gone, Belushi took Smith, Milstead and her boyfriend out to breakfast at Duke's, a diner on Santa Monica Boulevard. John ordered a cheese blintz, and after finishing it he started eating from Milstead's plate with his hands, putting on a Bluto show.

John was out of cash after breakfast, so he called the office of his manager, Bernie Brillstein, and was sent $600. Smith wondered how John always had so much cash. He generally seemed to have $1,000, and when he ran low he was resupplied at once by Brillstein's office. She asked him how it worked.

"There's several thousand dollars built into the [movie] contract," John told her. "Extra money for the length of the contract . . . not said, but that's what it's for."

At 10:13 that morning John called his wife in New York. She wasn't home, so he left a message: "Tell Judy I love her." Later he called his office in New York. Judy wasn't there, either, and he left the same message: "Tell Judy I love her."

Soon Belushi got a call from Nelson Lyon, a tall, heavyset, 43-year-old writer who enjoyed John's "anything-can-happen" exuberance and had heard that his old acquaintance was in town. John and Smith drove to Lyon's house. When Lyon saw Smith, he asked John about her.

"Oh, she's a good girl," he said. "She does a lot of errands."

They walked into a back room, where Smith shot herself with cocaine, compensating afterward with a shot of heroin. She then gave John a shot of coke. He was needing more and more of it to get the same feeling—highly dangerous, she realized, but she tried to keep the increases down.

"Will you do this for Nelson?" John asked.

Smith injected a modest amount of coke into his arm. He liked it so much that he shot up four times that afternoon. Later, Smith called her friend Alli, who was heavily involved in the local drug scene, to see whether more heroin was available. Alli said yes—she was going over to get some from her supplier that afternoon. Smith took $200 and drove Belushi's rented Mercedes to the supplier's house. He gave her about four tenths of heroin for the money.

At 9:45 that night Belushi went to meet with Michael Eisner, the president of Paramount. For days Eisner had been trying to talk John out of going forward with a script titled "Noble Rot," which he thought was terrible, suggesting instead a new project, making a comic film out of the sex manual "The Joy of Sex."

Eisner, his wife, Jane, and his assistant, Jeff Katzenberg, joined Belushi and Tino Insana, an old friend and comic acting colleague from Chicago, at a table at On the Rox, a private club on the Sunset Strip.

John was eating a lot, hamburgers and Chinese food, and he was leaving the table often. Eisner thought this a little strange, but maybe it was John's normal behavior. In any event, Eisner was trying to be optimistic. Perhaps something good would come out of this meeting.

After an hour they seemed to have reached an impasse on "The Joy of Sex," and Eisner and Katzenberg wanted to get home early. No more headway would be made that night.

It was 11 P.M., and a rerun of "Saturday Night Live" had just begun on the oversized TV screen at one end of the club. Eisner and his wife headed down the steps to the parking lot. He was glad to be leaving—the club reflected the seedy, low-life side of Hollywood that he tried to avoid.

Suddenly Belushi appeared in the parking lot.

"You've got to see this," he pleaded. "One of my best . . . please, please." He almost had to drag them back to the television. It was a show that had aired three years earlier, in November, 1978.

A few minutes later Eisner and his wife returned to their car. Jane found John incredibly sad.

"I feel as though I've just seen 'Sunset Boulevard,' " she said, referring to the 1950 Paramount classic in which Gloria Swanson played an aging, washed-up silent screen star who lived to watch reruns of her old films.

The morning of March 4, from his bungalow at the Chateau Marmont, Belushi called April Milstead.

"I want to see Cathy," he said, referring to Catherine Smith. Fifteen minutes later he called Milstead again. "Have you found Cathy?" he asked. Milstead promised to try harder.

Belushi drove to the house of Gary Watkins, an old friend and cocaine supplier, and called his wife, Judy, in New York.

"I'm sorry I didn't come home Sunday," John began. "I'm going to stay for a meeting"—with Paramount executives.

At about 1 o'clock that afternoon, Belushi called Milstead again. Had she found Smith? Milstead said Smith would be over in half an hour.

"Great. Fine," John said. "I'll be right over."

While Milstead waited she got a phone call from her mother. They were still chatting when Smith arrived and let herself in. Then John arrived.

She quickly got off the phone and kissed John hello. He took half a gram of cocaine, put it on the television and said, "Here, this is for you." John had brought a lot of cocaine, and he and Smith shot up several times over the course of the next half-hour.

Belushi and Smith then left in his rented Mercedes. John gave her $300 to buy some more heroin. They'd get together again after she made the buy. She dropped him off at the house of one of his friends, Tino Insana.

Insana wasn't home, so Belushi waited around for a while. Insana and Belushi had written a movie treatment the previous summer, and John wanted to work on it some more.

Soon after Insana arrived home, Smith returned in the Mercedes, and she and John left. They shot some cocaine at Nelson Lyon's home, and then Belushi went to On the Rox.

From there he called Insana and said that he wanted to work on the script the next day. It was important to him. Since the first draft, which had been written mostly by Insana, John had been pushing for a crucial new scene. He wanted his character to be talked into shooting up heroin. To lend credibility to the scene, Belushi wanted to actually shoot up on camera.

Insana was not that anxious to work on the script. John sounded drunk or high. The script had too much to do with drugs, and Insana didn't like drugs. But he loved John and agreed to get together the next day.

Belushi had been trying all week to get in touch with Richard Bear, a piano player and cocaine supplier. Bear had finally agreed to meet with him that night and showed up at On the Rox. They talked about John's idea to shoot up on the screen. They shared some cocaine.

Soon Smith and Lyon arrived, and John walked back to the club's private office, a small, seedy room that looked like an attic. With a nod he signaled Smith and Lyon to join him. John handed Smith some cocaine. She prepared the cocaine, shot herself and then shot Lyon and John.

Around midnight Robert De Niro walked in. John asked him to come back to his bungalow when On the Rox closed. At about 2 A.M. John went down to the parking lot to get his Mercedes. They would continue the party back at his place.

As John, Smith and Lyon waited for Belushi's rental car, John saw someone selling drugs. He bought a gram of coke for $100. They got into the car, and Smith drove, heading east down Sunset Boulevard, until John asked her to pull over.

"I'm going to get sick," he said, opening the door. He threw up, heaving and gasping. Lyon had done the same a while earlier in the washroom at On the Rox.

When they arrived at the Chateau Marmont, Lyon and Smith helped John in. He went into the bathroom and threw up again.

"John, are you all right?" Smith asked. "What are you sick from?"

"I don't know," he said. "I ate all this greasy food." He and Smith then left the bungalow.

At about that time comedian Robin Williams stopped at On the Rox and was told by a parking lot attendant that Belushi and De Niro were looking for him. Williams phoned De Niro at the Chateau Marmont and was told that they were all meeting at John's.

Williams was at the bungalow when Belushi and Smith returned. From the instant Smith walked through the door, Williams was uncomfortable. He had never seen John with such a crusty woman; she had been around.

Williams did not consider himself an innocent, but Smith was frightening. She and Lyon seemed somewhat out of place in John's life, at least from what Williams had seen. And the room was so tacky and messy—dozens of wine bottles were open and scattered around. Williams wondered what John was doing and why.

John grabbed his guitar and strummed a few chords. He didn't find the sound he was looking for and put it down. He stood up and got out some cocaine, and Williams had a little. Then John sat down and his head just dropped, as if he had fallen asleep or passed out. In about five seconds he lifted his head.

"What's up?" Williams asked. He had never seen anyone go out like that and then come back so quickly. "Are you okay?"

"Yeah. Took a couple of 'ludes," John said distractedly, referring to Quaaludes.

Williams decided it was time to go. He felt sorry for John and thought that if he knew him better he'd try to find out what was going on, maybe even recommend that John get away from this strange company and decadent room. But that was just a thought that flashed by. Williams realized he was an outsider. He got up and said goodnight.

Later, De Niro entered Belushi's bungalow through the sliding glass door in the back. He found Smith trashy and was surprised that John was with such a woman. He also felt that John seemed wired. There wasn't much to say, so he headed back to his room. It was shortly after 3 A.M.

John told Smith he felt cold and turned up the heat.

"I want everyone out," he told Smith.

Lyon was the only other person left. In the last 2½ days Lyon had taken at least 12 shots of cocaine or a "speedball" mixture of coke and heroin. He felt lousy and exhausted. In many ways the evening had been boring, not like the exciting times that he and John had when they were not using drugs this way. As Lyon got up to leave, John asked to borrow $10 from him.

John asked Smith to stay. From his pocket he produced a little more coke, which Smith mixed with some heroin. She gave herself the first shot, then made a speedball for John—half a tenth each of cocaine and heroin. John got up and took a shower, and she washed his back. They sat up in bed for a while and discussed the various scripts and movie deals John was involved in.

John said he felt chilly.

"Get under the covers," Smith said. "I'll turn up the heat." She tucked the blankets around him, then went into the living room and wrote a letter to an old friend in Toronto. She wanted to get back to her apartment, and wondered whether she could take John's car. She walked back into his bedroom. "Are you hungry?" she asked.

John mumbled something and waved her off.

Smith returned to the living room. Very strange noises—coughing and wheezing—were coming from the bedroom, so Smith went back again. John was making heavy, choked-up sounds. She pulled back the covers.

"John, are you all right?" she asked.

"Yeah," he said, waking up. "What's wrong?"

"You don't sound right. . . . Do you want a glass of water?"

She went to fill a glass, then came back and handed it to him. He took a couple of swallows and said his lungs were congested.

At about 10:15 A.M. Smith checked John again. He was sleeping now, snoring loudly, and seemed okay. She put the syringe and spoon they had been using in her purse. The maid might come to clean up, and she didn't want it found. She left the bungalow, took John's car and drove to Rudy's bar on Santa Monica to have a brandy and place a $6 bet on a horse.

At about noon Bill Wallace, Belushi's physical trainer, drove up to the bungalow with a typewriter and tape recorder that John wanted. Wallace noticed that John's car wasn't there. He went up to the door and knocked several times. There was no answer, so he let himself in with his key. He set the typewriter down and looked down the long hall to the back bedroom.

It seemed like someone was in the bed. If John were sleeping, he thought, there would be snoring. There wasn't even a hint of the familiar harsh, raspy breathing. The place was hot—a dry, breathless heat. The mess and squalor was John's.

Wallace felt a slight eeriness as he moved down the hall. Someone was gathered in a tight fetal position under the covers, with his head under a pillow. Wallace recognized John's form. He walked slowly to the side of the bed, reached over, touched John's shoulder and shook him gently.

"John," he said, "it's time to get up."

There was no response—no groan, no pulling back from the touch.

"John," Wallace said again, "time to get up."

Nothing. Wallace pulled the pillow away. John's lips were purple, and his tongue was hanging out. He was not moving.

Something like a flame ignited in Wallace. He had taught CPR, and recognized the signs. He flipped John's nude, heavy body over on its back. The right side, where blood had apparently settled, was dark and ghastly.

Wallace, his heart racing, reached into John's mouth with trembling fingers and drew out phlegm, which spilled and puddled on the bed sheet in a thick stain. There was a rancid odor. Wallace began mouth-to-mouth resuscitation. He tried for several minutes, training and horror in each motion.

John's body was cold, and his eyes contained nothing. There was no movement, no stirring of a breath, a nerve, a moan. John was dead.

MEANING

1. Does Woodward use this narrative to make a point? For example, does he imply that Catherine Evelyn Smith killed Belushi? Does he imply that Belushi planned his own death? Explain your reasons.
2. How would you characterize the last days of Belushi's life as portrayed by Woodward? Does this story serve as a "cautionary tale" about life in the fast lane? Do you think Woodward intends it as such?
3. Although a true story, this narrative seems at first glance to be about little more than self-destructive indulgence. Why do you think Woodward, who made his reputation as a *Washington Post* reporter who helped expose the Watergate scandal in the early 1970s, was drawn to this material? Does this story depict any themes or general ideas about life? What might they be?

METHOD

1. Woodward includes quite a lot of small details in this piece ("At 10:13 that morning John called his wife in New York. She wasn't home, so he left a message: 'Tell Judy I love her.'"). What effect do these details have? Do you think Woodward includes too much minutia? Which of Woodward's details seem to be most revealing of Belushi's story?
2. Woodward takes pains to keep himself outside the story, and to tell it from an objective, cameralike point of view. Why do you think he chose such a strategy? Wouldn't it have been more interesting to get inside Belushi's head? How much of Belushi's state of mind can be inferred from the conversations and actions Woodward reports?

AUDIENCE

1. Is the readership for such a story larger than that made up of John Belushi's fans? Why or why not?
2. Does this story produce any emotional reaction in you as a reader? If so, what is your reaction? If not, why not?

WRITING SUGGESTIONS

1. Narrate what you consider to be the crucial day (or few days) in someone's life. Choose a person well known to you, but one about whom you can write objectively. You may need to give your readers background information from time to time, but concentrate on the action of those important days. If it is possible, interview the person or his or her friends or family to obtain detail, remembered conversations, the "feel" of particular events. (As in the exercise earlier in this chapter, you may want to choose a person close at hand.)

2. Tell a true story that illustrates or embodies one or more themes or abstract ideas (as Woodward's story does the notion of "the price of success"). Don't write a parable with a clear moral—that's too easy. Instead, try to find a story that *suggests* ideas or themes without beating the reader over the head with them. Some theme ideas: failed friendship, the lure of success, life in the fast (or slow) lane, self-destruction, heroism, determination.

ADDITIONAL WRITING SUGGESTIONS

1. Write a narrative sketch of a person well known to you, one whose life is particularly interesting or unusual.
2. Interview your family and compile a timeline of the major events in its history. Narrate a portion of this story in detail for an exchange student who will be staying with the family.
3. Follow the directions for Suggestion 2, but place particular emphasis on the use of dialog and scenes. (You may need to narrow the scope of the narrative quite a bit.)
4. Interview a teacher or staff member who has worked at your school for a number of years. Then write a freelance piece for the student newspaper in which you tell the story of the school through your subject's experiences.
5. Write your own obituary, in the third person, emphasizing the narrative movement of your life; avoid static lists of facts. (You might want to consult the obit page of a big city newspaper for some models.)
6. Interview an older relative or friend who has had a brush with a powerful experience such as fame, wealth, bankruptcy, or death. Write the story of this experience as a short feature for the local newspaper.
7. If you work, interview several fellow employees, especially those who have been with the company a number of years. Through their eyes, tell the story of one of the firm's most interesting accomplishments or failures for an article in the company newspaper.

PART THREE

Writing to Analyze or Explain

ANALYSIS VS. ARGUMENT

Now we turn to a type of nonfiction whose purpose is more complex: analytical writing. Before doing so, however, it makes sense at this point to define the difference between it and another kind of writing with which it is sometimes confused: argument.

Analysis, as it is usually defined, means to study a subject, to take it apart in order to better comprehend it, and this, too, is our purpose in analytical writing. Certainly a finished analytical essay will have a point to make, and its author will want to make the point convincingly. The object of analytical prose, nevertheless, is increased understanding, not necessarily a change in the reader's opinions, beliefs, or actions.

As we define *argument* (and its associated types, criticism and persuasion), on the other hand, the writer's purpose *is* the stronger one of affecting change. Although analysis of facts or events will figure into an argument, its purpose is, nonetheless, distinct from that of explanation.

Although analysis rests on a base of objectivity, when we explain, evaluate, or interpret information for our reader, we allow more of our own views to enter our writing. Not all analytical prose is subjective, of course, but this purpose does allow more room for subjectivity than does purely informative writing. In argument, we carry our own views a step further and press them in partisan fashion.

Argument, although distinct from analytical writing, rests on sound analysis; and analysis, although different from reporting facts alone, includes information and depends on its accuracy.

8

ANALYTICAL WRITING

SOLVING PROBLEMS, ANSWERING QUESTIONS

Students often wonder why teachers assign papers. Why not simply give multiple-choice tests and save everyone a lot of aggravation? Aren't tests the best way to show how much, or how little, we know? Isn't the main purpose of education to pack our heads full of facts?

Certainly, testing has its place in college, and committing information to memory and having to recall it later is vital to learning. However, this is only part of the process of coming to understand a subject. Analyzing, evaluating, and explaining information—to ourselves and to others—is just as important. We learn best when we engage in an active struggle to master a subject through posing and solving problems, asking and answering questions.

As we shall see, analytical writing has much in common with its informational counterpart: Its effectiveness, too, depends on accuracy, clarity, balance; it can be fact-filled, resting on a sturdy informational footing. Yet when we write analytically, we do more than report or present facts. We attempt to *do* something with those facts—to understand them better, to place them in a context of meaning, to explain their significance. To write analytically means to take a body of information and to perform an operation on it, to inspect it closely for solutions and answers.

Like informational prose, analytical writing is all around us. Whether the subject is politics, current events, sports, or business, analytical writing is a common kind of nonfiction. Say, for example, that today's newspaper headline reads: STOCK PRICES TUMBLE; DOW INDUSTRIALS SLIDE 30 POINTS. Under the headline we will find a news report telling what happened, that trading on Wall Street was frantic, and that the market had suffered one of its worst declines in weeks. Elsewhere on the front page, or in the paper's business section, we are certain to find an article explaining why the bulls had a bad day. Perhaps investors were worried about higher interest rates; there was a renewed threat of war in the Middle East; recent government figures showed a large increase in wholesale prices; or the sun passed behind the moon. Whatever the case, the purpose of the analysis will be to explain the market drop in terms of a rational cause-and-effect relationship based on the assumption that events influence activity on the floor of the New York Stock Exchange. (We should note, further, that the article's purpose is not to convince us to sell our stocks and buy china dolls.)

Similarly, in hundreds of other newspapers, magazines, books, pamphlets, instruction manuals, textbooks, scholarly journals, we will be able to read about why the Middle East may erupt in war, how a new drug works better than aspirin and has fewer side-effects, why home computers will change our shopping habits, the difference between fixed- and adjustable-rate mortgages, various types of tomato plants and which will thrive in our climate, the similarities of two cultures' wedding rituals, the nature of existentialism—and on and on. In a world as complex as ours, the field of subjects fit for analysis can never be exhausted.

This very wealth of material, however, creates a problem. Not only are there innumerable subjects open to analysis, but each one of them can be in itself quite complicated. Say a writer encounters a subject that calls for further investigation. What does he or she do? Where to start? How to understand it? How does the writer get a handle on what may be a disorderly collection of bits of information with no apparent meaning?

THE RHETORICAL METHODS

As does anyone engaged in a craft, writers employ a few basic tools to get at their subjects. And, as we might expect, any useful tool or technique is a response to the demands of accomplishing a specific task. If analytical writing begins with a number of problems or questions, the writing process will involve our working toward answers. The problems with which we begin will determine the methods we use to solve them.

With what do we begin? A writer facing the job of analysis will usually want to discover something about one or more of the following matters:

1. The makeup, content, or physical appearance of a person or group, a place, an object, or group of objects
2. The essential characteristics or qualities of persons, places, objects, words, and ideas
3. The way something works or can be made to work
4. The likenesses and differences of two or more items of the same type or class
5. The categories into which a body of information can be divided and classified
6. The reason or the way one thing (or things) affects another (or others)
7. The figurative similarity of one subject to another in a different class

For each of these basic analytical problems, we have a way of thinking and writing—a kind of rhetorical crowbar—to pry subjects open and expose them to view. As we explain each, keep in mind that *the technique may be used in a variety of applications—in both short and long forms:* single sentences and paragraphs, sections of or entire works. We will first define each method and illustrate its use in a paragraph. In this chapter's readings we include examples of essays in which one of the methods is the dominant analytical focus.

Description

Although description is called a form of writing unto itself, it makes more sense to think of it as a technique. When we want to find out or to explain the makeup, content, or physical appearance of a person, place, or object, we attempt to *describe* it. Description usually appeals directly to our senses—sight, sound, touch, taste, or smell. The writer tries to render the subject in vivid, concrete language, to create a picture in the reader's mind. Sometimes, however, such as when we describe an emotion or state of mind, such concreteness may be harder to achieve.

Description usually falls into one of two broad categories: *objective* and *subjective.* Like third-person narrative, objective description tends to be more detached, concerned with impartial accuracy (the observer as a camera without distorting lenses or filters). Subjective description, on the other hand, allows a more direct expression of the writer's point of view. Here it is not the subject being described that dominates, but the writer's interaction with or experience of that subject. Subjective description is sometimes called impressionistic: It conveys the writer's impressions of or reactions to what's being described.

Whether a descriptive passage is objective, subjective, or a mixture of the two, effective description usually has a focus: It creates what rhetoricians call a dominant impression. That is, the descriptive detail is selected and organized to produce in the reader's mind a single effect. Here, for example, is a brief descriptive paragraph from Peter Matthiessen's *The Snow Leopard,* which recounts a difficult and at times frightening trek through the Himalaya Mountains:

> A rice-field path follows narrow dikes worn to grease by human feet. A mist along the mountains: heavy heat. The green rice, red huts, the red clothes of the women point up the darkness of these valleys. Away from the rivers, a rooster's cry cracks the still air, or an outraged human voice—a woman ranting at her buffalo, gone brooding in the pines, or the vacant laugh of a crazy man echoing outward toward the mountains.

These words are less effective as an objective rendering of a scene than they are as a description of Matthiessen's mood of unease, of being in an alien landscape. Notice the dominant impression conveyed by these words: *worn, heat, darkness, cry, cracks, still, outraged, ranting, brooding, va-*

cant, crazy, echoing. The author means to tell his readers that these mountains and their people are mysterious, even threatening, to his Western eyes and ears.

By contrast, here is a passage from a field guide to North American trees:

> Spruces grow straight and tall, tapering upward to a point. The branches are horizontal, often drooping. Since the wood is soft, fairly strong, and often free from knots, Spruce is a valuable timber tree. . . . All Spruces can be recognized by their needles, arranged in compact spirals around the twigs. Each needle is four-sided, nearly square in cross-section. The cones, always hanging down, mature in one season.

The dominant impression here is of the tree itself, objectively observed and described.

Both of these paragraphs illustrate the need for precise language in good description. In the first example, the phrase "dikes worn to grease by human feet" is especially vivid, as is "a rooster's cry cracks the still air" and "the vacant laugh of a crazy man echoing outward." Yet "green rice, red huts, the red clothes of the women" seems less exact than it might have been (although it does give the reader a sense that the visitor's eye is not yet fully trained, which may be what the author wants). In the second example, the precision of the language (especially the concrete nouns such as knots, timber, needles, spirals, twigs, cones) gives a strong visual impression of the spruce tree—so we'll recognize one when we see it.

Little that we do as writers can be more effective in bringing our readers into our work than crafting good description. And crafting is the word: It may take some extra work (such as resorting to dictionaries, encyclopedias, manuals, guides, and other reference sources) to make a descriptive sentence, passage, or piece really speak to your reader's senses and imagination.

Definition

Just as description helps us get at important aspects of people, places, and objects, *definition* asserts the essential nature of an object, value, idea, or word. When we define, we attempt to determine *what* something is—those qualities, characteristics, or elements that make it distinct. Whereas description appeals to our physical senses, typically, definition can be much more a matter of abstraction. Although it is almost always helpful to cite examples when we define (especially concrete illustrations, if appropriate), some values and ideas—frequently the most interesting ones—elude our attempts at concreteness. To discuss the essential features of concepts such as love, justice, the nature of reality, unhappiness, we may be impelled to use abstract language.

When writers need to define for the purpose of explaining or clarifying matters, they usually do so briefly; definition is not the main focus of their work but a means to an end. In other cases, however, especially when we want to explore a subject in greater depth, we may make definition the organizing principle of an extended treatment.

In the following example, the editors of *Consumer Guide* briefly define personal computers for readers who are assumed to be new to the subject:

> In the broadest sense, a personal computer is any product that contains a *microprocessor*. This technological wonder—about the size of a fingernail . . . contains tens of thousands of microscopic transistors, and is the real brains of a computer. . . . The dictionary calls a computer an electronic device that stores, retrieves, and processes information. . . . They look complicated, but all computers do, essentially, four things. Whatever their size, all computers use an *input* device for getting information in, a *processor* for working on the information, *memory* to store information, and an *output* device—usually a TV-like screen—for getting the new information out to you.

Notice that the passage tells you what the object is through naming its vital characteristics. Because it is a piece of physical hardware, it may be defined in precisely concrete terms.

Here, on the other hand, is a short excerpt from an extended definition, Joseph Epstein's *Ambition: The Secret Passion:*

> What is the worst that can be said—that has been said—about ambition? Here is a (surely) partial list:
>   To begin with, it, ambition, is often antisocial, and indeed is now outmoded, belonging to an age when individualism was more valued and useful than it is today. The person strongly imbued with ambition ignores the collectivity; socially detached, he is on his own and out for his own. . . . The ambitious individual, far from identifying himself and his fortunes with the group, wishes to rise above it. The ambitious man or woman sees the world as a battle; rivalrousness is his or her principal emotion: the world has limited prizes to offer, and he or she is determined to get his or hers. . . .

We should note that the author employs illustration to embody his abstractions, but words like antisocial, socially detached, rivalrousness, and so on, are, nevertheless, abstract. Still, how else might one get at the essential nature of such a hard-to-define concept?

Definition is an invaluable tool. Used carefully, it will help us establish the clear boundaries of our subjects, set forth our understanding of basic terms, and provide stable points of reference for our readers.

Process Analysis

When writing task calls for us to explain how something works or happens, or can be made to do so through our actions, we use the rhetorical method called *process analysis*. In form, process is similar to narration, telling a story, except that we usually think of processes as repeatable and stories as unique occurrences. In this book we have defined narrative as a fundamental *form* of nonfiction writing, shaping whole works in ways largely distinct from the shapes of essays and reports. Because narrative is so powerful a form for containing our experience, however, we frequently find it applied in smaller amounts, and it may not always be easy to distinguish between narrative passages and those that explain a process. Therefore, we will use the term *process* to refer to operations that may or may not involve human beings but which are not unique stories of human experience. (For example, the process by which a book reaches publication is not unique; if I tell my encounter with that process, though, investing it with the details of an individual human experience, I'm narrating a story.) We will continue to use the word *narrative* to mean the form (even if quite brief) in which people relate the events of their own or others' lives.

Process analysis, then, is used in one of two ways, depending on the writer's role as either observer or instructor. As observers, we attempt to explain how something comes, or has come, to be. As instructors, we tell our readers how they can bring something about. In the first instance, for example, we might study how a baby grows in its mother's womb; we isolate each stage of development and determine what happens during it. In the second case, we might write an instructive article for new parents on how to bathe, dress, and feed their infant.

Whether the task calls for us to observe or instruct (or perhaps combine the two), good process writing is a clear, step-by-step explanation of a sequence. In this passage from a book on investing, the authors explain what happens when people buy and sell stock:

> When a customer decides to buy or sell a stock he simply calls his local broker with the order. The broker then calls his firm's headquarters office in New York City, which in turn phones the order to a clerk in that firm's telephone booth on the exchange floor (unless, of course, the order comes directly to the floor by teletype). . . . When the clerk gets the order over the phone, he writes it out in a kind of shorthand and hands it to his *floor broker* to execute. . . . As he approaches the [specialist's] post, the broker looks at the price indicator and notes that the last sale of Rod and Reel took place at 18¾. . . .

The more complicated or lengthy the process, the greater the need for each step to be clearly defined. Here, for example, is a set of instructions for growing cucumbers:

> Where there is ample space and vines can sprawl, the simplest way is to plant cucumbers in hills, with several plants placed together. Space hills 4 feet apart each way and plant about 8 seeds per hill. Thin to the 3 strongest plants when the seedlings are about 4 inches high. Since cucumbers grow along rapidly once started, the ground should be prepared well in advance. Work a deep planting hole where each hill will be. Add a spadeful of well-rotted manure, and a generous handful of 5-10-10 or bonemeal and rock potash. Work in well and cover with soil before planting the seeds about an inch deep. The same soil preparation works well if the vines are to be trained on a support or grown in patio tubs.

Process analysis is sometimes combined with analysis of causes and effects, which also may call for discussion of sequence. As we shall see presently, however, the two methods are distinct, each suited to its own kind of analytical task.

Comparison and Contrast

Perhaps one of the most common methods of explanation and evaluation is to pinpoint similarities and differences between things. When we buy a new car, take a new job, move to a new town, we ask ourselves how it stacks up against other cars, jobs, and towns we have known. We compare and contrast political candidates, prices, and quality of food and consumer goods, travel routes, insurance policies, schools, and countless other things. Similarly, in writing we will find the method of comparison and contrast much used and widely applicable.

Before we can compare or contrast two or more things, however, we must be sure a common ground exists between them. We cannot, in a revised version of an old cliché, compare horses and apples. Identifying similarities and differences makes sense only if the persons, places, objects, or ideas in question share something essential or significant. The reason for this is that, as always in analyzing and explaining, we should want to discover what isn't already obvious or apparent. At first glance, for instance, we might think it interesting to compare or contrast the features of small town and big-city life. But what would be the point of such an analysis? Chances are we'd find the similarities few and the differences a matter of common knowledge. A much better use of the method might be to evaluate what two cities of the same size have to offer; that way, we could cite specific points ("Both towns have good school systems, but X has fewer parks, swimming pools, zoos, and other places children would like.") and avoid general or vague remarks ("Big cities are a lot noisier than small towns.").

Likewise, even when we have a fit subject for comparison or contrast, it is usually best to emphasize whichever features are the least known to the reader. That is, if the similarities are likely to be obvious, we should emphasize differences; if the differences are apparent, we should emphasize similarities. In many cases, too, a rough balance between comparison and contrast may be needed.

Depending on the length or complexity of the analysis, writers use two basic patterns of organization: *block* form (where each subject is treated separately) and *point-by-point* form (where the writer alternates between subjects according to a series of specific items). There are no hard and fast rules about when to use these patterns; it may take some experimenting to decide which one best serves your material. And, of course, the patterns can be combined (and frequently are) in full-length essays.

In the following passage, from his book *The Unsettling of America*, Wendell Berry analyzes the differences between "practical" and "liberal" education:

> The standard of liberal education is based upon definitions of excellence in the various disciplines. These definitions are in turn based upon example. One learns to order one's thoughts and to speak and write coherently by studying exemplary thinkers, speakers, and writers of the past. . . .
>
> The standard of practical education, on the other hand, is based upon the question of what will work, and because the practical is by definition of the curriculum set aside from issues of value, the question tends to be resolved in the most shallow and immediate fashion: what is practical is what makes money; what is most practical is what makes the most money. Practical education is an "investment," something acquired to be exchanged for something else—a "good" job, money, prestige. . . .
>
> It could be said that a liberal education has the nature of a bequest, in that it looks upon the student as the potential heir of a cultural birthright, whereas a practical education has the nature of a commodity to be exchanged for position, status, wealth, etc., *in the future*. A liberal education rests on the assumption that nature and human nature do not change very much or very fast and that one therefore needs to understand the past. . . .

Berry begins in block form, giving each term a paragraph, but then switches to an alternating or point form. In the block paragraphs, he characterizes or defines "practical" and "liberal"; in the final paragraph he brings the two together in sharp contrast.

As the tone of Berry's passage suggests, comparison and contrast can be used not only for objective analysis itself but for analytical support of an argument. Likewise, it is a common strategy in criticism, such as when we weigh two authors' treatments of subject or theme in works of fiction, poetry, and drama.

Division and Classification

Another way to get at a subject is to divide it into smaller parts or to classify it into useful categories.

When we *divide* something into its basic elements, we are better able to see how it is put together—we see it in greater depth. A class in auto repair, for example, would be useless if we didn't learn that cars are made up of several systems: engine, transmission, brakes, electrical system, cooling system, and so on. In studying writing, similarly, we divide forms into their components—such as the essay form into introduction, body, and conclusion—so that we have some control when we use them.

When we *classify*, on the other hand, we organize the parts of a subject according to common characteristics; we place the parts in discrete or separate categories. Science relies heavily on systems of classification, such as zoology's types of animal life, botany's types of plant life, astronomy's types of celestial bodies, and so on. In everyday life, too, systems of classification (and subclassification) are abundant: We categorize sports (team sports, individual sports, court games, field games), music (rock, jazz, blues, country), novels (detective, romance, spy thriller, family saga), investments (stocks, bonds, collectibles, real estate)—just about everything.

In both division and classification, it is vital that we keep the parts or classes distinct. Dividing an automobile into its front and back sections, for example, really won't help us understand how it works or to fix it when it breaks down (both front and back contain a number of different parts, so the division is incomplete and indistinct). Similarly, if we classify movies according to their popularity, degree of violence, and story quality, we're likely to find most films hard to place (many are violent and popular, many are violent but tell good stories, and so on). A sound system of division or classification, in other words, avoids overlapping, inconsistent parts or categories.

In the following example, excerpted from an essay on slang, editor Stuart Berg Flexner divides the English language into "several levels of vocabulary":

> *Standard Usage* comprises those words and expressions used, understood, and accepted by a majority of our citizens under any circumstances or degree of formality. Such words are well defined and their most accepted spellings and pronunciations are given in our standard dictionaries. . . .
>
> *Colloquialisms* are familiar words and idioms used in informal speech and writing, but not considered explicit or formal enough for polite conversation or business correspondence. Unlike slang, however, colloquialisms are used and understood by nearly everyone in the United States . . .
>
> *Dialects* are the words, idioms, pronunciations, and speech habits peculiar to specific geographical locations . . .
>
> *Cant, jargon,* and *argot* are the words and expressions peculiar to special segments of the population. *Cant* is the conversational, familiar idiom used and generally understood only by members of a specific occupation, trade, profession, sect, class, age group, interest group, or other sub-group of our culture. *Jargon* is the technical or even secret vocabulary of such a sub-group; jargon is "shop talk." *Argot* is both the cant and the jargon of any professional criminal group . . .

In addition to dividing our language into each of these parts, Flexner goes on to characterize each by using definition to draw distinctions. The last paragraph of this division is also an implied classification system, since the author defines slang as "the more popular portion of the cant, jargon, and argot" of various sub-groups. A different set of categories might be used as well: classifying slang according to its origin among musicians, college students, show business people, immigrants, soldiers, and so on.

Division and classification, used carefully, can greatly improve our understanding of a subject—changing a blur to a sharply focused and detailed picture.

Cause-and-Effect Analysis

In our complex and intricately interconnected world, nothing happens in a vacuum, and it seems that just about anything can produce a catastrophe. Assassinations can lead to world war, financial excesses to international economic depression, Cold War rhetoric to nuclear brinkmanship, Federal Reserve Board policy to widespread unemployment. Not all cause-and-effect relationships are unhappy, of course, but the bad ones occupy much of our attention. Hardly a day passes when we don't ask, "Why did *that* happen?" When we seek to understand the causal connections between things, to determine the relationships between events, we use *cause-and-effect analysis*.

Whatever our occupation or field of study, causal analysis is a principal method of investigation. It is used routinely in the sciences (through experiment), in the social sciences (through observation), in business (through market research and advertising), in sports (through strategy). Students use it regularly as a way of understanding subjects such as history, economics, and political science.

Because relationships between events tend to be complex instead of simple, causal analysis tests our ability to think clearly and carefully. Here are some of the tasks we face when writing an analysis of causes and effects:

Distinguishing facts from theories.   We need to know the difference between explanations based on evidence and ones that are more speculative. It's not that we should avoid speculation, but most causal writing begins with what can be known and supported before launching into hypothesis. Say, for example, that we want to explain the sharp drop in the number of college mathematics majors. Before we attribute it to "widespread math anxiety," we must also consider possible changes in the job market for math graduates, competition from computer science programs, shifts in the popularity of undergraduate majors, and so on. Math anxiety may actually be a big cause for the drop, but we can't assume so automatically.

Distinguishing prime from secondary or minor causes or effects.   In the above example, our investigation may show that the chief cause for declining math enrollment is competition from computer science departments, since students may see the latter as offering a more "practical" course of study. Other factors may contribute but be less important.

Distinguishing immediate from remote causes or effects.   Again, with our math example, past changes in teaching methods may have an influence on current enrollment but be much less immediate or close in time. (A remote cause or effect is not necessarily minor, however, and an immediate cause or effect is not automatically major.)

Considering causal sequence.   Often causes and effects interact in a chain of events in which a cause produces an effect that itself causes a further effect, and so on. To complete our illustration, it might very well be that the drop in math majors can itself produce a shortage of math teachers, fewer recruits for high-technology industries, and less pure math research. These things may, in turn, affect education, business, and science in future years.

A word of caution: Do not mistake sequence alone as proof of cause. One event may follow another in time but be unrelated to it. If I quit my job, for example, and the next day my wife files suit for divorce, I can't assume that the first action caused the second; it might be just as likely that both resulted from a long string of other problems.

Distinguishing necessary and sufficient causes.   Necessary causes are always needed to produce a given effect, but a necessary cause cannot always stand alone; a sufficient cause, on the other hand, can produce an effect without other causes being present. Smoking is a sufficient cause of lung disease, for instance (it can produce disease by itself), but it isn't a necessary cause (nonsmokers also can contract diseases of the lung). Likewise, vitamins are necessary for good health (we can't have it without them), but they aren't sufficient (vitamins by themselves aren't enough to produce good health).

In the following passage, anthropologists Richard E. Leakey and Roger Lewin explore the development of human intelligence as an effect of the group life of the higher primates:

> Intelligence is undoubtedly required for an animal to learn how to exploit the resources of its physical environment. But this does not match the skill demanded to operate successfully in the complex mercurial social milieu of group living: the location of a particularly fertile food source is soon placed in a mental map of the region; dealing with individuals whose reactions to the same event are variable depending on a myriad of circumstances is, however, much more demanding. So, it appears that the evolutionary process promotes its own progress: learning about the environment (which demands a certain intelligence) means living in a stable social milieu (which demands at least an equal and possibly a greater intelligence); as social intelligence increases, so too will the ability to learn; this in turn encourages an even longer social apprenticeship; and longer group living leads to more social intelligence. . . . This is not to suggest that social life was the prime mover in the evolution of human intelligence, but it would be difficult to argue that it did not play a very important role.

Leakey and Lewin's analysis shows primate social structure to be a necessary, if not sufficient, cause in the evolution of intelligence. (Elsewhere in their discussion, the authors consider primate anatomy and habitat as influences.) Note also their acknowledgment ("it would be difficult to argue") that their explanation, although based on hard information, is theoretical or speculative to a degree. Further, they consider a sequence of cause–effect–cause, and emphasize social life as a major and immediate influence on the development of intelligence.

Analogy and Metaphor

So far, the rhetorical devices we've discussed are *literal*—factual description, definition, process analysis, comparison, and so on. In much of the nonfiction we write, we will need to keep a literal perspective. Sometimes, however, the most effective way to analyze or explain a subject is through a nonliteral comparison or identity. This is especially true when the subject is difficult or unfamiliar. Earlier in this book, for example, we discussed the writing process in terms of three metaphors: exploring, playing, and building. Another writer, the novelist William Styron, has used a different comparison, an analogy. Writing a novel, he says, is "like walking from Paris to Madrid on your knees." Metaphors and analogies thus are very useful ways to give a subject life, to make it fresh or vivid.

Both analogy and metaphor emphasize the figurative similarities between things that are not literally alike. In analogy (and simile), we make an overt comparison: Presidential primary campaigns are like marathon races, riding the subway at rush hour is like being packed in a can of sardines, falling in love is like becoming a child again. In metaphor, we identify the two unlike things as if they were literally the same: "Today on Wall Street the bulls stampeded over the bears," "His mind is a maze of contradictions," "Marriage is a dance." In both, our goal is increased awareness and understanding. Because so many things in life are figuratively alike (and language itself is alive with metaphorical words and expressions), learning to see such nonliteral similarities will help us become more sensitive to and expressive about knowledge and experience.

As useful as metaphors and analogies are, however, they have their limits. Almost all figurative comparisons have a breaking point, where the literal differences between the two sides reassert themselves. Strong metaphors and analogies can be developed; weak ones fall apart right away. The stronger a metaphor or analogy, the more potential use it has as an analytical or explanatory device. Many common expressions are (or once were) vivid examples of the weak variety: "Getting my son to do anything is like pulling teeth," "Her life is no bed of roses," "Our boss is a real slavedriver." Such figurative comparisons collapse if we lean too hard on them. Many metaphors and analogies can withstand great pressure, however. In fact, the harder we press them, up to a point, the more revealing they may be. Here, for instance, is a brief passage from Norman Mailer's *Of a Fire on the Moon:*

To speak of the unconscious is to call up the set designer of one's imagination. He bows. Caverns and grottos appear, underwater palaces, the circles and amphitheaters of hell, the rites of barbarians in all the dark forest; we think of witches, and sniff the communions of mood in a church. Yes, the wealth of the theatre is here . . .

We have the sense that Mailer could continue expanding this metaphor—the unconscious as a theater—before reaching its useful limits, evoking our dream experience in the language of imagery of the stage.

In another example, mythology scholar Joseph Campbell, borrowing an analogy from the art of music, speaks of an idea he has "long and faithfully entertained":

. . . of the unity of the race of man, not only in its biology but also in its spiritual history, which has everywhere unfolded in the manner of a single symphony, with its themes announced, developed, amplified and turned about, distorted, reasserted, and, today, in a grand *fortissimo* of all sections sounding together, irresistibly advancing to some kind of mighty climax, out of which the next great movement will emerge.

The methods of metaphor and analogy, of course, can be used not only for brief illustration but for extended, full-length analysis, as the controlling focus of an explanatory essay. Whether brief or developed, however, strong, well-turned metaphors and analogies can be among a writer's most practical and valuable tools.

COMBINING THE METHODS

Just as most tools are best suited to a single task, we may need more than one to get a job done. In any piece of writing, we might use several rhetorical techniques to accomplish our purpose:

- In an analysis of communism and capitalism, for example, we'd certainly need definition and comparison/contrast; and, depending on the depth of the investigation, perhaps division or classification, process, or cause-and-effect analysis. In other words, in comparing or contrasting essential characteristics of each system (such as public versus private ownership) we would have to define terms; if we wanted to understand production and distribution of goods in each, we'd use process analysis and division; if we looked at types of communism and capitalism, we'd employ classification; and if we were interested in the historical forces that brought each about, we'd use cause-and-effect analysis.
- In an analysis of colleges or universities, we might classify them (public or private, vocational or liberal arts); we might describe their campuses ("a small, crowded square in the middle of downtown," "an expansive and uncluttered prairie setting, surrounded by corn fields"); we might compare their programs ("a good business college but among the weakest in science and math").

- In an analysis of recent fads in movies, we might classify or subclassify (types of comedies); we might compare and contrast (technical effects in "Star Wars" and "Star Trek" films); we might analyze cause and effect (the impact of younger audiences on the film industry).

Whatever our approach, and whatever tools or methods we select, when we write to analyze or explain, our goal is improved understanding—answers to questions. In the next chapter, then, we turn to an examination of the *process* of writing our way through an analysis, of posing effective questions and developing answers to them.

QUESTIONS

1. How is analytical writing different from writing that is chiefly informative?
2. What is the difference between subjective and objective description? Why should good description produce a dominant impression?
3. What role does definition play in analytical writing? What specific functions does it serve?
4. In what two ways may process analysis be used?
5. What is necessary before comparison-and-contrast analysis can be used effectively? Under what conditions would a writer emphasize only similarities or only differences?
6. What is the chief characteristic of a sound classification system? How is division different from classification?
7. What are some of the tasks writers face when using cause-and-effect analysis? What is the difference between necessary and sufficient causes?
8. How do metaphor and analogy differ from literal comparison? How do metaphor and analogy differ from each other?

EXERCISES

In each of the following exercises, write a paragraph or two in which you use a single rhetorical approach.

1. Describe one of the following and render it in vivid, concrete language: a friend's face, the view from your favorite window, an everyday object, a strong or disturbing feeling.

2. Define one of these terms, or one of your own choice: ambition, virtue, friendship, fear, happiness, love.

3. Analyze the process by which one: prepares to run a long distance, cooks spaghetti sauce, asks a stranger for a date. Or, analyze the process through which: a bank clears a check, a worker is evaluated for promotion, a fad develops and dies out.

---

4.   Ignoring the obvious similarities or differences, compare or contrast the most interesting, unusual features of: two types of popular music, two kinds of good people, two types of bad roommates, two similar types of food, drink, clothing, or other commodities.

5.   Systematically divide and classify (without overlapping categories): your paperback library, popular radio formats, high-tech audio components, collegiate hangouts, or livable cities.

6.   Analyze the causes *or* effects of: peer pressure, materialistic values, a bad attitude toward studying, nervousness, or insecurity.

7.   Using analogy or metaphor, explain one of the following in terms of something else: learning a new language, convincing an employer to hire you, breaking a bad habit, performing before an audience, leaving friends and family.

Readings

Born in 1940 in California, MAXINE HONG KINGSTON grew up among Chinese immigrants in Stockton, where her parents, also immigrants, ran a laundry. A graduate of the University of California at Berkeley, she taught high school in her home state and later moved to Hawaii, where she has lived since. She has published fiction, poetry, and nonfiction in, among others, The New Yorker, Iowa Review, *and* The New York Times Magazine. *Her two award-winning books of autobiography—*The Woman Warrior: Memories of a Girlhood Among Ghosts *(1976) and* China Men *(1980)—address in powerful, poetic language the experience of living amid two different cultures. In the following passage from* Woman Warrior, *Kingston describes a family memento in an attempt to better understand her mother.*

Mother

by Maxine Hong Kingston

Once in a long while, four times so far for me, my mother brings out the metal tube that holds her medical diploma. On the tube are gold circles crossed with seven red lines each—"joy" ideographs in abstract. There are also little flowers that look like gears for a gold machine. According to the scraps of labels with Chinese and American addresses, stamps, and postmarks, the family airmailed the can from Hong Kong in 1950. It got crushed in the middle, and whoever tried to peel the labels off stopped because the red and gold paint came off too, leaving silver scratches that rust. Somebody tried to pry the end off before discovering that the tube pulls apart. When I open it, the smell of China flies out, a thousand-year-old bat flying heavy-headed out of the Chinese caverns where bats are as white as dust, a smell that comes from long ago, far back in the brain. Crates from Canton, Hong Kong, Singapore, and Taiwan have that smell too, only stronger because they are more recently come from the Chinese.

Inside the can are three scrolls, one inside another. The largest says that in the twenty-third year of the National Republic, the To Keung School of Midwifery, where she has had two years of instruction and Hospital Practice, awards its Diploma to my mother, who has shown through oral and written examination her Proficiency in Midwifery, Pediatrics, Gynecology, "Medecine," and "Surgary," Therapeutics, Ophthalmology, Bacteriology, Dermatology, Nursing, and Bandage . . .

The school seal has been pressed over a photograph of my mother at the age of thirty-seven. The diploma gives her age as twenty-seven. She looks younger than I do, her eyebrows are thicker, her lips fuller. Her naturally curly hair is parted on the left, one wavy wisp tendrilling off to the right. She wears a scholar's white gown, and she is not thinking about her appearance. She stares straight ahead as if she could see me and past me to her grandchildren and grandchildren's grandchildren. She has spacy eyes, as all people recently from Asia have. Her eyes do not focus on the camera. My mother is not smiling; Chinese do not smile for photographs. Their faces command relatives in foreign lands—"Send money"—and posterity forever—"Put food in front of this picture." My mother does not understand Chinese-American snapshots. "What are you laughing at?" she asks.

The second scroll is a long narrow photograph of the graduating class with the school officials seated in front. I picked out my mother immediately. Her face is exactly her own, though forty years younger. She is so familiar, I can only tell whether or not she is pretty or happy or smart by comparing her to the other women. For this formal group picture she straightened her hair with oil to make a chin-length bob like the others'. On the other women, strangers, I can recognize a curled lip, a sidelong glance, pinched shoulders. My mother is not soft; the girl with the small nose and dimpled underlip is soft. My mother is not humorous, not like the girl at the end who lifts her mocking chin to pose like Girl Graduate. My mother does not have smiling eyes; the old woman teacher (Dean Woo?) in front crinkles happily, and the one faculty member in the western suit smiles westernly. Most of the graduates are girls whose faces have not yet formed; my mother's face will not change anymore, except to age. She is intelligent, alert, pretty. I can't tell if she's happy.

The graduates seem to have been looking elsewhere when they pinned the rose, zinnia, or chrysanthemum on their precise black dresses. One thin girl wears hers in the middle of her chest. A few have a flower over a left or a right nipple. My mother put hers, a chrysanthemum, below her left breast. Chinese dresses at that time were dartless, cut as if women did not have breasts; these young doctors, unaccustomed to decorations, may have seen their chests as black expanses with no reference points for flowers. Perhaps they couldn't shorten that far gaze that lasts only a few years after a Chinese emigrates. In this picture too my mother's eyes are big with what they held—reaches of oceans beyond China, land beyond oceans. Most emigrants learn the barbarians' directness—how to gather themselves and stare rudely into talking faces as if trying to catch lies. In America my mother has eyes as strong as boulders, never once skittering off a face, but she has not learned to place decorations and phonograph needles, nor has she stopped seeing land on the other side of the oceans. Now her eyes include the relatives in China, as they once included my father smiling and smiling in his many western outfits, a different one for each photograph that he sent from America.

He and his friends took pictures of one another in bathing suits at Coney Island beach, the salt wind from the Atlantic blowing their hair. He's the one in the middle with his arms about the necks of his buddies. They pose in the cockpit of a biplane, on a motorcycle, and on a lawn beside the "Keep Off the Grass" sign. They are always laughing. My father, white shirt sleeves rolled up, smiles in front of a wall of clean laundry. In the spring he wears a new straw hat, cocked at a Fred Astaire angle. He steps out, dancing down the stairs, one foot forward, one back, a hand in his pocket. He wrote to her about the American custom of stomping on straw hats come fall. "If you want to save your hat for next year," he said, "you have to put it away early, or else when you're riding the subway or walking along Fifth Avenue, any stranger can snatch it off your head and put his foot through it. That's the way they celebrate the change of seasons here." In the winter he wears a gray felt hat with his gray overcoat. He is sitting on a rock in Central Park. In one snapshot he is not smiling; someone took it when he was studying, blurred in the glare of the desk lamp.

MEANING

1. Kingston's purpose isn't to describe family photographs, but to get at something, to understand something, through a description of them. What does the author see in these photographs? What is she trying to

understand? Point out passages where Kingston explains or interprets with her description.

2. What does this essay tell you about Chinese and Chinese-American attitudes and culture? What concrete aspects of character does the author attribute to her mother and father?

METHOD

1. Which physical senses does Kingston appeal to in her description? Cite specific examples.
2. What is the dominant impression evoked by Kingston's descriptive approach? Is this impression largely physical or emotional?

AUDIENCE

1. For whom is Kingston writing? How do you know?
2. Does Kingston's essay help you understand the experience of Chinese emigrants? Which specific details and statements shed light on this complex subject?

WRITING SUGGESTION

Using description as an analytical tool, probe one of the following subjects for a deeper or more detailed understanding of it. As you look or listen closely, what do you notice that you may have previously overlooked? What do the concrete details of your subject reveal about its significance, importance, interest? Sample topics:

*   Old snapshots of family or friends
*   The local architecture of your town or campus
*   The sounds heard in the dorm at certain times of day
*   The sights and sounds of a wild party
*   What you see and hear on a favorite solitary walk

WILLIAM K. ZINSSER was born in New York in 1922 and is a graduate of Princeton University. After serving in the U. S. Army in North Africa and Italy during World War II, Zinsser joined the New York Herald Tribune *in 1946 as a feature writer. In his career at the* Herald Tribune, *he was drama editor, film critic, and editorial writer. He turned to freelancing full-time in 1959, and has since published numerous books and articles on a variety of subjects. Zinsser has taught at Yale University, where he was one of the first to offer a course in creative nonfiction writing. He has been a columnist for* Look *and* Life *magazines and a contributor to* The New Yorker. *His books include* The City Dwellers *(1962),* On Writing Well *(1980),* Writing with a Word Processor *(1983), and* Willie and Dwike: An American Profile *(1984). In the following essay from* On Writing Well, *Zinsser defines his notion of clutter—"the disease of American writing."*

Clutter

by William K. Zinsser

Fighting clutter is like fighting weeds—the writer is always slightly behind. New varieties sprout overnight, and by noon they are part of American speech. It only takes a John Dean testifying on TV to have everyone in the country saying "at this point in time" instead of "now."

Consider all the prepositions that are routinely draped onto verbs that don't need any help. Head up. Free up. Face up to. We no longer head committees. We head them up. We don't face problems anymore. We face up to them when we can free up a few minutes. A small detail, you may say—not worth bothering about. It *is* worth bothering about. The game is won or lost on hundreds of small details. Writing improves in direct ratio to the number of things we can keep out of it that shouldn't be there. "Up" in "free up" shouldn't be there. Can we picture anything being freed *up?* The writer of clean English must examine every word that he puts on paper. He will find a surprising number that don't serve any purpose.

Take the adjective "personal," as in "a personal friend of mine," "his personal feeling" or "her personal physician." It is typical of the words that can be eliminated nine times out of ten. The personal friend has come into the language to distinguish him from the business friend, thereby debasing not only language but friendship. Someone's feeling *is* his personal feeling—that's what "his" means. As for the personal physician, he is that man so often summoned to the dressing room of a stricken actress so that she won't have to be treated by the impersonal physician assigned to the theater. Someday I'd like to see him identified as "her doctor."

Or take those curious intervals of time like the short minute. "Twenty-two short minutes later she had won the final set." Minutes are minutes, physicians are physicians, friends are friends. The rest is clutter.

Clutter is the laborious phrase which has pushed out the short word that means the same thing. These locutions are a drag on energy and momentum. Even before John Dean gave us "at this point in time," people had stopped saying "now." They were saying "at the present time," or "currently," or "presently" (which means "soon"). Yet the idea can always be expressed by "now" to mean the immediate moment ("Now I can see him"), or by "today" to mean the historical present ("Today prices are high"), or simply by the verb "to be" ("It is raining"). There is no need to say, "At the present time we are experiencing precipitation."

Speaking of which, we are experiencing considerable difficulty getting *that* word out of the language now that it has lumbered in. Even your dentist will ask if you are experiencing any pain. If he were asking one of his own children he would say, "Does it hurt?" He would, in short, be himself. By using a more pompous phrase in his professional role he not only sounds more important; he blunts the painful edge of truth. It is the language of the airline stewardess demonstrating the oxygen mask that will drop down if the plane should somehow run out of air. "In the extremely unlikely possibility that the aircraft should experience such an eventuality," she begins—a phrase so oxygen-depriving in itself that we are prepared for any disaster, and even gasping death shall lose its sting. As for those "smoking materials" that she asks us to "kindly extinguish," I often wonder what materials are smoking. Maybe she thinks my coat and tie are on fire.

Clutter is the ponderous euphemism that turns a slum into a depressed socioeconomic area, a salesman into a marketing representative, a dumb kid into an underachiever and garbage collectors into waste disposal personnel. In New Canaan, Conn., the incinerator is now the "volume reduction plant." I hate to think what they call the town dump.

Clutter is the official language used by the American corporation—in the news release and the annual report—to hide its mistakes. When a big company recently announced that it was "decentralizing its organizational structure into major profit-centered businesses" and that "corporate staff services will be aligned under two senior vice-presidents" it meant that it had a lousy year.

Clutter is the language of the interoffice memo ("The trend to mosaic communication is reducing the meaningfulness of concern about whether or not demographic segments differ in their tolerance of periodicity") and the language of computers ("We are offering functional digital programming options that have built-in parallel reciprocal capabilities with compatible third-generation contingencies and hardware").

Clutter is the language of the Pentagon throwing dust in the eyes of the populace by calling an invasion a "reinforced protective reaction strike" and by justifying its vast budgets on the need for "credible second-strike capability" and "counterforce deterrence." How can we grasp such vaporous double-talk? As George Orwell pointed out in "Politics and the English Language," an essay written in 1946 but cited frequently during the Vietnam years of Johnson and Nixon, "In our time, political speech and writing are largely the defense of the indefensible. . . . Thus political language has to consist largely of euphemism, question-begging and sheer cloudy vagueness." Orwell's warning that clutter is not just a nuisance but a deadly tool did not turn out to be inoperative. By the 1960s his words had come true in America.

I could go on quoting examples from various fields—every profession has its growing arsenal of jargon to fire at the layman and hurl him back from its walls. But the list would be depressing and the lesson tedious. The point of raising it now is to serve notice that clutter is the enemy, whatever form it takes. It slows the reader and robs the writer of his personality, making him seem pretentious.

Beware, then, of the long word that is no better than the short word: "numerous" (many), "facilitate" (ease), "individual" (man or woman), "remainder" (rest), "initial" (first), "implement" (do), "sufficient" (enough), "attempt" (try), "referred to as" (called), and hundreds more. Beware, too, of all the slippery new fad words for which the language already has equivalents: overview and quantify, paradigm and parameter, input and throughput, peer group and interface, private sector and public sector, optimize and maximize, prioritize and potentialize. They are all weeds that will smother what you write.

Nor are all the weeds so obvious. Just as insidious are the little growths of perfectly ordinary words with which we explain how we propose to go about our explaining, or which inflate a simple preposition or conjunction into a whole windy phrase.

"I might add," "It should be pointed out," "It is interesting to note that"—how many sentences begin with these dreary clauses announcing what the writer is going to do next? If you might add, add it. If it should be pointed out, point it out. If it is interesting to note, *make* it interesting. Being told that something is interesting is the surest way of tempting the reader to find it dull; are we not all stupefied by what follows when someone says, "This will interest you"? As for the inflated prepositions and conjunctions, they are the innumerable phrases like "with the possible exception of" (except), "for the reason that" (because), "he totally lacked the ability to" (he couldn't), "until such time as" (until), "for the purpose of" (for).

Clutter takes more forms than you can shake twenty sticks at. Prune it ruthlessly. Be grateful for everything that you can throw away. Re-examine each sentence that you put on paper. Is every word doing new and useful work? Can any thought be expressed with more economy? Is anything pompous or pretentious or faddish? Are you hanging on to something useless just because you think it's beautiful?

Simplify, simplify.

MEANING

1. According to Zinsser, what are some of clutter's characteristics? How can you recognize it? Why is clutter to be avoided?
2. Does Zinsser's essay have a purpose beyond analyzing clutter? What might this second purpose be? Does it interfere with the main analytical purpose?
3. Does Zinsser's definition contain any moral or social implications? If so, what are they?

METHOD

1. Zinsser uses abundant examples to illustrate his thesis. Does he use any other rhetorical strategies? How, for example, would you describe this line: "every profession has its growing arsenal of jargon to fire at the layman and hurl him back from its walls"?
2. What tone does the author use in this essay? Does his tone seem appropriate to his subject? Why or why not?

AUDIENCE

1. What is your reaction to the author's strong, opinionated statements? Do you take them as opinions or facts?
2. Do you think Zinsser is fair in his remarks about the language of business and government? Defend your view.
3. Can you think of some examples of cluttered writing you know? Is clutter a problem in your own writing?

WRITING SUGGESTION

Using the author's essay as a model, analyze an idea with an eye toward defining it, fleshing it out in examples, weighing its significance. For this assignment you may wish to take off from your earlier definition exercise, or start fresh with one of the following topics (or one of your own suggested by these):

- simplicity
- complexity
- elegance
- imagination
- shoddiness
- competition
- loyalty
- class

GABE MIRKIN is one of America's leading experts on sports medicine. He was born in 1935 and received his undergraduate and medical degrees at Harvard University. A competitive marathon runner, Mirkin teaches courses in sports medicine at the University of Maryland and is a practicing physician in Silver Springs, Maryland. In addition to lecturing on athletic training and fitness, Mirkin contributes to a number of scholarly and popular publications, including Runner's World *and* The New England Journal of Medicine, *and is a regular commentator for CBS Radio's "Dr. Gabe Mirkin on Fitness" program. In 1978, Mirkin and co-author MARSHALL HOFFMAN (a journalist whose work has appeared in a number of national magazines, including* U.S. News & World Report *and* Nation's Business) *published* The Sportsmedicine Book, *from which the following excerpt is taken. In it they explain how a common and life-threatening process can attack the body during extreme heat or exertion, and what you should do when someone suffers a heat injury.*

Heatstroke

by Gabe Mirkin and Marshall Hoffman

There's a room in my office with almost a hundred trophies won in races since 1965.

One trophy, however, is far more dear to me than all the rest. It was my first and it says: "Four Mile Run 1965." It could have been my tombstone, because I almost died in that race.

In 1964, while completing a medical fellowship at Johns Hopkins, I decided to become a distance runner at age twenty-nine, after a ten-year layoff.

By June, I had been training and racing for nine months, but had never won a trophy.

As I waited at the starting line for the race in Arlington, Virginia, the midafternoon sun pushed the temperature to over 90 degrees. I noticed many of the top runners were absent and I should have suspected that something was amiss. It was my first race in the heat and at that time I knew nothing about competing in hot weather.

The transition from my air-conditioned home to the hot sun made me uncomfortable. Relying on medical texts, I had taken salt tablets daily. Since I had a chance to win my first trophy, I decided an "upper" would help and I took a 10-milligram amphetamine tablet an hour before the race. (That was my first and last amphetamine.)

As I checked out the competition, I noticed that I was the only runner without a white hat or handkerchief on my head. Foolishly, I had felt the extra weight would slow me down.

Right from the sound of the starter's gun, I pushed the pace. Several runners who had beaten me earlier were taking it easy. I thought they just couldn't keep up.

Early in the race, I passed Hugh Jascourt of Greenbelt, Maryland, the race director. I heard someone mumble to him about no water on the course. At three miles, I forced myself up to seventh place. Trophies were to be given to the top five.

I was not feeling well. My muscles were afire and my breath was labored from a burning feeling in my chest. My head started to ache and my feet were full of blisters. My mouth was parched and my tongue seemed to block my breathing.

We came up over a hill and I saw the finish line five hundred yards away. If I could catch two runners seventy yards ahead of me, I would have my trophy.

George Cushmac of Arlington, Virginia, was just ahead of me. I had never beaten him and was surprised to be so close. Drawing on my meager reserve, I broke into a sprint. George looked at me strangely as I went by. He didn't even try to hold me off.

My head was throbbing and I began seeing spots, but I pushed on.

As I neared Bruce Robinson I could hear him moaning and gasping. I stifled my wheezing so he wouldn't know how I was suffering and eased past him into fifth place.

As I hit the finish line, I lost my vision and fell to the ground. I knew something was seriously wrong. I couldn't breathe. My muscles burned. I had the most painful headache of my life.

My temperature must have been 110 degrees. I called for people to pour water on me. But no water was available. I lost consciousness, a victim of heatstroke.

With life-saving presence of mind, my wife had me carried to the shade and put me in shock position—feet elevated, head down. She poured our baby's milk over me. Others doused me with soft drinks and beer. Ice and water were obtained finally from a house nearby and the ice was rubbed on my skin.

After what my wife called an eternity, I awoke. My muscles were so tight I couldn't walk. To receive my fifth-place trophy, I had to be carried to the stand. It was a full three weeks before I could run again.

I know how lucky I am. A few years earlier, two high school runners had died of heatstroke during a ten-mile race in Virginia. Five years earlier, a cyclist died of heatstroke in the Olympics. Each August, football players die of heatstroke during practice.

Heatstroke is the sudden uncontrolled rise in body temperature caused by the inability of the temperature-regulating cells in the brain to increase the body's mechanisms of dissipating heat.

Normally these brain cells maintain your body temperature close to 98.6° F. They respond primarily to the temperature of the blood that passes through them, and when the temperature of the blood rises, they send signals through nerves to all parts of the body. This widens blood vessels near the surface of the skin so that more heat is given off, and decreases metabolic processes in internal organs so that less heat is produced.

Yet there is a point where the brain cells become damaged by the heat and lose their ability to function. The result: a heatstroke.

The greater your degree of dehydration, the more likely you are to develop heatstroke. The harder you exercise, the less dehydration you can tolerate. Dehydration decreases blood volume to the point where there's not enough blood to supply both the skin and internal organs such as the brain, liver, and muscles. Your body must make a choice and chooses the internal organs and muscles. Thus, the blood supply to the skin is shut off and your body temperature rises uncontrollably.

Heatstroke doesn't just happen. There's plenty of warning. Your lungs and muscles "catch fire." Your breathing becomes short and labored, and your mouth becomes parched. Your vision blurs, and dizziness and nausea set in. You may even start to think and act irrationally. One runner tried to punch me when I was trying to cool him.

If you continue to exercise, you stop sweating and your skin will become dry. It feels dry and clammy even though your body temperature may shoot up to 110° F. You will then become unconscious and unless you receive treatment immediately, you may die for these reasons:

> At this point your brain is being cooked and can be destroyed.
> Your blood volume, which is already less than normal, continues to decrease. You can lose so much fluid that there is not enough in your bloodstream to support circulation and you go into shock.
> The elevated temperature in your blood keeps it from clotting and blood leaks from the blood vessels into your brain, liver, kidneys, and heart and can damage them.

If you suspect that a person is suffering from heatstroke, call for medical help immediately. The victim can die before help arrives. Because the body's temperature is rising rapidly, you don't have much time.

Place the victim in the shock position with his head down and his legs elevated. The shock position will guarantee a supply of blood to the brain. Pour a lot of liquid—any liquid—all over the victim's body. Promoting evaporation is the key to lowering body temperature. Rubbing ice cubes on the skin is even more effective. Rubbing opens up the blood vessels in the skin and ice is more cooling than water.

Stop the treatment when the victim is wide awake, alert, and out of pain. If you continue the treatment after he is alert, you may drop his body temperature sharply and kill him.

Continue to watch the victim for at least an hour. If he becomes unconscious again, or starts to complain of headache, nausea, or dizziness, repeat the treatment. Several times I have revived patients and while they were talking to me, they have suddenly gone into convulsions, acted irrationally, or lapsed back into unconsciousness. This signals that their temperature is rising again. You must restart treatment and may have to repeat this procedure several times.

If a heatstroke victim doesn't revive in minutes, he may be dying. At this point, a trained medical person must administer special fluids into his veins. After the victim has been revived, he should be encouraged to drink large amounts of fruit juices and other potassium-rich drinks to replace fluids and minerals.

Heatstroke usually occurs in the early spring when athletes and fitness enthusiasts have not had time to acclimatize to the heat. It occurs most frequently on days when both the temperature and the relative humidity are high. High humidity slows the evaporation of sweat.

A victim of heatstroke is more likely to develop another one if he or she exercises vigorously again within a month. After that period, he or she is no more susceptible than others.

MEANING

1. What is heatstroke? How does it take place? What are its warning signals?
2. What should you do to treat a heatstroke victim? What is the one thing you *must* do to avoid killing him?

METHOD

1. Where does this piece shift from a "how it happens" analysis to a "how-to" explanation?
2. Does this essay employ any other rhetorical techniques? Which ones?

AUDIENCE

1. Although the latter half of this essay is given to a clinical explanation, the first half includes a very frightening incident from Mirkin's private life. What effect does this have on you as a reader? Is it more likely to make you read the clinical part?

2. Does this essay make you think twice about exercising strenuously in high heat and humidity? Do the authors intend the piece as an explanation *and* a warning?

WRITING SUGGESTIONS

1. Write a "how it happens" analysis on one of the following topics (or you may wish to go on from your process exercise earlier):
   - How people acquire values
   - How love develops
   - How children separate from parents
   - How a political party nominates a candidate
   - How advertisers build audiences for their products

2. Write a "how-to" explanation on one of these topics (or you may wish to choose your own):
   - How to apply first-aid to a burn victim
   - How to build self-esteem
   - How to get into shape
   - How to start a small business
   - How to break up with a boyfriend or girlfriend

Born in Hawaii in 1943, WILLIAM OUCHI attended Williams College and earned his MBA from Stanford University and his PhD from the University of Chicago. In addition to being a consultant for many corporations, he has taught at Chicago, Stanford, and the Graduate School of Management, University of Southern California. Ouchi's research led to the publication of his widely read book Theory Z: How American Business Can Meet the Japanese Challenge *(1981). Ouchi followed* Theory Z *with* The M-Form Society: How American Teamwork Can Capture the Competitive Edge *(1984). In "Japanese and American Workers," excerpted from* Theory Z, *Ouchi analyzes important differences in how work is viewed in the two cultures.*

Japanese and American Workers
by *William Ouchi*

Collective Values

Perhaps the most difficult aspect of the Japanese for Westerners to comprehend is the strong orientation to collective values, particularly a collective sense of responsibility. Let me illustrate with an anecdote about a visit to a new factory in Japan owned and operated by an American electronics company. The American company, a particularly creative firm, frequently attracts attention within the business community for its novel approaches to planning, organizational design, and management systems. As a consequence of this corporate style, the parent company determined to make a thorough study of Japanese workers and to design a plant that would combine the best of East and West. In their study they discovered that Japanese firms almost never make use of individual work incentives, such as piecework or even individual performance appraisal tied to salary increases. They concluded that rewarding individual achievement and individual ability is always a good thing.

In the final assembly area of their new plant long lines of young Japanese women wired together electronic products on a piece-rate system: the more you wired, the more you got paid. About two months after opening, the head foreladies approached the plant manager. "Honorable plant manager," they said humbly as they bowed, "we are embarrassed to be so forward, but we must speak to you because all of the girls have threatened to quit work this Friday." (To have this happen, of course, would be a great disaster for all concerned.) "Why," they wanted to know, "can't our plant have the same compensation system as other Japanese companies? When you hire a new girl, her starting wage should be fixed by her age. An eighteen-year-old should be paid more than a sixteen-year-old. Every year on her birthday, she should receive an automatic increase in pay. The idea that any one of us can be more productive than another must be wrong, because none of us in final assembly could make a thing unless all of the other people in the plant had done their jobs right first. To single one person out as being more productive is wrong and is also personally humiliating to us." The company changed its compensation system to the Japanese model.

Another American company in Japan had installed a suggestion system much as we have in the United States. Individual workers were encouraged to place suggestions to improve productivity into special boxes. For an accepted idea the individual received a bonus amounting to some fraction of the productivity savings realized from his or her suggestion. After a period of six months, not a single suggestion had been submitted. The American managers were puzzled. They had heard many stories of the inventiveness, the commitment, and the loyalty of Japanese workers, yet not one suggestion to improve productivity had appeared.

The managers approached some of the workers and asked why the suggestion system had not been used. The answer: "No one can come up with a work improvement idea alone. We work together, and any ideas that one of us may have are actually developed by watching others and talking to others. If one of us was singled out for being responsible for such an idea, it would embarrass all of us." The company changed to a group suggestion system, in which workers collectively submitted suggestions. Bonuses were paid to groups which would save bonus money until the end of the year for a party at a restaurant or, if there was enough money, for family vacations together. The suggestions and productivity improvements rained down on the plant.

One can interpret these examples in two quite different ways. Perhaps the Japanese commitment to collective values is an anachronism that does not fit with modern industrialism but brings economic success despite that collectivism. Collectivism seems to be inimical to the kind of maverick creativity exemplified in Benjamin Franklin, Thomas Edison, and John D. Rockefeller. Collectivism does not seem to provide the individual incentive to excel which has made a great success of American enterprise. Entirely apart from its economic effects, collectivism implies a loss of individuality, a loss of the freedom to be different, to hold fundamentally different values from others.

The second interpretation of the examples is that the Japanese collectivism is economically efficient. It causes people to work well together and to encourage one another to better efforts. Industrial life requires interdependence of one person on another. But a less obvious but far-reaching implication of the Japanese collectivism for economic performance has to do with accountability.

In the Japanese mind, collectivism is neither a corporate or individual goal to strive for nor a slogan to pursue. Rather, the nature of things operates so that nothing of consequence occurs as a result of individual effort. Everything important in life happens as a result of teamwork or collective effort. Therefore, to attempt to assign individual credit or blame to results is unfounded. A Japanese professor of accounting, a brilliant scholar trained at Carnegie-Mellon University who teaches now in Tokyo, remarked that the status of accounting systems in Japanese industry is primitive compared to those in the United States. Profit centers, transfer prices, and computerized information systems are barely known even in the largest Japanese companies, whereas they are a commonplace in even small United States organizations. Though not at all surprised at the difference in accounting systems, I was not at all sure that the Japanese were primitive. In fact, I thought their system a good deal more efficient than ours.

Most American companies have basically two accounting systems. One system summarizes the overall financial state to inform stockholders, bankers, and other outsiders. That system is not of interest here. The other system, called the managerial or cost accounting system, exists for an entirely different reason. It measures in detail all of the particulars of transactions between departments, divisions, and key individuals in the organization, for the purpose of untangling the interdependencies between people. When, for example, two departments share one truck for deliveries, the cost accounting system charges each department for part of the cost of maintaining the truck and driver, so that at the end of the year, the performance of each department can be individually assessed, and the better department's manager can receive a larger raise. Of course, all of this information processing costs money, and furthermore may lead to arguments between the departments over whether the costs charged to each are fair.

In a Japanese company a short-run assessment of individual performance is not wanted, so the company can save the considerable expense of collecting and processing all of that information. Companies still keep track of which department uses a truck how often and for what purposes, but like-minded people can interpret some simple numbers for themselves and adjust their behavior accordingly. Those insisting upon clear and precise measurement for the purpose of advancing individual interests must have an elaborate information system. Industrial life, however, is essentially integrated and interdependent. No one builds an automobile alone, no one carries through a banking transaction alone. In a sense the Japanese value of collectivism fits naturally into an industrial setting, whereas the Western individualism provides constant conflicts. The image that comes to mind is of Chaplin's silent film "Modern Times" in which the apparently insignificant hero played by Chaplin successfully fights against the unfeeling machinery of industry. Modern industrial life can be aggravating, even hostile, or natural: all depends on the fit between our culture and our technology. . . .

A Difference Of Tradition

The *shinkansen* or "bullet train" speeds across the rural areas of Japan giving a quick view of cluster after cluster of farmhouses surrounded by rice paddies. This particular pattern did not develop purely by chance, but as a consequence of the technology peculiar to the growing of rice, the staple of the Japanese diet. The growing of rice requires the construction and maintenance of an irrigation system, something that takes many hands to build. More importantly, the planting and the harvesting of rice can only be done efficiently with the cooperation of twenty or more people. The "bottom line" is that a single family working alone cannot produce enough rice to survive, but a dozen families working together can produce a surplus. Thus the Japanese have had to develop the capacity to work together in harmony, no matter what the forces of disagreement or social disintegration, in order to survive.

Japan is a nation built entirely on the tips of giant, suboceanic volcanoes. Little of the land is flat and suitable for agriculture. Terraced hillsides make use of every available square foot of arable land. Small homes built very close together further conserve the land. Japan also suffers from natural disasters such as earthquakes and hurricanes. Traditionally homes are made of light construction materials, so a house falling down during a disaster will not crush its occupants and also could be quickly and inexpensively rebuilt. During the feudal period until the Meiji restoration of 1868, each feudal lord sought to restrain his subjects from moving from one village to the next for fear that a neighboring lord might amass enough peasants with which to produce a large agricultural surplus, hire an army and pose a threat. Apparently bridges were not commonly built across rivers and streams until the late nineteenth century, since bridges increased mobility between villages.

Taken all together, this characteristic style of living paints the picture of a nation of people who are homogeneous with respect to race, history, language, religion, and culture. For centuries and generations these people have lived in the same village next door to the same neighbors. Living in close proximity and in dwellings which gave very little privacy, the Japanese survived through their capacity to work together in harmony. In this situation, it was inevitable that the one most central social value which emerged, the one value without which the society could not continue, was that an individual does not matter.

To the Western soul this is a chilling picture of society. Subordinating individual tastes to the harmony of the group and knowing that individual needs can never take precedence over the interests of all is repellent to the Western citizen. But a frequent theme of Western philosophers and sociologists is that individual freedom exists only when people willingly subordinate their self-interests to the social interest. A society composed entirely of self-interested individuals is a society in which each person is at war with the other, a society which has no freedom. This issue, constantly at the heart of understanding society, comes up in every century, and in every society, whether the writer be Plato, Hobbes, or B. F. Skinner. The question of understanding which contemporary institutions lie at the heart of the conflict between automatism and totalitarianism remains. In some ages, the kinship group, the central social institution, mediated between these opposing forces to preserve the balance in which freedom was realized; in other times the church or the government was most critical. Perhaps our present age puts the work organization as the central institution.

In order to complete the comparison of Japanese and American living situations, consider a flight over the United States. Looking out of the window high over the state of Kansas, we see a pattern of a single farmhouse surrounded by fields, followed by another single homestead surrounded by fields. In the early 1800s in the state of Kansas there were no automobiles. Your nearest neighbor was perhaps two miles distant; the winters were long, and the snow was deep. Inevitably, the central social values were self-reliance and independence. Those were the realities of that place and age that children had to learn to value.

The key to the industrial revolution was discovering that non-human forms of energy substituted for human forms could increase the wealth of a nation beyond anyone's wildest dreams. But there was a catch. To realize this great wealth, non-human energy needed huge complexes called factories with hundreds, even thousands of workers collected into one factory. Moreover, several factories in one central place made the generation of energy more efficient. Almost overnight, the Western world was transformed from a rural and agricultural country to an urban and industrial state. Our technological advance seems to no longer fit our social structure: in a sense, the Japanese can better cope with modern industrialism. While Americans still busily protect our rather extreme form of individualism, the Japanese hold their individualism in check and emphasize cooperation.

MEANING

1. Why were the Japanese workers embarrassed by the American customs of piecework and the suggestion box? What two interpretations does Ouchi offer for these incidents?
2. What are the essential features of Japanese collectivism? Why does it seem to mesh well with industrial production?
3. How do Japanese geography, culture, and history influence collective values? Likewise, how are American work values influenced by United States history and culture?

METHOD

1. Although Ouchi's focus is comparison, he includes other rhetorical methods in his analysis. Which ones?
2. Does Ouchi pass judgment on the two cultures he's studying? Does he imply a judgment?

AUDIENCE

1. Japanese–American competition has been in the news for a long time, and will likely remain so. What are your feelings about this issue? Do you think American manufacturing should pattern itself more after Japanese methods? Why or why not?
2. If you have experience in the workplace, do you agree with Ouchi's implication that American workers don't "hold their individualism in check"? To what extent are collective or cooperative values present in American industry or business?

WRITING SUGGESTION

Analyze a subject that seems to fall naturally into opposing camps. You'll want to determine what the two sides have in common, and where they differ. You'll want to emphasize (as does Ouchi) those things that aren't readily apparent or obvious and not worth mentioning. Don't begin writing with your answer or conclusion in mind. Rather, ask yourself some questions about this subject: Where do the similarities or differences seem important? What can I learn by analyzing these points? What conclusion does my analysis lead me toward?

Suggested topics:

- Collectivist vs. competitive values
- The quality of American and Japanese cars
- British vs. American rock bands
- Clean living vs. burning the candle at both ends
- Dependent vs. independent lifestyles

GAIL SHEEHY was born in 1937 and is a graduate of the University of Vermont. A freelance journalist, she has published work in a wide variety of magazines, including Esquire, McCall's, Rolling Stone, *and* The New York Times Magazine. *Sheehy is also the author of several bestselling books of nonfiction, among them* Lovesounds *(1970),* Hustling *(1973), and* Pathfinders *(1981). In* Passages *(1976), from which this excerpt is taken, Sheehy analyzes the developmental stages of adulthood. Her book did much to increase people's awareness that the ''crises'' of growing older are normal and quite common. In the following essay, Sheehy outlines the general categories or passages she details further in her book.*

Predictable Crises of Adulthood

by Gail Sheehy

We are not unlike a particularly hardy crustacean. The lobster grows by developing and shedding a series of hard, protective shells. Each time it expands from within, the confining shell must be sloughed off. It is left exposed and vulnerable until, in time, a new covering grows to replace the old.

With each passage from one stage of human growth to the next we, too, must shed a protective structure. We are left exposed and vulnerable—but also yeasty and embryonic again, capable of stretching in ways we hadn't known before. These sheddings may take several years or more. Coming out of each passage, though, we enter a longer and more stable period in which we can expect relative tranquillity and a sense of equilibrium regained. . . .

As we shall see, each person engages the steps of development in his or her own characteristic *step-style*. Some people never complete the whole sequence. And none of us "solves" with one step—by jumping out of the parental home into a job or marriage, for example—the problems in separating from the caregivers of childhood. Nor do we "achieve" autonomy once and for all by converting our dreams into concrete goals, even when we attain those goals. The central issues or tasks of one period are never fully completed, tied up, and cast aside. But when they lose their primacy and the current life structure has served its purpose, we are ready to move on to the next period.

Can one catch up? What might look to others like listlessness, contrariness, a maddening refusal to face up to an obvious task may be a person's own unique detour that will bring him out later on the other side. Developmental gains won can later be lost—and rewon. It's plausible, though it can't be proven, that the mastery of one set of tasks fortifies us for the next period and the next set of challenges. But it's important not to think too mechanistically. Machines work by units. The bureaucracy (supposedly) works step by step. Human beings, thank God, have an individual inner dynamic that can never be precisely coded.

The Developmental Ladder

Although I have indicated the ages when Americans are likely to go through each stage, and the differences between men and women where they are striking, do not take the ages too seriously. The stages are the thing, and most particularly the sequence.

Here is the briefest outline of the developmental ladder.

PULLING UP ROOTS. Before 18, the motto is loud and clear: "I have to get away from my parents." But the words are seldom connected to action. Generally still safely part of our families, even if away at school, we feel our autonomy to be subject to erosion from moment to moment.

After 18, we begin Pulling Up Roots in earnest. College, military service, and short-term travels are all customary vehicles our society provides for the first round trips between family and a base of one's own. In the attempt to separate our view of the world from our family's view, despite vigorous protestations to the contrary—"I know exactly what I want!"—we cast about for any beliefs we can call our own. And in the process of testing those beliefs we are often drawn to fads, preferably those most mysterious and inaccessible to our parents.

Whatever tentative memberships we try out in the world, the fear haunts us that we are really kids who cannot take care of ourselves. We cover that fear with acts of defiance and mimicked confidence. For allies to replace our parents, we turn to our contemporaries. They become conspirators. So long as their perspective meshes with our own, they are able to substitute for the sanctuary of the family. But that doesn't last very long. And the instant they diverge from the shaky ideals of "our group," they are seen as betrayers. Rebounds to the family are common between the ages of 18 and 22.

The tasks of this passage are to locate ourselves in a peer group role, a sex role, an anticipated occupation, and ideology or world view. As a result, we gather the impetus to leave home physically and the identity to *begin* leaving home emotionally.

Even as one part of us seeks to be an individual, another part longs to restore the safety and comfort of merging with another. Thus one of the most popular myths of this passage is: We can piggyback our development by attaching to a Stronger One. But people who marry during this time often prolong financial and emotional ties to the family and relatives that impede them from becoming self-sufficient.

A stormy passage through the Pulling Up Roots years will probably facilitate the normal progression of the adult life cycle. If one doesn't have an identity crisis at this point, it will erupt during a later transition, when the penalties may be harder to bear.

THE TRYING TWENTIES.   The Trying Twenties confront us with the question of how to take hold in the adult world. Our focus shifts from the interior turmoils of late adolescence—"Who am I?" "What is truth?"—and we become almost totally preoccupied with working out the externals. "How do I put my aspirations into effect?" "What is the best way to start?" "Where do I go?" "Who can help me?" "How did *you* do it?"

In this period, which is longer and more stable compared with the passage that leads to it, the tasks are as enormous as they are exhilarating: To shape a Dream, that vision of ourselves which will generate energy, aliveness, and hope. To prepare for a lifework. To find a mentor if possible. And to form the capacity for intimacy, without losing in the process whatever consistency of self we have thus far mustered. The first test structure must be erected around the life we choose to try.

Doing what we "should" is the most pervasive theme of the twenties. The "shoulds" are largely defined by family models, the press of the culture, or the prejudices of our peers. If the prevailing cultural instructions are that one should get married and settle down behind one's own door, a nuclear family is born. If instead the peers insist that one should do one's own thing, the 25-year-old is likely to harness himself onto a Harley-Davidson and burn up Route 66 in the commitment to have no commitments.

One of the terrifying aspects of the twenties is the inner conviction that the choices we make are irrevocable. It is largely a false fear. Change is quite possible, and some alteration of our original choices is probably inevitable.

Two impulses, as always, are at work. One is to build a firm, safe structure for the future by making strong commitments, to "be set." Yet people who slip into a ready-made form without much self-examination are likely to find themselves *locked in.*

The other urge is to explore and experiment, keeping any structure tentative and therefore easily reversible. Taken to the extreme, these are people who skip from one trial job and one limited personal encounter to another, spending their twenties in the *transient* state.

Although the choices of our twenties are not irrevocable, they do set in motion a Life Pattern. Some of us follow the locked-in pattern, others the transient pattern, the wunderkind pattern, the caregiver pattern, and there are a number of others. Such patterns strongly influence the particular questions raised for each person during each passage. . . .

Buoyed by powerful illusions and belief in the power of the will, we commonly insist in our twenties that what we have chosen to do is the one true course in life. Our backs go up at the merest hint that we are like our parents, that two decades of parental training might be reflected in our current actions and attitudes.

"Not me," is the motto, "I'm different."

CATCH-30.   Impatient with devoting ourselves to the "shoulds," a new vitality springs from within as we approach 30. Men and women alike speak of feeling too narrow and restricted. They blame all sorts of things, but what the restrictions boil down to are the outgrowth of career and personal choices of the twenties. They may have been choices perfectly suited to that stage. But now the fit feels different. Some inner aspect that was left out is striving to be taken into account. Important new choices must be made, and commitments altered or deepened. The work involves great change, turmoil, and often crisis—a simultaneous feeling of rock bottom and the urge to bust out.

One common response is the tearing up of the life we spent most of our twenties putting together. It may mean striking out on a secondary road toward a new vision or converting a dream of "running for president" into a more realistic goal. The single person feels a push to find a partner. The woman who was previously content at home with children chafes to venture into the world. The childless couple reconsiders children. And almost everyone who is married, especially those married for seven years, feels a discontent.

If the discontent doesn't lead to a divorce, it will, or should, call for a serious review of the marriage and of each partner's aspirations in their Catch-30 condition. The gist of that condition was expressed by a 29-year-old associate with a Wall Street law firm:

"I'm considering leaving the firm. I've been there four years now; I'm getting good feedback, but I have no clients of my own. I feel weak. If I wait much longer, it will be too late, too close to that fateful time of decision on whether or not to become a partner. I'm success-oriented. But the concept of being 55 years old and stuck in a monotonous job drives me wild. It drives me crazy now, just a little bit. I'd say that 85 percent of the time I thoroughly enjoy my work. But when I get a screwball case, I come away from court saying, 'What am I doing here?' It's a *visceral* reaction that I'm wasting my time. I'm trying to find some way to make a social contribution or a slot in city government. I keep saying, 'There's something more.'"

Besides the push to broaden himself professionally, there is a wish to expand his personal life. He wants two or three more children. "The concept of a home has become very meaningful to me, a place to get away from troubles and relax. I love my son in a way I could not have anticipated. I never could live alone."

Consumed with the work of making his own critical life-steering decisions, he demonstrates the essential shift at this age: an absolute requirement to be more self-concerned. The self has new value now that his competency has been proved.

His wife is struggling with her own age-30 priorities. She wants to go to law school, but he wants more children. If she is going to stay home, she wants him to make more time for the family instead of taking on even wider professional commitments. His view of the bind, of what he would most like from his wife, is this:

"I'd like not to be bothered. It sounds cruel, but I'd like not to have to worry about what she's going to do next week. Which is why I've told her several times that I think she should do something. Go back to school and get a degree in social work or geography or whatever. Hopefully that would fulfill her, and then I wouldn't have to worry about her line of problems. I want her to be decisive about herself."

The trouble with his advice to his wife is that it comes out of concern with *his* convenience, rather than with *her* development. She quickly picks up on this lack of goodwill: He is trying to dispose of her. At the same time, he refuses her the same latitude to be "selfish" in making an independent decision to broaden her own horizons. Both perceive a lack of mutuality. And that is what Catch-30 is all about for the couple.

ROOTING AND EXTENDING.   Life becomes less provisional, more rational and orderly in the early thirties. We begin to settle down in the full sense.

Most of us begin putting down roots and sending out new shoots. People buy houses and become very earnest about climbing career ladders. Men in particular concern themselves with "making it." Satisfaction with marriage generally goes downhill in the thirties (for those who have remained together) compared with the highly valued, vision-supporting marriage of the twenties. This coincides with the couple's reduced social life outside the family and the in-turned focus on raising their children.

THE DEADLINE DECADE.   In the middle of the thirties we come upon a crossroads. We have reached the halfway mark. Yet even as we are reaching our prime, we begin to see there is a place where it finishes. Time starts to squeeze.

The loss of youth, the faltering of physical powers we have always taken for granted, the fading purpose of stereotyped roles by which we have thus far identified ourselves, the spiritual dilemma of having no absolute answers—any or all of these shocks can give this passage the character of crisis. Such thoughts usher in a decade between 35 and 45 that can be called the Deadline Decade. It is a time of both danger and opportunity. All of us have the chance to rework the narrow identity by which we defined ourselves in the first half of life. And those of us who make the most of the opportunity will have a full-out authenticity crisis.

To come through this authenticity crisis, we must reexamine our purposes and reevaluate how to spend our resources from now on. "Why am I doing all this? What do I really believe in?" No matter what we have been doing, there will be parts of ourselves that have been suppressed and now need to find expression. "Bad" feelings will demand acknowledgment along with the good.

It is frightening to step off onto the treacherous footbridge leading to the second half of life. We can't take everything with us on this journey through uncertainty. Along the way, we discover that we are alone. We no longer have to ask permission because we are the providers of our own safety. We must learn to give ourselves permission. We stumble upon feminine or masculine aspects of our natures that up to this time have usually been masked. There is grieving to be done because an old self is dying. By taking in our suppressed and even our unwanted parts, we prepare at the gut level for the reintegration of an identity that is ours and ours alone—not some artificial form put together to please the culture or our mates. It is a dark passage at the beginning. But by disassembling ourselves, we can glimpse the light and gather our parts into a renewal.

Women sense this inner crossroads earlier than men do. The time pinch often prompts a woman to stop and take an all-points survey at age 35. Whatever options she has already played out, she feels a "my last chance" urgency to review those options she has set aside and those that aging and biology will close off in the *now foreseeable* future. For all her qualms and confusion about where to start looking for a new future, she usually enjoys an exhilaration of release. Assertiveness begins rising. There are so many firsts ahead.

Men, too, feel the time push in the mid-thirties. Most men respond by pressing down harder on the career accelerator. It's "my last chance" to pull away from the pack. It is no longer enough to be the loyal junior executive, the promising young novelist, the lawyer who does a little *pro bono* work on the side. He wants now to become part of top management, to be recognized as an established writer, or an active politician with his own legislative program. With some chagrin, he discovers that he has been too anxious to please and too vulnerable to criticism. He wants to put together his own ship.

During this period of intense concentration on external advancement, it is common for men to be unaware of the more difficult, gut issues that are propelling them forward. The survey that was neglected at 35 becomes a crucible at 40. Whatever rung of achievement he has reached, the man of 40 usually feels stale, restless, burdened, and unappreciated. He worries about his health. He wonders, "Is this all there is?" He may make a series of departures from well-established lifelong base lines, including marriage. More and more men are seeking second careers in midlife. Some become self-destructive. And many men in their forties experience a major shift of emphasis away from pouring all their energies into their own advance-ment. A more tender, feeling side comes into play. They become interested in developing an ethical self.

RENEWAL OR RESIGNATION.   Somewhere in the mid-forties, equilibrium is regained. A new stability is achieved, which may be more or less satis-fying.

If one has refused to budge through the midlife transition, the sense of staleness will calcify into resignation. One by one, the safety and supports will be withdrawn from the person who is standing still. Parents will be-come children; children will become strangers; a mate will grow away or go away; the career will become just a job—and each of these events will be felt as an abandonment. The crisis will probably emerge again around 50. And although its wallop will be greater, the jolt may be just what is needed to prod the resigned middle-ager toward seeking revitalization.

On the other hand . . .

If we have confronted ourselves in the middle passage and found a re-newal of purpose around which we are eager to build a more authentic life structure, these may well be the best years. Personal happiness takes a sharp turn upward for partners who can now accept the fact: "I cannot expect *anyone* to fully understand me." Parents can be forgiven for the burdens of our childhood. Children can be let go without leaving us in collapsed silence. At 50, there is a new warmth and mellowing. Friends become more important than ever, but so does privacy. Since it is so often proclaimed by people past midlife, the motto of this stage might be "No more bullshit."

MEANING

1. What is the main characteristic of each of Sheehy's life-stages?
2. Does Sheehy's system apply to all economic and social classes? Are there some people for whom such a system might not apply?
3. Each of the author's categories is fairly broad. Are they too broad? Does she include enough specific examples to support each one? Do you sense any overlap in her categories?
4. Does Sheehy's analysis imply an attitude toward the process of change and growth? If so, what might it be?

METHOD

1. How effective is the author's introduction? Does it help set the stage for her classification system? Why?
2. What is the effect of Sheehy's use of dialog and rhetorical questions ("Is this all there is?")? Do these remarks help to make the analysis more understandable or interesting? How so?
3. Although this is a classification system primarily, what other rhetorical method provides structure to the essay?
4. What is the effect of the last line? Is this language appropriate to such a study?

AUDIENCE

1. From what you know, how accurate is Sheehy's system of stages? Would you change it in any way? How?
2. Have you known anyone who fits any of these categories? How close does Sheehy come to hitting the mark?

WRITING SUGGESTIONS

1. Choose one of Sheehy's stages and analyze it carefully, asking yourself if it might be further broken down into subcategories. If one stage doesn't work, try another.

2.   Develop your own system of division or classification by analyzing one of
     these subjects (or one you're more interested in):
     • Romance novels
     • Horror movies
     • The stages in a worker's life
     • Education
     • Desirable men or women
     • Career choices
     • Worries

*Born in Philadelphia in 1918, LEONARD SILK has had a distinguished career as a
teacher, economist, and journalist. He graduated from the University of Wisconsin and
took his PhD at Duke University. After a five-year stint as a United States government
economist in Washington and Paris, Silk joined the staff of* Businessweek *magazine in
1954, where he served as an editor until 1959 and as a senior editor until 1966, when he
became a member of the magazine's board of directors. Since 1970 he has been a member
of the editorial board of and a columnist for* The New York Times. *Silk has served on
several public and private commissions and has been a lecturer at the New School for
Social Research and at New York University. He is author of many books, among them:*
Nixonomics *(1971);* Capitalism: The Moving Target *(1973);* The Economists
(1976); and, with his son, Mark Silk, The American Establishment *(1980). In the
following excerpt from* Economics in Plain English *(1978), Silk explains the cause-
and-effect relationships that governs markets.*

Markets

by Leonard Silk

All economics is divided into two major parts:

MICROECONOMICS (micro = small): The part concerned with the behavior of people and organizations in particular markets; and

MACROECONOMICS (macro = great): The part concerned with the
operation of a nation's economy as a whole.
[Here] we look at microeconomics, the study of particular markets, of
which the two most fundamental concepts are *supply* and *demand.*

SUPPLY: The varying amounts of any good that its producers or owners
are willing to offer at different prices. . . . [To] the economist supply is not
a point (a fixed amount) but a curve that relates quantity to price.

In the case of supply, price and quantity are ordinarily positively correlated; higher prices call forth increased supplies. Some suppliers are "price takers"; they must accept as given the price for their product that is set in the market. Among price takers are the producers of corn and wheat, leather and hides, coal and concrete, alcohol and ammonia, bricks and lime—products which are relatively homogeneous and which have many producers, so that it is easy for customers to substitute the output of one producer for that of another.

But some producers, called "price searchers," have a greater measure of control over a market and look for customers willing to pay the prices they set. Price searchers include local builders or merchants or candy concessionaires in a movie theater who can raise their prices above what outside competitors charge—because their customers find it inconvenient or more costly (including time and transportation costs) to go elsewhere. Some price searchers are big producers, like General Motors or the Aluminum Corporation of America, who are dominant forces in a wide market. And some are producers of highly specialized and desirable goods, such as Gucci shoes, Steuben glass, IBM computers, particular books, films, pharmaceuticals, musical instruments, etc.

Producers of different goods have varying degrees of "elasticity of supply"—the additional quantity they are willing to offer at higher prices. A few products have zero-elasticity of supply; there is only one Hope diamond, and no matter how much anyone is willing to pay, there will never be more than one Hope diamond—or one Mona Lisa, one Acropolis, one Marlon Brando. The market can bid the price of them sky-high without increasing the supply.

But few goods are unique. Some are extremely elastic in their supply; you can get as many extra paper clips, cans of dog food, stockings, or copies of a best-selling book as you like, with little or no increase in price, or even a reduction in price over time.

Supplies of most goods are more elastic in the long run than in the short, because it takes time for producers to expand their plant for making more of the product to meet increasing demand. Many goods will fall in price as the volume of production increases, due to "economies of scale" resulting from better technology, savings on materials, lower fixed costs, etc.; this has been the case with radio and TV sets, ball-point pens, calculators, computers, and chickens.

The general public and most politicians underestimate the elasticity of supply; they don't seem to believe, for example, that higher prices will bring forth more oil, or that increased supplies will keep oil prices from going through the roof. Nor do they believe that lifting rent controls in New York will bring more housing—including existing housing—on the market.

Price is determined by the interaction of supply and . . .

DEMAND: The quantity of any good that would be bought at different prices. Generally speaking, the higher the price of anything, the less of it will be demanded.

One's desire for a good is not the same as one's demand for it. Desire has to be backed by money and a willingness to spend the money to become demand. When the price of a good falls, a person may or may not actually buy more of it, depending on what he thinks an extra unit of that good is worth "at the margin"—on what economists call its "marginal utility."

Characteristically, goods have "diminishing marginal utility"—that is, the more you have of any particular good, the less you are willing to pay for an additional unit of it. If you have one auto, a second car may be worth considerably less to you, and a third may be worth far less than the cost of owning and operating one more car. A few products may seem to possess "increasing marginal utility," so that the more you get, the more you want—like eating pistachio nuts or drinking beer or smoking cigarettes. But sooner or later, diminishing marginal utility appears to set in. Even a billionaire may find that he has no appetite for that seventh villa, that third yacht, or that sixth wife. An exception may be drugs like heroin, on which somebody is "hooked." But these are pathological cases. Avid collectors of art, stamps, or rare books may also be slightly pathological—their appetites grow with consumption, rather than diminish.

Normally consumers, rich, poor, or middle class, vary their consumption patterns in response to prices going up or down for two basic reasons:

THE SUBSTITUTION EFFECT: Using more of a now less expensive product and less of a more expensive one. If gasoline prices and taxes on "gas-guzzling monsters" go up, we may substitute smaller cars for larger ones, extra miles of commuting by bus for commuting in our own cars, or even apartments in town for houses in the suburbs or exurbs. One might even substitute status-enhancing clothes or jewelry for status-enhancing cars.

Shoppers routinely substitute cheaper chicken for dearer veal, Ivory for Duz (or vice versa), etc., juggling new market prices and marginal utilities endlessly.

THE INCOME EFFECT: The effect of a price increase or decrease on the real income of a consumer. A price increase causes one's real income to decline, a price cut makes it rise.

With a price *decrease*, the consumer has more money to spend either on that good or on other goods. Ordinarily, a price cut on a particular good makes it seem like a bargain, and that pleasant experience often leads us to buy more of it. Similarly, a price *increase* is experienced as unpleasant, and usually causes us to buy less of it—unless, as we noted in the case of Giffen's Paradox,* the income effect of a price increase is such that one

*When consumers *increase* purchases of inferior goods as prices rise (Ed.).

must consume more of the "inferior good" (potatoes or spaghetti or bread) whose prices have risen, as a substitute for the "superior goods" (steak or lobster or entertainment) which one can no longer afford.

The substitution and income effects, taken together, determine the elasticity of demand for any product. The demand for coffee, wine, oil, and food products (taken collectively, not individually) is relatively *inelastic*; producers who realize this often try to restrict supply in order to get or keep their prices up; the Arab oil embargo of 1973 was a perfect demonstration of how, in the face of highly inelastic demand, oil producers were able to restrict supply and greatly raise prices.* Wine growers in France and milk producers in Wisconsin have been known to spill their products on the ground in order to keep prices up, in the face of inelastic demand. Their aim is to keep a small increase in supply from causing a huge drop in price—and in their own incomes.

THE PRICE MECHANISM: Markets come into equilibrium at the price at which supply (the quantity offered) equals demand (the quantity demanded).

Sellers are satisfied (in the sense that they are selling all they want to sell at that price, and would not want to sell more at a lower price) and all buyers are satisfied (in the sense that they are buying all they want at that price and would not want more at a higher price).

Market prices may move up or down (or remain the same) in response to a host of factors causing shifts in supply (the whole supply curve) or demand (the whole demand curve) or both together.

Bad weather makes prices go up—not just the prices of agricultural products, but of a great many other goods, ranging from steel to nightgowns, because of interruptions of production, breakdowns in transportation, power failures, etc.

Changes in technology cause shifts in supply curves; a more efficient way of making transistors brings down the prices of calculators, computers, radios, television sets, record players, recorders. Increases in the scale of production, as we have seen, often bring down certain product prices.

Shrinking oil and mineral reserves contract supply, and prices move up. "Diseconomies" resulting from shrinking scales of production, as when the market for handmade pocketbooks, horsedrawn carriages, grandfather clocks, custom tailoring, and handmade furniture contracts, push up the prices of such products not only absolutely, but relatively far above what they were in the old days, when skilled labor was cheaper and more abundant.

Similarly, many factors can cause demand curves to swing up or down— booms or busts in the national economy, affecting the incomes of con-

---

*The cut in oil supply was only about 10 percent—but oil prices were quadrupled, with slight effect on consumption.

sumers; changes in taste—a President may increase the national taste for chamber music or hominy grits, a popular singer may increase (or decrease) the taste for orange juice; changes in "joint demand"—a fall-off in movie attendance may shrink the demand for popcorn, a rise of interest in skiing may increase the demand for liniment and orthopedic surgery; changes in fashion—the Hamptons may be in, Newport may be out; changes in the seasons, changes in military threats, changes in the livability or stench and danger of cities, changes in the public mood toward hope or despair, excitement or boredom—in brief, changes.

The price mechanism sensitively catches and reacts to all such changes. If equilibrium prices of particular goods move up, more will be produced—because benefits to producers will tend to exceed costs by a wider margin—and human and material resources will tend to shift to those uses.

If equilibrium prices of other goods move down, less of them will be produced, as the cost-benefit ratio for producers is squeezed, and resources shift away to other uses, where the cost-benefit ratios (measured by profits) are higher.

Similarly, consumers will drop out of a market (or buy less in it) as their own cost-benefit ratio declines with a rising price of a particular product. Conversely, they will buy more of a product when their cost-benefit ratio improves.

This is how a market economy allocates its goods and services; the price mechanism constantly flickers out millions and millions of signals. These bits of precisely articulated information help producers to decide what to produce and consumers what to consume, in order to make more money or increase their satisfactions.

MEANING

1. Silk explains a number of cause-and-effect relationships in his essay. What are some of these?
2. What effect does increased price usually have on the supply of a good? What effect does increased price usually have on demand?
3. What is the substitution effect? What causes it? What is the income effect? How is it related to changes in price?
4. How does the price mechanism work? What are some general factors that affect supply and demand?

METHOD

1. Although Silk is chiefly concerned with analyzing and explaining cause-and-effect relationships, in order to do so he must employ other rhetorical devices as support. What is the most prominent one?

2.   This selection is taken from Silk's book *Economics in Plain English*. What are some of the things the author does to keep his explanation understandable?

AUDIENCE

1.   This essay is written for readers unfamiliar with economics. Do you think it succeeds in explaining its subject clearly for such an audience? Why or why not?
2.   Can you think of some concrete examples from your experience that would illustrate Silk's points? Similarly, if you were to gauge the effects of such market forces on your own life, what might they be?

WRITING SUGGESTION

Analyze one of the following subjects for its cause-and-effect relationships. You may wish to focus on either causes or effects as a way of narrowing your work. As usual, try to avoid belaboring the obvious or well-known aspects of the subject, and see if you can't discover something new about it. Cite specific instances and examples to support your explanation. Sample topics:

- Fashions in dress, speech, consumption (choose one)
- Conflict between friends or family members
- Exercise and dieting
- Advertising and product sales
- The decline in the average size of new families
- Choosing a major in college
- Going against your own best judgment
- Deficit spending by the government

LEWIS THOMAS, born 1913, followed in his father's footsteps by becoming a doctor. He attended Princeton University as an undergraduate, and studied medicine at Harvard, where he earned his MD. Primarily a research scientist, Dr. Thomas has also had a career as a medical administrator and essayist. His first collection of pieces, originally written for his column "Notes of a Biology Watcher" in The New England Journal of Medicine, *was published as* The Lives of a Cell *in 1974 and won a National Book Award. Since then, Thomas has published additional collections of essays—*The Medusa and the Snail *(1979) and* Late Night Thoughts on Listening to Mahler's Ninth Symphony *(1984)—as well as an autobiography,* The Youngest Science, *in 1983. In "On Societies as Organisms," from* The Lives of a Cell, *Thomas analyzes the figurative similarities between the insect world and the human realm of scientific investigation.*

On Societies as Organisms

by Lewis Thomas

Viewed from a suitable height, the aggregating clusters of medical scientists in the bright sunlight of the boardwalk at Atlantic City, swarmed there from everywhere for the annual meetings, have the look of assemblages of social insects. There is the same vibrating, ionic movement, interrupted by the darting back and forth of jerky individuals to touch antennae and exchange small bits of information; periodically, the mass casts out, like a trout-line, a long single file unerringly toward Childs's. If the boards were not fastened down, it would not be a surprise to see them put together a nest of sorts.

It is permissible to say this sort of thing about humans. They do resemble, in their most compulsively social behavior, ants at a distance. It is, however, quite bad form in biological circles to put it the other way round, to imply that the operation of insect societies has any relation at all to human affairs. The writers of books on insect behavior generally take pains, in their prefaces, to caution that insects are like creatures from another planet, that their behavior is absolutely foreign, totally unhuman, unearthly, almost unbiological. They are more like perfectly tooled but crazy little machines, and we violate science when we try to read human meanings in their arrangements.

It is hard for a bystander not to do so. Ants are so much like human beings as to be an embarrassment. They farm fungi, raise aphids as livestock, launch armies into wars, use chemical sprays to alarm and confuse enemies, capture slaves. The families of weaver ants engage in child labor, holding their larvae like shuttles to spin out the thread that sews the leaves together for their fungus gardens. They exchange information ceaselessly. They do everything but watch television.

What makes us most uncomfortable is that they, and the bees and termites and social wasps, seem to live two kinds of lives: they are individuals, going about the day's business without much evidence of thought for tomorrow, and they are at the same time component parts, cellular elements, in the huge, writhing, ruminating organism of the Hill, the nest, the hive. It is because of this aspect, I think, that we most wish for them to be something foreign. We do not like the notion that there can be collective societies with the capacity to behave like organisms. If such things exist, they can have nothing to do with us.

Still, there it is. A solitary ant, afield, cannot be considered to have much of anything on his mind; indeed, with only a few neurons strung together by fibers, he can't be imagined to have a mind at all, much less a thought. He is more like a ganglion on legs. Four ants together, or ten, encircling a dead moth on a path, begin to look more like an idea. They fumble and shove, gradually moving the food toward the Hill, but as though by blind chance. It is only when you watch the dense mass of thousands of ants, crowded together around the Hill, blackening the ground, that you begin to see the whole beast, and now you observe it thinking, planning, calculating. It is an intelligence, a kind of live computer, with crawling bits for its wits.

At a stage in the construction, twigs of a certain size are needed, and all the members forage obsessively for twigs of just this size. Later, when outer walls are to be finished, thatched, the size must change, and as though given new orders by telephone, all the workers shift the search to the new twigs. If you disturb the arrangement of a part of the Hill, hundreds of ants will set it vibrating, shifting, until it is put right again. Distant sources of food are somehow sensed, and long lines, like tentacles, reach out over the ground, up over walls, behind boulders, to fetch it in.

Termites are even more extraordinary in the way they seem to accumulate intelligence as they gather together. Two or three termites in a chamber will begin to pick up pellets and move them from place to place, but nothing comes of it; nothing is built. As more join in, they seem to reach a critical mass, a quorum, and the thinking begins. They place pellets atop pellets, then throw up columns and beautiful, curving, symmetrical arches, and the crystalline architecture of vaulted chambers is created. It is not known how they communicate with each other, how the chains of termites building one column know when to turn toward the crew on the adjacent column, or how, when the time comes, they manage the flawless joining of the arches. The stimuli that set them off at the outset, building collectively instead of shifting things about, may be pheromones released when they reach committee size. They react as if alarmed. They become agitated, excited, and then they begin working, like artists.

Bees live lives of organisms, tissues, cells, organelles, all at the same time. The single bee, out of the hive retrieving sugar (instructed by the dancer: "south-southeast for seven hundred meters, clover—mind you make corrections for the sundrift") is still as much a part of the hive as if attached by a filament. Building the hive, the workers have the look of embryonic cells organizing a developing tissue; from a distance they are like the viruses inside a cell, running off row after row of symmetrical polygons as though laying down crystals. When the time for swarming comes, and the old queen prepares to leave with her part of the population, it is as though the hive were involved in mitosis. There is an agitated moving of bees back and forth, like granules in cell sap. They distribute themselves in almost precisely equal parts, half to the departing queen, half to the new one. Thus, like an egg, the great, hairy, black and golden creature splits in two, each with an equal share of the family genome.

The phenomenon of separate animals joining up to form an organism is not unique in insects. Slime-mold cells do it all the time, of course, in each life cycle. At first they are single amebocytes swimming around, eating bacteria, aloof from each other, untouching, voting straight Republican. Then, a bell sounds, and acrasin is released by special cells toward which the others converge in stellate ranks, touch, fuse together, and construct the slug, solid as a trout. A splendid stalk is raised, with a fruiting body on top, and out of this comes the next generation of amebocytes, ready to swim across the same moist ground, solitary and ambitious.

Herring and other fish in schools are at times so closely integrated, their actions so coordinated, that they seem to be functionally a great multi-fish organism. Flocking birds, especially the seabirds nesting on the slopes of offshore islands in Newfoundland, are similarly attached, connected, synchronized.

Although we are by all odds the most social of all social animals—more interdependent, more attached to each other, more inseparable in our behavior than bees—we do not often feel our conjoined intelligence. Perhaps, however, we are linked in circuits for the storage, processing, and retrieval of information, since this appears to be the most basic and universal of all human enterprises. It may be our biological function to build a certain kind of Hill. We have access to all the information of the biosphere, arriving as elementary units in the stream of solar photons. When we have learned how these are rearranged against randomness, to make, say, springtails, quantum mechanics, and the late quartets, we may have a clearer notion how to proceed. The circuitry seems to be there, even if the current is not always on.

The system of communications used in science should provide a neat, workable model for studying mechanisms of information-building in human society. Ziman, in a recent *Nature* essay, points out, "the invention of a mechanism for the systematic publication of *fragments* of scientific work may well have been the key event in the history of modern science." He continues:

> A regular journal carries from one research worker to another the various . . . observations which are of common interest. . . . A typical scientific paper has never pretended to be more than another little piece in a larger jigsaw—not significant in itself but as an element in a grander scheme. *This technique, of soliciting many modest contributions to the store of human knowledge, has been the secret of Western science since the seventeenth century, for it achieves a corporate, collective power that is far greater than any one individual can exert* [italics mine].

With some alternation of terms, some toning down, the passage could describe the building of a termite nest.

It is fascinating that the word "explore" does not apply to the searching aspect of the activity, but has its origins in the sounds we make while engaged in it. We like to think of exploring in science as a lonely, meditative business, and so it is in the first stages, but always, sooner or later, before the enterprise reaches completion, as we explore, we call to each other, communicate, publish, send letters to the editor, present papers, cry out on finding.

MEANING

1. What is the basic analogy in Thomas's essay—that is, what is being figuratively compared to what? What is the *focus* of the analogy—what is being explained?
2. According to Thomas, how are insects like human beings?
3. How are colonies of insects like single organisms or creatures?
4. How is the process of scientific knowledge-gathering like the collective behavior of insect organisms?

METHOD

1. Thomas is playful and personal in his language and tone. Can you find some examples of this easygoing quality?
2. How does Thomas's obvious learning affect his explanation? Does he communicate his analysis clearly? Find several sentences that you think are very clear, and then find a few that you may have trouble understanding. Upon rereading, do these sentences seem clearer?
3. Does Thomas's use of scientific terms do serious damage to your understanding of his essential point? You should check the dictionary for the meaning of unfamiliar words. Some examples: ganglion [par. 5]; organelles, genome [par. 8]; amebocytes [par. 9].

AUDIENCE

1. Lewis Thomas publishes many of his essays in *The New England Journal of Medicine*, a professional medical journal. Is "On Societies as Organisms" aimed solely at this professional audience? What about the essay may make it appealing to the general reader?
2. What is your sense of Thomas's view of nature? Of man's place in nature? Of man's importance in the cosmic scheme of things? Do you share any of Thomas's feelings?

WRITING SUGGESTION

Analyze one of the following subjects from a metaphorical or figurative perspective. (You might review some of the analogies or metaphors you developed in response to Discussion Question 1 in Chapter 2, "The Writing Process.") In this assignment, ask yourself what might be gained through a figurative rather than a literal explanation. Let your imagination run as you try various possibilities. Some topic ideas:

* Achieving success
* Being disappointed
* Resolving a dilemma
* Serving on a committee
* Training for performance or competition
* Cheating
* Falling in love
* Growing up

ADDITIONAL WRITING SUGGESTIONS

1. Make a list of ideas, problems, questions, or other concerns about which you have a genuine curiosity. Choose a topic from among these for development as an analytical essay, and confine yourself to use of a single rhetorical method as a controlling device. In your prewriting, try to determine which method will give you the most leverage in exposing your subject, and draft your essay as an extended application of the method you select. (The topics on page 214 may help you get started.)
2. Review the writing suggestions after each reading in this chapter and choose three or four that really interest you. Then consider which of the rhetorical methods might be useful as ways to think and write about these subjects. Try your hand at writing an analytical essay that combines at least *two* rhetorical approaches, as in the examples on pages 149 and 150. (More on combining methods in the following chapter.)

9

ANALYTICAL ESSAYS

DISCOVERING THE THESIS

As we saw in Chapter 6, essays are a basic and useful form for presenting information. Also, we saw that essays make a point—the thesis—about their subjects. In Chapter 8 we considered analytical writing in general, as a medium to understand or explain information. We now take a closer look at the *process* of writing directed toward analysis and interpretation.

Just as in the informative essay, the thesis of an analytical essay controls it and forms the core around which we build our work. As we have seen, however, we rarely begin the writing process knowing all we think or want to say. Rather, a focus emerges as we write. In analytical essays, this is all the more apparent: We begin with a subject and try to make some sense out of it, usually by asking (and trying to answer) questions. We write to discover and support a thesis—in this case the analytical point we decide to make. The thesis is not what we start with but what we *arrive at*; it is our answer to the problem or question with which we began.

Granted, in some instances we may already know a body of information well enough to begin writing with a specific point in mind. Experienced writers, for example, may at times abbreviate the "groping about in the darkness" stage of the process because they've already done much thinking and writing on a subject. Even professionals, however, can't guarantee that the thesis they start with won't take some surprising new shape as they work on it.

Analytical essays begin where informative ones end; they press facts for answers. And as we exert this pressure, we may not know what will result. We may find that things we thought were true aren't, that our first guess at an answer falls far short, that the deeper we investigate a subject, the more complex it becomes—and the less amenable to quick and easy treatment. We will find ourselves thinking hard as we write, and that our initial questions spawn many more.

WRITING AN ANALYTICAL ESSAY: AN EXAMPLE OF THE PROCESS

Let's look at some of what goes on when we write to analyze, evaluate, or explain. In this illustration, we don't want merely to demonstrate how to use a certain rhetorical device (comparison, for example). Rather, *our goal is to address a subject for our own or our readers' greater understanding*. We may, therefore, use any appropriate device available to us, even if our essay becomes heavily influenced by only one or two.

A Problem or Question

Before we have a reason to analyze, there must be a body of information (facts and opinions) that presents us or our reader with some difficulty: Why did the Vietnam War last so long? What happens when cells don't function normally? Will industrial planning help our economy? What are the best methods of child rearing? How can I improve the energy efficiency of my house? The difficulty may be broad or general, vague or ill defined: The problem of divorce. The inflation issue. The highway death toll. Substance abuse. Heart disease. The changing role of religion. In either case, the writer scrutinizes the subject with an eye toward getting inside it.

In the writing we do for college courses, more often than not the subject is provided. We may be assigned papers on Freud's theory of the ego, Shakespeare's comedies, the reform movement in United States politics, and so on. (The student's role here is not much different from that of a freelance or staff writer who receives an "assignment" from an editor.) Still, even if a writing task is guided by limits on subject, purpose, form, or content, we must, nevertheless, be creative in generating ideas within these bounds.

For our example, let's assume that we have been given a topic and are to write an analytical essay for an audience of fellow students. (We may consult reference sources for support, but this is not primarily a research assignment; we should base the essay on what we know or can uncover without launching a long investigation.) Each essay will be unique, each one a reflection of that writer's encounter with the subject. Our goal is to increase our own and our readers' grasp—to explain or clarify something for our own or their sake.

The problem: Success in the work world—getting a good job after college.

Preliminary Writing

We have the assignment and a deadline. Now what?

As we saw in earlier chapters, preliminary writing helps get the process rolling. We jot down ideas, make lists, ask questions, brainstorm:

Here I am writing words on a piece of paper and I have absolutely no idea where to go with this. I don't know anything well enough to analyze it! Isn't that why I'm in college? Why *am* I in college? To get an education. Why? To get a job. What job? Who knows?

- Analyze the problem of getting a job after college. The problem of success (big issue with a lot of people I know). Everybody says it's not what you know but who you know. *Connections.* Is that true? Don't lots of people get good jobs without any connections at all? (Brother's friend—got a job on a soap opera six months after moving to New York. Didn't know a soul when he got off the bus.)
- How do people get good jobs? Good question.
- What *is* a good job? Definition: A good job is one that you really like, even if the pay's low. You never hate to show up for work. You feel personally satisfied by it.
- How do you know what jobs you'll like if you've never had them? How can you prepare for a career you've only seen from the outside? I suppose some people are born knowing what they want to be or do. But what if you don't know? That raises the problem of what kind of school to attend. If you already know, you can choose a school that trains you for the job or career. If you don't know, then what? Take liberal arts for a couple of years and hope you find out.

If we stop for a minute and read what we have so far, we find that some loose pre-writing has already raised a few points worth noting: (1) You don't necessarily need connections to get a good job; (2) good jobs make you happy; and (3) career or job choice is tied to education. Some of this may be obvious, or it may need more development. At least we have something, however, and that should make going on a little easier:

- What do most college students already know about getting jobs? That you have to be responsible, that you have to dress appropriately, stuff like that. I'm not very interested in writing a "How to Get a Job" essay, telling people to be on time for interviews, etc. Too dry.
- What *am* I interested in about this topic? Actually, I think about it a lot, and am getting some pressure from my folks to take a bunch of computer courses. I'm not interested in computers! I mean, they're fine, but I'm not in love with them. I don't think I want to spend my life sitting at some terminal somewhere. Another problem: getting a job in a field you don't really care much about. This connects with the "good job" definition: A bad job is one you're not interested in.
- What is the single most important thing in trying to get a job? I don't know. Maybe—
- What is the difference between a job and a career? Probably how much you're involved in it. You can have a really good job and still not think of it as a career. A career is something you devote a major part of your life to. Except a lot of people change careers all the time now. I still think a career is a bigger deal than a job.
- Am I getting anywhere?

Let's stop again. Our thinking seems to be heading in a pretty clear direction: toward the idea that jobs and careers are different things, and that a career choice is not to be taken lightly. Note that we've already used several rhetorical devices: definition (what is a good job?), division (work as jobs and careers), comparison (good vs. bad jobs), cause and effect (how career choice influences decisions about education). All of these matters call for more, of course. We can see, however, that *our finished essay may need a number of rhetorical approaches* to be complete. Since we have a direction, let's stay with it, continuing to write freely:

> It seems that people have two basic choices, or else there are two kinds of people. Some people plan for a career and really put it at the center of their life, and other people sort of get jobs haphazardly. *(On the other hand, some people stumble into terrific careers, without any planning. This is getting too complicated! Maybe* luck *is more important than anything.)* Anyway, when you consider the problem of work after college, you have to face these two choices or paths. Are you going to plan, or are you going to stumble around? Maybe the best thing is to do a little of both. Maybe the thing is to plan as much as you can, but also to be open to new ideas that come along. I suppose whatever you do, it depends on the kind of person you are. Some people are really driven to accomplish things, to become doctors and lawyers. Other people just want to get through school with a minimum of pain. But if I were to ask, "What is the single most important factor in getting a job after college?"—the answer (*I think*) would be: deciding what kind of person you were. Looking into yourself. Figuring out your personality or character.

- Maybe I can get somewhere with this. Sample: The problem of choosing a job or career goal is really a matter of first analyzing yourself. Who are you, and what do you *really* want out of life?
- But what are some other factors that might be just as important?
- Another title or topic: Deciding on a career—some of the problems you face
- What do people really think about when choosing a career? Money. Job security. That jobs are available. How many people can choose a career just because it will make them happy? Not many, probably. Maybe more people should. Life is too short to spend it doing something you hate.
- Which of these questions am I going to answer?
- So far I have: (1) What is a good job or career? (2) What's the most important thing in choosing a career? (3) Can you combine personal desires with a limited job market?
- All of these sort of go together, actually.
- I'm totally stumped.

If we stop again and stand back from what we've written, we may see more than that last line. In fact, our scribbling has generated a number of valuable ideas. We can't go on with this forever, unfortunately; the deadline draws ever nearer. We have several distinct points—enough to warrant digging deeper into each.

Narrowing For Depth And Shape

Let's list what we have:

Topic: Career choice
  Points to develop:
  • What is a good job (*career*)? Define each?
  • Difference between job and career
  • Which one is better for you? Which do you want?
  • How does job market affect choice?
  • Illustration: My brother's actor friend

All of these things *do* go together. You can't really explain the problem of career choice or being successful without including all these aspects. Could I make that my thesis?

We have stumbled across a potentially significant idea. As we've thought and written about the issue of choosing a career, a complex picture has begun to take shape. *Why not put that very complexity at the center of our explanation?* If it doesn't work, we can try a different tack.

Next, we might try to briefly expand each point:

1. *Work.* What is it? something you have to do, also something you want to do. Work can be divided into jobs and careers. Most people have to do some kind of work, so the difference is important.
2. *Jobs vs. careers.* Jobs are jobs. Something to do to earn money. Jobs are necessary, but not always personally satisfying. People quit jobs and get new ones. You think of it as not part of your real life. Careers are more personal. Bigger part of your life. Also they can take a lot more effort to get (doctor, lawyer). Harder to change careers. Also, careers can take over your life. (*Maybe two kinds of people in this part?*)
3. *Which do you want?* (*Two kinds of people?*)
4. *Effect of job market.* Competition. Pressure to go where jobs are (conform). Lure of big money? Worry about unemployment? Desire to stop going to school before career goal is reached?
5. *Illustration:* A person who decided what he wanted and went after it (*luck?*). Try to remember details.

Since we now have a sense of potential content, let us try to shape this material in a trial outline or two:

Topic: The complexity of career choice
Intro: • Lead: General question about careers?
             Statistics? (*Look up*)
             Definition?
         • Thesis

Body: • Two kinds of people
          • What is work?
          • Difference between job and career
          • Effect of job market
          • Which one do you want? Self-analysis
Conclu: • Story about brother's friend?
I don't know. Try another one:
Intro: • Lead: Story about brother's friend (*more interesting; illustrates topic*)
          • Thesis
Body: • Work: Two categories
          • Jobs vs. careers: Define and compare
          • Effects of job market
          • Which one do you want? Self-analysis
Conclu: • Two kinds of people? Two paths?
          • ? Need something else . . . *success?*

We've come far enough now to try our hand at writing the essay.

First Draft

Whether we proceed immediately or come back after a break, we should first review our notes and working outline. The better the feeling we have for the essay's possible shape, the smoother our work will be. We don't have to start with the lead section (some writers leave it for last), but here we shall illustrate how a draft introduction can get the rest of the first draft moving. We can always revise it later.

And so we begin. Working title:

JOBS AND CAREERS: TWO PATHS

Jim Kinney decided to become an actor when he was a student at Southern Illinois University. He tried out for the lead in *Hamlet,* and when he got it he was bitten by the show business bug. During the rest of his school career, Jim performed in many plays and was voted best actor his junior and senior year. His parents thought he was being foolish for wanting to become a professional actor. They wanted him to get a degree in business administration. After graduation, he went home for a while, but soon decided it was time to head for Broadway. He bought a bus ticket to New York, and six months after he arrived, he was hired as an extra on "All My Children," a television soap opera.

What happened to Jim is unusual, of course. Most actors have to wait for years to be hired, and many never are. But Jim's decision illustrates a problem all students face at one time or another: what to do when they graduate. It is one of the most complicated decisions they will ever make and involves many different things. (*Too vague—revise later.*)

Most students—most people—have to do some kind of work for a living (unless they are rich). We may not like the idea, but that's the way it is. It seems that everybody has two paths to choose from: getting a job or making a career. Some students just want to get through school with a minimum of pain, but others are driven to accomplish things (*more?*). At some point, every student has to decide where he or she fits. But how are you supposed to decide that? It may depend on how people view work in their lives.

What is the difference between a job and a career? Most people think of jobs as necessary evils (*does this repeat?*). A job is something you need, but it might not be personally satisfying. Jobs are something you can quit and not feel that you've ruined your life. On the other hand, a career is something you choose. It is a more personally satisfying way to earn a living. Most people can't quit a career without feeling that a major change is taking place. Because a career is a big part of a person's life, it can take a lot of effort to prepare for and keep. It can even take over your life, pushing family and friends to the sidelines.

Choosing between a job and a career is not simple. Even if you know what you want to be, the competition for jobs or careers may be enormous. Often, students feel pressured into picking a career just because jobs are opening up or because a certain major or degree might be more marketable. Students may go into a field they really don't like or understand, only to find out later that they made a big mistake. On the other hand, though, it's pretty hard to completely ignore the job market when choosing a school or a major.

With all this to think about, how is a student to decide? How can you tell which path is for you? Probably the single most important thing for anyone to do is self-analysis. What kind of person are you? What are you really interested in? What is important to you? What makes you the most happy? It's probably impossible to make a decision about how you want to spend your life without deciding first who you really are. (*How do you do* that? *Do I have to write another essay on that subject?*) And even if you know yourself very well, it could still be hard to make up your mind about a career or job.

(*Just got an idea for a conclusion!*)

Everybody wants to be successful—but what is success? It has a lot to do with luck, and with making an attempt. Deciding what you want to be could be quite similar to deciding who you want to marry (or if you want to get married at all). It might take a long time, and you might have a lot of bad experiences, but if you try hard and keep your fingers crossed—who knows?

Before attempting a revision, we should take a critical look at what we have. What can we say about this first draft?

First, the lead paragraph seems to work pretty well. It gets the essay off to a fast start and gives the reader something concrete to take hold of. (Rhetorical device: brief chronological narrative.)

Next, the thesis statement (par. 2) is very rough, too broad and vague to focus the essay effectively. If our main point is that career decisions are complex or multifaceted, we should name those facets to give the reader some sense of what the essay will cover. (Although a broadly stated thesis is appropriate in many cases, here merely to assert that career decisions are complex tells the reader little.) Before revising the thesis, however, we must ask if the whole essay suits us, if we are satisfied with its overall approach.

Generally, the piece gets at the difficulty of choosing work, but something is missing—it lacks a certain sharpness. What are we trying to say? What is the point and how are we developing it?

The thrust of this essay is not just that choices are complex. Upon rereading, we see that what really concerns us is another idea: the importance of self-knowledge. Success in the world of work may depend most of all on knowing who we are and how we look at things. If we revise the essay with this idea at its center, we should improve its content and further clarify our understanding of the problem.

Second Draft

Let's try a revised outline first:

Intro:
- Lead: Story as is
- Thesis: Success comes from self-knowledge (career choice really at least three different decisions).

Body:
- Attitudes toward work (divide jobs/careers)
- Attitudes toward job market pressures
- Attitudes toward self (interest, fulfillment, etc.)

Conclu:
- Marriage analogy?

Leaving our original lead untouched for the moment, we begin revision at paragraph 2:

What happened to Jim is unusual, of course. Most actors have to wait years for their first paying job, and many never land one. But Jim's decision to pursue an acting career illustrates the complexity of a problem all students face sooner or later. Deciding on a career—seeking success in the work world—is really at least three different decisions, each one based on self-knowledge. (*Leave as broad statement?*)

The first decision a student must face is his or her attitude toward work. Unless we are independently wealthy, we will need to work for a living. Two paths lie before us: a job or a career. To many people, a job—anything that puts money in the bank—is enough. From this point of view, a job is a necessary evil: It might not be personally satisfying, but at least you can quit and not feel that you've ruined your life. After all, you can always get another job. A career, on the other hand, is something you choose, something you feel attached to because you're interested in it. Most people can't quit a career without feeling that their life is changing drastically. But because a career is a big part of a person's life, it can take a lot of effort to prepare for and keep. And it can even dominate your life, pushing family and friends to the sidelines. So the question is, how important do you want work to be in your life?

The second decision a prospective worker faces is how he or she will react to pressure from the job market. With competition for jobs and careers so fierce, many students will go where the most jobs are just to avoid unemployment. Often, perhaps too often, people go into a field they don't really like or understand, only to find out later that they made a big (and sometimes irreversible) mistake. But who has the strength to completely ignore the job market when choosing a possible career? Many things, such as which school we attend and which major we study, hinge on our career plans, and those are affected by market conditions. So here the question is, how brave are you? Are you willing to enter a field where every job opening is mobbed by hundreds of applicants? (*diction?*)

Finally, anyone starting out toward a life of work has to face the ultimate decisions: Who are you and what do you really want out of life? Do you want money? Do you want free time? Do you want city life or country life? What is important to you? What makes you happy? What makes you bored to death? If you had complete freedom, how would you spend your time? In answering these questions, people have to consider their values and their dreams. They have to face the question of their true identity—not the mask they put on for society, but their real self, the person they live with all the time, alone.

Even if a person faces these three decisions and tries to make them honestly, there is not a guarantee that success will follow. Everybody wants to be successful, to make the right choice, but luck is also involved. People change, and the decision you make today might not look so good tomorrow. It could be that deciding on a career is like deciding who you want to marry (or if you even *want* to get married). It might take years, and you might have some bad experiences, but if you keep trying and cross your fingers—who knows? You might just be successful.

Time to take another look. How does this draft differ from the first? Is it any better? What else could we do to improve it?

The first thing we notice is that *the second draft has a much clearer thesis and structure.* The thesis divides the topic into three parts and relates each to a common ground. Although it leaves the three decisions unnamed, this thesis still controls the essay firmly because it does two important things: (1) *It makes an analytical connection or relation;* and (2) *it sets forth a brief outline of organization and content.* (We should expect the main point of an analytical essay to be more than a factual statement; it should attempt to explain, to "put things together." Any effective thesis also must give the essay direction and limits.)

Further, each body paragraph in this essay is shaped around a clear topic sentence and developed within its bounds. Although we may wish to do more work on each paragraph, structure and content seem workable.

The conclusion, somehow, still needs something. It would be easy enough to just restate the thesis, but we want the conclusion to do more. Although it may require summary or restatement, the conclusion should *complete the essay's design with emphasis.* In our example, the final paragraph introduces a new idea: that making a career choice is like finding a spouse. This analogy can work, but it needs to be developed out of the essay rather than tacked onto it. Is there a link we can use? One obvious choice is to bring Jim Kinney back for a final bow:

> Even if a person faces these three decisions and tries to make them honestly, there is no guarantee of success. Jim Kinney was lucky; he fell in love with acting, and the attraction was strong enough to support his decisions. But everyone is not so lucky. Some people have to spend many years looking for the right person—or the right career. But who knows? If you cross your fingers and keep looking, you just might be successful.

Still not perfect, maybe, but it's coming along. There is still more work to be done—"close" revision for language, style, polish, as well as editing and proofing a final draft—but we now have an analytical essay, a piece of writing with a definite shape, content, and explanatory point.

A FINAL NOTE ON THE METHOD

The essay we composed for illustration is only one of a great many possibilities on our topic. Other writers might have chosen to delve deeper into the meaning of the word *success,* others the mechanics of job searching, and others the changing economic or market environment. We chose to follow our interest, to write our way into this subject according to what concerned us, exploring as we went. In that process we uncovered a number of worthwhile ideas, and we found a focus for those ideas and an appropriate arrangement for them. Although we make no claim for the eternal greatness of the essay that emerged, it does (we hope) add some small bit of clarity to the subject.

In the analytical process, we found that many rhetorical methods came in handy, not only as potential patterns for organizing the essay, but as *ways of thinking and writing about the subject in all stages of the essay's development*, from pre-writing through later drafts. We eventually came to use *brief narration, division, contrast, cause and effect,* and *analogy* in the second revision. If we had set out to apply only one rhetorical technique to the topic, we might have developed a decent essay, but our analysis might have suffered. That is, we may have needlessly limited our capacity, thrown away a potentially useful tool before we were sure it was unnecessary.

Anything that helps us understand, helps us reveal what we hadn't suspected, or helps us explain to someone else what we've discovered, is too valuable to discard. It makes sense, then, to keep these devices—all of them—within easy reach.

QUESTIONS

1. In an analytical essay, what does the thesis result from?
2. What usually starts the analytical process? What calls the analytical process into being?
3. How can the rhetorical methods be helpful throughout the analytical-writing process?

EXERCISES

1. Read through the Writing Suggestions at the end of this chapter and choose two or three (or your own topics) that most interest you. Following the example of analytical writing in our discussion, do a page or two of preliminary writing on each subject. Take down all your ideas, pursue the questions your curiosity raises, write your way into the topic according to your interest in it. Try to break the topic apart with any rhetorical methods that seem suitable.

2. For each batch of notes above, try narrowing for depth and shape. List major points, and briefly expand each, as in our example. Which of these have the potential for greater development? Do any further ideas, questions, or related topics come to mind?

3. Now sketch some possible outlines around the answers you've begun to develop. Are your notes giving way to a controlling idea—an analytical response to the problems or questions with which you started?

Readings

RANDY WAKITSCH was born in 1963 in Johnsburg, Illinois, a small town north of Chicago. He is a graduate of Johnsburg High School and Loras College, Dubuque, Iowa. As a high school student, Wakitsch was twice voted Journalist of the Year and served as editor of the Johnsburg Weekly News, *the school paper. He also played varsity sports and was president of his chapter of the National Honor Society as a senior. While in college, Wakitsch majored in writing and was active in campus ministry, particularly retreat work, music ministry, and liturgy planning. He was an assistant editor of* The Lorian, *the college newspaper, and a contributor to its pages, and wrote for* The Carpenter's Square, *the campus ministry newsletter. Upon graduation from Loras in 1985, Wakitsch entered graduate school to study theology and prepare for the priesthood. In this essay, the author poses a question—and offers a tentative answer—about the nature of "fathers."*

Are All Priests Really Fathers?

by Randy Wakitsch

Roman Catholics have a funny habit. They refer to the men of the professional clergy as their "fathers." Some church members call them "Father So-and-So" out of respect for their position within the church's hierarchy. Others say it automatically whenever they see a man wearing a black suit and the collar because "they've always been called that." We sometimes use the title because it goes right along with the job description, the clothes and the seminary training, not because the men themselves are fatherly.

Why are priests called fathers? St. Irenaeus said that a teacher is a father and a disciple is a son. And of course, the church also cites passages of scripture from the letters of Saints Peter and Paul. The Apostles are referred to as the first "teachers" of spiritual things so that the people of the growing Christian church could be "reborn into the likeness of Christ." As the church progressed through history, it began to call the Apostles and disciples of the first seven centuries "the Fathers of the Church." As one theologian writes, the Fathers are "the parents at whose knee the Catholic Church of today was taught her belief."

The title originally belonged only to the bishops, because they baptized everyone and were the "chief teachers" during the early years of the church. The superiors of religious houses and convents were named "abbots," a title which was derived from "abba," the Aramaic word for "father." Even the title of "pope" came from the Greek word "pappas."

As the population of Christians continued to increase and the bishops began to feel the pressure of tending to a larger church, priests were also named "fathers," especially as ministers of the sacrament of penance. Still, the clergy's main duty was to be "teachers."

According to spiritualists, priests are called fathers because, in ministering the sacraments of baptism and eucharist, they assist God in giving "divine life" to His spiritual family.

Until now, priests are fathers because of their teaching position and because of their function as ministers of the sacraments. However, one cannot look past the actual title. What should it mean to be the father of a "parish family"?

Just like the doctor of medicine who is so titled because he has a degree (not because he is "one who teaches" as the word "doctor" really means), the priest is tagged as "Father," even if he does not live up to the fatherly image.

During my two years as a college student, I have become close to several

Randy Wakitsch, "Are All Priests Really Fathers?" Used by permission.

of the priests on campus, and I consider them to be friends. However, I have become especially close to an elderly priest who is not only a very wise Biblical scholar, but a tender and compassionate man. He is, indeed, the only priest whom I know personally that I refer to as "Father," because he fits the description. In fact, I introduced him to my parents as "my father at college."

I'm certain that there are people who have said to their pastor, "You know, you've been like a father to me. You've listened when I needed to be listened to; you've advised me when I needed advice; and you've offered your shoulder when I needed to cry." The Father acted as a father.

Commonly referred to as "the Reverend So-and-So" in official correspondence, the priest is hardly ever called that in everyday conversation. The title carries an image of the holy man with flowing black robes, a breviary stuck under his arm, and his hands piously joined together. Instead, "father" is a much more affectionate term. A father guides and leads his family members; he does not act holy and reverent. A pious monk keeps to himself, but a father deals with people and has a pastoral function.

Another reason why people may have begun to call the priests "father" is half out of pity. The celibate is not allowed to marry and have children of his own, so the community, in respect for that, names the priest as its "spiritual father." However, in this case, people say "Father" because of the celibate state of the clergy, not necessarily because they are fatherly.

The real father figure is a man who is respected for his good qualities and achievements and who is trusted for his reliability and responsibility. He is one who cares for and directs his "children" with affection. Does a young man who gets a college degree, puts in four years at a theology school and is ordained necessarily have the qualities of a father? Why is he automatically called a father (besides the traditional reasons)? Must not he first deal with the people of his "family" to earn their respect and trust?

We tend to slap titles on people in authority, but slapping is often done in haste. Should we call a learned man of the priesthood a father if he is not fatherly? Should we call one who is foolish "wise"?

MEANING

1. What is the controlling idea or thesis of Wakitsch's essay? Is it stated directly, or implied? How would you state it in your own words?
2. What is the subject of Wakitsch's analysis? Is there a subject beyond the concept of "fatherliness" addressed in this essay? If so, what is it?
3. Is Wakitsch critical of the priesthood as an institution? Why or why not?

METHOD

1. Which rhetorical modes (or modes of thought) does the author employ? Is the essay dominated by a single one?
2. Wakitsch writes in the first person. Does this prevent his essay from being an objective appraisal of his subject? To what extent, if any, is the essay slanted or biased?

AUDIENCE

1. Do you agree with the author's ideas on authority and the deference we pay it? Why or why not?
2. Is the author—himself a Roman Catholic and candidate for the priesthood—speaking to a broad or narrow audience? To what extent can non-Catholics appreciate Wakitsch's discussion of names and authority?

WRITING SUGGESTION

Write an analytical essay in which you address one of the following topics: What it means to be a _____. (Choose one, below.)

- Teacher
- Student
- Parent
- Lover
- Friend
- Leader

- Citizen
- Criminal
- Hero
- Man
- Woman

GEORGE LAKOFF was born in 1941 and was educated at the Massachusetts Institute of Technology and Indiana University, where he earned his PhD. Lakoff has been a research fellow and lecturer at Harvard University and has taught linguistics at the University of Michigan, Ann Arbor. Currently, he is on the faculty of the linguistics department at the University of California, Berkeley. Lakoff contributes to a number of scholarly journals and is the author of Irregularity in Syntax *(1970).*

Born in 1949, MARK JOHNSON studied at the University of Kansas and the University of Chicago, where he earned his PhD. He teaches philosophy at Southern Illinois University, Carbondale, and was a visiting professor at Berkeley in 1979. His articles on philosophy of language, aesthetics, and ethics have appeared in a number of scholarly journals, and he is the editor of Philosophical Perspectives on Metaphor *(1981). In the following excerpt from their book* Metaphors We Live By *(1980), Lakoff and Johnson examine the nature of metaphorical language and explain how metaphors reveal an aspect of human thought and experience.*

Concepts We Live By

by George Lakoff and Mark Johnson

Metaphor is for most people a device of the poetic imagination and the rhetorical flourish—a matter of extraordinary rather than ordinary language. Moreover, metaphor is typically viewed as characteristic of language alone, a matter of words rather than thought or action. For this reason, most people think they can get along perfectly well without metaphor. We have found, on the contrary, that metaphor is pervasive in everyday life, not just in language but in thought and action. Our ordinary conceptual system, in terms of which we both think and act, is fundamentally metaphorical in nature.

The concepts that govern our thought are not just matters of the intellect. They also govern our everyday functioning, down to the most mundane details. Our concepts structure what we perceive, how we get around in the world, and how we relate to other people. Our conceptual system thus plays a central role in defining our everyday realities. If we are right in suggesting that our conceptual system is largely metaphorical, then the way we think, what we experience, and what we do every day is very much a matter of metaphor.

But our conceptual system is not something we are normally aware of. In most of the little things we do every day, we simply think and act more or less automatically along certain lines. Just what these lines are is by no means obvious. One way to find out is by looking at language. Since communication is based on the same conceptual system that we use in thinking and acting, language is an important source of evidence for what that system is like.

Primarily on the basis of linguistic evidence, we have found that most of our ordinary conceptual system is metaphorical in nature. And we have found a way to begin to identify in detail just what the metaphors are that structure how we perceive, how we think, and what we do.

To give some idea of what it could mean for a concept to be metaphorical and for such a concept to structure an everyday activity, let us start with the concept ARGUMENT and the conceptual metaphor ARGUMENT IS WAR. This metaphor is reflected in our everyday language by a wide variety of expressions:

ARGUMENT IS WAR

Your claims are *indefensible.*
He *attacked every weak point* in my argument.
His criticisms were *right on target.*
I *demolished* his argument.
I've never *won* an argument with him.
You disagree? Okay, *shoot!*
If you use that *strategy,* he'll *wipe you out.*
He *shot down* all of my arguments.

It is important to see that we don't just *talk* about arguments in terms of war. We can actually win or lose arguments. We see the person we are arguing with as an opponent. We attack his positions and we defend our own. We gain and lose ground. We plan and use strategies. If we find a position indefensible, we can abandon it and take a new line of attack. Many of the things we *do* in arguing are partially structured by the concept of war. Though there is no physical battle, there is a verbal battle, and the structure of an argument—attack, defense, counterattack, etc.—reflects this. It is in this sense that the ARGUMENT IS WAR metaphor is one that we live by in this culture; it structures the actions we perform in arguing.

Try to imagine a culture where arguments are not viewed in terms of war, where no one wins or loses, where there is no sense of attacking or defending, gaining or losing ground. Imagine a culture where an argument is viewed as a dance, the participants are seen as performers, and the goal is to perform in a balanced and aesthetically pleasing way. In such a culture, people would view arguments differently, experience them differently, carry them out differently, and talk about them differently. But *we* would probably not view them as arguing at all: they would simply be doing something different. It would seem strange even to call what they were doing "arguing." Perhaps the most neutral way of describing this difference between their culture and ours would be to say that we have a discourse form structured in terms of battle and they have one structured in terms of dance.

This is an example of what it means for a metaphorical concept, namely, ARGUMENT IS WAR, to structure (at least in part) what we do and how we understand what we are doing when we argue. *The essence of metaphor is understanding and experiencing one kind of thing in terms of another.* It is not that arguments are a subspecies of war. Arguments and wars are different kinds of things—verbal discourse and armed conflict—and the actions performed are different kinds of actions. But ARGUMENT is partially structured, understood, performed, and talked about in terms of WAR. The concept is metaphorically structured, the activity is metaphorically structured, and, consequently, the language is metaphorically structured.

Moreover, this is the *ordinary* way of having an argument and talking about one. The normal way for us to talk about attacking a position is to use the words "attack a position." Our conventional ways of talking about arguments presuppose a metaphor we are hardly ever conscious of. The metaphor is not merely in the words we use—it is in our very concept of an argument. The language of argument is not poetic, fanciful, or rhetorical; it is literal. We talk about arguments that way because we conceive of them that way—and we act according to the way we conceive of things. . . .

Arguments usually follow patterns; that is, there are certain things we typically do and do not do in arguing. The fact that we in part conceptualize arguments in terms of battle systematically influences the shape arguments take and the way we talk about what we do in arguing. Because the metaphorical concept is systematic, the language we use to talk about that aspect of the concept is systematic.

We saw in the ARGUMENT IS WAR metaphor that expressions from the vocabulary of war, e.g., *attack a position, indefensible, strategy, new line of attack, win, gain ground,* etc., form a systematic way of talking about the battling aspects of arguing. It is no accident that these expressions mean what they mean when we use them to talk about arguments. A portion of the conceptual network of battle partially characterizes the concept of an argument, and the language follows suit. Since metaphorical expressions in our language are tied to metaphorical concepts in a systematic way, we can use metaphorical linguistic expressions to study the nature of metaphorical concepts and to gain an understanding of the metaphorical nature of our activities.

To get an idea of how metaphorical expressions in everyday language can give us insight into the metaphorical nature of the concepts that structure our everyday activities, let us consider the metaphorical concept TIME IS MONEY as it is reflected in contemporary English.

TIME IS MONEY

You're *wasting* my time.
This gadget will *save* you hours.
I don't *have* the time to *give* you.
How do you *spend* your time these days?
That flat tire *cost* me an hour.
I've *invested* a lot of time in her.
I don't *have enough* time to *spare* for that.
You're *running out* of time.
You need to *budget* your time.
Put aside some time for ping pong.
Is that *worth your while?*
Do you *have* much time *left?*
He's living on *borrowed* time.

You don't *use* your time *profitably.*
I *lost* a lot of time when I got sick.
Thank you for your time.

Time in our culture is a valuable commodity. It is a limited resource that we use to accomplish our goals. Because of the way that the concept of work has developed in modern Western culture, where work is typically associated with the time it takes and time is precisely quantified, it has become customary to pay people by the hour, week, or year. In our culture TIME IS MONEY in many ways: telephone message units, hourly wages, hotel room rates, yearly budgets, interest on loans, and paying your debt to society by "serving time." These practices are relatively new in the history of the human race, and by no means do they exist in all cultures. They have arisen in modern industrialized societies and structure our basic everyday activities in a very profound way. Corresponding to the fact that we *act* as if time is a valuable commodity—a limited resource, even money— we *conceive of* time that way. Thus we understand and experience time as the kind of thing that can be spent, wasted, budgeted, invested wisely or poorly, saved, or squandered.

MEANING

1. According to Lakoff and Johnson, why is metaphor an important aspect of our language and thought systems?
2. How does metaphor govern the way we think? What effect does it have on our perceptions and behavior?
3. What is the thesis of this essay, and where is it stated? What evidence do the authors supply to support their assertion?

METHOD

1. Which rhetorical methods do the authors employ in their explanation? Does any one dominate? If so, which one?
2. Lakoff and Johnson present a difficult subject in clear language. Still, they want to be as objectively precise as possible. Are there places in this essay you find difficult to follow? Upon rereading, are they still hard to understand? If a problem exists, is it due to the authors' presentation or to the subject itself? Why?

AUDIENCE

1. From the tone and style of this essay, what can you tell about the audience to whom it's addressed?

2. Do you agree with the authors' assertions about the nature of ordinary thought? Does an essay like this have practical as well as academic value? Why or why not?

WRITING SUGGESTIONS

1. In another chapter of the book *Metaphors We Live By,* Lakoff and Johnson list a number of other basic metaphorical concepts that structure our everyday experience. Write an analytical essay on one or more of these concepts, and see if you can't determine their influence on ordinary thought or behavior. Sample metaphors (you may want to investigate others of your own choice, too):
    *   Theories (and arguments) are buildings.
    *   Ideas are food.
    *   Ideas are organisms, either people or plants.
    *   Ideas are fashions.
    *   Love is madness, magic, war.
    *   Significant is big.

2. Here are some other common metaphors. Analyze one or more for its flexibility, influence, and so forth.
    *   Life is a game.
    *   Politics is a sport.
    *   Marriage is a war (or an uneasy truce).
    *   Business competition is war.
    *   Love is heaven.
    *   Happiness is money, power, fame.

DANIEL J. BOORSTIN was born in 1914 in Atlanta, Georgia. He was educated at Harvard, Oxford, and Yale Universities, and earned his law degree from Yale in 1940. Boorstin has taught history at Harvard and the University of Chicago, where he spent the bulk of his academic career. In 1969, he became director of the National Museum of History and Technology of the Smithsonian Institution, Washington, D.C., and in 1975 was appointed to head the Library of Congress. He has received numerous awards and honors, including the Pulitzer Prize for History. Boorstin is best known as the author of many widely read books of history, including his massive trilogy The Americans, *the first volume of which was published in 1958, and the third in 1973. Among his other works:* The Lost World of Thomas Jefferson *(1948);* The Image: A Guide to Pseudo-Events in America *(1964);* The Exploring Spirit *(1976); and* The Discoverers *(1983). The author has also edited the University of Chicago's* History of American Civilization *and has been editor of American history for the* Encyclopedia Britannica, *as well as a contributor to such publications as* Harper's, The New York Times Book Review, *and* Fortune. *In the following chapter from* The Americans: The Democratic Experience *(Vol. 3 of the trilogy), Boorstin examines the impact television has had on our national life.*

Extending Experience:
The New Segregation

by Daniel J. Boorstin

Émile Zola's observation that "you cannot say you have thoroughly seen anything until you have got a photograph of it," now applied a hundred-fold in the world of television. By the late twentieth century the man on the spot, the viewer of the experience where it actually happened, began to feel confined and limited. The full flavor of the experience seemed to come only to the "viewer," the man in the television audience. Suddenly, from feeling remote and away the televiewer was painlessly and instantaneously transported *into* the experience. Television cameras made him a ubiquitous viewer. The man there in person was spacebound, crowd-confined, while the TV viewer was free to see from all points of view, above the heads of others, and behind the scenes. Was it he who was *really* there?

Making copies of experience, sights and sounds, for *later* use was one thing. Conquering space and time for instantaneous viewing was quite another, and even more revolutionary.

Before the Civil War, Morse's telegraph had hastened the pace of business and was speeding news to the papers within a day after it happened. When Bell's telephone was displayed at the Philadelphia Centennial Exposition in 1876, in the very year that Alexander Graham Bell had received his first telephone patent, it was still a great curiosity. Only two years later the first telephone appeared in the White House, under President Rutherford B. Hayes. Scores of inventors, including Thomas A. Edison and Emile Berliner, improved the telephone. By the early twentieth century the telephone had become an everyday convenience, and Bell's company, overtaking U.S. Steel, had grown to be the largest corporation in the United States. On remote farms and ranches, medical care by telephone saved the life of many a child—and incidentally saved the doctor a long ride, in the days when doctors still commonly made house calls. New businesses were started by Go-Getters who sold their goods exclusively by telephone, having discovered that customers who had formed the habit of throwing away their "junk mail" would still answer every ring. The telephone (like the typewriter, which was perfected at about the same time) provided a whole new category of jobs for women.

By the time the fifty-millionth American telephone was ceremoniously placed on President Dwight D. Eisenhower's desk, it was unusual for any

American family to be out of reach of the telephone. The business of government was conducted by phone. The United States possessed more than half the telephones in the world, and by 1972 nearly a half-billion separate phone conversations were being carried on in the United States each day. Still, the telephone was only a convenience, permitting Americans to do more casually and with less effort what they had already been doing before. People found it easier to get their message to other individuals whom they wanted to reach.

Television was a revolution, or more precisely, a cataclysm. For nobody "wanted" television, and it would create its own market as it transformed everyday life. It extended simultaneous experience, created anonymous audiences even vaster and more universal than those of radio, and incidentally created a new segregation.

Back in the 1920's . . . young David Sarnoff had had difficulty persuading his RCA colleagues that radio had an all-American future. Earlier commercial forms of communication had routed a message to a specific addressee. He believed that this novelty could prove to be radio's special virtue. And Sarnoff imagined a democratized world of anonymous addressees. His own experience must have impressed on him the advantages of this way of communicating. In April 1912, when Sarnoff was manning the wireless station which Wanamaker's in New York had installed as a publicity stunt to keep in touch with their store in Philadelphia, by chance he had caught the wireless message: "S.S. *Titanic* ran into iceberg. Sinking fast." He quickly established communication with another steamer, which reported that the *Titanic* had sunk and that some survivors had been picked up. While President William Howard Taft ordered all other stations to remain silent, the twenty-year-old Sarnoff stayed at his post for seventy-two hours, taking the names of survivors which, along with the name of Sarnoff, became front-page news.

Five years later, when working for the American Marconi Company, Sarnoff urged the marketing of "a simple 'Radio Music Box.' " His plan, he noted, "would make radio a 'household utility' in the same sense as the piano or phonograph." In 1920 he proposed a plan for manufacturing these radio music boxes for $75 apiece, and prophesied that at least one million families would buy them within three years. He proposed that money would be made from selling advertising in *Wireless Age* (a magazine that RCA had bought), which would carry an advance monthly schedule of the programs to be broadcast. Sarnoff's optimistic production schedule for the one million sets proved conservative. Radio was launched on a career that transformed the American entertainment world, as well as the world of advertising and news reporting.

By 1930, advertisers were spending $60 million annually on the radio, a figure that was to be multiplied tenfold in the next ten years. Thirty years after the granting of the first commercial broadcasting license to KDKA

(Pittsburgh) in 1920, there were more than two thousand stations and more than 75 million receiving sets. Before World War II, the annual production of radio sets numbered 10 million. By 1960 the national average showed three radio sets per household.

Radio had remained primarily an "entertainment" and "news" medium, allowing people to enjoy the melodrama of "soap serials," the jokes of Jack Benny, Fred Allen, and Bob Hope, the songs of Bing Crosby, the breathless sportscasting of Grantland Rice. The newscaster himself—H. V. Kaltenborn or Lowell Thomas—was a kind of "performer" who told the radio listener in solemn or lively tones what it was really like to be there.

Television opened another world. It did not simply multiply the sources of news and entertainment, it actually multiplied experience. At the TV set the viewer could see and hear what was going on with a rounded immediacy. Simultaneity was of the essence. When you took a picture you had to wait to have it developed; when you bought a phonograph record you knew in advance how it would sound. But now on TV you could share the suspense of the event itself. This new category of experience-at-a-distance would transform American life more radically than any other modern invention except the automobile.

On the surface, television seemed simply to combine the techniques of the motion picture and the phonograph with those of the radio, but it added up to something more. Here was a new way of mass-producing the moment for instant consumption by a "broadcast" (i.e., undefinable and potentially universal) community of witnesses. Just as the printing press five centuries before had begun to democratize learning, now the television set would democratize experience, incidentally changing the very nature of what was newly shared.

Before, the desire to share experience had brought people out of their homes gathering them together (physically as well as spiritually), but television would somehow separate them in the very act of sharing. While TV-democratized experience would be more equal than ever before, it would also be more separate. TV segregation confined Americans by the same means that widened their experience. Here was a kind of segregation that no Supreme Court ruling could correct, nor could it be policed by any federal commission. For it was built into the TV set.

This was again the familiar consequence of having a centralized and enlarged source, now not merely for running water or running electricity. Just as Rebecca no longer needed to go to the village well to gather her water (and her gossip), so now, too, in her eighth-floor kitchenette she received the current of hot and cold running images. Before 1970, more than 95 percent of American households had television sets. Now the normal way to enjoy a community experience was at home in your living room at your TV set.

In earlier times, to see a performance was to become part of a visible audience. At a concert, in a church, at a ball game or a political rally, the audience was half the fun. What and whom you saw in the audience was at least as interesting as and often humanly more important than what you saw on the stage. While she watched her TV set, the lonely Rebecca was thrust back on herself. She could exclaim or applaud or hiss, but nobody heard her except the children in the kitchen or the family in the living room, who probably already knew her sentiments too well. The others at the performance took the invisible form of "canned" laughter and applause. The mystery of the listening audience which had already enshrouded radio now became the mystery of the viewing audience. The once warmly enveloping community of those physically present was displaced by a world of unseen fellow TV watchers. Who else was there? Who else was watching? And even if they had their sets turned on, were they *really* watching?

Each of the millions of watching Americans was now newly segregated from those who put on the program and who, presumably, were aiming to please him. Television was a one-way window. The viewer could see whatever *they* offered, but nobody except the family in the living room could know for sure how the viewer reacted to what he saw. Tiny island audiences gathered nightly around their twinkling sets, much as cave-dwelling ancestors had clustered around their fires for warmth and safety, and for a feeling of togetherness. In these new tribal groups, each child's television tastes were as intimate a part of family lore as whether he preferred ketchup or mustard on his hamburger. With more and more two-TV families (even before 1970 these were one third of all American households) it became common for a member of the family to withdraw and watch in lonely privacy. Of course, broadcasters made valiant and ingenious efforts to fathom these secrets, to find out what each watcher really watched, what he really liked and what he really wanted. But the broadcasters' knowledge was necessarily based on samples, on the extrapolation of a relatively few cases, on estimates and guesses—all merely circumstantial evidence.

There was a new penumbra between watching and not-watching. "Attending" a ball game, a symphony concert, a theatrical performance or a motion picture became so casual that children did it while they wrote out their homework, adults while they played cards or read a magazine, or worked in the kitchen or in the basement. The TV watcher himself became unsure whether he was really watching, or only had the set on. Experience was newly befogged. The most elaborate and costly performances ceased to be special occasions that required planning and tickets; they became part of the air conditioning. Radio, too, had become something heard but not necessarily listened to, and its programming was directed to people assumed to be doing something else: driving the car, working at a hobby, washing the dishes. Car radios, which numbered 15 million in 1950, exceeded 40 million by 1960. With the rise of the transistor, miniaturized radio sets were carried about on the person like a fountain pen or a purse, to assuage loneliness wherever the wearer might be.

Newly isolated from his government, from those who collected his taxes, who provided public services, and who made the crucial decisions of peace or war, the citizen felt a frustrating new disproportion between how often and how vividly political leaders could get their messages to him and how often and how vividly he could get *his* message to them. Except indirectly, through the opinion polls, Americans were offered no new avenue comparable to television by which they could get their message back. Private telegrams began to become obsolete. The citizen was left to rely on the telephone (which might respond to his call with a "recorded message") or on a venerable nineteenth-century institution, the post office.

By enabling him to be anywhere instantly, by filling his present moment with experiences engrossing and overwhelming, television dulled the American's sense of his past, and even somehow separated him from the longer past. If Americans had not been able to accompany the astronauts to the moon they would have had to read about it the next morning in some printed account that was engrossing in retrospect. But on television, Americans witnessed historic events as vivid items of the present. In these ways, then, television created a time myopia, focusing interest on the exciting, disturbing, inspiring, or catastrophic instantaneous *now*.

The high cost of network time and the need to offer something for everybody produced a discontinuity of programming, a constant shifting from one sort of thing to another. Experience became staccato and motley. And every act of dissent acquired new dramatic appeal, especially if it was violent or disruptive. For this lost feeling of continuity with the past, the ineffective TV antidote was Old Movies.

Television, then, brought a new vagueness to everyday experience: the TV watcher became accustomed to seeing something-or-other happening somewhere-or-other at sometime-or-other, but all in Living Color. The common-sense hallmarks of authentic firsthand experience (those ordinary facts which a jury expected from a witness to prove that he had actually experienced what he said) now began to be absent, or only ambiguously present, in television experience. For his TV experience, the American did not need to go out to see anything in particular: he just turned the knob, and then wondered while he watched. Was this program live or was it taped? Was it merely an animation or a simulation? Was it a rerun? Where did it originate? When, if ever, did it really occur? Was it happening to actors or to real people? Was that a commercial?—a spoof of a commercial?—a documentary?—or pure fiction?

Almost never did the viewer see a TV event from a single individual's point of view. For TV was many-eyed, alert to avoid the monotony of any one person's limited vision. While each camera gave an image bigger and clearer than life, nobody got in the way. As the close-up dominated the screen, the middle distance dissolved. The living-room watcher saw the player in left field, the batter at the plate, or rowdies in a remote bleacher more sharply than did the man wearing sunglasses in the stands. Any casual kook or momentary celebrity filled the screen, just like Humphrey Bogart or President Nixon. All TV experience had become theater, in which any actor, or even a spectator, might hold center stage. The new TV perspective made the American understandably reluctant to go back to his seat on the side and in the rear. Shakespeare's metaphors became grim reality when the whole world had become a TV stage.

In this supermarket of surrogate experience, the old compartments were dissolved. Going to a church or to a lecture was no different from going to a play or a movie or a ball game, from going to a political rally or stopping to hear a patent-medicine salesman's pitch. Almost anything could be watched in shirt sleeves, with beer can in hand. The experience which flowed through the television channels was a mix of entertainment, instruction, news, uplift, exhortation and guess what. Successful programming offered entertainment (under the guise of instruction), instruction (under the guise of entertainment), political persuasion (with the appeal of advertising) and advertising (with the charm of drama). The new miasma, which no machine before could emit, and which enshrouded the TV world, reached out to befog the "real" world. Americans began to be so accustomed to the fog, so at home and solaced and comforted by the blur, that reality itself became slightly irritating because of its sharp edges and its clear distinctions of person, place, time, and weather.

As broadcasting techniques improved, they tended to make the viewer's experience more indirect, more controlled by unseen producers and technicians. Before, the spectator attending a national political convention would, simply by turning his head, decide for himself *where* he would look, but the TV watcher in the living room lacked the power to decide. Cameramen, directors, and commentators decided for him, focusing on this view of a brutal policeman or that view of a pretty delegate. As these conventions became guided tours by TV camera, the commentators themselves acquired a new power over the citizen's political experience, which was most vividly demonstrated at the Democratic National Convention in Chicago in 1968. Even as the American's secondhand experience came to seem more real and more authentic, it was more than ever shaped by invisible hands and by guides who themselves upstaged the leading performers and became celebrities.

Television watching became an addiction comparable only to life itself. If the set was not on, Americans began to feel that they had missed what was "really happening." And just as it was axiomatic that it was better to be alive than to be dead, so it became axiomatic that it was better to be watching *something* than to be watching nothing at all. When there was "nothing on TV tonight," there was a painful void. No wonder, then, that Americans revised their criteria for experience. Even if a firsthand experience was not worth having, putting it on TV might make it so.

Of all the wonders of TV, none was more remarkable than the speed with which it came. Television conquered America in less than a generation, leaving the nation more bewildered than it dared admit. Five hundred years were required for the printing press to democratize learning. And when the people could know as much as their "betters," they demanded the power to govern themselves. As late as 1671, the governor of Virginia, Sir William Berkeley, thanked God that the printing press (breeder of heresy and disobedience!) had not yet arrived in his colony, and he prayed that printing would never come to Virginia. By the early nineteenth century, aristocrats and men of letters could record, with Thomas Carlyle, that movable type had disbanded hired armies and cashiered kings, and somehow created "a whole new democratic world." Now with dizzying speed, television had democratized experience. It was no wonder that like the printing press before it, television met a cool reception from intellectuals and academics and the other custodians of traditional avenues of experience.

MEANING

1.   What is the thesis of Boorstin's essay? Where does he state it?
2.   What are the major effects Boorstin attributes to the spread of television? What has happened to "everyday experience," according to him?
3.   Is Boorstin's analysis critical of television? If so, what specific accusations does he level against it?
4.   What is Boorstin's conclusion? Does his essay contain any implications beyond the subject of TV?

METHOD

1.   Boorstin employs a variety of rhetorical strategies in this essay. Cite specific examples of where and how he uses each.
2.   Boorstin attributes feelings and behavior to Americans as a group. Does he offer enough support for these generalizations? With which of them would you take issue?

AUDIENCE

1.   Boorstin is a historian, and he writes for a general audience. Can you point to some passages in this essay where he clearly speaks to the general reader?

2. Do you agree with the author's characterization of television and its effects? How might you defend television against Boorstin's claims?

WRITING SUGGESTIONS

1. Perform your own analysis of the nature or effects of TV in public or private life. Try to use as much concrete evidence as you can from your own or others' experience rather than speculating on possibilities.
2. Analyze the nature and impact of another invention. Some sample topics:
   - Personal computers
   - Home video equipment
   - Personal, pocket tape-players
   - Subscription computer databases
   - Cable TV systems

ADDITIONAL WRITING SUGGESTIONS

Each of the topics below is a general issue or problem that may be profitably opened to analytical writing and thinking. In choosing one to pursue, you might want to do some pre-writing and brainstorming on those that interest you most. List questions about these subjects as you write, and ask yourself what analytical lines of thought seem most attractive or revealing. As your ideas take shape, sketch a tentative thesis and outline. Use the rhetorical strategies as ways to approach thinking and writing about these subjects, not as goals unto themselves.

- The dilemmas of youth
- Individuality
- Living in groups
- Drugs and athletics
- Political activism
- The role of sex in a person's life
- Fantasy in films and popular novels
- Generation gaps
- Men and women
- The fairness of economic competition
- The future of the workplace
- Personal relationships
- Healthy or unhealthy habits or attitudes
- Elders
- Institutions (church, government, military)
- Traditions and customs
- Careers
- Status

Note: These are general subjects. You will have to narrow your focus considerably as you move through your analysis.

10

ANALYTICAL NARRATIVES

MAKING SENSE OF EXPERIENCE: BIOGRAPHY AND HISTORY

Although the essay is an immensely flexible form (we shall see other applications in subsequent chapters), it does have limits. In rendering concrete human experience, the narrative or story form may be more appropriate—and just as flexible in its own ways. This distinction also holds true when a writer's purpose goes beyond informing to analyzing or explaining. In analytical narrative, we not only report what happened, but we attempt to make sense of it.

Consider, for example, the nonfiction genres of biography and history. Making sense of lives and events—whether we do so in brief or extended narratives—means more than just providing information. Biographers and historians usually *interpret* their subjects; they explain the meaning of events, their significance to the people who lived through them, and their importance to us as readers. In this sense, writers of analysis, in either narrative or essay form, seek the same goal of increased understanding. In narrative, however, the writer's focus is the dynamic movement of life, of persons, families, communities, nations.

In biography, we seek an understanding of one person's life beyond the sequence of events that constitute it. Because our lives are complex and ultimately private, however, the biographer's task is not easy. We must try to sort out the motives for our subject's actions, discover his or her values, goals, fears. We must attempt to see the subject's life from his or her point of view, from the inside, but at the same time avoid unwarranted speculation or conjecture. Our goal is to find out the truth about a person's life, however elusive that truth may prove to be.

In writing of history, too, we want to understand the larger life of societies or periods of time beyond mere facts. We want to get at the situations, forces, and decisions that underlie events—to determine shapes or patterns in what may otherwise seem random occurrences. And, as in biography, we want to characterize people, groups, and periods to reveal their essential or important qualities, to "fix" them in our minds.

Granted, the writing of biography and history are typically professional tasks undertaken in longer forms such as articles and books. Yet much biography and history is produced on a less grand scale—in families, organizations, institutions, businesses, and, increasingly, in college courses. Narrative, too, is an often-used form in newspaper and magazine feature stories, articles that combine informing and explaining.

Although, as we have said, the essay is the workhorse of college writing, it is not the whole stable. In the wider world of nonfiction, certainly, the narrative form has extensive applications. We include this chapter to give a balanced view of nonfiction, and to encourage you to try your hand at it, even though analytical narrative may play a smaller role than some other forms in your college writing.

APPLYING ANALYTICAL METHODS TO NARRATIVE

In writing analytical narrative, we combine the principles of analytical writing (Chapter 8) with those of narrative form (Chapter 7). It is not that we tell the story but interrupt it with explanation from time to time (although such a mixture of elements is possible). Rather, we attempt to weave the two strands of story and interpretation into a single thread. At times we may emphasize one or the other, but overall we aim to produce a uniform work—*a story told from an analytical point of view.*

Analytical narrative shares much with the other kinds of writing we have looked at so far: Like report writing, it depends on accurate information. Whether the facts (first-hand, gathered through research interviews or observation, or a combination) a writer uses are known to him or her, they are the necessary object of the analysis, upon which all else depends. Further, the writer must select from the gathered information those pieces that seem most important. (No work of analytical narrative, no matter how comprehensive, can include everything about its subject, so some selecting will be inevitable.)

Like essay writing, analytical narrative is one's personal encounter with a subject. As a result, different writers will approach the same subject in different ways. Biographers and historians, for example, usually seek an objective understanding of their subjects—yet two writers on the same topic may disagree greatly on matters of fact, interpretation, or significance. The truth the writer seeks may depend on the angle of his or her approach toward it. Also, as in writing analytical essays, composing an analytical narrative is a matter of discovering the content, shape, and emphasis we think most pleasing or appropriate for our work.

Like informative narrative, analytical narrative evokes the texture of life being lived. With its focus on the concrete aspects of experience—

individual persons and acts, specific places and times, particular conflicts and agreements—and the use of dialog, flashback, scenic construction and description, it gives us the look and feel of life, the illusion that it is unfolding before our very eyes.

Within the narrative form, then, writers seek to construct from their materials a meaningful *version* of human experience, to give us a sense of life and time that satisfies our curiosity. First, writers must satisfy their own, however, and here the principles of analytical writing come into play.

We saw that analyzing a subject is largely a process of asking and seeking answers to questions. We saw, further, that certain basic strategies of thought and writing—the rhetorical methods—are useful tools for opening subjects to our scrutiny. In analyzing lives and events, it should not surprise us that the same strategies apply. The difference is that the subject of our questions may be fluid—in a state of flux—thus complicating the answers. Our approach remains, however, one using whatever tools may be useful: description, definition, comparison, division, process or causal analysis, and so on.

For example, imagine how difficult it would be to give a meaningful account of someone's life, say a friend, without answering some basic questions:

- What is this person like? (Describe basic or unique features of personality.)
- Has he or she always been this way? (Analyze developmental process and compare current features to earlier ones.)
- What has the subject accomplished? (Divide achievements into categories or classify types.)
- What motivates this person? (Analyze causal relationships between subject's actions and possible influences that helped shape them.)
- What does the subject believe? (Define values, religious or world view, personal philosophy.)

All of this might be necessary *before* we could begin to put any of it into narrative form, before we could tell a story in which events and interpretation were integrated, or woven together. As always in the writing process, we accumulate material as we work, and from this we select and build. In the case of analytical narrative, we must come to know the subject well enough to construct a final draft that incorporates both the story and our understanding of it.

To write an analytical narrative, then, we follow the narrative-writing process and apply the tools of analysis at each stage. We analyze our material *as* we gather, select, and arrange it. We aim for a final draft that combines narrative and explanation. Here are some points to consider:

1. Audience.   What analytical slant or focus will interest the audience most? What is the audience likely to be most curious about? What information does the reader already know, and how much of it needs to be explained, clarified, revised, or expanded? Of the new information to be gathered and presented, what needs explanation and what can be reported without comment?

2. Getting the story.   As we gather facts, background material, the opinions of others, and so on, what questions of our own come to mind? Can these analytical questions be answered through further research, interviews, or first-hand observation? (The questions on page 217 are one example.)

3. Assembling a chronology.   Can we establish any meaningful links between events? Which events are clearly related (by supporting evidence), and which are open to various or different explanations?

4. Organizing for interest.   How does our curiosity or analytical focus affect choices for the lead and the narrative's overall structure? How may we tell the story to best present its meaning as we understand it?

5. Using description, dialog, and scenes.   How can our choices here help illustrate or reveal our interpretation? What key details, conversations, and events best support our views?

6. Revising.   As we reread and rework our material, how might we further clarify and sharpen both the narrative and analytical lines? Where can we bring them even closer together?

Writing biography or history, even in short forms, is a complex, *synthetic* process calling for the storyteller's art and the essayist's curiosity. By learning to write analytical narrative, we begin to build our writing skill toward greater flexibility and power, and toward a more subtle, intricate rendering of the life about which we write.

QUESTIONS

1. What are some common uses for analytical narrative? What does analytical narrative do?
2. How is analytical narrative similar to report writing? What does it share with essay writing?

3. What role do the rhetorical methods play in the process of putting together an analytical narrative?

EXERCISES

As a pre-writing activity for the writing assignments that follow this chapter's readings:

1. List the names of several people you know well whose lives would make interesting subjects for biography. Then, for each person, list as many analytical questions as you can think of, as in the chapter discussion. Use the rhetorical strategies as a base, but don't limit yourself to using only them. Write down everything you or your reader might want to find out about your subject.

2. As above, list several subjects about which you have firsthand knowledge for possible historical treatment, and follow with analytical questions for each. Some sample topics: your home town, your college or university, a club or organization you belong to, a harrowing or dramatic event (fire, flood, tornado, death in the family) and its aftermath.

3. Go over your notes for the previous exercises and ask yourself which of these subjects you're most interested in pursuing. Then reread your notes for that subject. What have you written that will help distinguish your prospective story from one that only informs? In other words, have you taken an analytical, questioning attitude? What about your subject *needs* explanation or interpretation? (The answer to this question should help lead you to a narrower focus.)

Readings

"ADAM SMITH" is the pen name of George J. W. Goodman, author, journalist, and television commentator. He was born in 1930 and is a graduate of Harvard. A Rhodes Scholar, he has published books and articles on a number of subjects, but most of his writing has been about the world of business and economics. As Adam Smith, Goodman has had four best sellers: The Money Game *(1967),* Supermoney *(1972),* Powers of Mind *(1975), and* Paper Money *(1981). One of the founders of* New York *magazine, Goodman has also written for* The Atlantic, Esquire, *and others. He is currently an editorialist for the PBS program "The Nightly Business Report," and he moderates his own "Adam Smith's Money World," also on PBS. In the following selection from* Paper Money, *Smith recounts the story of the hyperinflation of 1920s Germany and analyzes its significance.*

The Great Inflation

by Adam Smith

The New York Times printed a letter from a lawyer, once a sixties activist, who wrote this: "I don't understand what's going on. I make a good salary, but the prices of houses and apartments seem outrageous. Money doesn't mean anything. Your income goes up, but taxes go up and expenses go up and the rest goes right out of your wallet. I don't think anybody's in control; it feels like things are out of control."

This lament is common. There is an archetypal fear at work here, just beyond the realm of consciousness. The fear is of losing what you have. For Americans of previous generations, "losing what you have" meant losing a job and not being able to get another, or losing the family farm to drought, dust, and the bankers. There is probably a group of cells somewhere in the cerebral cortex that resonates to the fear of the unknown, of the enemy tribe over the horizon, of strange men on horseback burning farms. The current form of this fear is relatively new to Americans now alive: it is that the currency is losing its value, becoming meaningless. We are told that Americans have changed their economic behavior in the past five years; they have stopped saving, and they spend even when there is no immediate necessity to spend. Europeans know the symbol of meaningless currency: it is the wheelbarrow full of money, the image of the Great Inflation in Germany in the 1920s. The Great Inflation not only helped bring Hitler to power; the memory of it has an effect even today, and it has some lessons for us.

Before World War I Germany was a prosperous country, with a gold-backed currency, expanding industry, and world leadership in optics, chemicals, and machinery. The German mark, the British shilling, the French franc, and the Italian lira all had about equal value, and all were exchanged four or five to the dollar. That was in 1914. In 1923, at the most fevered moment of the German hyperinflation, the exchange rate between the dollar and the mark was one trillion marks to one dollar, and a wheelbarrow full of money would not even buy a newspaper. Most Germans were taken by surprise by the financial tornado.

"My father was a lawyer," says Walter Levy, an internationally known German-born oil consultant in New York, "and he had taken out an insurance policy in 1903, and every month he had made the payments faithfully. It was a twenty-year policy, and when it came due, he cashed it in and bought *a single loaf of bread.*" The Berlin publisher Leopold Ullstein wrote that an American visitor tipped their cook one dollar. The family convened, and it was decided that a trust fund should be set up in a Berlin bank with the cook as beneficiary, the bank to administer and invest the dollar.

In retrospect, you can trace the steps to hyperinflation, but some of the reasons remain cloudy. Germany abandoned the gold backing of its currency in 1914. The war was expected to be short, so it was financed by government borrowing, not by savings and taxation. Fifty years later, the United States did not finance the Vietnam War by savings and taxation because its leaders thought that Vietnam was only a limited involvement and would be over quickly. In Germany prices doubled between 1914 and 1919, just as they have here in the past ten years.

The parallels are limited. Germany had lost a war. Under the Treaty of Versailles it had already made a reparations payment in gold-backed marks, and it was due to lose part of the production of the Ruhr and of the province of Upper Silesia. The Weimar Republic was politically fragile.

But the bourgeois habits were very strong. Ordinary citizens worked at their jobs, sent their children to school and worried about their grades, maneuvered for promotions and rejoiced when they got them, and generally expected things to get better. The prices that had doubled from 1914 to 1919 were doubling again during just five months in 1922. Milk went from 7 marks per liter to 16; beer from 5.6 to 18. There were complaints about the high cost of living. Professors and civil servants complained of getting squeezed. Factory workers pressed for wage increases. An underground economy developed, aided by a desire to beat the tax collector.

On June 24, 1922, right-wing fanatics assassinated Walter Rathenau, the moderate, able foreign minister. Rathenau was a charismatic figure, and the idea that a popular, wealthy, and glamorous government minister could be shot in a law-abiding society shattered the faith of the Germans, who wanted to believe that things were going to be all right. Rathenau's state funeral was a national trauma. The nervous citizens of the Ruhr were already getting their money out of the currency and into real goods— diamonds, works of art, safe real estate. Now ordinary Germans began to get out of marks and into real goods. Pianos, wrote the British historian Adam Fergusson, were bought even by unmusical families. Sellers held back because the mark was worth less every day. As prices went up, the amounts of currency demanded were greater, and the German central bank responded to the demands. Yet the ruling authorities did not see anything wrong. A leading financial newspaper said that the amounts of money in circulation were not excessively high. Dr. Rudolf Havenstein, the president of the Reichsbank—equivalent to the Federal Reserve—told an economics professor that he needed a new suit but wasn't going to buy one until prices came down.

Why did the German government not act to halt the inflation? It was a shaky, fragile government, especially after the assassination. The vengeful French sent their army into the Ruhr to enforce their demands for reparations, and the Germans were powerless to resist. More than inflation, the Germans feared unemployment. In 1919 Communists had tried to take over, and severe unemployment might give the Communists another chance. The great German industrial combines—Krupp, Thyssen, Farben, Stinnes—condoned the inflation and survived it well. A cheaper mark, they reasoned, would make German goods cheap and easy to export, and they needed the export earnings to buy raw materials abroad. Inflation kept everyone working.

So the printing presses ran, and once they began to run, they were hard to stop. The price increases began to be dizzying. Menus in cafés could not be revised quickly enough. A student at Freiburg University ordered a cup of coffee at a café. The price on the menu was 5,000 marks. He had two cups. When the bill came, it was for 14,000 marks.

"If you want to save money," he was told, "and you want two cups of coffee, you should order them both at the same time."

The presses of the Reichsbank could not keep up, though they ran through the night. Individual cities and states began to issue their own money. Dr. Havenstein, the president of the Reichsbank, did not get his new suit. A factory worker described payday, which was every day at 11:00 A.M.: "At eleven o'clock in the morning a siren sounded and everybody gathered in the factory forecourt where a five-ton lorry was drawn up loaded brimful with paper money. The chief cashier and his assistants climbed up on top. They read out names and just threw out bundles of notes. As soon as you had caught one you made a dash for the nearest shop and bought just anything that was going." Teachers, paid at 10:00 A.M., brought their money to the playground, where relatives took the bundles and hurried off with them. Banks closed at 11:00 A.M.; the harried clerks went on strike.

Dentists and doctors stopped charging in currency and demanded butter or eggs, but the farmers were holding back their produce. "We don't want any Jew-confetti from Berlin," a chronicler quotes a Bavarian farmer. The flight from currency that had begun with the buying of diamonds, gold, country houses, and antiques now extended to minor and almost useless items—bric-a-brac, soap, hairpins. The law-abiding country crumbled into petty thievery. Copper pipes and brass armatures weren't safe. Gasoline was siphoned from cars. People bought things they didn't need and used them to barter—a pair of shoes for a shirt, some crockery for coffee. Berlin had a "witches' Sabbath" atmosphere. Prostitutes of both sexes roamed the streets. Cocaine was the fashionable drug. In the cabarets the newly rich and their foreign friends could dance and spend money. Other reports noted that not all the young people had a bad time. Their parents had taught them to work and save, and that was clearly wrong, so they could spend money, enjoy themselves, and flout the old.

The publisher Leopold Ullstein wrote: "People just didn't understand what was happening. All the economic theory they had been taught didn't provide for the phenomenon. There was a feeling of utter dependence on anonymous powers—almost as a primitive people believed in magic—that somebody must be in the know, and that this small group of 'somebodies' must be a conspiracy."

When the one-thousand-billion-mark note came out, few bothered to collect the change when they spent it. By November 1923, with one dollar equal to one trillion marks, the breakdown was complete. The currency had lost meaning.

What happened immediately afterward is as fascinating as the Great Inflation itself. The tornado of the mark inflation was succeeded by the "miracle of the Rentenmark." A new president took over the Reichsbank, Horace Greeley Hjalmar Schacht, who came by his first two names because of his father's admiration for an editor of the *New York Tribune*. The Rentenmark was not Schacht's idea, but he executed it, and as the Reichsbank president, he got the credit for it. For decades afterward he was able to maintain a reputation for financial wizardry. He became the architect of the financial prosperity brought by the Nazi party.

Obviously, though the currency was worthless, Germany was still a rich country—with mines, farms, factories, forests. The backing for the Rentenmark was mortgages on the land and bonds on the factories, but that backing was a fiction; the factories and land couldn't be turned into cash or used abroad. Nine zeros were struck from the currency; that is, one Rentenmark was equal to one billion old marks. The Germans wanted desperately to believe in the Rentenmark, and so they did. "I remember," said one Frau Barten of East Prussia, "the feeling of having just one Rentenmark to spend. I bought a small tin bread bin. Just to buy something that had a price tag for one mark was so exciting."

All money is a matter of belief. *Credit* derives from Latin, *credere*, "to believe." Belief was there, the factories functioned, the farmers delivered their produce. The central bank kept the belief alive when it would not let even the government borrow further.

But although the country functioned again, the savings were never restored, nor were the values of hard work and decency that had accompanied the savings. There was a different temper in the country, a temper that Hitler would later exploit with diabolical talent. Thomas Mann wrote: "The market woman who without batting an eyelash demanded a hundred million for an egg lost the capacity for surprise. And nothing that has happened since has been insane or cruel enough to surprise her."

With the currency went many of the lifetime plans of average citizens. It was the custom for the bride to bring some money to a marriage; many marriages were called off. Widows dependent on insurance found themselves destitute. People who had worked a lifetime found that their pensions would not buy one cup of coffee.

Pearl Buck, the American writer who became famous for her novels of China, was in Germany in 1923. She wrote later: "The cities were still there, the houses not yet bombed and in ruins, but the victims were millions of people. They had lost their fortunes, their savings; they were dazed and inflation-shocked and did not understand how it had happened to them and who the foe was who had defeated them. Yet they had lost their self-assurance, their feeling that they themselves could be the masters of their own lives if only they worked hard enough; and lost, too, were the old values of morals, of ethics, of decency."

The fledgling Nazi party, whose attempted coup had failed in 1923, won 32 seats legally in the next election. The right-wing Nationalist party won 106 seats, having promised 100-percent compensation to the victims of inflation and vengeance on the conspirators who had brought it. A British economist who had been in his country's delegation at the peace treaty had written a polemic called *The Economic Consequences of the Peace.* Fired from the Treasury, John Maynard Keynes wrote brilliant, quick-tempered articles to London papers, recalling his foresight.

Since our own time of economic nightmare was not when a currency lost its meaning but when men lost jobs—the Depression—we have not had the German fear of losing what you have because of explosion of the currency. We are far more likely to have a soggy British-style inflation than a frenzied German-style hyperinflation featuring wheelbarrows full of money. But the lessons of the Great Inflation go beyond the simple formula of the monetarists—that if the money supply is limited, all will be well. The lessons have to do with belief and instinct. When Americans create a mania for housing—not building houses, but bidding up housing at the rate of $100 billion a year, as they have done in the past five years—they are losing belief in their currency as a store of value.

Why does everyone talk so obsessively about houses? What can be so interesting about bricks and mortar and plumbing and wiring? It isn't the houses themselves, the architecture, the layout, the traffic patterns, the kitchens, how we shape the houses and how they shape us, that is the obsessive topic. It's the prices. The reason there is so much talk about condos and co-ops and houses is that there is a new twist to the old adage "A house is not a home." When is a house not just a home? When it is a way to flee the currency.

MEANING

1. How was the Great Inflation an outgrowth of Germany's involvement in World War I?
2. How did the Great Inflation pave the way for Hitler's rise to power in the 1930s?

3. What similarities does Smith imply between German life in this period and contemporary life in the United States? What are the chief differences you see?
4. According to Smith, what is the real basis of monetary value?

METHOD

1. How does Smith build the narrative momentum of this story? What story-telling techniques does he use to draw the reader into the action and make it exciting?
2. Apart from the narrative shape of this piece, what other rhetorical strategies or devices does Smith use? Where does he emphasize the unfolding of the story, and where his interpretation or explanation of it?
3. Why does Smith frame his story with an introduction and conclusion referring to the United States economy?

AUDIENCE

1. Smith, like many of the writers in this book, is concerned with reaching a large audience. What specific clues can you find in "The Great Inflation" that tell you the author is addressing the general public?
2. Do you agree with Smith that any parallels between the German situation and our own economic woes "are limited"? To what extent has economic crisis played a role in your life or the lives of your family?

WRITING SUGGESTIONS

1. Using your pre-writing exercises as a starting point, begin to develop an analytical narrative about your subject. Following Adam Smith's lead, explain and interpret the story as you tell it, emphasizing important points along the way. By the end of the story, your reader should know not only what happened but why it was significant.
2. As in the suggestion above, compose an analytical narrative based on your knowledge of history. Choose a topic you're familiar with (although you may need to refresh your memory with research). As does Smith, limit yourself to a single event or related sequence of events, and try to integrate your explanation with the telling of the story. Some topic ideas: the Kennedy assassination, the peace movement, Watergate, the Great Depression, the moon shot.

IRVING HOWE was born in 1920 in New York and attended City College. He began his teaching career at Brandeis University in 1953, and in 1961 moved to Stanford University. Two years later Howe returned to the east coast to teach at Hunter College,

where he became a distinguished professor in 1970. He is the author of many books of
literary criticism and has written about the United States labor movement and the
American Communist Party. Howe has edited the journal Dissent *since 1953 and has*
been a contributor to such publications as Partisan Review, Commentary, Harper's,
The New Republic, *and* The New York Times Book Review. *He has also written*
an autobiography, A Margin of Hope *(1982). Howe's lifelong interest in Jewish his-*
tory and literature resulted in World of Our Fathers *(1976), which recounts the ordeal*
of Jewish immigrants in the United States. In the following selection, taken from that
book, Howe tells the story of Lillian Wald, a woman who had an enormous impact on the
poor of New York's Lower East Side.

The Implacability of Gentleness

by Irving Howe

No act of individual kindness could change immigrant life as it needed to
be changed, yet such acts, when they occurred, were received with a
warmth, almost an excess of gratitude. Lillian Wald (1867–1940), the nurse
who founded the Henry Street Settlement, grew within her lifetime into a
figure of legend, known and adored on every street.

She came to the East Side in 1893, a German-Jewish young woman of
twenty-six who had been raised in a comfortable bourgeois family, a
"spoiled child" as she later kept insisting, still largely innocent of the suf-
ferings of life. Her father had been an optical dealer in Rochester, New
York, and Lillian had gone to "Miss Cruttenden's English-French Boarding
and Day School for Young Ladies." She had wanted to enter Vassar at
sixteen, but someone at the college ruled that she was too young. If Vassar
didn't want her, she would go elsewhere—to another life.

Several years later, Lillian Wald entered the New York Hospital's School
of Nursing, learning there what she needed to learn, not least an unflinch-
ing and unsentimental capacity for living near pain. In 1893, after a frustrating interval at an orphan asylum where the children were ill-treated,
she began running a class in home nursing for East Side women. One day a
little girl came up to Miss Wald, asking that she visit someone sick at home.
Lillian Wald followed the child to a dismal two-room apartment that
housed a family of seven plus a few boarders. "Within half an hour" she
had made the central decision of her life: she would move to the East Side,
there to give her life as nurse, settlement-house leader, and companion to
the afflicted.

There are two kinds of fastidious people, those who recoil from messes
and those who stay to clean them up. Lillian Wald stayed, not out of ex-

alted sentiments or angelic temperament, but because there was work to be done and no one else seemed likely to do it. She stayed at a time when only a handful of social workers paid any attention to the place, and long before it took on associations of glamour or nostalgia.

Together with another nurse, Mary Brewster, Lillian Wald lived and worked in a fifth-floor apartment at 27 Jefferson Street, with the single indulgence of a private bathtub. Lavinia Duck, soon to be a fellow nurse at the Henry Street Settlement, visited these tiny rooms and found the "chief solicitude" of Miss Wald and Miss Brewster to be a wish "to make their own impression as friendly souls before whom all the confidence and problems of living might be safely opened. Their nursing was their open sesame."

The two young women made themselves available to anyone asking for help; they charged a trifle to those who could afford it and gave services freely to those who could not. "I came with very little program of what could or should be done," said Lillian Wald; she kept her eyes open, saw the magnitude of need, rushed to whoever called for help, and persuaded others to join her. "I went into every room in the front and rear tenements, set the dwellers to sweeping, cleaning, and burning the refuse. In some rooms swill thrown on the floor, vessels standing unemptied after the night's use. I saw the housekeeper, who promised cooperation in keeping the place cleaner, and I impressed on her that I would repeat the rounds next day and frequently thereafter."

Her tasks were endless. Children with summer bowel complaints that sent infant mortality rates soaring; children with measles, unquarantined; children "scarred with vermin bites"; a case of "puerperal septicaemia, lying on a vermin-infested bed without sheets or pillow-cases"; a pregnant mother with a crippled child and two others living on chunks of dry bread sent in by neighbors; people "ill from organic trouble and also from poor food."

In October 1893 she was writing, "We have found several cases of typhoid fever, and in every case succeeded in overcoming hospital prejudice, accompanying patients to the hospital wards and doing what we could to satisfy their first uneasiness." Sometimes Miss Wald or Miss Brewster would stay deep into the night with patients for whom the very idea of a hospital struck terror. When patients were too sick to be moved, they would fetch surgeons to the apartment, help with operations, and then provide aftercare. It was all terrible enough during these depression years, but "we are not discouraged, and the more intimately we come to know these poor Russian Jews the more frequently we are rewarded with unexpected gleams of attractiveness."

Substantial help came from Jacob Schiff, the German-Jewish philanthropist. Between him and Lillian Wald arose a curious relationship: he helped defray costs on condition that his part be kept secret and she send him monthly letters detailing her activities. Could so intelligent a man as Schiff have thought it necessary to keep check on so selfless a woman as Lillian Wald? Perhaps; but it seems happier to suppose that he asked for these reports out of an admiring recognition that her simple sentences bore a moral substance to be treasured.

Visit and care of typhoid patient, 182 Ludlow Street. Visit to 7 Hester Street where in rooms of Nathan S. found two children with measles. After much argument succeeded in bathing these two patients and the sick baby. The first time in their experience. They insisted no water and soap could be applied to anyone with measles for seven days.

Gave tickets for Hebrew Sanitarium excursion to Mrs. Davis and three children, Mrs. Schneider and five children for Tuesday's excursion but five of the seven children are nearly naked, I am convinced, have no apparel in their possession. So we will make their decent appearance possible for the picnic.

Many of these people have kept from begging and it is not uncommon to meet families, to whom not a dollar has come in in seven months—the pawn shop tickets telling the progress of their fall, beginning some months back with the pawning of a gold watch, ending with the woman's waist.

The multitude of unemployed grows and many who had been able to live for the first few months [of 1893] are now at the end of their resources. However we are glad in one respect, that having no money to engage the midwife they allow us to furnish doctors . . . who do intelligent good work.

In a rear tenement, top floor, on Allen Street, a doctor found a woman, a Mrs. Weichert, crazy and ill with pneumonia and typhoid; cared for by her 14 year old daughter. She had been crazy for some time and the husband and child had kept it secret, fearing she would be forcibly taken to an asylum were it known. Though she died in a few days, I shall always be glad that one doctor told us in time so that she was made human and decent, bedding given and the child assisted to making her dwelling fit for habitation before her end.

Lily Klein very ill with pneumonia for whom we procured medical attention and nursed. The child died but the night before Miss Brewster had remained with the child all night. She was ineligible for hospital as she had whooping cough. Father deserted and mother worn out, was not safe to leave a child so ill with.

Annie P., 44 Allen Street, front tenement, second floor. Husband Louis P. came here three years ago and one year ago sent for wife and three children. From that time unfortunately, his trade, that of shoemaker, became less remunerative. She helped by washing and like labor, but two months ago he deserted her, though she stoutly maintains he returned to Odessa to get his old work back. The youngest, Meyer P., age five years, fell from the table and injured his hip. He lay for 7 months in the Orthopedic Hospital, 42nd Street; he was discharged as incurable and supplied with a brace. . . . The mother is absolutely tied by her pregnant condition; the cripple is in pain and cries to be carried. They had no rooms of their own but paid $3 a month to Hannah A., a decent tailoress, who allowed the family to sleep on her floor. . . . Sunday I saw them. Monday I filed application with Montefiore Home for Meyer's admission. . . . Tuesday I went to Hebrew Sheltering Guardian Society, saw

Superintendent, and obtained promise of place for the two well children by Thursday. . . . Thursday afternoon we washed and dressed the two children, and I left them in the afternoon at the Asylum, leaving my address for the Superintendent so that he might know their friend in case of need. They have absolutely no one in America but their mother.

Once and for all, she gave her heart to those "poor Russian Jews" (even, with time, learning some Yiddish words and phrases). "We are full of the troubles of our neighbors," reads an early letter, and it would remain that way to the end. When the papers printed denunciations of immigrants who had joined food riots, Lillian Wald fought against these slurs upon her neighbors. When these neighbors started to form trade unions, she sided with them openly.

Some of the immigrants kept themselves apart from Miss Wald's nurses—there were rumors they were secret agents proselytizing for Christianity—but others started climbing the five flights to their apartment, asking for help, sometimes just wanting to talk. Mary Brewster had to quit: she was overworked, and her health failed. A growing number of nurses came to volunteer, some taking the fifteen-dollar-a-week salary and some quietly returning it. Miss Wald began looking for a larger place, to be used entirely by what had come to be called the Nurse's Settlement. She found a house at 265 Henry Street and moved in. For a time she kept the name Nurse's Settlement—it was really the best name—but had to give way to the pleas of a boy's athletic club attached to 265 Henry, which could no longer bear the teasing of opponents on the baseball field: "Hey, noices! Noices!" So they called the place the Henry Street Settlement.

The Settlement kept growing: by 1898, eleven full-time staff, nine of them nurses; by 1900 fifteen nurses; by 1906, twenty-seven nurses. As her work succeeded, Miss Wald's power grew, and she used it shrewdly and to keen effect. She persuaded the city to start a program of public nursing—the very phrase was hers. She persuaded the Board of Education to put nurses into the schools. She worked hard on committees opposing child labor; joined the movement for more playgrounds; badgered the mighty and wheedled the rich for money, telling them not about her theories (it is doubtful she had any) but about "little Louie, the deplorable condition of whose scalp is denying him the blessings of education"; joined the suffragettes, though not militantly; became an active pacifist in the First World War, brushing past unpopularity as if it were one of those unfortunate neighbors needing help. Ready as she was to charm millionaires for help, she never allowed that to stand in the way of her persuasions. In the 1910 cloakmakers' strike, she aligned herself firmly with the strikers—where else could she be? They were her neighbors. Within the Jewish world, she was especially skillful at creating links between the Germans and east Europeans, gaining the confidence of the former in behalf of aid to the latter.

A reporter for the New York *Press* wrote of her: "Picture to yourself a woman still in the freshness of youth: tall and well-proportioned. . . . The mouth is tender, sensitive, sympathetic. The chin says, 'I will. . . .' The would-be violator of sanitary regulations calls her 'She-Who-Must-Be-Obeyed.' . . . The poor, invalid Yiddish mother claims her as an intimate friend. . . ." Jacob Riis adds to the picture: "The poor trust her absolutely, trust her head, her judgment, and her friendship. She arbitrates in a strike, and the men listen. . . . When pushcart peddlers are blackmailed by the police, she will tell the mayor the truth, for she knows."

By 1916 the Settlement owned half a million dollars in property and had extended its activities far beyond the original task of nursing. Still, that task remained a central one, the annual budget for the Visiting Nurses Service coming to $150,000 and the more than one hundred nurses making 227,000 visits a year. Large as it now was, the Settlement kept its personal tone, run along the principles of anarchic matriarchy.

Miss Wald was the ideal Fabian. Shrewd, practical, dry-eyed, she had a genius for the concrete, seeing life as it was and wanting to make it better. There was no shrinking, no condescension, no idylizing, no sentimentalism, no preening, little theorizing, nothing but work, hard and endless and free from contaminations of self. Writing an article about the Settlement toward the end of her life, she began with a simple question: "Have you ever seen a hungry child cry?" It was a question that haunted all her years, driving her incessantly, making her into a "do-gooder"—a phrase that can never be used lightly by anyone who comes to know what Lillian Wald did for those "poor Russian Jews" stranded in America.

By some later perspectives, Lillian Wald missed a good deal in life. She never married, she seems to have had no intense personal relationships, she yielded her emotions to all about her, she showed small inclination toward self-scrutiny or introspectiveness. If these were the costs of her life, the rewards were at least as high. In the experience of thousands, she made a difference; on the consciousness of her contemporaries, she left a mark. Like the other superb women of her generation who plunged into the work they saw in front of them—women like Jane Addams, Rose Schneiderman, Lavinia Duck, Florence Kelley—she made a mockery of all the idle chatter about a "woman's place." "The subtle and persistent saintliness of these social workers was in the end more deadly than all the bluster of business. Theirs was the implacability of gentleness."

MEANING

1. According to Howe, why did Lillian Wald decide to devote her life to caring for the poor?
2. What are some of Wald's most revealing personal traits? Does Howe explain the apparent contrast between Wald's early "spoiled" life and her later selflessness?

3. What were some of Wald's major accomplishments? What is Howe's overall assessment of her significance?

4. What image of New York's Lower East Side emerges from this story?

METHOD

1. Does Howe integrate his interpretation of Wald's life with the telling of her story? Where does he do the major part of his analysis?

2. Why do you think the author includes a long excerpt from one of Wald's personal reports? What does this add to the narrative? Does it have any ill effect?

3. What do you sense is Howe's attitude toward Lillian Wald? Is it objective? Does it interfere with Howe's assessment of Wald's importance?

AUDIENCE

1. Howe's portrait is taken from *World of Our Fathers,* a book about Jewish immigrants. Do you think the audience for this story is limited by its ethnic focus? What about Wald's life makes it interesting or significant for a general audience?

2. How do you react when you read about unusually devoted or determined people like Wald and Brewster?

3. Have you ever made a snap decision, like Wald's "within half an hour," which affected your life or others' for years afterward? What brought this decision about?

WRITING SUGGESTIONS

1. Using your biographical pre-writing exercise as a takeoff point, develop a brief, focused biographical sketch of your subject. Try to blend your understanding of the story's importance with your telling of it. Like Howe, include concrete detail and description with your analysis.

2. Tell the story of a historical figure you find particularly admirable. What single accomplishment best typifies the subject's life? What kinds of information and explanation is your reader likely to find noteworthy?

ADDITIONAL WRITING SUGGESTIONS

1. Interview a friend or classmate to learn about a significant event in that person's life. Write a biographical sketch of your subject; narrate the crucial moments and explain why they were important. (Be sure to ask pointed, analytical questions during your interview, so your subsequent interpretation will be based on specific statements.)

2. As in the suggestion above, interview people close at hand who were involved in some important project in your town, at school, or at work. Ask them what took place and why it was unusual, controversial, necessary, and so on in an effort to understand the event as well as its significance. Write the story succinctly and explain as you narrate.

3. Narrate an important sequence of events from your own life, but write in the third person, and try to be as objective as any biographer would. Don't assume you already know a full interpretation of the story; apply the same sort of analytical reasoning to it that you would if it were about someone else. Why is the story meaningful to your audience? What makes it an interesting subject for biography?

PART FOUR

Writing to Convince

ARGUMENT, CRITICISM, PERSUASION

The battle of good against evil has always been a favorite subject in art and literature, especially in the popular forms of film, fiction, and, of course, television. Similarly, the drama of ritualized combat in professional sports and games holds millions of us in thrall, some to the point of being labelled fanatics. And in the daily life of politics and international relations, verbal, and actual, war is a given. There seems an abundance of evidence that human beings love to witness, or engage in, a good fight, even if it threatens their own survival. We seem to inhabit a world where conflict rules, and where each of us must answer the question "Which side are you on?" with increasing frequency.

Such a characterization may seem extreme to some, understated to others. And that, perhaps, is part of the point. People have differing views about the world they live in—different opinions about truth, value, action. They struggle to advance the views they hold, usually in opposition to someone else's. They act to influence or convince other persons to change their differing attitudes or behavior. Regrettably, the methods people have used for this purpose have included lies, threats, and physical force. The presence of such tactics in our world may give some indication of the importance people place on the correctly aligned viewpoint.

In this part, we will look at three common kinds of writing that seek to affect us in some way, to influence our actions or to convince us to embrace an idea. The first, *argument*, relies on the rational aspects of people, their ability to reason logically from assumptions and draw conclusions from evidence. The second, *criticism*, is an application of argumentative technique to specific subjects, such as literature, music, film, as well as general concerns, such as political or cultural values. The third, *persuasion*, often has the same goal as the first two but may employ certain "nonrational" methods, such as appealing to our emotions, ethical or religious beliefs or values, patriotism, superstitions, and so on.

Although argument and criticism are the most common in college writing, all three types play major parts in the world of nonfiction, and it is rare that any of them occurs in a pure state—without some influence from the others. For example, an argument, however rationally executed, may be heartfelt or emotionally based (the opposing sides of the abortion issue, for example). Critics sometimes resort to distortion, name-calling, and other tactics of propagandists, thereby producing a kind of expressive writing (see Part V) masquerading as criticism. Persuasion may affect an appearance of unbiased rationality (the corporate "report" in the guise of a TV commercial) as a device.

There is no continuum of value between argument and persuasion, as some may think; argument is not "better" than persuasion, nor persuasion by definition sinister or sneaky. Sound arguments have been used to ad-

234

vance questionable purposes (protecting national security as a reason for breaking-and-entering), and some kinds of persuasion appeal to the very best in our character by seeking to lift our sights to noble causes. Each kind of writing has its appropriate, and inappropriate, uses; we study each to learn how best to use it to influence or convince our readers, and to learn how others use each kind to do the same to us.

All three forms of nonfiction—reports, essays, and narratives—can be vehicles for changing readers' attitudes and actions. The evidence contained in a report, for example, can have a powerful effect; and a well-told story, likewise, can move readers toward a desired goal. Nonetheless, we will focus chiefly on the essay in the next three chapters, as the form most often used to carry an argumentative or persuasive point.

11

ARGUMENT

DISPUTES, GOALS, AND AUDIENCES

The other night on television, two political candidates, each running for his party's nomination for the presidency, faced each other across a table. Candidate X claimed that candidate Y had received illegal campaign funds; Y claimed that X did not represent the "true voice" of the party; X insisted that Y's policies, if carried out, would return the country to a state of economic stagnation; Y argued that X's Senate votes had done real damage to poor people and that he (X) should hang his head in shame. The candidates told jokes at each other's expense, defamed each other's character, and spoke glowingly of their own accomplishments. Each was the best choice to beat the incumbent.

The debate between the two men was complex, a mix of argument, criticism, persuasion—and evasiveness. Three things, at least, were clear to viewers, however: the nature of the dispute, each side's goal, and the role of the audience. These three elements will be present in any situation where the need for argument or persuasion arises.

First, the nature of the dispute. In order for argument to be necessary, there must be an explicit or implicit disagreement (or potential one). In the political debate, the disagreement between the candidates was total, at least apparently. But what, specifically, did they dispute? Here are some common categories of disagreement*:

1. *Matters of fact.* Did Y receive illegal funds? Is X lying? If Y got the money, did he know it was dirty? Does X know that Y didn't knowingly accept back-room donations?

2. *Matters of theory.* Are Y's policies bad for the economy? Have X's votes done harm to the poor? Are one man's ideas better than the other's?

3. *Matters of belief.* What does the party really stand for, and who best embodies this set of values? What assumptions do all party members share? Are they the correct assumptions?

*Nancy R. Comley, David Hamilton, Carl H. Klaus, Robert Scholes, and Nancy Sommers, *Fields of Writing* (New York: St. Martins, 1984), 445–447.

4. Matters of action. Once the nominee is chosen, what's the best strategy for winning the election? How can the party be reunited? What should the candidate promise to do as president?

We must first determine what is at issue. Where does the disagreement lie? (In critical argument, often, the dispute is implicit or potential; that is, the critic argues a position that may imply an opposing one, even if the latter hasn't been expressed.) Is it a major difference or a minor one? Is it superficial or technical, or is it a matter of principle?

Second, the goal. When we make an argument, we assert a position aimed at influencing others, and we defend or support our stand with reasons (logic and evidence). What sort of influence do we want to exert? Our goal is tied to the nature of the dispute, and usually will be one or more of the following:

1. To affect opinions or attitudes by arguing *for* a position we advocate
2. To change attitudes by arguing *against* an opposing view
3. To influence behavior by arguing *for* a certain course of action
4. To affect behavior by arguing *against* the actions of others

Sometimes, in seeking to influence beliefs, refute the theories, arguments, or policies of others, or rally support for an idea or cause, we may end up doing several, or all, of these things. To make a case successfully, for example, it may be necessary to first demolish the opposing one. But many kinds of argument are limited to only one of these goals.

Third, the audience. Because argument (and criticism and persuasion) seeks to influence, we can't succeed without knowing *whom* we want to affect and where they stand with respect to us. We must have some idea of the distance the argument is meant to cross. There will be a range of actual or potential disagreement (and agreement) based largely on the amount of shared assumptions between the two sides. We can describe it as falling between the extremes of general agreement and total disagreement on what the opponents accept as true:

1. General agreement on assumptions. In this instance, both parties share common values, world views, and a basic understanding of reality (at least in the given case). Disagreement may exist over specific facts, ideas, or actions, but within the context of a broad ground of agreement.

2. Incomplete agreement on assumptions. Here, the parties stand apart to some degree, holding somewhat opposing views about basic questions. Their disagreement, therefore, will be deeper and more difficult to bridge.

3. Complete disagreement on assumptions. Although certainly an extreme situation, total disagreement is not uncommon. Here, the opposing sides refuse to acknowledge any common ground at all. Each side sees the other as evil incarnate, and it may be difficult even for them to listen to, much less accept, the other's position.

In assessing our audience, we must estimate this degree of shared belief and construct the argument accordingly. In the first case, we may not need to belabor assumptions but instead move right to the heart of the specific difference; in the second instance, we may first need to establish which assumptions are shared before going on to make our points; in the third situation, we may need to question our own assumptions or to give serious effort to seeing the other side's before any possibility of progress may develop.

In our example of the political debate, even though the two men oppose each other, each is trying to convince the audience of viewers, not his opponent. In an argumentative essay, we may face a similar situation as we write not so much to the opposing side as to a third-party viewer or listener. Still, this is the person or group we wish to influence, and our judgments about that audience—its intelligence, moral character, seriousness, rationality—combined with our analysis of the dispute and the goal we seek, are the guidelines for the argument we will write.

USING LOGIC AND EVIDENCE

Good arguments are more than mere expressions of opinion. Our opinions may be silly or irrational, based on instinct or whimsy; we have a right to hold them, but they may not stand the tests of argument. Good arguments, rather, are carefully designed structures built on solid information and sound analysis. It is for this reason that we come to argument after first considering informing and analyzing.

Arguments are also something else, however. They are attempts at certainty. Just as in the logical proof of a theorem in geometry, arguments are our attempts to prove the validity of our assertions. A convincing argument has "the ring of truth" to it, and the strength to change a mind. Arguments marshal this strength through the use of logic and evidence.

The idea that people can know or determine the truth is probably as old as human consciousness, but it was not until the time of Aristotle, in the 4th century B.C., that we formulated a system of logical rules that could yield dependable results. As logic was developed and refined, especially in ancient Greek civilization and in the scientific revolution of the 16th and 17th centuries, human reasoning took two different but complementary forms: induction and deduction. Reasoning is a process, like writing, and each of these two *ways* of reasoning leads toward conclusions, but takes its own path.

Induction

Perhaps the most basic form of reasoning is that based on direct experience and observation. When we *generalize* from a body of specific information, we are using *inductive reasoning.*

Induction begins with facts, evidence, and instances, and moves toward general conclusions—statements that describe or predict the nature of other, similar instances. For example, say I have taken a job in New York and now must find an apartment. I look through the ads, make some calls, visit some places. The first apartment I see has two rooms, no view, and costs $900 per month. The next place is worse, and just as expensive. Then I visit a clean but unexciting one-bedroom for $1300, utilities extra. And so on. By the end of my first day of apartment hunting, I should be able to draw some general conclusions about Manhattan apartments: Good ones are very hard to find and are very expensive; bad ones are easier to find and are outrageously overpriced. I don't have to see every vacant flat in New York to make these inferences; a sample of all available information is enough (in this case) to support some tentative generalizations.

As we can see from this illustration, too, inductive reasoning is not foolproof. In some cases, we may find our conclusions affected by additional evidence, and we may need to revise our inferences to account for the new data. It may be hard to know exactly when a generalization is warranted or, indeed, *if* one is. The evidence we have collected doesn't *prove* our conclusion about it; it merely supports the likelihood or probability that our statement is true.

Because induction doesn't give us certainty, then, we must be careful not to *overgeneralize* or go beyond what the evidence suggests. In some cases, our information will support an *unqualified* statement: "The history of the stock market shows that it fluctuates, that it never goes up or down forever." (This is a general conclusion about the nature of the market, likely to remain true indefinitely.) In other cases, however, an accurate conclusion will need to be *qualified* or limited: "While real estate values have increased dramatically in past years, and may continue to do so, some evidence suggests that prices have peaked." (This is a statement that accounts for differences or inconsistencies in evidence.)

In inductive reasoning, the quality of our evidence or support is all-important. Our facts must be clear, accurate, and reliable—able to be checked and verified by others, if necessary—and they must be substantive, not based on speculation. That is why science and scholarship, for example, which rely heavily on accumulated evidence, have developed elaborate systems for collecting and documenting information. Only if the evidence is reliable will reliable conclusions be possible.

Finally, the amount of evidence must be sufficient to support the generalization. Unfortunately, there are no rules for gauging sufficiency; we must instead rely on common sense to tell us when we have enough. In some cases, one fact can support a generalization: We need witness only one nuclear explosion to know that a nuclear war would produce a holocaust. In other instances, such as in opinion polls, even a very large collection of data won't support an unqualified conclusion. In marshaling evidence, then, it pays to maintain an objective, even skeptical, view, and to question the facts as might an unfriendly critic. If you can satisfy the potential objections of your opposition, chances are your argument will be sufficiently supported.

Deduction

In *deductive reasoning,* instead of starting with individual facts and generalizing from them, we begin with general assumptions and *derive specific conclusions.* We do this by applying a general statement to a particular situation.

For example, say that I apply my general conclusion about apartment hunting in New York to a specific case: I've found a place that's reasonably priced but only so-so in appeal; should I take it or keep looking and risk losing it? What would be the logic in taking it?

> *General statement:* Decent, moderately priced apartments are rare in this town.
> *Specific case:* This is a decent, moderately priced apartment.
> *Conclusion:* This apartment is rare.

I've started to reason my way toward a decision, depending on my stamina and time available to keep looking. Perhaps I should carry the logic one step further:

> *General statement:* Rare apartments take time and energy to find, and people with a limited supply of either probably should lock up the first good place they see.
> *Specific case:* I am a person with limited time and energy, and this is a good place.
> *Conclusion:* I probably should lock this place up.

When we think something through like this, we usually aren't conscious of these steps. Reasoning deductively is second nature to us. When we break down the process of deduction, however, we can see that certain rules apply to it, that it works correctly only in certain ways, and that incorrect reasoning will produce faulty conclusions.

The structure of deduction we've just seen above is called the *syllogism.*

When properly used, the syllogism is a device that can yield certainty—unlike the process of inductive reasoning, which cannot result in absolute proof. With the syllogism, however, we can know whether our conclusions are valid and true.

Syllogisms, when expressed formally, have three parts: the general statement, or *major premise*; the specific case, or *minor premise*; and the *conclusion*. In everyday speaking and writing, we usually convert the formal syllogism to an "if, then" statement, such as, "If I want to get a good job, then I must first get a good education." As a formal syllogism, this line of reasoning would develop as follows:

Major premise: Most good jobs require a high level of education.
Minor premise: I want a good job.
Conclusion: Therefore, I must attain a high level of education.

The major premise of a deductive argument acts as a "given"; for the purposes of the argument, we assume it to be true. In some cases, the major premise is itself the result of a previous deductive or inductive process; in others, it is assumed to be true without proof. For example, in Aristotle's classic syllogism, "All men are mortal; Socrates is a man; therefore, Socrates is mortal," the major premise, "All men are mortal," is a generalization derived from observation, an *inductive* conclusion. It also serves, however, as the foundation of a *deductive* argument about an individual man (a specific case), Socrates. On the other hand, we might make the following argument:

Major premise: All lives have meaning.
Minor premise: Socrates has a life.
Conclusion: Socrates' life has meaning.

In this syllogism, the major premise, "All lives have meaning," is assumed to be true without proof, for the sake of argument. We can't really conclude from evidence that all lives have meaning; rather, we *postulate* it, state it as a self-evident or believed truth.

Whether we begin with an assumption or a conclusion derived from a previous argument, if both the major and minor premises of the syllogism are true, and if we follow a valid line of reasoning, the conclusion of the argument will be both true and valid. However, an argument may produce a true but invalid conclusion (a true statement reached through faulty reasoning) or a valid but untrue one (a false statement deduced through correct reasoning). Let's look at each of these possibilities.

In a sound argument, both premises are true, and the minor premise refers to a specific instance *within* the general class of instances covered by the major premise:

Major premise: Green, leafy vegetables are good for you.
Minor premise: Spinach is a green, leafy vegetable.

Here, both conditions are satisfied; therefore, the only conclusion we can draw is: Spinach is good for you. No other conclusion is possible. The argument is both true and valid—true because both statements can be accepted without objection, valid because the second statement is a specific case of the class or set of instances (green, leafy vegetables) covered by the first.

In a faulty argument, one that is invalid or untrue, one or both of these conditions has not been met. Here, for example, is a valid (correctly reasoned) but untrue argument:

Major premise: All politicians are corrupt.
Minor premise: Senator Jones is a politician.
Conclusion: Senator Jones is corrupt.

In this case (conventional belief aside), the major premise is untrue—it cannot be convincingly demonstrated. Still, the argument is perfectly valid since the minor premise cites a specific instance of the generality.

Here, on the other hand, is a true but invalid argument:

Major premise: All rock bands play music.
Minor premise: Talking Heads plays music.
Conclusion: Talking Heads is a rock band.

All the statements are true; the conclusion is true. But the argument is not valid because the minor premise does *not* cite an instance of the generality. The premises are *unrelated*. We might just as well say, for the minor premise, "The Chicago Symphony plays music." Following our same line of thought, we'd have to conclude that "The Chicago Symphony is a rock band," an example of an invalid syllogism leading to an untrue conclusion.

There is one more possibility in which logic and sense break down completely, the invalid and untrue argument:

Major premise: Wealthy people are happy.
Minor premise: I am happy.
Conclusion: I am a wealthy person.

Not only are the premises unrelated, but the major premise is untrue—in this case an overgeneralization, unqualified by common sense. The conclusion, then, is both false and invalid.

These examples point up the importance of starting with premises you can defend as true (against possible objections), and of applying the general or major premise to a specific case directly related to it. If you develop arguments that meet these conditions, the soundness of your reasoning should compel your reader to accept your conclusions—to be convinced.

Combining Induction and Deduction

In the real world, where we apply reason to ordinary, concrete situations, we don't segregate induction and deduction but instead use them together, as complementary features of one process. Induction, we have said, can provide the generalization or major premise for a deductive argument. Inductive reasoning, however, can also support the minor premise of a syllogism, lending the weight of evidence to a sound theoretical argument.

Consider, for instance, the argument for stricter anti-drunk-driving laws. The evidence of alcohol-related fatalities is certainly strong, but by itself doesn't imply a specific response to the problem. To do that, we must first analyze how society has confronted other, similar problems, determine whether these methods have worked, and ask if experience can guide us toward a solution. In other words, we must discover what we assume to be true about social ills and remedies before we can apply our knowledge to a specific problem.

After some thought, we might list a few basic assumptions:

- Laws help regulate social behavior.
- When society faces a major social problem, it usually passes a law against it.
- Laws don't always work, but they do most of the time.
- Society has a right, even a duty, to protect itself against dangerous individuals.
- Society has a right to make lawbreakers accountable for their actions, even if it means passing very strict laws.

And we might go on to list some specific characteristics of the drunk-driving problem, based on inductive reasoning from evidence:

- Drunk driving is a very serious social ill.
- Drunk drivers are extremely dangerous individuals.
- Many drunk drivers are willful lawbreakers, often speeding, driving recklessly, and ignoring traffic conditions and directions.

Having outlined some general assumptions and some specific problems, we can now form a logical argument—or see, at least, if one can be built. Rather than use the formal syllogism at this stage, however, let's try the more informal "if, then" structure:

- If laws help regulate social behavior, and if drunk driving is social behavior, then laws should help regulate it.

- If society deals with social problems by passing laws against them, and if drunk driving is a social problem, society will probably pass a law against it, sooner or later.
- If society has a right to protect itself against dangerous people, and if drunk drivers are dangerous people, then society has the right to protect itself against them.
- If society has the right to pass very strict laws in order to make lawbreakers accountable for their actions, and if drunk drivers are willful lawbreakers, then society has the right to pass strict laws making them accountable for their actions.

Have we developed a potentially sound argument here? It seems so, but we must evaluate our premises for truthfulness to make certain that the condition of validity has been met. Let us state the argument formally:

Major premise: Society has the right to pass strict laws in order to make law-breakers (people who may be potentially dangerous to others) accountable for their actions.
Minor premise: Drunk drivers willfully break traffic laws, and endanger other people by speeding, driving recklessly, ignoring conditions, and so on.
Conclusion: Society has the right to pass strict laws making drunk drivers accountable for their actions.

Are the premises true? Upon a second look, the major premise is not as precise as it might be. Although it seems generally accurate, it could be expanded and sharpened:

Major premise: People in society, through their elected representatives, have the right to impose laws for the regulation of social conduct; they also have the right to impose strict penalties on those who willfully disobey the law, and to make them accountable for their actions, especially when the lawbreaker presents a threat to public safety.

This statement now seems fairly solid. It constitutes a reasonable assumption. The minor premise has been overstated, however. A more qualified sentence will be easier to defend as true:

Minor premise: Drunk drivers, many of whom willfully disobey traffic laws, thereby seriously endangering others, present a threat to public safety.

This statement now seems truthful, able to withstand objection.

If we are satisfied that the premises are true, are they logically related? Does the minor premise cite a specific instance of the major? Yes. The generality includes all lawbreakers, and the specific case is one type of lawbreaker. Therefore, the language of the conclusion will change to reflect the change in the original assumption:

Conclusion: People in society have the right to impose strict penalties on drunk drivers and to make them accountable for their actions.

ORGANIZING AN ARGUMENTATIVE ESSAY

As we've seen in previous chapters, essays have a basic structure of introduction, body, and conclusion—but possess enormous flexibility within this form. We've also seen that formal essays (such as those written for college courses) tend to state a controlling idea, or thesis, early on, usually at the end of the introductory paragraph or section. This pattern, because it is clear and straightforward, also works very well for arguments:

> *Intro:*   Nature of dispute or disagreement
>   Thesis: Conclusion of argument
> *Body:*   Support: Evidence and inductive reasoning, or
>   :   Logic—deductive reasoning, or
>   :   Combination
> *Conclusion:*   Restatement of thesis or closing comment

Successful argumentative essays also often address opposing views, however, and offer counterarguments or rebuttals; the essay's body of support may include these, either before or after the central argument.

There is another pattern, however (mentioned briefly in Chapter 3), which can sometimes serve to make arguments even stronger. In this structure, the writer leaves the thesis unstated—holds it back for the last paragraph, often the very last sentence, so that the main point of the argument gets the maximum emphasis. Essays patterned this way have the shape of syllogisms, and their conclusions have the irrefutable logic and force of deductive proof.

Newspaper editorial writers and columnists are fond of this design for argument, and they take their lead from one of the most effective essays ever written, The Declaration of Independence. In this revolutionary document, powerfully eloquent yet simple and clear, Jefferson sets forth the argument for secession, building his case as a syllogism:

> *Major premise:* People institute governments among themselves to secure the basic human rights of life, liberty and the pursuit of happiness, and when any form of government becomes destructive to these ends, the people have a right to alter or to abolish it.
> *Minor premise:* The government of King George III of Great Britain, in a history of repeated injuries and usurpations, has become destructive to our basic human rights.

> *Conclusion:* Therefore, we the people of the Colonies have a right to alter or to abolish it, and so declare ourselves absolved from all allegiance to the British Crown.

The force of this argument results not only from its valid logic, but from the strength of the major premise (that people have a basic right to self-determination) and the evidence in support of the minor premise, the list of King George's crimes. By the time we reach the end of this brief masterpiece—the conclusion of the argument and the thesis of the essay—we are convinced, as was the world in 1776.

Structuring an argumentative essay as a syllogism—starting with assumptions, applying those principles to specific cases and supporting with evidence, and developing the conclusion or main point from these premises—creates a kind of suspense. It has the effect of drawing the reader in and walking him or her through your reasoning process, so that both of you come to the same conclusion at the same time. By creating suspense or doubt and then resolving it at the end, you give the reader an *experience* of thought, not just the results of it, and your essay thus may be more memorable and emphatic.

If we were to develop an outline for our drunk-driving argument, then, we might come up with the following:

> *Intro:* Lead with striking or disturbing fact, incident.
> Characterize the problem.
> *Body:* State major premise (and explain support for).
> State minor premise (including evidence of threat to public safety, statistics, expert testimony).
> Consider counterarguments or objections to premises.
> *Conclusion:* Main point (explain)
> Closing remark for emphasis?

Some kinds of argument, such as critical essays (see Chapter 12), are better served by the thesis/support pattern, especially when the argument is longer or more complicated—research papers, for instance. Such essays are primarily *inductive* in that the thesis is really the conclusion the evidence points to and supports. The organization of the body of an inductive essay can take a number of shapes: a list of points, as in the inductive portion of the Declaration of Independence; or the various single and combined patterns of the rhetorical methods—comparison, contrast, classification, cause and effect, and so on. In this sense, the body of the essay presents the results of analysis to support the argumentative point.

The structure you choose will depend on the complexity of the argument, the degree to which it relies on concrete facts and analysis (induction) or theoretical logic (deduction), and the effect you want to produce in your reader's mind. As always, you may have to try a few strategies before finding the best one.

TESTING ARGUMENTS FOR FALLACIES

Thinking and writing logically takes concentration. Because not all of us have perfect concentration all the time, however, we may lapse now and then into *fallacy*, an unclear, illogical, inappropriate, or incomplete line of reasoning. People in everyday speech and conversation regularly short-circuit logic with fallacy: "I'd never take a course from that teacher—he's such a slob." "If we could only get rid of the Russians, our problems would be solved." "I'm going on that new diet—my favorite actress uses it." When we commit words to paper, however, such thoughtlessness can destroy any possibility of our convincing our audience. Less than in talk, logical lapses in writing seem to be lighted in neon.

Here are some of the most common thought-errors.

Oversimplification

Although it is a temptation in a complex world, oversimplification distorts the truth, denies its complexity. When we blame *all* world tensions on the Soviets, we tell less than the whole story. When we say that drug problems are caused by a lack of spiritual values, the same thing. Oversimplification can take a variety of forms: (1) *either/or reasoning*—insisting that every issue is a matter of the good side versus the bad side, with no middle ground; (2) *mistaking sequence for causation*—assuming that an action or event is causative merely because it preceded an event in time (example: The assassination of John F. Kennedy caused the social turmoil of the Sixties); (3) *unsupported or unqualified generalization*—making a sweeping statement that ignores evidence that might weaken it: "Poor people are just lazy." "The space program is a total waste of money." "They don't make movies like they used to."

Circular Reasoning/Begging the Question

When we assume the very conclusion we want to prove, we argue in a circle or beg the question. For example, if I assume that capital punishment is wrong because it is murder, I have ended exactly where I began—saying capital punishment is wrong because it is wrong (since murder is wrong by definition). If I want to prove capital punishment to be wrong, I have to show that it belongs to a group of actions that can be shown to be wrong (in other words, use deduction). Circular reasoning can sound deceptively like valid logic—unless you learn to recognize it; but we all have ample opportunity to do that, since it makes up a large part of our daily discourse: "We must raise taxes because the government needs money!" "Rock video is destroying the minds of youth because it presents lurid, unhealthy images!" "If only he would stop drinking, his alcohol problem would disappear!"

Non Sequitur

Non sequitur (in Latin, "it does not follow") is a gap in thinking or reasoning. We saw in our discussion of deduction that valid conclusions follow from logically related premises. In *non sequitur*, one statement follows another without logical connection: "Vietnam was an immoral war—no wonder so many veterans are suffering delayed-stress syndrome." "The welfare system is a disaster; that's why the budget deficit is so high."

Ad Hominem Argument (Name Calling)

Another Latin phrase, meaning "at the man," *ad hominem* argument attacks the person rather than his ideas. A person is not an assertion or a position, however, and attacking character can never be an argument, only a way of skirting one. We may resort to it in a moment of desperation, but it is always self-defeating and usually makes us look worse than the person we're attacking.

Argument from Poor or Inappropriate Authority

In inductive arguments especially, in which evidence is crucial, citing strong authority can bolster a case, but citing weak or misplaced authority will have the opposite effect. Legitimate sources should be professionals or recognized experts in the fields for which they speak, and they must be identified, not kept in the shadows. A victim of armed assault, for example, might offer evidence of a specific case, but would not automatically qualify as an authority on gun control.

Arguing from Analogy

Analogy and metaphor, as we've seen, can be useful tools of explanation or analysis, but because they compare basically dissimilar things *figuratively*, they do not offer factual or literal proof. I cannot, for instance, argue against taxation by claiming that the state is a pirate plundering the wealth of helpless innocents.

A final word: In our everyday thinking and writing, we infer conclusions from evidence and assumptions we take to be true without question. Although this is necessary for us to be able to function in the world, our ability to think and argue critically and objectively grows as we become aware of, and willing to question, accepted truth. The great creative leaps of civilization have come from men and women who doubted certain "facts" and assumptions, and who argued instead from positions that challenged conventional belief. The process of reasoning through induction and deduction, then, is not merely a mechanical method of demonstration. Like writing, it is a *creative* process, a way of rational exploration and discovery.

QUESTIONS

1. What three elements are present in any argumentative situation?
2. Most disputes fall into one or more of four basic categories. What are these?
3. What factor most influences the degree of dispute between opponents?
4. What is inductive reasoning? What are some qualities of sound induction? What pitfall should you watch for?
5. What is deductive reasoning? How does it differ from induction?
6. What logical structure does deductive reasoning use?
7. How can you tell if a deductive argument is invalid, untrue, or both?
8. How may induction and deduction be combined? How are they combined in the Declaration of Independence?
9. Why does one popular structure for argument reverse the standard pattern of stating the thesis first? What is gained by placing the main point at the end of a deductively reasoned essay?
10. What are some common argumentative fallacies? Can you invent your own illustration for each?

EXERCISES

1. What kinds of inductive evidence would help support the following conclusions? Cite specific examples.

- Education leads to higher income.
- The Big Bang theory seems to be reasonable.
- Capitalist economies tend to have boom and bust cycles.
- Child abuse leaves lasting emotional scars on victims.
- Mass movements can bring about social change.
- History has been heavily influenced by great individuals.
- Exercise produces certain physiological benefits.

2.   Which of these generalizations need qualification? Why? Which ones won't stand up at all? Why?

- Children are irresponsible.
- Politicians can't be trusted.
- Divorce is caused by weakening community values.
- The more nuclear weapons we have, the safer we are from attack.
- Film violence is harmless.
- College courses have no use on the job.
- The government has all the power.

3.   What conclusions can you draw from the following if–then arguments? Which conclusions will be valid, which true, and which both valid and true? Why?

- If money buys happiness, and I have money, then . . .
- If cigarettes cause cancer, and I smoke cigarettes, then . . .
- If all people are equal, and Jack and Bill are equal, then . . .
- If might makes right, and I have might, then . . .
- If all ancient philosophers are dead, and Socrates is dead, then . . .
- If all cities are expensive to visit, and San Francisco is a city, then . . .

4.   How would you construct a deductive argument for the following conclusions? What assumptions underlie these conclusions?

- I have the right to make my own decisions.
- Mr. Smith is not a good teacher.
- The draft registration law is not fair.
- The United States Olympic team should be funded by the government.
- That girl made the biggest mistake of her life by sleeping with her boyfriend.
- Anyone caught with a concealed weapon should face a long prison sentence.

5.   What argumentative fallacies are embedded in the following statements?

- If you wouldn't be so bull-headed, maybe you'd agree with me!
- The average voter has no influence—it's no wonder so many people don't vote.
- My buddy at work told me to buy this stock. It's going through the roof!
- If the government raises taxes, it will be the final blow to the person in the street who's already taken a brutal beating.
- Don't vote Republican—they were behind the Watergate scandal.
- In this country, you're either a patriot or a traitor.
- No wonder Jill left school—she lost her scholarship.

Readings

Born in Czechoslovakia, MARIE WINN grew up in New York and is a graduate of Radcliffe College. She has written numerous books and articles about children, among them The Plug-In Drug *(1977), an influential analysis of the effects of television on children and families, and* Children Without Childhood *(1983), from which the following selection is taken. In it, Winn argues that childhood has changed radically in American society, but that the change need not be permanent if parents are willing to respond to it.*

The New Middle Ages

by Marie Winn

Today, after several centuries of childhood as an estate carefully separated from adulthood, it begins to appear that we are returning to a long-ago pattern of undifferentiation—a New Middle Ages, we might call it.

There is little doubt that since the 1960s children have come to resemble adults more closely than they have done for centuries. In the clothes they wear, the language they use, and the things they know, in all aspects of their daily behavior, children today seem less childlike.

Consider the change that has overtaken children's leisure time. Centuries ago, children and adults played games together in the streets and sang songs and listened to stories together indoors. In later times, children and adults went off in divergent directions. Today, in the New Middle Ages, children read books about prostitution and see movies about adult marital problems. They listen to music with a strong sexual beat. And adults and children are again united in their most important leisure-time deployment. No longer do kids play while adults engage in more grown-up activities: young and old alike these days spend most of their free time watching television.

Consider the complex code of manners that developed slowly over the centuries, serving to separate children's behavior sharply from adults'. There is no law decreeing that what develops slowly cannot be "undeveloped" quickly, perhaps even within a few decades. The shame and revulsion that it took civilized folks so long to acquire seem to have taken them only a single generation to loosen and in some cases slough off entirely. A new openness prevails. Today we learn from our therapists to feel more ashamed of our repressions than of "letting it all hang out." In the New Middle Ages parents no longer have dinner alone by candlelight while children eat in the nursery, learning the proper way to use their forks and knives. Now the whole family can go out and eat with their fingers at the Kentucky Fried Chicken place down the street.

Consider the demise of sexual innocence among children. We know that the casual integration of children into adult society in the Middle Ages included few sexual prohibitions. Today's nine- and ten-year-olds watch pornographic movies on cable TV, casually discourse about oral sex and sadomasochism, and not infrequently find themselves involved in their own parents' complicated sex lives, if not as actual observers or participants, at least as advisers, friendly commentators, and intermediaries. Yet another portent of the New Middle Ages.

Consider that curious medieval convention of sending children away from home at an early age to live in other people's houses. Until as late as the eighteenth century, children as young as seven years old were sent off for training to households similar to their own. At the same time that people sent their own children away, they took other people's children into their own homes. In this way the primary ties between parents and children were broken early. According to our current understanding of child psychology, such a deprivation and loss would serve to make children more docile and malleable, less exuberant and childlike. Had they remained at home their natural psychological vigor, their healthy egocentrism, might have made them resist their parents' demands for work and services, just as children today frequently go to great lengths to avoid doing any work around the house.

Today too the primary ties are broken early for great numbers of children. Now, instead of sending the children away, it is the parents who go away, their exits precipitated by separation, divorce, or work requirements. The consequences for the children, however, are similar to those that accompanied the child departures of old: depression, a loss of vigor, and the end of childhood as a period of carefree dependence.

Consider, finally, the recent change in the popular iconography of childhood—that is, the way children are represented in movies and books and especially in television programs and commercials. Just as on television today we see children transformed by make-up, clothing, facial expressions, and gestures (sexually suggestive dancing, for instance) into pseudo-adults, so we may begin to understand the strange distortion of children in medieval paintings and drawings that made them look like small, dwarflike adults rather than children. The recognition of childhood as a separate and different state from adulthood did not then, and does not today, suit the inner purposes of society.

It has become fashionable to idealize the distant past, to suppose that when children were integrated into society they were somehow better off. Yet critics of the current nostalgia point out evidence of widespread sexual exploitation, neglect, and abuse of children in the medieval period. Similarly, as we make the transition from an era in which children were separated and protected from adult hardships to one in which they are once again incorporated early into a more casual and undifferentiated society, we cannot fail to observe that child abuse and child exploitation are once again on the increase and that the lives of great numbers of children have not improved but instead have worsened.

It may indeed prove that children have become increasingly useful to adults in modern society as their roles have changed from innocent, dependent, "special" creatures to secret and not-so-secret sharers of adult life's inevitable burdens. But from the viewpoint of children themselves, whether the strengths they may derive from their earlier preparation for adulthood will compensate for the loss of that carefree childhood that people once believed children deserve and require remains in doubt. But there is no doubt that childhood is harder today. As a fifteen-year-old girl who looks back on a past that included a parental divorce, experimentation with marijuana from sixth grade on, and a troubling experience with sex in eighth grade remarked: "All the kids I see are in a rush to grow up, and I don't blame them. I don't think childhood is a golden age at all. I wouldn't want to be a child again."

This is not to suggest that childhood in the bygone Age of Protection was a continuously blessed, happy state. Rare indeed was the child who did not experience jealousy or terror or shame or anger or any of the other myriad forms of human misery at some time during the childhood years. In his book *Growing Up,* for example, journalist Russell Baker describes his childhood during the Depression years, darkened by poverty, marital discord, illness, and death. And yet he is able to write: "The occasional outbursts of passion that flickered across my childhood were like summer storms. The sky clouded suddenly, thunder rumbled, lightning flashed and I trembled a few moments, then just as swiftly the sky turned blue again and I was basking contentedly again in the peace of innocence." It is not by chance that when Baker paints a scene to describe the overriding mood of his childhood days he peoples it with adults sitting on a porch, rocking and pronouncing beliefs such as "Children should be seen and not heard," interrupting their gossip with reminders that "Little pitchers have big ears." For it was not the complete absence of unhappiness in those early years that allowed him to look back on his childhood as an island of peace and innocence. It was the secure certainty that he was a child and that adults were adults, and that in spite of the wretchedness he might glimpse in their world he could still remain, in his different state, untouched by it. This is the essence of adult protectiveness: transmitting to children the sense that they are separate and special and under the adults' careful supervision. This understanding allowed children of the past, even those growing up a mere ten or fifteen years ago, to enjoy the simple pleasures of childhood—of play, imagination, curiosity, and pursuit of adventure—in the most adverse circumstances.

Can the boundaries between adulthood and childhood be once again restored? Can parents today, who sense uneasily that something is missing, try to re-create the different sort of childhood that they themselves once enjoyed? In an Age of Preparation, can individual parents hope to buck the tide and try to bring their children up protectively?

The social processes that helped bring about children's new integration into adult life—changes in family stability, most notably, together with women's liberation and the proliferation of television as a dominant part of children's lives—cannot be reversed. We will never return to the old-style family with the bread-earning father and the childlike, stay-at-home mother minding the house and kids. Nor would we desire such a step backward. The liberation movement has brought a new maturity and independence to women, forcing them, sometimes against their deepest instincts, to seek to fulfill a greater potential than they had understood in the past. The hope of a simple turning of the tide is an unrealistic and indeed a retrogressive one. Nevertheless, while social change cannot be reversed, perhaps it can be modified and made to work better for families.

Perhaps an understanding of the irreversible consequences of family breakdown on children may cause men and women to readjust some of their original goals for marriage. If their objectives are primarily self-fulfillment, sexual excitement, a deeply gratifying adult relationship, then it might be advisable for them to think twice about embarking on a family in the first place. The thought of a family mainly as a source of fulfillment and gratification for the marriage partners does not bode well for children's future. Parents need to understand that the successful raising of a family requires a greater focus on the well-being of the children and that they must sacrifice some of their own ambitions, desires, and strivings for personal happiness if the children are to grow up well. It may be the future holds the possibility of a variety of partnerships for men and women, only some of which will be seen as conducive to the raising of children.

Perhaps an understanding that early childhood is not the only important stage of childhood, that the middle years are equally important, may lead parents to compromise their career and social ambitions and devote more time and attention, more care and supervision, to their post-toddler children, capable and unchildlike though they may seem. As child-development specialist Annie Herman proposes, the early childhood years may not necessarily be the most crucial ones, in spite of the orthodox view that the personality is formed during those years. "There is a certain resilience in early childhood," she explains, "but this resilience slowly disappears. When you are resilient you bounce back. Thus young children can recover from physical and mental trauma quickly and can put things aside and turn to other things. But as they grow older their resilience is diminished. At this point the child becomes far more vulnerable to outside experience. Now the child can suffer permanent damage."

Perhaps an understanding of the importance of play in children's lives, not only to the child directly as a source of a particular kind of satisfaction but as an activity that helps define the child as a childlike creature, thus promoting more protective treatment by adults, will provoke parents to take a stronger stand in controlling their children's television viewing, television being the single great replacement of play among today's children.

Perhaps an understanding that children and adults are *not* equal, and that children do not prosper when treated as equal, will encourage parents to take a more authoritative—authoritative, not authoritarian—position in the family.

Perhaps the recognition that a highly complicated civilization cannot afford to shorten the period of nurture and protection of its immature members will restore a real childhood to the children of coming generations.

MEANING

1. Is Winn arguing primarily for something, against something, or both? How can you tell?
2. If you condensed this argument into a single assertion, what would it be? Does Winn make such a statement anywhere in the essay?
3. What does Winn dispute in this essay? Is it largely a matter of fact, theory, belief, or action?
4. Does Winn's essay contain any overt or unstated biases? If so, what are some of them? What other assumptions rule her argument?

METHOD

1. Does Winn's argument rely primarily on either deduction or induction? How does she use these forms of reasoning in her essay?
2. What specific evidence does Winn cite to support her assertions? Does her evidence support her conclusions about it?

AUDIENCE

1. Does Winn convince you that childhood has been lost and that it must be regained? Where is her argument strongest, or weakest, from your view?

2.   Does your childhood conform to Winn's description? How close is she to giving an accurate portrait of modern childhood? Would the evidence from your own life be grounds for a counterargument?

WRITING SUGGESTIONS

1.   Compose an argument that refutes Winn's major assertion. Your counter-assertion might be something like: Children need to be exposed to reality early, and the sooner the better (or perhaps a somewhat less extreme version of this). Try to pattern your essay after Winn's, and present an opposing view point by point.
2.   Argue in defense of the assertion: Exposure to the adult world does not automatically destroy childhood; children still can be children even though they know more and more about the problems and experiences of adulthood. What form of reasoning is best suited to such a defense? How can you strengthen the argument with evidence?

Born in 1941, STEPHEN JAY GOULD is a teacher, writer, and scientist. He graduated from Antioch College in 1963 and earned his PhD from Columbia University. A paleontologist, Gould teaches at Harvard University and writes on science for several publications, including Natural History *magazine and* The New York Review of Books. *Among his books:* Ever Since Darwin *(1977);* The Panda's Thumb *(1980);* The Mismeasure of Man *(1981); and* Hen's Teeth and Horses's Toes *(1983). In the following selection from* Ever Since Darwin, *Gould argues against the claim that evidence can be found supporting a link between intelligence and race.*

Racist Arguments and IQ

by Stephen Jay Gould

Louis Agassiz, the greatest biologist of mid-nineteenth-century America, argued that God had created blacks and whites as separate species. The defenders of slavery took much comfort from this assertion, for biblical prescriptions of charity and equality did not have to extend across a species boundary. What could an abolitionist say? Science had shone its cold and dispassionate light upon the subject; Christian hope and sentimentality could not refute it.

Similar arguments, carrying the apparent sanction of science, have been continually invoked in attempts to equate egalitarianism with sentimental hope and emotional blindness. People who are unaware of this historical pattern tend to accept each recurrence at face value: that is, they assume that each statement arises from the "data" actually presented, rather than from the social conditions that truly inspire it.

The racist arguments of the nineteenth century were based primarily on craniometry, the measurement of human skulls. Today, these contentions stand totally discredited. What craniometry was to the nineteenth century, intelligence testing has been to the twentieth. The victory of the eugenics movement in the Immigration Restriction Act of 1924 signaled its first unfortunate effect—for the severe restrictions upon non-Europeans and upon southern and eastern Europeans gained much support from results of the first extensive, and uniform application of intelligence tests in America— the Army Mental Tests of World War I. These tests were engineered and administered by psychologist Robert M. Yerkes, who concluded that "education alone will not place the negro [sic] race on a par with its Caucasian competitors." It is now clear that Yerkes and his colleagues knew no way to separate genetic from environmental components in postulating causes for different performances on the tests.

The latest episode of this recurring drama began in 1969, when Arthur Jensen published an article entitled, "How Much Can We Boost IQ and Scholastic Achievement?" in the *Harvard Educational Review*. Again, the claim went forward that new and uncomfortable information had come to light, and that science had to speak the "truth" even if it refuted some cherished notions of a liberal philosophy. But again, I shall argue, Jensen had no new data; and what he did present was flawed beyond repair by inconsistencies and illogical claims.

Jensen assumes that IQ tests adequately measure something we may call "intelligence." He then attempts to tease apart the genetic and environmental factors causing differences in performance. He does this primarily by relying upon the one natural experiment we possess: identical twins reared apart—for differences in IQ between genetically identical people can only be environmental. The average difference in IQ for identical twins is less than the difference for two unrelated individuals raised in similarly varied environments. From the data on twins, Jensen obtains an estimate of environmental influence. He concludes that IQ has a heritability of about 0.8 (or 80 percent) *within* the population of American and European whites. The average difference between American whites and blacks is 15 IQ points (one standard deviation). He asserts that this difference is too large to attribute to environment, given the high heritability of IQ. Lest anyone think that Jensen writes in the tradition of abstract scholarship, I merely quote the first line of his famous work: "Compensatory education has been tried, and it apparently has failed."

I believe that this argument can be refuted in a "hierarchical" fashion—that is, we can discredit it at one level and then show that it fails at a more inclusive level even if we allow Jensen's argument for the first two levels:

Level 1: The equation of IQ with intelligence. Who knows what IQ measures? It is a good predictor of "success" in school, but is such success a result of intelligence, apple polishing, or the assimilation of values that the leaders of society prefer? Some psychologists get around this argument by defining intelligence operationally as the scores attained on "intelligence" tests. A neat trick. But at this point, the technical definition of intelligence has strayed so far from the vernacular that we can no longer define the issue. But let me allow (although I don't believe it), for the sake of argument, that IQ measures some meaningful aspect of intelligence in its vernacular sense.

Level 2: The heritability of IQ. Here again, we encounter a confusion between vernacular and technical meanings of the same word. "Inherited," to a layman, means "fixed," "inexorable," or "unchangeable." To a geneticist, "inherited" refers to an estimate of similarity between related individuals based on genes held in common. It carries no implications of inevitability or of immutable entities beyond the reach of environmental influence. Eyeglasses correct a variety of inherited problems in vision; insulin can check diabetes.

Jensen insists that IQ is 80 percent heritable. Princeton psychologist Leon J. Kamin has done the dog-work of meticulously checking through details of the twin studies that form the basis of this estimate. He has found an astonishing number of inconsistencies and downright inaccuracies. For example, the late Sir Cyril Burt, who generated the largest body of data on identical twins reared apart, pursued his studies of intelligence for more than forty years. Although he increased his sample sizes in a variety of "improved" versions, some of his correlation coefficients remain unchanged to the third decimal place—a statistically impossible situation.* IQ depends in part upon sex and age; and other studies did not standardize properly for them. An improper correction may produce higher values between twins not because they hold genes for intelligence in common, but simply because they share the same sex and age. The data are so flawed that no valid estimate for the heritability of IQ can be drawn at all. But let me assume (although no data support it), for the sake of argument, that the heritability of IQ is as high as 0.8.

Level 3: The confusion of within- and between-group variation. Jensen draws a causal connection between his two major assertions—that the

---

*I wrote this essay in 1974. Since then, the case against Sir Cyril has progressed from an inference of carelessness to a spectacular (and well-founded) suspicion of fraud. Reporters for the London *Times* have discovered, for example, that Sir Cyril's coauthors (for the infamous twin studies) apparently did not exist outside his imagination. In the light of Kamin's discoveries, one must suspect that the data have an equal claim to reality.

within-group heritability of IQ is 0.8 for American whites, and that the mean difference in IQ between American blacks and whites is 15 points. He assumes that the black "deficit" is largely genetic in origin because IQ is so highly heritable. This is a *non sequitur* of the worst possible kind—for there is no necessary relationship between heritability within a group and differences in mean values of two separate groups.

A simple example will suffice to illustrate this flaw in Jensen's argument. Height has a much higher heritability within groups than anyone has ever claimed for IQ. Suppose that height has a mean value of five feet two inches and a heritability of 0.9 (a realistic value) within a group of nutritionally deprived Indian farmers. High heritability simply means that short farmers will tend to have short offspring, and tall farmers tall offspring. It says nothing whatever against the possibility that proper nutrition could raise the mean height to six feet (taller than average white Americans). It only means that, in this improved status, farmers shorter than average (they may now be five feet ten inches) would still tend to have shorter than average children.

I do not claim that intelligence, however defined, has no genetic basis—I regard it as trivially true, uninteresting, and unimportant that it does. The expression of any trait represents a complex interaction of heredity and environment. Our job is simply to provide the best environmental situation for the realization of valued potential in all individuals. I merely point out that a specific claim purporting to demonstrate a mean genetic deficiency in the intelligence of American blacks rests upon no new facts whatever and can cite no valid data in its support. It is just as likely that blacks have a genetic advantage over whites. And, either way, it doesn't matter a damn. An individual can't be judged by his group mean.

If current biological determinism in the study of human intelligence rests upon no new facts (actually, no facts at all), then why has it become so popular of late? The answer must be social and political. The 1960s were good years for liberalism; a fair amount of money was spent on poverty programs and relatively little happened. Enter new leaders and new priorities. Why didn't the earlier programs work? Two possibilities are open: (1) we didn't spend enough money, we didn't make sufficiently creative efforts, or (and this makes any established leader jittery) we cannot solve these problems without a fundamental social and economic transformation of society; or (2) the programs failed because their recipients are inherently what they are—blaming the victims. Now, which alternative will be chosen by men in power in an age of retrenchment?

I have shown, I hope, that biological determinism is not simply an amusing matter for clever cocktail party comments about the human animal. It is a general notion with important philosophical implications and major political consequences. As John Stuart Mill wrote, in a statement that should be the motto of the opposition: "Of all the vulgar modes of escaping from the consideration of the effect of social and moral influences upon the

human mind, the most vulgar is that of attributing the diversities of conduct and character to inherent natural differences."

MEANING

1. Against what is Gould arguing? Can you state the major assertion of his
    argument in your own words? Does he make a direct statement of this
    assertion? What is in dispute here?
2. According to Gould, there are two basic flaws in the argument that genes
    determine individual intelligence. What are these two flaws?
3. Why does Gould bring in the issue of intelligence tests? Why does he
    object to them?
4. What is the political significance of racist arguments?
5. A number of Gould's words may be difficult for you. Some suggestions
    for the dictionary: egalitarianism [par. 2], hierarchical [6], vernacular [7],
    heritability [8].

METHOD

1. How does Gould show the flaw in Jensen's IQ argument? Explain the
    example in par. 12 (line 7, p. 259), for instance.
2. Is Gould's argument generally inductive, deductive, or a combination?
    Support your view.
3. Does Gould employ any rhetorical strategies in addition to his use of logic
    and evidence? If so, which ones? How does he use them?

AUDIENCE

1. Whom is Gould writing to convince? Is an avowed racist likely to be influ-
    enced by Gould's argument? Why or why not?
2. How do you react to Gould's case against racist arguments? Has this
    essay had an effect on your thinking about racial issues? Is this essay
    likely to change your behavior in any way?

WRITING SUGGESTION

Using a combination of induction and deduction (evidence, for example, to support
the minor premise of a syllogism), construct an argument either for or against one
of these propositions:

*   Women should be paid less than men for the same work.
*   Rape should be a crime punishable by death.

- Government should be able to deduct child-support payments from fathers' paychecks.
- Police should have the power to search suspicious people without a warrant.
- Every person between the ages of 18 and 30 should have to spend one year in some form of public or military service.

Remember: Whom are you trying to convince? What objections will an opponent likely raise? Is your evidence consistent and your reasoning sound?

JONATHAN SCHELL was born in New York. He attended Harvard University and the University of California, Berkeley, and is currently a staff writer for The New Yorker. *His first book,* The Village of Ben Suc *(1967), is an account of an American battle with the Viet Cong during the Vietnam War. Another of Schell's works,* The Time of Illusion *(1976), considers United States politics between 1969 and 1974. Schell's most widely read book is* The Fate of the Earth *(1982), first serialized in* The New Yorker *and a significant expression of the anti-nuclear movement. In it, Schell mounts a controversial yet moving appeal for action against nuclear arms. He followed this book with another on the same subject,* The Abolition *(1984), a detailed proposal for such action. In this excerpt from* The Fate of the Earth, *Schell argues against the generally accepted theory of deterrence.*

The Fault in Deterrence Doctrine

by Jonathan Schell

The central proposition of the deterrence doctrine—the piece of logic on which the world theoretically depends to see the sun rise tomorrow—is that a nuclear holocaust can best be prevented if each nuclear power, or bloc of powers, holds in readiness a nuclear force with which it "credibly" threatens to destroy the entire society of any attacker, even after suffering the worst possible "first strike" that the attacker can launch. Robert McNamara, who served as Secretary of Defense for seven years under Presidents Kennedy and Johnson, defined the policy, in his book "The Essence of Security," published in 1968, in the following terms: "Assured destruction is the very essence of the whole deterrence concept. We must possess an actual assured-destruction capability, and that capability also must be credible. The point is that a potential aggressor must believe that our assured-destruction capability is in fact actual, and that our will to use it in retaliation to an attack is in fact unwavering." Thus, deterrence "means the certainty of suicide to the aggressor, not merely to his military forces, but to his society as a whole." Let us picture what is going on here. There are two possible eventualities: success of the strategy or its failure. If it succeeds, both sides are frozen into inaction by fear of retaliation by the other side. If it fails, one side annihilates the other, and then the leaders of the second side annihilate the "society as a whole" of the attacker, and the earth as a whole suffers the consequences of a full-scale holocaust, which might include the extinction of man. In point of fact, neither the United States nor the Soviet Union has ever adopted the "mutual-assured-destruction" doctrine in pure form; other aims, such as attempting to reduce the damage of the adversary's nuclear attack and increasing the capacity for destroying the nuclear forces of the adversary, have been mixed in. Nevertheless, underlying these deviations the concept of deterring a first strike by preserving the capacity for a devastating second strike has remained constant. The strategists of deterrence have addressed the chief issue in any sane policy in a nuclear-armed world—the issue of survival—and have come up with this answer: Salvation from extinction by nuclear weapons is to be found in the nuclear weapons themselves. The possession of nuclear weapons by the great powers, it is believed, will prevent the use of nuclear weapons by those same powers. Or, to put it more accurately, the threat of their use by those powers will prevent their use. Or, in the words of Bernard Brodie, a pioneer in nuclear strategy, in "The Absolute Weapon: Atomic Power and World Order," a book published in 1946: "Thus far, the chief purpose of our military establishment has been to win wars. From now on its chief purpose must be to avert them. It can have almost no other useful purpose." Or, in the classic, broad formulation of Winston Churchill, in a speech to the House of Commons in 1955: "Safety will be the sturdy child of terror, and survival the twin brother of annihilation."

This doctrine, in its detailed as well as its more general formulations, is diagrammatic of the world's failure to come to terms with the nuclear predicament. In it, two irreconcilable purposes clash. The first purpose is to permit the survival of the species, and this is expressed in the doctrine's aim of frightening everybody into holding back from using nuclear weapons at all; the second purpose is to serve national ends, and this is expressed in the doctrine's permitting the defense of one's nation and its interests by threatening to use nuclear weapons. The strategists are pleased to call this clash of two opposing purposes in one doctrine a paradox, but in actuality it is a contradiction. We cannot both threaten ourselves with something and hope to avoid that same thing by making the threat—both intend to do something and intend not to do it. The head-on contradiction between these aims has set up a crosscurrent of tension within the policies of each superpower. The "safety" that Churchill mentions may be emphasized at one moment, and at the next moment it is the "terror" that comes to the fore. And since the deterrence doctrine pairs the safety and the terror, and makes the former depend on the latter, the world is never quite sure from day to day which one is in the ascendant—if, indeed, the distinction can be maintained in the first place. All that the world can know for certain is that at any moment the fireballs may arrive. I have said that we do not have two earths, one to blow up experimentally and the other to live on; nor do we have two souls, one for reacting to daily life and the other for reacting to the peril to all life. But neither do we have two wills, one with which we can intend to destroy our species and the other with which we can intend to save ourselves. Ultimately, we must all live together with one soul and one will on our one earth.

For all that, the adoption of the deterrence doctrine represented a partial recognition that the traditional military doctrine had become an anachronism—a doctrine that was suited well enough to the pre-nuclear world but lost all application and relevance when the first nuclear bomb flashed over the New Mexico desert. In assessing the advance made by deterrence, we must acknowledge how radically it departed from traditional military doctrine. Traditional military doctrine and nuclear doctrine are based on wholly different factual circumstances, each set of which corresponds to the technical realities of its period. Traditional military doctrine began, as I have suggested, with the premise that the amounts of force available to the belligerents were small enough to permit one side or the other to exhaust itself before both sides were annihilated. Nuclear doctrine, on the other hand, begins with the premise that the amounts of force are so great that both sides, and perhaps all mankind, will be annihilated before either side exhausts its forces. Like postulates in geometry, these two premises determine the entire systems of thought that follow, and no discussion of military strategy can make any sense unless one clearly specifies which premise one is starting from. But, as I pointed out at some length at the outset of these observations, there is no longer room for doubt that in our time the second premise is the correct one.

The chief virtue of the doctrine of nuclear deterrence is that it begins by accepting this basic fact of life in the nuclear world, and does so not only on the rhetorical plane but on the practical plane of strategic planning. Hence, it acknowledges that victory can no longer be obtained in a contest between two well-armed nuclear powers, such as the United States and the Soviet Union. Senator Barry Goldwater wrote a book, published in 1962, whose title was "Why Not Victory?" To this question the strategists of deterrence have a decisive answer: Because in the present-day, nuclear world "victory" is oblivion. From this recognition flows the conclusion, arrived at by Brodie in 1946, that the sole purpose of possessing nuclear strategic arms is not to win war but to prevent it. The adoption of the aim of preventing rather than winning war requires the adoption of other policies that fly in the face of military tradition. One is abandonment of the military defense of one's nation—of what used to be at the center of all military planning and was the most hallowed justification of the military calling. The policy of deterrence does not contemplate doing anything in defense of the homeland; it only promises that if the homeland is annihilated the aggressor's homeland will be annihilated, too. In fact, the policy goes further than this: it positively requires that each side leave its population open to attack, and make no serious effort to protect it. This requirement follows from the basic logic of deterrence, which is that safety is "the sturdy child of terror." According to this logic, the safety can be only as great as the terror is, and the terror therefore has to be kept relentless. If it were to be diminished—by, for example, building bomb shelters that protected some significant part of the population—then safety would be diminished, too, because the protected side might be tempted to launch a holocaust, in the belief that it could "win" the hostilities. That is why in nuclear strategy "destruction" must, perversely, be "assured," as though our aim were to destroy, and not to save, mankind.

In strategic terms, the requirement that the terror be perfected, and never allowed to deteriorate toward safety, translates into the requirement that the retaliatory force of both sides be guaranteed—first, by making sure that the retaliatory weapons cannot be destroyed in a first strike, and, second, by making sure that the society of the attacking power *can* be destroyed in the second strike. And since in this upside-down scheme of things the two sides will suffer equally no matter which one opens the hostilities, each side actually has an interest in maintaining its adversary's retaliatory forces as well as its own. For the most dangerous of all the configurations of forces is that in which one side appears to have the ability to destroy the nuclear forces of the other in a first strike. Then not only is the stronger side theoretically tempted to launch hostilities but—what is probably far more dangerous—the other side, fearful of completely losing its forces, might, in a crisis, feel compelled to launch the first strike itself. If on either side the population becomes relatively safe from attack or the retaliatory strike becomes vulnerable to attack, a temptation to launch a first strike is created, and "stability"— the leading virtue of any nuclear balance of power—is lost. As Thomas Schelling, the economist and noted nuclear theorist, has put it, in "The Strategy of Conflict," a book published in 1960, once instability is introduced on either side, both sides may reason as follows: "He, thinking I was about to kill him in self-defense, was about to kill me in self-defense, so I had to kill him in self-defense." Under deterrence, military "superiority" is therefore as dangerous to the side that possesses it as it is to the side that is supposedly threatened by it. (According to this logic, the United States should have heaved a sigh of relief when the Soviet Union reached nuclear parity with it, for then stability was achieved.) All these conclusions follow from the deterrence doctrine, yet they run so consistently counter to the far simpler, more familiar, and emotionally more comprehensible logic of traditional military thinking—not to mention instinct and plain common sense, which rebel against any such notion as "assuring" our own annihilation—that we should not be surprised when we find that the deterrence doctrine is constantly under challenge from traditional doctrine, no matter how glaringly at odds with the facts traditional doctrine may be. The hard-won gains of deterrence, such as they are, are repeatedly threatened by a recrudescence of the old desire for victory, for national defense in the old sense, and for military superiority, even though every one of these goals not only would add nothing to our security but, if it should be pursued far enough, would undermine the precarious safety that the deterrence doctrine tries to provide.

If the virtue of the deterrence policy lies in its acceptance of the basic fact of life in the nuclear world—that a holocaust will bring annihilation to both sides, and possibly the extinction of man as well—its defect lies in the strategic construct that it erects on the foundation of that fact. For if we try to guarantee our safety by threatening ourselves with doom, then we have to mean the threat; but if we mean it, then we are actually planning to do, in some circumstance or other, that which we categorically must never do and are supposedly trying to prevent—namely, extinguish ourselves. This is the circularity at the core of the nuclear-deterrence doctrine; we seek to avoid our self-extinction by threatening to perform the act. According to this logic, it is almost as though if we stopped threatening ourselves with extinction, then extinction would occur. Brodie's formula can be reversed: if the aim of having nuclear forces is to avert annihilation (misnamed "war" by him), then we must cling for our lives to those same forces. Churchill's dictum can be reversed, too: If safety is the sturdy child of terror, then terror is equally the sturdy child of safety. But who is to guarantee which of the children will be born? And if survival is the twin brother of annihilation, then we must cultivate annihilation. But then we may *get* annihilation. By growing to actually rely on terror, we do more than tolerate its presence in our world: we place our trust in it. And while this is not quite to "love the bomb," as the saying goes, it decidedly is to place our faith in it, and to give it an all-important position in the very heart of our affairs. Under this doctrine, instead of getting rid of the bomb we build it ever more deeply into our lives.

The logical fault line in the doctrine runs straight through the center of its main strategic tenet—the proposition that safety is achieved by assuring that any nuclear aggressor will be annihilated in a retaliatory strike. For while the doctrine relies for its success on a nuclear-armed victim's resolve to launch the annihilating second strike, it can offer no sensible or sane justification for launching it in the event. In pre-nuclear military strategy, the deterrent effect of force was a useful by-product of the ability and willingness to wage and win wars. Deterrence was the shadow cast by force, or, in Clausewitz's metaphor, the credit that flowed from the ability to make the cash payment of the favorable decision by arms. The logic of pre-nuclear deterrence escaped circularity by each side's being frankly ready to wage war and try for victory if deterrence failed. Nuclear deterrence, however, supposedly aims solely at forestalling any use of force by either side, and has given up at the outset on a favorable decision by arms. The question, then, is: Of what object is nuclear deterrence the shadow? Of what cash payment is it the credit? The theoretical answer, of course, is: The retaliatory strike. Yet since in nuclear-deterrence theory the whole purpose of having a retaliatory capacity is to deter a first strike, one must ask what reason would remain to launch the retaliation once the first strike had actually arrived. Nuclear deterrence requires one to prepare for armed conflict not in order to "win" it if it breaks out but in order to prevent it from breaking out in the first place. But if armed conflict breaks out anyway, what does one do with one's forces then? In pre-nuclear times, the answer would have required no second thought: it would have been to strive for the decision by arms—for victory. Yet nuclear deterrence begins by assuming, correctly, that victory is impossible. Thus, the logic of the deterrence strategy is dissolved by the very event—the first strike—that it is meant to prevent. Once the action begins, the whole doctrine is self-cancelling. In sum, the doctrine is based on a monumental logical mistake: one cannot credibly deter a first strike with a second strike whose *raison d'être* dissolves the moment the first strike arrives. It follows that, as far as deterrence theory is concerned, there is no reason for either side not to launch a first strike.

What seems to be needed to repair the doctrine is a motive for retaliation—one that is not supplied by the doctrine itself and that lies outside its premises—but the only candidates are those belonging to traditional military doctrine; namely, some variation of victory. The adherents of nuclear victory—whatever that would be—have on occasion noted the logical fallacy on which deterrence is based, and stepped forward to propose their solution: a "nuclear-war-fighting" capacity. Thus, the answer they give to the question of what to do after the first strike arrives is: Fight and "win" a "nuclear war." But victory does not suddenly become possible simply because it offers a solution to the logical contradiction on which the mutual-assured-destruction doctrine rests. The facts remain obdurately what they are: an attack of several thousand megatons will annihilate any country on earth many times over, no matter what line of argument the strategists pursue; and a "nuclear exchange" will, if it is on a large scale, threaten the life of man. Indeed, if victory were really possible there would have been no need for a deterrence strategy to begin with, and traditional military strategy would have needed no revision. This "solution" is therefore worse than the error it sets out to remedy. It resolves the contradiction in the deterrence doctrine by denying the tremendous new reality that the doctrine was framed to deal with, and that all of us now have to deal with on virtually every level of our existence. Consequently, this "solution" could lead us to commit the ultimate folly of exterminating ourselves without even knowing what we were doing. Aiming at "victory," we would wind up extinct.

MEANING

1. What is deterrence doctrine? State its central principle in your own words.
2. According to Schell, what is the basic flaw in deterrence doctrine? Why is it a flaw?
3. Why does Schell think deterrence doctrine is dangerous?

METHOD

1. Is Schell's argument against deterrence doctrine largely inductive or deductive? Why do you say so?
2. Does Schell's attitude toward the subject of nuclear deterrence seem unbiased, or does this essay perhaps reveal something about the author's subjective opinions? Cite specific passages in support of your answer.
3. What other rhetorical devices does Schell use to develop his essay?

AUDIENCE

1. Who is Schell's audience? Is he writing to convince the framers of nuclear strategy, or the general reader? How do you know?
2. Do you agree or disagree with the author's argument? Has Schell altered your thinking about this issue? In what areas do you disagree with him?

WRITING SUGGESTIONS

1. Draft a deductive counterargument to Schell's in which you defend the doctrine of nuclear deterrence. Be sure to reread Schell's essay carefully and try to address his major points—especially that deterrence doctrine is based on a logical contradiction.
2. Write a deductive argument for or against one of the following assertions:
   - The United States should have strict immigration quotas.
   - The Equal Rights Amendment is logical and necessary.
   - Communities should have the right to ban pornography.
   - The right to pray in school should be guaranteed by the Constitution.
   - The United States should cut off all foreign aid to undemocratic governments.

Remember: Who is your audience? What assumptions underlie your argument? Which of these assumptions does your reader share? Which will he or she likely dispute? Can you convince your audience to accept the assumptions from which you will draw your conclusion? Will the conclusion follow logically from those assumptions?

ADDITIONAL WRITING SUGGESTIONS

1. Are there any issues you find yourself debating with friends? If so, choose the one that interests you most and try to put your case about it into words—an argumentative essay for the student newspaper, or a long letter to the editor of a city paper.
2. Find an editorial or column with which you disagree and write an essay refuting it. Study the argument carefully and address each point with your own evidence and assumptions.
3. Write an argument for or against one of these proposals:
   - Publishing student evaluations of teachers
   - Raising the national drinking age to 21
   - Doing away with the home mortgage tax deduction
   - Raising the speed limit to 70 m.p.h.
   - Instituting a national test for all high school graduates
   - Legalizing drugs
   - Changing the presidential term to a single, six-year one, no reelection
   - Making airbags mandatory in all new cars
   - Reducing the minimum wage so employers can hire more workers

12

CRITICISM

CRITICISM AS A FORM OF ARGUMENT

Argumentative writing, as it occurs in newspaper editorials, columns, essays, position papers, and so on, usually addresses matters of fact, theory, belief, or action. It is concerned with the "nonfiction" world of ideas and experience. Within the everyday world, however, there is another realm— a world of created objects: books, movies, pieces of music, works of art and architecture, theatrical works and performances. When writers turn to these created works as subjects of argument, they engage in *criticism*— writing to evaluate an object and influence the reader's view of its merit.

Criticism is not a negative term, although it has negative connotations to many. Critics do find fault with their subjects, but writing critically is much more than toting up weaknesses. Rather, we attempt to study the book, film, painting, song, to understand it and form a knowledgeable opinion of it, and to present this opinion as an argument aimed at convincing others.

Because criticism is argument, usually in essay form, all the guidelines for argument (Chapter 11) apply to it. It may begin with basic assumptions as a context for individual works (deductive reasoning), or it may generalize from specific evidence (inductive reasoning). More often than not, criticism will apply general critical principles (criteria) to evidence in order to reach a judgment of a work's worth, originality, effectiveness or quality. Because criticism also typically does rely heavily on evidence, critical arguments will differ according to the writer's decisions about which facts to emphasize, play down, or ignore.

Criticism can be a very personal kind of argumentative writing, because our experience of a play, novel or movie is subjective. Our point of view will affect the experience and what we write about it, and although most critics try (as they should) to be fair in their judgments, pure objectivity is not only difficult to attain but undesirable. We assume criticism will be shaped by the writer's perspective, but it will not be *about* that perspective. Good critical writing keeps its focus on the object, the thing in question, and builds a convincing case for or against it.

Critical argument often has a very practical purpose. The reader of a critical review or essay may be a potential consumer of the object under scrutiny, wondering whether to buy the record, see the film, read the book, visit the building. The writer's job, then, will be to speak to the audience's concerns. Even in the more scholarly forms of criticism, where the object may be familiar to us, the critic tries to breathe new life into it, to make us understand or appreciate it in some new way.

Finally, not all critical arguments are equal, not all opinions valid. Some critical arguments may fall prey to fallacy (see previous chapter); they may be based on questionable assumptions or on incomplete or inconsistent evidence. Their assertions may be frivolous or trivial, or obvious, or superficial. They may begin and end with the same unquestioned, unexamined opinion. By the same token, however, even a superbly reasoned and brilliantly written argument is not the last word. For, in the world of criticism, there are few final or absolute truths—just good cases.

BASIC APPROACHES TO CRITICISM

Because criticism seeks both meaning and judgment, analysis and a decision, it looks at objects in the light of certain general ideas. As critical writers, when we study an object we attempt to analyze the elements that constitute it—to see which elements are present, how they work (or don't) together, and what relationships, if any, they may have with things that lie outside the work itself.

Here is a brief list of some of the elements writers analyze in various objects of criticism:

Fiction (short stories and novels): Plot, character, setting, theme, tone, narrator's point of view, dramatic conflict
Drama: Plot, character, setting, theme
Dramatic performance: Staging, acting, pacing, casting
Poetry: Imagery, sound, diction, style, rhythm, form, theme
Film: Story elements (plot, character, theme, etc.); cinematic elements (direction, pacing, cinematography, special effects)
Music: Sound, form, lyrics, style
Art: Subject, form, composition, technique, visual impact
Architecture: Scale, form, materials, design, stylistic influences

What writers do with their analysis, however, depends on which critical approach they take. We can divide criticism into two general varieties: that which concentrates on the object itself, and that which views the object in relation to other factors not contained within the work. Each approach has its own criteria.

Looking at the Work Itself

When we examine a created work—novel, symphony, skyscraper, or poem—as a unique object, something with a life of its own, apart from its maker's intentions, we try to understand and judge the work as if it were a world unto itself. For the purposes of the critical argument, there is nothing "outside" the work, no author, no composer or designer, no history or society, that can color our interpretation. We attempt to view the object as a self-sufficient whole, and to come to a decision about its internal, or intrinsic, nature.

Although this may sound an extreme or unrealistic critical view, it's an idea whose influence has been, and continues to be, deep and widespread. In fact, it is common practice for us, even in our everyday conversations about books, movies, records, and so on, to discuss works as isolated objects with value in and of themselves. Our first impulse is to consider the thing: Is it worthwhile? Is it junk? Do I like it? Does it work? Does it have a pleasing design? Does it make me think?

Still, as these questions indicate, we can't criticize in a void. Even when our focus is the object itself, we must apply some critical principles, some criteria, to it before we can conclude anything about it. Despite differences between fields of critical study (literary versus film criticism, for instance), the criteria we use should help us make basic decisions common to all critical inquiry. No matter what object we study, then, we face certain fundamental questions, and we apply critical principles to the object in order to answer these questions.

In general, critical writers address some or all of the following issues:

Impact.   Any created work will produce some reaction in the viewer, listener, or reader. As critics, we not only experience the impact of the work, but we analyze and judge it. Was the effect strong, weak, or somewhere between? Did the work draw us toward it or push us away? Was our reaction consistent, did it change with time, did it increase or decrease in intensity? Were we moved to laughter, tears, terror, pity, joy? Were parts of the work stronger or weaker than others? Did the work stay with us afterward, or did we immediately forget it? Did it give us *pleasure?* What was pleasing, or displeasing, about it?

In gauging the impact of a work, in analyzing our subjective experience of it, we address perhaps the most basic critical question, the starting point of all critical thought: emotional response. However, sound criticism does not stop with mere like or dislike. Critics want to understand *why* they had the reaction they did, whether it was valid or based on misunderstanding, and how their responses affect their judgment. Moreover, only through analysis, through the process of critical thought and writing, may our initial reaction give way to a more complex or subtle one.

Beauty.   Certainly an object's beauty (or lack of it) will be part of its impact, but beauty is itself a separate critical focus. When we analyze and judge a work's aesthetic qualities, we look at its *form, design,* or *composition.* Is the work unified and consistent? Do the parts fit together in an orderly pattern that the observer can understand? Is the work balanced, so that it stands solidly, or do some of its parts seem overweighted or thin in comparison to the rest? Is the work presented in an appealing way, or is it harsh or jarring to the senses? (Works may have these latter qualities and yet be beautiful.) Is it fully formed, developed, and concluded? Do we have a sense of *completeness* about it, that nothing about it need be changed?

Because the perception of beauty is so personal, critical arguments on this issue will differ widely. Also, aesthetic standards change, and artists often delight in experimenting with them, treating them with contempt, perhaps doing away with them altogether. (Pablo Picasso, Igor Stravinsky, James Joyce, and other revolutionary moderns, for instance, completely redefined beauty in the arts of painting, music, and fiction by creating new standards, which themselves later came under assault.) How we judge beauty will depend on our assumptions about what it is, as well as on our willingness to experience new kinds of beauty for which we may not be prepared.

Truth.   Created works such as novels, movies, plays, musical compositions, and others, are not true in the sense that they give us verifiable facts. Rather, they present us with an image or expression of reality (even if the reality of dream or imagination). The truth of a work is not the degree to which it corresponds to the real world (although works of nonfiction and realistic fiction are judged by this standard), but how well it corresponds to *itself.* Does the work create a believable world? Is the work true to its own assumptions? (That is, does it have integrity?) Is it honest? Does it contradict itself? Can we enter the world the work creates and feel that our experience is genuine?

A work's truth is difficult to know or judge. However, if a movie, short story, song, painting, poem, or other work, gives us an *unselfconscious* experience, chances are it is truthful. By unselfconscious experience we mean one that doesn't announce itself to us while we're having it. Rather, we fall into the world the work expresses, as though its world and our world were one and the same. (Works that fail this test aren't necessarily untruthful; they may have other problems.) Even if the experience lasts only an instant, it is intensely absorbing, and for that instant we lose ourselves to the work.

Meaning.   No less difficult a critical question is asking what a work means. How can we possibly know? What it means to me may have nothing to do with what it means to you. Meaning is perhaps the most subjective of these issues, but it may be the most important as well. In a sense, meaning is the ultimate judgment we can make about something, as we assign it great, profound, or enduring meaning, or none at all. When we limit our view to the object itself, however, without the context of history, society, biography, or a specific theory of interpretation, its meaning lies in its openness—its ability to suggest new ideas each time we view, hear, or read it.

When a work has meaning for us, it tells us something about life, the world, human nature, and the mysteries of being, in a way only that work can. It gives us a unique and significant way of viewing our experience; it adds value to our lives. Perhaps most of all, meaningful works surprise us with an impact, beauty, or truth we didn't know we needed but now find indispensable.

Craft.   Of course, the care with which something is made can't be removed from its other qualities, but few critical judgments can be complete without a look at craftsmanship. Some works may have great potential but are poorly executed (see also our discussion in Chapter 4). In others, lack of care, skill, or talent may completely undermine the project. Does the object reflect the serious intent of its maker, or is it shoddy, poorly conceived, or hastily put together? Is its sole purpose to take advantage of faddishness or gullibility? Has it been made only to be consumed and thrown away?

Craft is a vital quality of any created work, from a knitted sweater to a blockbuster motion picture. In fact, the work is realized *through* its craft, so the energy and care the maker brings to the task directly affect our critical judgment. Good craftsmanship is more than a means to an end, however. It is itself a value, something to be achieved for its own sake.

Looking at the Work in Relation to Other Factors

Examining a novel, poem, or musical piece as if it were a world unto itself can give us a subtle, comprehensive understanding of the object. While such study is necessary for critical inquiry, it has obvious limits. Often, we want to understand created works as they reflect or embody specific values, ideas, periods of time, experiences, or systems of thought. In other words, we want to place the work in a context, to view it in relation to something apart from itself.

Many fields of knowledge can be useful frames of reference for criticism, but several are among the most common and widely applicable:

Mythology and religion.   When we view a work against the background of myth or religion, we analyze its use of themes, stories, symbols, universal or archetypal characters and situations, images, or values. We ask to what extent the work draws its power from mythic or religious sources, how important these references are for us to fully understand the work, and to what degree the work achieves its own mythic or religious impact. This context of belief—whether the myths of hunters and planters, early civilizations, classical Greece and Rome, or the Judeo-Christian religious tradition—has inspired, and continues to do so, much of the art, music, literature, and architecture of our culture. Thus it may be impossible to adequately criticize a work without considering its mythic or religious roots.

History and biography.   Another popular method of criticism treats the created object as an outgrowth of a specific historical period, social setting, or maker's life. Here the critic seeks to define relationships between the work and actual events, customs, world views, and experiences that affect it. We ask to what extent a work is based on historical fact, how the values, manners, and outlooks of people may influence it, and to what degree it expresses its maker's private history and concerns. When we take this approach, we acknowledge that concrete times, places, and events can be powerful sources of subjects, styles, and modes of thought and expression. We further recognize that, as the world changes, the objects people create also change.

Theory and ideology.   Although the backgrounds of belief and time lend much to our critical understanding, they may not tell us all we want to know. A third school of criticism (actually it's many different schools) applies specific systems of thought or philosophy to created works. Such systems include psychoanalytic theory (the ideas of Freud, Jung, and others), philosophy (e.g., existentialism), anthropology, linguistics, and political ideology (e.g., Marxism). The psychoanalytic approach to literature, for instance, tends to see stories as expressions of our unconscious life, of dreams, desires, or universally shared human experiences. Certain schools of linguistic or philosophical analysis view literary works not so much as expressions of life as complex systems of signs—almost as codes to be broken or deciphered. Ideological criticism usually condemns as corrupt any works that fail to adhere to its ideological premises. As critics, we may find these systems interesting or valuable, but we should remember that the perspectives they provide aren't absolute. Each has its own assumptions about the nature of things, and is, therefore, limited to only a partial description.

Although it may take some time before you, as a student writer, become adept at practicing criticism—especially from the vantage point of these three contexts—much of the criticism you read will have been written from one or more of these perspectives. You will be a better critic of that criticism if you are aware of its assumptions.

SOCIAL AND CULTURAL CRITICISM

Until now we have spoken only of created works as subjects of critical inquiry. Another brand of critical nonfiction deserves mention, however. When writers address the larger questions of our common life—how or why we live as we do, or should live—with an eye toward analysis and judgment, they engage in social or cultural criticism.

Social and cultural critics view lifestyles, values, and cultural practices and patterns *as if* these were created objects. They try to describe, analyze, and argue the merit of behavior, attitudes, and policies—of social and cultural assumptions and their consequences. Though it is not necessarily their job to do so, these writers often suggest remedies or alternatives based on their critiques.

As do all critics, writers on society and culture examine their evidence from a specific point of view. Many of the approaches we've just reviewed work equally well for social or cultural subjects. (You will see some examples in the readings that conclude this chapter.) Freudian psychology, for instance, may shed some light on contemporary lifestyles. Anthropology may help us understand the need for solutions to urban crowding. Or, a strict moral or political ideology may point up serious flaws in business or governmental practices. Just about any frame of reference can be (or already has been) used for writing about society and culture, although some with better success than others.

Likewise, there seems to be an unlimited number of subjects open to this kind of scrutiny. Critics have addressed the effect of mass agriculture on family life and social and moral values; they have condemned the decline of literacy and intelligence; they have attempted to expose capitalism as barbaric; they have criticized our views of certain illnesses and tied these views to the nature of language; they have shown us the racist elements in our culture; they have exhorted us to ban nuclear weapons, ensure women's rights in the Constitution, wipe out pornography, increase our savings rate, install airbags in automobiles, and protect our wildlife.

In fact, social and cultural criticism brings us back to where we began, with conflict, argument, and debate. For this form of critical endeavor may be among the highest or most important kinds of argumentative writing—that which addresses the vital issues of the day, and which often can shape and change the values, actions, and goals of the society or culture it confronts.

QUESTIONS

1. What field of subjects does criticism usually address?
2. Why and how is criticism a form of argument? Why is criticism often both personal and practical?
3. What are some of the issues a critic confronts when he or she looks at the work itself?
4. What fields of knowledge are often used as frames of reference for criticism?

EXERCISES

1. Find some examples of criticism in popular newspapers and magazines. Assess how each essay approaches its subject—whether it relies on evidence primarily, whether it seems less an argument than a personal opinion, and whether it concentrates on the object itself or relates it to external factors. Some convenient sources of review–criticism: any big city paper such as *The New York Times, Chicago Tribune,* or *Los Angeles Times;* newsmagazines such as *Time* and *Newsweek;* special audience magazines such as *Rolling Stone, New York, The New Yorker, Atlantic, Harper's,* or *The New Republic.*

2. Find two critical reviews of the same movie, novel, TV show, and compare them. Which seems to be the better argument? Where do the writers agree and disagree? Which review gives the best sense of the object itself?

3. The next time you read fiction, watch a movie or television show, or listen to music, try to apply some of the critical principles discussed in this chapter. As you read or watch, be alert for: (1) The impact of the work on you as an audience. What's your first reaction? Does the work give you pleasure? Why or why not? (2) The work's beauty or aesthetic nature. Does the work seem to have been designed for a certain reason or purpose? Does the form seem complete and understandable? (3) The work's truthfulness. Does the object draw you into itself and create an imaginary but consistent world? Or do you feel outside the work, looking in? (4) The work's meaning. Does the object convey a meaning to you? Is the meaning surprising or refreshing—a new slant? Will the object be memorable? (5) The work's craftsmanship. How well made is the object? Did the people who put it together take their time, or is it junk?

4. Write your own list of essential critical standards. When you read novels, attend plays and movies, watch TV, or listen to music, what things do you look for? How do you define quality or importance, impact, beauty, truth, and meaning in created works? How do you know when something is good or bad? How do you know that you like it, or don't?

Readings

PAULINE KAEL *was born in 1919 and is a graduate of the University of California at Berkeley. She began her writing career in 1953 as a freelancer, and became film critic for* Life *magazine in 1965. Writing about films for* McCall's *and later for* The New Republic, *she went to work for* The New Yorker *in 1968 and has been there since, except for a brief stint as a consultant for Paramount Pictures. She is a regular lecturer on college campuses and has received numerous awards for her work, including a National Book Award in 1974. Among her books of film criticism:* I Lost It at the Movies *(1965);* Going Steady *(1970);* Deeper into Movies *(1973);* Reeling *(1976); and* When the Lights Go Down *(1980). Kael's enthusiastic attitude toward movies is one of her hallmarks, and her essays about film have provoked strong reactions from readers. In the following review of ''Indiana Jones and the Temple of Doom,'' Kael mounts a strong argument for the kind of movie entertainment this film represents.*

A Breeze

by Pauline Kael

The great thing about a tall tale on the screen is that you can be shown the preposterous and the implausible. In ''Indiana Jones and the Temple of Doom,'' the director Steven Spielberg is like a magician whose tricks are so daring they make you laugh. He creates an atmosphere of happy disbelief: the more breath-taking and exhilarating the stunts are the funnier they are. Nobody has ever fused thrills and laughter in quite the way that he does here. He starts off at full charge in the opening sequence and just keeps going. There isn't a let-down anywhere in it. A friend of mine denounced the picture as ''heartless;'' another friend called it ''overbearing.'' In a sense, they're right, but they're also off the beam. This kind of story-telling doesn't have to be heartfelt; it just has to hold your interest (and delight you). ''Indiana Jones'' is a series of whoppers—it depends on verve and imagination to concoct the next big fib. And it leaps from one visual exaggeration to another—overbearingness is part of its breakneck style. (If it were modest and unassuming, it would fall apart.)

Set in 1935, ''Indiana Jones and the Temple of Doom'' probably has to be called a pre-sequel, or prequel, to ''Raiders of the Lost Ark,'' which was set in 1936, but it isn't pulpy in the way that ''Raiders'' was. It doesn't have the serious undercurrents that ''Raiders'' had; it's less ''sincere''—and that's what is so good about it. The two films have the same adventurer-archeologist hero, Dr. Indiana Jones (Harrison Ford), who wears a brown fedora and carries specs and a bullwhip. Indy seems more assured now, and more formidable physically—he's a professor with the chest of a horse. The plot is minimal this time: the action starts in Shanghai, at the Obi Wan night club, where the lusty blond Willie (Kate Capshaw), in a spangled crimson gown, struts in front of a line of tap-dancing chorus girls and belts out the film's keynote song, "Anything Goes," in English and Chinese. After a scramble at the club that features a diamond, a dose of poison, a vial of antidote, a lazy Susan, a pack of Oriental gangsters, and a rickshaw, and turns into a full-blown masterpiece of cheerful slapstick, Willie and Indy and his tiny, daredevil sidekick, the Chinese orphan Short Round (Ke Huy Quan), make a fast getaway by plane and drop off (literally) in India. There they are greeted by an elderly tribal chieftain who believes they have come in response to his prayers to Siva. He takes them to his blighted village; the land is arid, and the starving villagers are in mourning. The sacred stone that they believe conferred blessings on them has been stolen, and their children have disappeared. The three agree to go on a mission to retrieve the stone and the children, and the chieftain provides them with elephants to ride, and guides. The quest takes the three to the sumptuous palace of an odious boy maharajah (where the gold-digger Willie breathes the atmosphere of wealth and is momentarily in ecstasy), and from there, by underground passageway, to the temple where the villainous high priest Mola Ram (Amrish Puri), the leader of the Thugs, presides over human sacrifices to the goddess Kali. (The name Mola Ram is an anagram for Malomar; the Thugs—expert stranglers and sneaks—and the evil cult of Kali will be familiar to people who have seen the 1939 adventure comedy "Gunga Din.")

The subject of a movie can be momentum. It has often been the true—even if not fully acknowledged—subject of movies. In "Indiana Jones and the Temple of Doom," it's not merely acknowledged, it's gloried in. The picture has an exuberant, hurtling-along spirit. Spielberg tried kinetic comic-strip routines in his "1941" and couldn't quite make them work; here comparable routines come off just about perfectly. Spielberg uses old wheezes like the lazy Susan and you're charmed by it, remembering how, as a kid, you were nuts about these spinning discs. "Indiana Jones" is the kind of comedy in which the hero, in the middle of terrifying circumstances, and with his foot smoking, yells for water, and a deluge comes at him. The film sets the comic-book context for the hyperbolic perils that the three central characters get into, and keeps us laughing at the very fact that they don't get a chance to catch their breath. The whole movie is designed as a shoot-the-chutes, and toward the end, when the heroic trio, having found the sacred stone and freed the stolen children from the maharajah's mines, are trying to escape in a tiny mine car, and a shift in camera angles places us with them on a literal roller-coaster ride, the audience laughs in recognition that that's what we've been on all along. Yet Spielberg seems relaxed, and he doesn't push things to frighten us. The movie relates to Americans' love of getting in the car and just taking off—it's a breeze . . . .

This entire flying-carpet movie, with its comic-strip frames, is a pastel tourist paradise, as if a kid had filled in the numbered spaces to show what colored pencils can do. The look of it is itself funny. (Older kids may think the picture is a demonstration of what mattes can do.) Part of the fun of moviegoing for children is in getting wise to what's fake and what isn't. There are so many degrees of "reality" and fakery involved here that it could almost have been designed to keep them guessing; the stunt work and the laboratory special effects seem inseparable, and at the close of the Shanghai night-club sequence there's a fall through several canopies which evokes the lineage of modern movie trickery—the Douglas Fairbanks, Sr., pictures, and the famous opera-house shot in "Citizen Kane," and every cowboy movie in which the hero jumped from a building into a wagon or onto his horse. "Indiana Jones" plays with the whole idea of movie magic. This spirit of play (which I felt was present only intermittently in "Raiders") makes possible some glimmering storybook effects that probably weren't planned at all and were achieved only half-consciously. When our three find their route from the palace to the temple, they go through a passageway carpeted with creepy, crawly things. But this isn't a gross-out. Our reaction is a mixture of horror and awe, because the shining, symmetrical insects look like crawling jewels. They're—perhaps inadvertently— beautiful. And when some of them fall from the walls and are tangled in Willie's frizzy reddish-gold hair they're like the precious gems she has always wanted. The picture has fun-house skeletons and a night scene with a shooting star (a Spielberg signature); it has startling twists and sometimes small poetic curves. When Short Round wants to get into the speeding, out-of-control little mine car that Willie is in and a huge villain is clinging to, he uses the man's body as a staircase and climbs right up. It's pure Buster Keaton; that's real magic.

The stunts are brought off with incredible precision. (The way the editor, Michael Kahn, clips shots, you can almost hear him chuckling.) But plot points are occasionally fuzzy. There's a bit of information planted early on: Willie tells Indy that her father made his living as a magician, and so when the three are hiding in the temple (they're posed so that the scene is an homage to a shot in "Gunga Din") and they look down into the vast cave where Mola Ram is conducting the rituals of Kali-worship and plucking the heart out of a man's chest—and as the man is consigned to fire, his heart, held high in Mola Ram's hand, bursts into flame—everything is prepared for Willie to spot Mola Ram as a con man who had a heart up his sleeve.

But that revelation never comes, and since Lucas's special-effects company, Industrial Light & Magic, has become virtuosic about simulating the look of flesh being torn into, the poetic flourish of the burning heart may be too "real" for some viewers. The movie is set in a make-believe world, with cross-references to both Lucas's and Spielberg's other films, but this sequence is said to frighten some people, and there has been talk on television and in the press of making the film's PG classification more restrictive.

It's my impression that almost invariably the media stir up a fuss about the wrong movies. If you take a child to Disney's "Dumbo," this is what the child sees: Dumbo's mother—a circus elephant—is so angry at kids who taunt Dumbo and pull his ears that she attacks them, and as a result she is beaten and locked in a cage for mad elephants. Dumbo is left on his own, and the other elephants humiliate him constantly. He's made into an elephant clown, and during a routine he's left at the top of a fireman's ladder in a burning house, crying elephant tears, because the human clowns fail to rescue him. His only friend is another outcast—the mouse Timothy. Each sequence is brought up to its maximum psychological resonance, and when a child projects himself into this vat of bathos and moroseness it's agony: the situations on the screen have immediate correlations with his own terrors. But what correlatives could there be in "Indiana Jones and the Temple of Doom"? It doesn't take advantage of childhood traumas. With its "Road to Morocco" sensibility, it constantly makes fun of itself, and it's as remote from children's real-life fears as Sabu's escapades in "The Thief of Bagdad." The emotional mechanism of "Dumbo" is to make what happens to the cartoon animals real to kids; the emotional mechanism in "Indiana Jones" is to make what happens to the human characters unreal. And the hero carries you through—you know Indy won't die. Grownups who are upset by the menu at the banquet must be forgetting how cheerfully kids have traditionally sung such macabre ditties as "The worms crawl in, The worms crawl out, The worms play pinochle on your snout, And one little worm, Who's not too shy, Climbs into your ear, And out your eye" and "Great green globs of greasy grimy gophers' guts, Mutilated monkeys' meat, Little birdies' dirty feet, Great green globs of greasy grimy gophers' guts, And I forgot my spoon, Aw shucks."

The fuss in the media may be caused simply by the fact that there's something slightly off in the tone and the timing of the cult-of-Kali sequence. All through the picture, the comedy dominates the thrills, but here, when, at Mola Ram's instigation, Willie is put inside a contraption that looks like a deep-fat fryer, lowered partway down toward a pit of red-hot molten lava, and raised and lowered several times, Spielberg's control seems to slacken. The sequence is tense but flat; Willie has no wisecracks to deliver, and even her shrieks (which we've learned to laugh at affectionately) aren't very funny.

Spielberg's work in this movie is being called mechanical, but there are machines and then there are Rube Goldberg machines. Just because the slapstick requires brilliant timing (and the director's genius for composition) doesn't mean it's cold or impersonal. Possibly some people have got that idea because Spielberg shies away from giving the audience full, clear satisfaction. When the rotten Mola Ram pours some horrible guck down Indy's throat, Indy fights it but is held down; the scene suggests a child's fear of a dose of medicine. The guck—a "potion"—puts Indy in Mola Ram's power; he's in a trance, and we wait to see what will get him to snap out of it, but Spielberg doesn't point up the instant of awakening (though it appears to be the result of Short Round's quick thinking). And although Ke Huy Quan's Short Round is a nifty conception—this grasshopper-size kid is smarter and more resourceful than Indy, and a good case could be made for his being the true (and invulnerable) hero of the adventure—his victory over the boy maharajah isn't given the rush of feeling that the moment seems to call for. The name Short Round is an homage to Samuel Fuller, who used that nickname for the Korean kid in his 1950 movie "The Steel Helmet;" for Fuller, action is everything—and that's the acknowledgment being given here—but Fuller also piles on moral sentiment. Spielberg doesn't, and although that's part of his elegance as a moviemaker, he slights the emotional resolution of the plot. Having made the visual point that after the children were stolen from their village the land became a desert where nothing grew, he almost owes us a drenching downpour and lush vegetation to signify the children's return. It isn't quite satisfying to see them united with their families on land that looks only a little greener. Spielberg's not providing a formal closure makes the film's structure seem weaker than it is. He polishes off routines like that five-minute gag perfectly, but he may be a little embarrassed about giving us the same kind of pleasure on the larger plot points. He just comes to the end of the story and stops. Still, this is the most sheerly pleasurable physical comedy I've seen in years. And I'm grateful that Spielberg doesn't give the audience a chance to revel in how noble Indy is.

The only thing that really bothered me about the movie was the John Williams score, which is always selling excitement; it's too heavy for the tone of the film, and it's set too loud. Although there isn't much talk, the film gives you such a lot to respond to that the non-stop music produces overload; you feel as if you'd been listening to a crowd roar for two hours. (And for almost the full time you are: the audience's enthusiasm is uncontainable.) Away from the discomfort of the sound, the movie plays even better, in memory. But that sound level isn't anything as simple as a miscalculation; it's more like a guarantee. There is still the question of why a director as skillful as Steven Spielberg should make a succession of "ultimate" roller-coaster movies. (He has indicated that he may do a third in the Indiana Jones series.) It can't just be that he wants the money. It must go deeper. What I think makes this movie so overwhelming that some people recoil from it is that there is an emotional drive in it. The picture's momentum may be congruent with Spielberg's own impetus. Having had the most meteoric rise of any young director in the history of movies, he may feel that he has to push on to ever more inventive fantasies. He has made the most successful movie of all time ("E.T.") and three of the runners-up ("Jaws," "Close Encounters of the Third Kind," and "Raiders of the Lost Ark"). His own career is a roller coaster. How can he make a picture about "normal" life? He has only his childhood to draw upon. As an adult, he rides a fantasy wilder than anything in his movies.

MEANING

1. What is Kael's main point about "Temple of Doom"? What assumptions underlie the case she makes? Does she state these assumptions directly? Where?
2. What is Kael's counterargument to those critics who have condemned the movie's violent scenes? What assumptions underlie this position?
3. What is Kael's major objection to the film? Does it involve the film's subject or its execution?
4. Does Kael assess the film's impact, beauty, truth, meaning, and craft? Cite passages where she addresses any of these points.

METHOD

1. In addition to reviewing the film, Kael gives her readers quite a lot of information about it. Where does she include important facts, and why does she include them? For the readers' sake? To bolster her argument? For both reasons?
2. Kael is a careful writer, yet her style is "breezy"—very personal and relaxed. What effect does such a style have on her authority as a critic? Does she seem to be in complete command of her facts and opinions?
3. Is the author's argumentative method primarily inductive, deductive, or a combination? Explain.

AUDIENCE

1. Kael, who reviews movies for *The New Yorker*, writes extensive, detailed critical essays. Does the audience for such criticism overlap with the audience for movies like "Temple of Doom"? If Kael isn't writing for the 12-year-old fan of Indy Jones, whom is she writing for?

2. If you have seen this film, do you agree with Kael's critical review? If you saw the movie but didn't like it, has Kael's case for it changed your opinion? Do movie reviews in general affect your decisions about which films to see?

WRITING SUGGESTIONS

1. Using Kael's essay as a model, review a contemporary film or TV movie while looking carefully at each of the five critical elements we've discussed.
2. If you have a favorite movie, one you've seen several times and know well, write a review (as in Suggestion 1) in which you try to capture your final judgment of it.

KATHLEEN A. KILNOSKI was born in 1959 in Council Bluffs, Iowa. She attended public elementary and junior high schools there, and graduated as valedictorian from St. Albert Catholic High School in 1977. She then attended Grinnell College, in Grinnell, Iowa, where she majored in American Studies and under whose sponsorship she spent a semester in London. Graduating Phi Beta Kappa, Kilnoski earned her honors B.A. from Grinnell in 1981. In the spring of 1985, she graduated from the University of Iowa with a degree in law. In the essay below, Kilnoski considers the shared vision of two contemporary authors' recent works, Wendell Berry's The Unsettling of America *and Christopher Lasch's* The Culture of Narcissism. *She assesses their impact and their implications for current social values.*

Conquistadors and Narcissists: Nomads of American Culture

by Kathleen A. Kilnoski

Whether voyaging across the Atlantic, trekking over the plains, or blasting to the moon, Americans have for centuries been a people in motion. Though many politicians, entrepreneurs, and intellectuals applaud mobility as the ensign of progress, Wendell Berry and Christopher Lasch see only pathology in the unchecked wanderlust that characterizes American culture. Berry's conquistador and Lasch's narcissist, though not identical, are similarly unsettled physically, as well as morally. Moreover, both Berry and Lasch concur that America's march for progress is instead a course leading to cultural entropy.

The conquistador and the narcissist detach themselves from physical ties to their land and their work. The conquistador does not "look upon the land as a homeland," Berry argues. Instead he views the land as a resource ready to be exploited by his efficient, profit-making technologies. Unlike a good farmer, who puts his land to "kindly use," the exploiter uses up the land and moves on. In a nation run by specialists, says Berry,

> The concept of country, homeland, dwelling place becomes simplified as "the environment"—that is, what surrounds us. Once we see our place, our part of the world, as *surrounding* us, we have already made a profound division between it and ourselves.

Land is an alien, and because the conquistador sees only its otherness, he abandons his responsibility to use it kindly in his attempt to control it completely.

Lasch also alludes to the unsettled ties which Americans have to their homes and their work. Like Berry, he argues that the historical "withdrawal of many work processes from the home" erodes the connections to both family and work. No longer do parents teach children skills they need in the workplace, for technology has turned most jobs into trivial, meaningless motions. The narcissist equates success not with achievement at his work but with mobility. The most successful corporate executive is no longer a loyal organization man but is anti-organizational, ready to use his workplace as a steppingstone to a position with even more status and power.

Berry and Lasch, then, regard the attitude of moderns to their workplace as a cause of their physical unsettledness. By mistakenly thinking that "work is beneath human dignity," Berry asserts, Americans "have made it our overriding ambition to escape work, and as a consequence have debased work until it is only fit to escape from." One can imagine Berry's rural conquistador migrating to the city to escape the drudgery of the farm, only to be swallowed up by the trivial work of Lasch's urban bureaucracy.

The physical rootlessness of the conquistador and narcissist mirrors an equally pervasive moral and psychic rootlessness. This moral vicissitude affects both the individual and the larger community. The exploitive conquistador appears to have no moral code. He clouds his perception of his actions by adopting a system of "internal accounting" rather than "external accounting." By limiting his view to the facts and figures espoused by agribusiness experts, he blinds himself to the fact that agribusiness practices have external costs to land and to society:

> It is by internal accounting that the modern American agricultural program may be thought "the best, the most logical and the most successful." External accounting brings us to a very different conclusion. External accounting

pushes us back into our moral tradition, which asks us to consider that we are members of the human community and are therefore bound to help or harm it by our behavior.

In moving away from his "moral tradition," in adopting a world view that is myopic rather than far-sighted, the conquistador absolves himself of the responsibility for the long-term effects of his behavior and drifts, according to Berry, toward cultural disaster.

The narcissist likewise has a warped moral sensibility. Parents abandon their child-rearing duties to experts, "surrogate parents responsible not to the family but to the state, to private industry, or to their own codes of professional ethics." The only function parents retain is to love, not discipline, their offspring. Lasch relates further that "the parents' failure to serve as models of disciplined self-restraint or to restrain the child does not mean that the child grows up without a superego." He grows up instead with a superego composed of anxiety and a falsely large sense of self but void of any true moral code.

Without an established morality or a sense of place, American nomads are wandering toward cultural entropy, from a state of organization and differentiation to a state of chaos and sameness. The increasing specialization and bureaucratization of society, while appearing to create ever more differentiation, has, says Lasch, "made life predictable and even boring." Americans live in an "overorganized society" in which the boundaries of authority are submerged and lost. Berry reiterates that the expert's "attempt at total control is an invitation to disorder. And the rule seems to be that the more rigid and exclusive is the specialist's boundary, and the stricter the control within it, the more disorder rages around it."

In simplifying our relationship to the land to one of exploitation instead of one of nurture and husbandry, in simplifying our relationship to work to one of escape and debasement rather than one of fulfillment, we set the stage for chaos. Both Berry and Lasch agree that Americans are wandering toward a cultural crisis which can be stopped only if we build communities of settled households which share a common morality of healthy interdependence.

MEANING

1. What are the two main similarities between Berry's conquistador and Lasch's narcissist? (Check the dictionary if these terms are not clear to you.)
2. What are the chief characteristics of the conquistador, according to Kilnoski? What does she say defines the narcissist?
3. What is the "cultural crisis" against which Kilnoski sees both authors warning us?

METHOD

1. How is this essay organized? Point out specific key words and phrases the author uses to keep the reader following her critical line of thought. How does she use evidence to support her ideas?
2. To what extent does Kilnoski judge or evaluate the two books? Does she imply such a judgment or evaluation in her essay?
3. Does Kilnoski appear to agree or disagree with Berry's and Lasch's critique of American society? Where does she most openly reveal her own critical opinion on the subject these authors address?

AUDIENCE

1. Does Kilnoski speak to a broad or narrow audience? Which of her readers are likely to agree with her thesis, and which to disagree? Why?
2. Do you agree with Kilnoski that many of us are "nomads" wandering toward "a state of chaos and sameness"? What counter-criticism would you offer if you disagree?

WRITING SUGGESTIONS

1. One of the authors Kilnoski discusses appears in the following chapter (Wendell Berry, "The Unsettling of America"). Read Berry's essay and write your own evaluation and criticism of it, especially your sense of its impact, beauty, truth, or meaning.
2. Write a review–criticism of two books, movies, pieces of art, musical pieces, or similar works that share a common subject, theme, or perspective. Keeping the criteria in #1 above in mind, compare or contrast them with an eye toward evaluating their worth or significance.

CHARLES KRAUTHAMMER was born in New York in 1950. He studied political science and economics at McGill University, and then went on to become a Commonwealth Scholar at Balliol College, Oxford University, where he studied politics. A man of various interests and talents, Krauthammer also earned an M.D. from Harvard University in 1975. He practiced psychiatry, conducted research, and published a number of scientific papers, but returned to the political sphere in 1980, when he became speech writer to Walter Mondale. He joined The New Republic *in 1981 as Associate Editor, and specialized in social criticism and foreign affairs. He is currently a Senior Editor of that magazine. In the essay below, Krauthammer reviews the enormously popular* Jane Fonda's Workout Book *from a distinctly political perspective.*

The Body Politic

by Charles Krauthammer

Like all classics that harmonize form and content, this book about food (and how to burn it off) comes in the form of a sandwich. The bulky middle consists of stacks of good, lean meat: page upon page of beautiful women, stretched out in various athletic poses to illustrate The Workout. The meat is packed between two whole-wheat slices of politics Fondue: at the beginning a long, autobiographical confessional in which Jane Fonda explains her long ascent from bulimia and *Barbarella* to exercise and activism; and, at the end, a disquisition on how The Workout alone cannot bring true fitness until pollution, job stress, and corporate growth ("concentration means inflation") are stopped, or, alternatively put, until economic democracy reigns. Heretofore, economic democracy (Tom Hayden's term for a kind of grass-roots democratic socialism) was justified on the grounds of equality or social justice. Now The Workout provides an entirely new rationale: it purifies the pores. And who knows? Given the phenomenal success of this book and the current fitness craze, it could be that Mrs. Hayden has finally found the basis for an authentic American socialism: body worship.

But Jane could use a better scriptwriter. The three-part coda reads like left-over background research from her recent movies. One chapter is devoted to the villainy of food moguls (c.f., *The Electric Horseman*), another to the arrogance of industrial polluters *(The China Syndrome)*, and the third to the stress-inducing perils of office work *(Nine to Five)*. The agitprop homilies suffer in translation from the screen. They turn a book with otherwise excellent chapters on "Beginner's Abdominals" and "Advanced Buttocks" into a Big Mac of trendy Hollywood politics, stuffed with every radical cliché of the last fifteen years. *Hayden Meets Holism* would have been a better title. Those who missed out on limited editions of *Pumping Iron with Engels* or *In Sneakers: Michael Harrington Speaks* will appreciate this book. It manages the acrobatic feat of linking every woolly trend imaginable: acupuncture, "natural" medicine, anti-corporatism, chiropractic, nutrition, a new feminism ("our right to physical as well as economic, political and social equality"), cancer phobia, economic democracy, lean thighs, community control, and an aversion to sugar. The only thing missing is a call for nuclear disarmament. Not to worry. The Workout came out just before that wave crested. Look for it in the revised edition.

The opening slice of whole wheat, "Lessons Learned: A Body Abused," is Jane's story. It is literally her oral history, a chronicle of all the things— foods, drugs, ideas—she has stuffed into herself. Her theme is that since the day she was born she has internalized (her favorite word) things from the outside; her refrain, an ironic twist on Adam's complaint, is that others—usually men—made her eat it.

> Like many young girls, I internalized this message [that women are judged by their looks] and, in an effort to conform to the sought-after female image, I abused my health, starved my body and ingested heaven-knows-what chemical drugs.

She certainly did some weird things. In boarding school she went on eating-vomiting binges, a condition called bulimia, though to Jane's credit she did so long before it became fashionable. Jane's complaint is that her school never taught her not to; it crammed her instead with a "tedious general science course." She later graduated to pep pills and diuretics, and for that she is very sore at doctors. Until she met her "wonderful naturopathic" doctor, "no one had ever explained that there were other ways of losing weight besides starvation diets, Dexadrine, and diuretics." Apparently, it never independently occurred to her to try eating less and exercising more. "Looking back, I realize that to a large extent I was a victim of medical malpractice."

One could almost feel sorry for her were it not for her whiny tone and perpetual claim to the status of victim. And if it weren't for her portrayal of herself as a fearless crusader for the idea of taking responsibility for one's own life. It seems that her every choice was foisted on her by . . . society. Why was she so obsessively worried about her looks, a universal anxiety for which she might at least be a bit grateful since it accounts for the sales of her book? "I was so conditioned to thinking of myself as fat that later, when I was really thin, I could never convince myself that I was thin enough." And how does the now-liberated Fonda explain floating naked through the film *Barbarella?* "I was completely unaware of the extent to which I had internalized the cultural pressures that associated a woman's success with sex. . . . " She must have missed the film.

Is it too impolite to suggest that her current "activist" incarnation is yet another internalization? Does this woman never stop eating? Having ingested the values first of Roger Vadim and now of Tom Hayden, she delivers with mind-numbing seriousness the startling message that one should never take one's values from others and, in particular, that women should never accept sexual stereotypes that make them appendages to men. A curious message for a book that peddles Tom Hayden's ideas wrapped in Jane Fonda's body.

The Workout has turned into more than just a number-one best seller. It has become a fitness industry. There is a Workout record album, a Workout videocassette, and a string of Workout salons. On the whole, it is a remarkable piece of entrepreneurship: the right idea at the right time in the right package. It is a pity that Jane doesn't just take the money and run. We admire people who can turn an idea into a bundle. But to call Fonda a capitalist success story is to embarrass her. For one thing, it then becomes hard to distinguish her from other profit-makers (who play the villain in her political fables). For another, having gone holistic, she feels compelled to demonstrate that everything she does is interrelated and in the service of the highest ideals. She goes to great lengths to plead that her interest in fitness is but another expression of her humanistic politics. That is what lifts The Workout from the level of just another best seller (like *Garfield Gains Weight)*, or profits-from-vanity industry (like Estée Lauder's) to the level of historical artifact. Where else can one find a straight-faced attempt to give fitness an ideology, to tie exercise to progressive politics?

> I do not claim that a strong, healthy woman is automatically going to be a progressive, decent sort of person. Obviously, other factors are involved in that. But I am sure that one's innate intelligence and instinct for good can be enhanced through fitness.

One would ordinarily pass over this nugget as just another sign of Fonda's loopy thinking, if it didn't point up a singular irony of holistic Haydenism. Body worship is traditionally the province of the political right. This is not the first time we have had a fitness craze. In *The Healthy Body and Victorian Culture* (Harvard University Press), Bruce Haley describes a similar "national mania" for athletics and fitness that engulfed Britain in the second half of the last century and coincided with the birth of social Darwinism and the rise of British jingoism. In our century, Fascism took the idea of physical purity, yoked it to racist fantasies, and pressed them both into the service of fanatic nationalism. On the face of it, the new notion that fitness makes for goodness is as absurd as the old one that fitness justifies survival. If I follow Fonda's defense of the new dispensation, and it isn't always easy, it seems that physical self-development is necessary for women to liberate themselves from (you guessed it) internalized sexual stereotypes and become (right again!) whole persons. But surely any sentient observer can see that the fitness craze has little to do with gender and much to do with class. Exercise is the new middle-class hobby—working people get their exercise on the job—supplanting meditation and sex, the principal diversions of the 1970s. My theory is that meditation and sex are simply not narcissistic enough for the 1980s. Meditation is solipsistic, to be sure, but it is directed toward some higher consciousness and thus contains some element of relatedness. And sex ordinarily requires at least two people. Exercise, on the other hand, is uniquely self-absorbing and asocial. None of this, of course, is to argue against deep knee-bends. Exercise doesn't need social justification. It is fun, it makes your heart race, and it even may help you live longer. To pretend that it is more than that is to travel beyond silliness into cynicism.

In *The Road to Wigan Pier* George Orwell noted dourly,

the horrible—the really disquieting—prevalence of cranks wherever Socialists are gathered together. One sometimes gets the impression that the mere words 'Socialism' and 'Communism,' draw towards them with magnetic force every fruit-juice drinker, nudist, sandal-wearer, sex-maniac, Quaker, 'Natural Cure' quack, pacifist, and feminist in England.

He took pains to make clear that he was "arguing *for* socialism, not *against* it." But he added, "as with the Christian religion, the worst advertisement for Socialism is its adherents."

Economic democrats, beware Adidas socialism.

MEANING

1. Can you summarize Krauthammer's chief objection to Fonda's book? What does he say is the hidden purpose of the book?
2. Why does Krauthammer insist that the fitness craze is an issue of social class?
3. Why does the author suspect the linking of physical fitness and political ideology?
4. Is the target of Krauthammer's criticism just Fonda's book, or is it larger than that?

METHOD

1. Krauthammer takes a close look at the book itself, but he also considers factors outside it. What are some of these? What two principal ones does he consider? How do these externals affect the author's argument?
2. How would you describe Krauthammer's tone and attitude in this essay? Are his remarks about Fonda as a person a valid part of his criticism of her book? Why or why not?
3. Does the author present a political ideology of his own in this review?

AUDIENCE

1. Krauthammer's essay appeared in a liberal political journal, *The New Republic*, whose readers are likely to share similar attitudes. What clues does the author provide that he's writing for a sympathetic audience? How would Fonda, or someone in her political camp, be likely to react to this review?
2. To what extent do you agree with the author's assertion that exercise is "the new middle-class hobby," or that it is "uniquely self-absorbing and asocial"? What does Krauthammer imply in these remarks?
3. Has fitness become a political or social value? Is the world being divided into two groups, the fit and the unfit?

WRITING SUGGESTIONS

1. Review a current movie or TV show from a religious or political perspective. Some sample topics: Materialism on "Dallas" or "Dynasty," religious themes in "E.T." or "Close Encounters."
2. If you're familiar with *Jane Fonda's Workout Book* and disagree with Krauthammer, write a counterreview, but be sure to address his claims about the book's political ideology.

ADDITIONAL WRITING SUGGESTIONS

1. Find a number of reviews of a movie or program you like, or dislike, much. Choose the review you agree with least, and write your own to counter its major points.
2. Write a critical argument about a public figure from show business, government, sports, education, the law, and so on whose fame or notoriety focuses or embodies social issues about which you are concerned.
3. Write a critical review of any of the following for an audience of your fellow students:
   - Novel or short story
   - Movie
   - Music video
   - Record album
   - Computer software
   - Restaurant or pub
   - Museum
   - Theatrical performance
   - Musical performance
   - New building

4. Write a critical essay, for a general audience, on one of these social or cultural issues:
   - Changing forms of popular culture
   - Changing family and social lifestyles
   - Alcoholism among young people
   - The role of mass media in everyday life
   - The place of religion in public education
   - The problem of child abuse
   - Lingering racial bigotry
   - Individualism and social responsibility

13

PERSUASION

HOW PERSUASION DIFFERS FROM ARGUMENT

Think about times you've tried to convince someone—parents, brothers and sisters, friends or loved ones—to do something. Was rational argument your first tactical choice? If so, suppose logic failed. What did you do then? And if you began with an appeal that was not rational argument, what kind was it?

Before we learn to speak, and long before we learn the skills of inductive and deductive reasoning, we acquire any number of effective, if primitive, persuasive techniques: crying, smiling, pointing, grabbing. We learn to convince others by asserting ourselves. As we grow, we develop increasingly sophisticated strategies for getting what we want: making promises or threats, offering gifts, begging, flattering, insulting. Later, as we mature, we learn the socially accepted, conventional forms for using these elemental tactics. We learn what works and what doesn't.

If argument is defined by fairly strict rules about the use of logic and evidence, persuasion is quite the opposite. Broadly speaking, persuasion employs whatever means will best accomplish the desired end, and that makes it a wide open but morally complex undertaking. In persuasive writing, we are not limited by objective tests for rationality—or even, necessarily, a concern for the truth. (Much advertising and political propaganda will attest to this.) Our purpose is to move the audience toward some goal, and the methods we choose will depend on what we think will work, at least within the boundaries of our ethical standards.

We find persuasive writing in many forms and in all walks of life: sermons, speeches, advertisements, love letters, corporate reports, official statements of government, and, of course, religious, military, and political propaganda. In many instances, persuasion and argument will be mixed—logic for our rational, persuasion for our nonrational, sides. Just as argument relies on certain fundamental devices, however, persuasion has its own assortment of techniques:

Connotative language (loaded words). Many words in a language will suggest meanings beyond the objects they name, and our reactions to such "loaded" words may be strongly positive or negative. Words such as love, hate, liberty, brotherhood, life, death, and so on call up feelings and memories—a whole range of thoughts and emotions. We respond to them with our hearts and stomachs as much as with our minds. Because of this, they are potentially powerful tools of manipulation: "Make our restaurant your *home* away from home." "You'll *love* our new line of lipsticks." "We must *defend* the *cause* of *justice* against the *forces* of *evil* and *death!*"

Figurative language (metaphor, simile, analogy).   As we've already seen, figurative language can help to explain complex or difficult subjects. Because it is suggestive and expressive, however, it can also serve to convince us. In fact, the very qualities of metaphor, simile, and analogy that make them *argumentative fallacies* (see Chapter 11) make them potentially strong *nonrational* devices. Although we can't prove that two dissimilar things are actually alike, the mere assertion of similarity can produce an effect almost as strong as proof: "My opponent has shown himself to be a *snake*—*slithering* between the issues, *silently advancing* on its *prey*, the *innocent* voters of this district!" "Try our new toilet tissue—it's *soft* as a *summer's day.*" "The Pentagon bureaucracy is *like a man with a lobotomy:* it acts without awareness of its actions, *mindlessly.*"

Description and narration.   Few things are more persuasive than direct, concrete language that evokes experience. Connotative and figurative language can do that, but so can literal description and narration, for either positive or negative effect. Opponents of war, for instance, may use horrifying images or stories to convince us, while proponents may dwell on descriptions of the homeland and tales of valor in its defense. Description and narration, because they depend on the writer's selection of detail and language, can be easily *slanted* to emphasize the desirable and omit the rest.

Tone, mood, and style.   Just as in the persuasive strategies we use when speaking or holding a conversation, the attitude we adopt—the way we present ourselves—will affect our audience's response. The tone of a persuasive piece may be *friendly,* even intimate, as though writer and audience have already reached some agreement; it may be *authoritative,* conveying a sense of unquestioned expertise; it might be *sarcastic,* mocking or ridiculing a person, place, or idea; it might be *sentimental,* highly charged with nostalgic or romantic emotions. Certain tones of voice seem to have become standardized, almost automatic or unconscious, such as the sound of promotional writing—advertising and public relations—which must be uniformly *happy, confident, optimistic,* and *upbeat.* The mood of persuasive prose, likewise, can range from this *sweetness-and-light* spirit of sales talk to the *dark, melodramatic, menacing* language of totalitarian propaganda. The style the writer uses to convey tone and mood may range from the *simple* and *plain-spoken* to the *pretentious, pompous,* and *bombastic.*

Since persuasion can be used for good or for ill, then, let's look at the two most common bases from which persuasive appeals are built: emotions and ethics.

APPEALS BASED ON EMOTIONS

In February 1950, when Senator Joseph R. McCarthy announced to the public that the United States State Department had been infiltrated by over 200 "card-carrying Communists," he was helping to kick off a period of accusation and recrimination that later came to bear his name. He was appealing to a widespread fear, and whether the fear of Soviet spies in government could be confirmed by evidence was beside the point. McCarthy's campaign to thrust himself into the limelight succeeded wonderfully despite his lack of proof. Mere assertion of the threat, expressed in appropriately lurid and sensational language, was enough to give the Senator power to hold the attention of the media for months and to wreck or damage scores of lives. Though McCarthy's charges were groundless, they were undeniably persuasive.

Thirteen years later, when Martin Luther King, Jr., led his Freedom March to the Lincoln Memorial in Washington, D.C. and told the world, "I have a dream," he was appealing to a widespread hope. King's speech expressed that hope, but it also aimed to convince those who did not support civil rights for blacks that the time had finally come for full equality of the races. His words are charged with religious and patriotic fervor, and they reach an emotional crescendo as he builds to a resounding assertion of the destiny of all peoples to be free.

Both King and McCarthy, though they are as far apart in style and substance as two men can be, base their persuasive appeal on *emotion*—in McCarthy's case, fear, paranoia, and hate; in King's, hope, courage, and love. They persuade by making their audience *feel* something strongly, by giving them an emotional experience.

Because the range of human emotion is so wide, it provides the broadest base for persuasive writing. Here, for example, are just a few of the emotions familiar to us: *desire, pride, jealousy, anger, joy, greed, satisfaction, tenderness, dread, sympathy, sadness, elation, zeal, passion, inspiration, grief, shame, worry, envy, longing,* and *contentment.* Because human emotions do run deep, however, as these words clearly show, they must be handled with care—as should anything volatile. The emotional response of the audience may be unpredictable, and a carelessly worded appeal may backfire. Joseph McCarthy's hysterical harping, for example, eventually became too much for people to bear, while Martin Luther King's powerful but tightly controlled rhetoric helped earn him a place as one of history's masterful orators.

When basing a persuasive appeal on emotions, then, it pays to be aware of some general guidelines. Remember, in persuasion your goal is not necessarily to "beat" the opposing side, but to bring it over to yours.

Consider the audience.   As always, gauging likely audience reaction is your starting point. Do you share any common ground, something you could build upon? Does the audience hold a strong opinion that isn't likely to be swayed? If so, where is this view most vulnerable to doubt or second thoughts? What emotional assumptions does your reader or listener go by? That is, what is likely to provoke a favorable response, without question? What are the audience's sympathies and biases?

Avoid excessive language.   In most cases, gross exaggeration, misrepresentation, preposterous claims, or a panic-stricken tone won't work except for the most gullible audience. People, these days, are fairly sensitive to hype, so surrounded are we by it. The great persuaders, from Jesus to Gandhi, didn't use language as a blunt instrument; rather, they spoke and wrote with subtlety, often with irony and understatement.

Don't talk down.   Give your audience some credit. The one tone or attitude people seem to resent most, and thus are likely to respond to least favorably, is condescension (although this fact has failed to register with many of those who write and produce television commercials). Successful persuasion addresses the audience respectfully and allows it to bring its own subjectivity to the meeting of opposing sides.

Use the power of suggestion.   All persuasion is suggestive in that it warns us what will happen if we don't act, or shows us the benefits we'll receive if we do. (Notice, for example, how the promise of increased sexual allure has come to dominate almost all forms of advertising.) In fact, persuasion may work best by offering us attractive possibilities that our imagination can't resist.

APPEALS BASED ON ETHICS

While an emotional appeal speaks to feelings that may or may not be morally justifiable (certain emotions, such as hate, envy, greed, and so on, are usually considered *im*moral), a persuasive appeal to *ethics*, on the other hand, does depend on our sense of right and wrong. Ethical appeals address the audience's moral principles or values, those things we believe "ought" to guide our conduct and that of others.

The ethical base for persuasion can be the writer's own moral rectitude and reputation (Gandhi's success, for example, was due in large part to his unimpeachable character), or it can be the moral values of the audience. More often than not, however, the ethics of both speaker and listener are brought into play, as in the preacher's sermon to the congregation. The speaker presents him- or herself as morally conscientious and thus to be believed, and seeks to arouse the listener to moral awareness and action.

In this sense, the appeal based on ethics may include the support of deductive argument. Those closely held values and beliefs about right and wrong are, in a way, moral *assumptions* or *premises:* "Murder is always wrong." "Murder is justified in self-defense." "Marriage partners should be faithful to each other; to do otherwise is immoral." "A parent has a right to strike his or her child." "Physical violence against anyone, especially one's own children, is never right." When we speak to these beliefs, it is usually in the context of some specific issue or problem, and we apply our moral principles to it. For instance, the ethical appeal against capital punishment might go as follows:

> *Moral principle:* Murder is always wrong.
> *Specific issue:* Capital punishment is murder.
> *Conclusion:* Capital punishment is always wrong.

Thus, although the substance of the appeal is ethical, it takes the form of a syllogism (if you accept the truth of both premises). What keeps this appeal ethically based is the minor premise: Capital punishment is murder. This statement is itself a kind of moral assumption about the definition of capital punishment, with which not all would agree.

The list of guidelines for emotional appeal can be modified slightly for persuasion based on ethics:

Audience.   What are your readers' moral assumptions? Do you share them? Which ethical principles would you, or your audience, *never* abandon, and which are open to discussion?

Language.   Moral or ethical discourse ranges from the simple and earnest language of everyday life to the hellfire-and-brimstone imagery still heard from many pulpits. Chances are your audience will prefer the former, unless, of course, they are in the mood for a revival.

Attitude.   As above, avoid haranguing your audience with morally pretentious or self-important pronouncements. Although you do present an ethical standard, you want to *narrow* the distance between yourself and the reader, not increase it. Appeal to your audience's better side without denouncing its real or implied weaknesses.

Suggestion.   As in emotional appeal, ethical persuasion guides us toward a desired end but doesn't lead us by the nose. The effective speaker from a moral platform makes the path of virtue seem irresistible, but leaves the first step to us.

PERSUASION, CONFLICT, AND PROPAGANDA

As subjects of persuasion—the audience at whom it's directed—we are the prize in the battle for hearts and minds. As we persuade others, so will others try to persuade us.

In a world of powers and interests, and of conflict between them, persuasion becomes more than a method for convincing individuals to do or think one thing or another. It becomes a tool for the manipulation and control of large numbers of people, sometimes whole societies, as in the real world of Hitler's Germany, and the imaginary one of Orwell's *1984*.

Persuasion of this sort does not try to bridge the gap between sides. Instead, it accepts the "us versus them" description of the world and seeks to perpetuate it. It fosters tribalism and a fear of groups other than one's own. It also elevates persuasive rhetoric to the realm of absolute truth; its claims and appeals become *facts*, standards of eternal value to be defended against attacking enemies.

Such in-group–out-group propaganda, regrettably, is not limited to fascist, totalitarian regimes. Free societies use it, too, perhaps a bit more subtly, perhaps not. (The anti-Japanese propaganda in United States War Department-sponsored Hollywood movies during World War II, for instance, now seems embarrassingly blatant.) Can we even know the difference between "propaganda" and "truth"? After all, one person's "totalitarian regime" is another's "socialist republic"; one's "right-wing extremism" is another's "conservative political philosophy"; one's "capitalist economic system" is another's "organized plundering of the world's resources."

There may be no answer to our question. For most of us, our ability to persuade is a function of our depth of belief. What we believe to be true is, for us at least, not propaganda. What the other guy says, however, may very well be, even if he claims to believe it himself.

QUESTIONS

1. How is persuasive writing different from argument?
2. What are some basic techniques of persuasive writing? Give at least one example of each.
3. What are some common emotions to which persuasive writing appeals?
4. How can we persuade through an appeal based on ethics?
5. What are some basic guidelines for writing persuasion?

EXERCISES

1.   Find some examples of persuasive writing or speech in sources readily at hand. Evaluate their use of connotative and figurative language, slanted description or narration, and use of tone, mood, and style. Some types of persuasive writing you might look for: print and electronic advertising, speeches (as published in *Vital Speeches* or major newspapers such as *The New York Times)*, the remarks of political figures or candidates for office as quoted in news stories, the quoted remarks of "official spokespersons" for business and government, and the leaflets or other materials of private organizations seeking recruits. To what extent is the language in these examples loaded with words that produce strong positive or negative reactions? Does the writer or speaker use certain figures of speech (metaphor, analogy) to help persuade you? Does the writer use description or narration to produce particular effects? Does the tone, mood, or style of the writing play an important part in its impact? Finally, is the piece appealing to emotions, ethics, or some combination of the two?

2.   Think back over your past and try to remember those times when you read or saw something that had a strong persuasive effect on you. What was it about the book, movie, speech, or advertisement that caused the effect? What did it change about you? Your feelings? Opinions? Behavior? How long-lasting was the change? If the change was fleeting, why do you think it was so? If it stayed with you, why did it? Have you ever been so dramatically affected by persuasion that you became almost literally "a different person"? (Along these same lines, have you ever had a strongly persuasive influence on another person or group? How did you bring about this change?)

3.   Think of some instances from everyday experience in which you use persuasive tactics. Are you aware when you attempt to persuade others, or do you do so instinctively? Are you aware when others attempt to persuade you?

Readings

Born in 1929 and assassinated on April 4, 1968, MARTIN LUTHER KING, JR., was one of the United States' most admired and influential civil-rights leaders of our time. A native of Atlanta, Georgia, King was the son of a Baptist minister and went on to follow in his father's footsteps. He was educated at Morehouse College, Crozer Theological Seminary, Boston University, and Chicago Theological Seminary, and earned doctorates at both Boston and Chicago. He was ordained at his father's church in 1947 and was pastor of the Dexter Avenue Baptist Church, Montgomery, Alabama, from 1954 to 1960. He founded the Southern Christian Leadership Conference (SCLC) in 1957, and served as its director until his death. King was co-pastor, with his father, of Ebenezer Baptist Church in Atlanta from 1960. In the mid-1950s, King led bus boycotts, sit-ins, and marches to protest segregation, spearheading the civil-rights movement that was eventually to sweep the country and result in the landmark legislation of the 1964 Civil Rights Act and the Voting Rights Act of 1965. For his work, King was awarded the Nobel Peace Prize in 1964. In the following historic address, delivered in August of 1963 at the end of his march to commemorate the 100th anniversary of Lincoln's Emancipation Proclamation, King makes a moving plea to the nation to end racial injustice once and for all.

I Have a Dream

by *Martin Luther King, Jr.*

Five score years ago, a great American, in whose symbolic shadow we stand today, signed the Emancipation Proclamation. This momentous decree came as a great beacon of light of hope to millions of Negro slaves who had been seared in the flames of withering injustice. It came as a joyous daybreak to end the long night of their captivity.

But one hundred years later, the Negro still is not free. One hundred years later, the life of the Negro is still sadly crippled by the manacles of segregation and the chains of discrimination.

One hundred years later, the Negro lives on a lonely island of poverty in the midst of a vast ocean of material prosperity. One hundred years later, the Negro is still languished in the corners of American society and finds himself an exile in his own land. So we have come here today to dramatize a shameful condition.

In a sense we have come to our nation's capital to cash a check. When the architects of our republic wrote the magnificent words of the Constitution and the Declaration of Independence, they were signing a promissory note to which every American was to fall heir. This note was a promise that all men, yes, black men as well as white men, would be granted the unalienable rights of life, liberty, and the pursuit of happiness.

It is obvious today that America has defaulted on this promissory note insofar as her citizens of color are concerned. Instead of honoring this sacred obligation, America has given the Negro people a bad check; which has come back marked "insufficient funds."

But we refuse to believe that the bank of justice is bankrupt. We refuse to believe that there arc insufficient funds in the great vaults of opportunity of this nation. So we have come to cash this check—a check that will give us upon demand the riches of freedom and the security of justice.

We have also come to this hallowed spot to remind America of the fierce urgency of now. This is no time to engage in the luxury of cooling off or to take the tranquilizing drug of gradualism. Now is the time to make real the promises of democracy. Now is the time to rise from the dark and desolate valley of segregation to the sunlit path of racial justice. Now is the time to lift our nation from the quick sands of racial injustice to the solid rock of brotherhood. Now is the time to make justice a reality for all of God's children.

It would be fatal for the nation to overlook the urgency of the movement and to underestimate the determination of the Negro. This sweltering summer of the Negro's legitimate discontent will not pass until there is an invigorating autumn of freedom and equality. 1963 is not an end but a beginning. Those who hope that the Negro needed to blow off steam and will now be content will have a rude awakening if the nation returns to business as usual.

There will be neither rest nor tranquility in America until the Negro is granted his citizenship rights. The whirlwinds of revolt will continue to shake the foundations of our nation until the bright day of justice emerges.

But there is something that I must say to my people who stand on the warm threshold which leads into the palace of justice. In the process of gaining our rightful place we must not be guilty of wrongful deeds.

Let us not seek to satisfy our thirst for freedom by drinking from the cup of bitterness and hatred. We must forever conduct our struggle on the high plane of dignity and discipline. We must not allow our creative protest to degenerate into physical violence. Again and again we must rise to the majestic heights of meeting physical force with soul force.

The marvelous new militancy which has engulfed the Negro community must not lead us to a distrust of all white people, for many of our white brothers, as evidenced by their presence here today, have come to realize that their destiny is tied up with our destiny and they have come to realize that their freedom is inextricably bound to our freedom. This offense we share mounted to storm the battlements of injustice must be carried forth by a bi-racial army. We cannot walk alone.

And as we walk, we must make the pledge that we shall always march ahead. We cannot turn back. There are those who are asking the devotees of civil rights, "When will you be satisfied?" We can never be satisfied as long as the Negro is the victim of the unspeakable horrors of police brutality.

We can never be satisfied as long as our bodies, heavy with the fatigue of travel, cannot gain lodging in the motels of the highways and the hotels of the cities. We cannot be satisfied as long as the Negro's basic mobility is from a smaller ghetto to a larger one.

We can never be satisfied as long as our children are stripped of their selfhood and robbed of their dignity by signs stating "for whites only." We cannot be satisfied as long as a Negro in Mississippi cannot vote and a Negro in New York believes he has nothing for which to vote. No, we are not satisfied, and we will not be satisfied until justice rolls down like waters and righteousness like a mighty stream.

I am not unmindful that some of you have come here out of excessive trials and tribulation. Some of you have come fresh from narrow jail cells. Some of you have come from areas where your quest for freedom left you battered by the storms of persecution and staggered by the winds of police brutality. You have been the veterans of creative suffering. Continue to work with the faith that unearned suffering is redemptive.

Go back to Mississippi; go back to Alabama; go back to South Carolina; go back to Georgia; go back to Louisiana; go back to the slums and ghettos of the Northern cities, knowing that somehow this situation can, and will be changed. Let us not wallow in the valley of despair.

So I say to you, my friends, that even though we must face the difficulties of today and tomorrow, I still have a dream. It is a dream deeply rooted in the American dream that one day this nation will rise up and live out the true meaning of its creed—we hold these truths to be self evident, that all men are created equal.

I have a dream that one day on the red hills of Georgia, sons of former slaves and sons of former slave-owners will be able to sit down together at the table of brotherhood.

I have a dream that one day, even the state of Mississippi, a state sweltering with the heat of injustice, sweltering with the heat of oppression, will be transformed into an oasis of freedom and justice.

I have a dream my four little children will one day live in a nation where they will not be judged by the color of their skin but by content of their character. I have a dream today!

I have a dream that one day, down in Alabama, with its vicious racists, with its governor having his lips dripping with the words of interposition and nullification, that one day, right there in Alabama, little black boys and black girls will be able to join hands with little white boys and white girls as sisters and brothers. I have a dream today!

I have a dream that one day every valley shall be exalted, every hill and mountain shall be made low, the rough places shall be made plain, and the crooked places shall be made straight and the glory of the Lord will be revealed and all flesh shall see it together.

This is our hope. This is the faith that I go back to the South with.

With this faith we will be able to hew out of the mountain of despair a

302 Writing to Convince

stone of hope. With this faith we will be able to transform the jangling discords of our nation into a beautiful symphony of brotherhood.

With this faith we will be able to work together, to pray together, to struggle together, to go to jail together, to stand up for freedom together, knowing that we will be free one day. This will be the day when all of God's children will be able to sing with new meaning—"my country 'tis of thee; sweet land of liberty; of thee I sing; land where my fathers died, land of the pilgrim's pride; from every mountain side, let freedom ring"—and if America is to be a great nation, this must become true.

So let freedom ring from the prodigious hilltops of New Hampshire.

Let freedom ring from the mighty mountains of New York.

Let freedom ring from the heightening Alleghenies of Pennsylvania.

Let freedom ring from the snow-capped Rockies of Colorado.

Let freedom ring from the curvaceous slopes of California.

But not only that.

Let freedom ring from Stone Mountain of Georgia.

Let freedom ring from Lookout Mountain of Tennessee.

Let freedom ring from every hill and molehill of Mississippi, from every mountainside, let freedom ring.

And when we allow freedom to ring, when we let it ring from every village and hamlet, from every state and city, we will be able to speed up that day when all of God's children—black men and white men, Jews and Gentiles, Catholics and Protestants—will be able to join hands and to sing in the words of the old Negro spiritual. "Free at last, free at last; thank God Almighty, we are free at last."

MEANING

1. What is King's thesis in this speech? Point out specific passages in which his language reveals an emotional or an ethical base.
2. What does King mean that the Constitution and the Declaration of Independence were "a promissory note to which every American was to fall heir"? Why does he choose the metaphor of money?
3. Is there a note of warning or threat in this speech, or merely a statement of fact about the plight of blacks? Defend your answer.
4. Why does King identify his dream with "the American Dream"?

METHOD

1. Reread King's address and look for specific examples of loaded words, metaphor, description, and especially tone and mood. Does King's use of all these techniques produce a single effect? How would you describe it?
2. From what sources does King draw his rhetorical style? What echos, in other words, do you hear in these words?

AUDIENCE

1. When King delivered this address, he was speaking to a massive throng of followers. What clues does he give that he wants his audience to include many other people—even the entire nation?
2. Have you seen a film of King delivering "I Have a Dream"? To what extent do his voice and physical presence increase the effectiveness of his words?
3. If you are familiar with the public remarks of other social activists or political or religious leaders, how would you describe their language and style?

WRITING SUGGESTIONS

1. Write a speech in which you address a contemporary issue about which you feel very strongly. Base your appeal primarily on either emotions or ethics, and try your hand at using the persuasive strategies we've discussed.
2. Using King's address as a model, write your own "I Have a Dream," in which you speak about a keenly felt injustice. Describe your vision of a better world—a world you want to persuade your listeners is well within reach.

Founded in 1925 by Harold Ross, a native of Aspen, Colorado, The New Yorker *magazine soon became a showcase for many of the world's best writers of fiction, poetry, humor, and nonfiction. In the latter category, the magazine has published some of the most influential journalism of our day, and it continues to be a leader in its coverage of current affairs. In addition,* The New Yorker, *especially in its "Talk of the Town" section, details local concerns, and in its "Notes and Comment," a lead essay or editorial, it frequently addresses matters of morals, politics, and other issues. In the following anonymous essay, the author probes the dilemma of the alms-giver, and the proper moral response to a panhandler.*

How Much Is Enough?

A friend writes: If an insane man showed you fifteen people he was about to execute, and told you he'd free ten if you would shoot the remaining five, what would you do? If your wife was dying, and the only way to save her was to break into a pharmacy and steal medicine you couldn't afford to buy, would you? Psychologists use questions like these to confront their subjects with "moral dilemmas;" sometimes the questions are bandied about at dinner tables where the conversation has turned from foreign films. Dilemmas they assuredly are, but oddly comforting ones, for they banish problems of values and ethics to the realm of the unlikely. Even on the West Side I.R.T., the chances are you won't meet a lunatic with fifteen hostages.

But—these days—you will almost certainly come across poor people cadging change. One raggedy man works the northbound No. 2 train every morning. Down the aisle he stumbles, shoving his Dixie Cup under every nose. At Times Square, a filthy, vacant-looking man asks people for a nickel as they climb the stairs to Forty-second Street. In the lee of a doorway at Town Hall, an old fellow in a knitted cap, with a paper sack containing an empty bottle by his feet, addresses passersby with the plea "Help me out." All over this city, people beg, and an inadvertent by-product of their hunger and thirst is the daily imposition of actual moral choices on the begged-from—choices that they can't avoid even by looking far off down the avenue and pretending not to hear, for that, of course, is a choice.

Faced with an outstretched palm, I usually dig a fist into my pocket to search for change and at the same time keep walking at a brisk midtown pace. The ambivalence is mighty. If a dime is lying loose in my pocket and if the tide has not carried me out of range, then perhaps. Otherwise, I wander on, a little angry with myself, offering a few salves to my conscience. "He'd only spend it on booze." Well, of course. The wind is cold, he has no place to spend the night, and half his life has already been drunk away. What else could he buy that would so powerfully take the edge off his misery? "I don't have any change." But I do have a dollar. Men were asking for dimes during the *Depression*, when dinner was a quarter.

No one likes giving alms, or almost no one. Even St. Francis of Assisi, who eventually learned to like *asking* for handouts, balked in his early days when he was confronted with beggars. A biographer records that one old woman used to approach him each day: "And it happened that in the newly converted young soul there rose a repugnance and a resistance—a repugnance to the dirt and misery of the old woman, a resistance to her troublesome ways and to her persistency." That same revulsion against liquor-soaked, foul-smelling, stubborn people explains some of the pain that panhandlers cause the panhandled. But there is also the bother that comes with accountability. For people of good conscience—not those who like to believe, and explain, that derelicts are derelicts because they are lazy, or those who snarl at elderly winos that they should get jobs—the confrontation with a beggar is distressing and annoying because it presents in the unshaven, unwashed flesh a problem more comfortably dealt with when it appears on the evening news. I can handle problems that are capitalized, like Nuclear Peril, or Racism, or Poverty; that is to say, I know the proper and accepted responses that a person of good conscience is expected to make to those quandaries. But when a bum sticks out his hand it is no longer Poverty, or, for that matter, poverty. It is a poor person, and telling him my truths—"Income should be better distributed," "Reagan is unfair"—won't even enlighten him; he drinks in those facts with every swig of Olde English "800." Worse, the perennially comforting notion that nothing much can be done—at least, not by one person—which may very well be true when one is talking about Poverty, means little when one is dealing with a poor person. He lacks money to buy dinner and a drink; I have enough cash in my wallet to stand him to a dozen dinners and a case of muscatel. If I give him some of my money, his problem will disappear for a night, which is quite a long time.

But when I do kick in, it doesn't ease my mind much. Giving anything implies acceptance of the notion that I can be of some help, at which point the limits of that help, short of my reducing myself to real poverty, become impossible to set. People who can't see that misery exists all around them and people who believe misery to be absolutely intractable can't be faulted for doing nothing to alleviate it. But sometimes I give quarters to strange men. What excuse do I have for not giving them more?

MEANING

1. What is the persuasive aim of this essay? Is it stated directly? Is it clear?
2. What are the "actual moral choices" panhandlers present? Has the author resolved the moral dilemma he or she addresses?
3. What is the basis of the author's appeal? Does it matter that he or she is anonymous? Is the appeal stronger or weaker for it?
4. What reaction does the author wish to provoke in the reader?

METHOD

1. Does this writer employ any obvious persuasive techniques? Which ones? Does the author use any of the techniques of argument?
2. How would you characterize the tone of this piece? (Think carefully about this—the tone here may be more complicated than it first seems.)
3. Do the writer's graphic descriptions of panhandlers work at cross-purposes with his or her persuasive point?

AUDIENCE

1. To whom is the writer speaking? Is it the "people who can't see that misery exists all around them and people who believe misery to be absolutely intractable"?

2.   Are you more likely to give money "to strange men" after having read this essay? Does the piece persuade you to be more accepting of pan-handlers or concerned about the poverty-stricken or homeless?

WRITING SUGGESTION

Write an extended "letter to the editor" in which you take an *indirect* approach to persuasion. You might choose a topic about which you feel ambivalent or split. What is the struggle with which the issue confronts you? Is it one your audience is likely to share? Can you speak to both sides of the problem and still indicate a desirable or ideal course of action?

Born in 1934, WENDELL BERRY is a farmer, teacher, poet, novelist, essayist, and defender of land and the values of responsible agriculture. He was educated at the University of Kentucky, where he received his B.A. and M.A. degrees. Among Berry's books: A Place on Earth *(novel; 1967, revised 1983);* Farming: A Handbook *(1970);* A Continuous Harmony: Essays Cultural and Agricultural *(1972);* The Country of Marriage *(1973);* The Unsettling of America: Culture and Agriculture *(1977); and* The Gift of Good Land: Further Essays Cultural and Agricultural *(1981). Berry taught at the University of Kentucky from 1964 to 1977, when he left his post to write and farm full-time. He has been a contributor to magazines such as* Nation, Prairie Schooner, *and others. In the following essay, the opening chapter of* The Unsettling of America, *Berry sets forth his strong position that traditional agricul-tural practices are not only wasteful and destructive of land, but express a more pro-found, far-reaching problem at the heart of our cultural values.*

The Unsettling of America

by *Wendell Berry*

So many goodly citties ransacked and razed; so many nations destroyed and made desolate; so infinite millions of harmelesse people of all sexes, states and ages, massacred, ravaged and put to the sword; and the richest, the fairest and the best part of the world topsiturvied, ruined and defaced for the traffick of Pearles and Pepper: Oh mechanicall victories, oh base conquest.

Montaigne

One of the peculiarities of the white race's presence in America is how little intention has been applied to it. As a people, wherever we have been, we have never really intended to be. The continent is said to have been discovered by an Italian who was on his way to India. The earliest explorers were looking for gold, which was, after an early streak of luck in Mexico, always somewhere farther on. Conquests and foundings were incidental to this search—which did not, and could not, end until the continent was finally laid open in an orgy of goldseeking in the middle of the last century. Once the unknown of geography was mapped, the industrial marketplace became the new frontier, and we continued, with largely the same motives and with increasing haste and anxiety, to displace ourselves—no longer with unity of direction, like a migrant flock, but like the refugees from a broken ant hill. In our own time we have invaded foreign lands and the moon with the high-toned patriotism of the conquistadors, and with the same mixture of fantasy and avarice.

That is too simply put. It is substantially true, however, as a description of the dominant tendency in American history. The temptation, once that has been said, is to ascend altogether into rhetoric and inveigh equally against all our forebears and all present holders of office. To be just, however, it is necessary to remember that there has been another tendency: the tendency to stay put, to say, "No farther. This is the place." So far, this has been the weaker tendency, less glamorous, certainly less successful. It is also the older of these tendencies, having been the dominant one among the Indians.

The Indians did, of course, experience movements of population, but in general their relation to place was based upon old usage and association, upon inherited memory, tradition, veneration. The land was their homeland. The first and greatest American revolution, which has never been superseded, was the coming of people who did *not* look upon the land as a homeland. But there were always those among the newcomers who saw that they had come to a good place and who saw its domestic possibilities. Very early, for instance, there were men who wished to establish agricultural settlements rather than quest for gold or exploit the Indian trade. Later, we know that every advance of the frontier left behind families and communities who intended to remain and prosper where they were.

But we know also that these intentions have been almost systematically overthrown. Generation after generation, those who intended to remain and prosper where they were have been dispossessed and driven out, or subverted and exploited where they were, by those who were carrying out some version of the search for El Dorado. Time after time, in place after place, these conquerors have fragmented and demolished traditional communities, the beginnings of domestic cultures. They have always said that what they destroyed was outdated, provincial, and contemptible. And with alarming frequency they have been believed and trusted by their victims, especially when their victims were other white people.

If there is any law that has been consistently operative in American history, it is that the members of any *established* people or group or community sooner or later become "redskins"—that is, they become the designated victims of an utterly ruthless, officially sanctioned and subsidized exploitation. The colonists who drove off the Indians came to be intolerably exploited by their imperial governments. And that alien imperialism was thrown off only to be succeeded by a domestic version of the same thing; the class of independent small farmers who fought the war of independence has been exploited by, and recruited into, the industrial society until by now it is almost extinct. Today, the most numerous heirs of the farmers of Lexington and Concord are the little groups scattered all over the country whose names begin with "Save": Save Our Land, Save the Valley, Save Our Mountains, Save Our Streams, Save Our Farmland. As so often before, these are *designated* victims—people without official sanction, often without official friends, who are struggling to preserve their places, their values, and their lives as they know them and prefer to live them against the agencies of their own government which are using their own tax moneys against them.

The only escape from this destiny of victimization has been to "succeed"—that is, to "make it" into the class of exploiters, and then to remain so specialized and so "mobile" as to be unconscious of the effects of one's life or livelihood. This escape is, of course, illusory, for one man's producer is another's consumer, and even the richest and most mobile will soon find it hard to escape the noxious effluents and fumes of their various public services.

Let me emphasize that I am not talking about an evil that is merely contemporary or "modern," but one that is as old in America as the white man's presence here. It is an intention that was *organized* here almost from the start. "The New World," Bernard DeVoto wrote in *The Course of Empire*, "was a constantly expanding market . . . . Its value in gold was enormous but it had still greater value in that it expanded and integrated the industrial systems of Europe."

And he continues: "The first belt-knife given by a European to an Indian was a portent as great as the cloud that mushroomed over Hiroshima . . . . Instantly the man of 6000 B.C. was bound fast to a way of life that had developed seven and a half millennia beyond his own. He began to live better and he began to die."

The principal European trade goods were tools, cloth, weapons, ornaments, novelties, and alcohol. The sudden availability of these things produced a revolution that "affected every aspect of Indian life. The struggle for existence . . . became easier. Immemorial handicrafts grew obsolescent, then obsolete. Methods of hunting were transformed. So were methods—and the purposes—of war. As war became deadlier in purpose and armament a surplus of women developed, so that marriage customs changed and polygamy became common. The increased usefulness of women in the preparation of pelts worked to the same end . . . . Standards of wealth, prestige, and honor changed. The Indians acquired commercial values and developed business cults. They became more mobile . . . .

"In the sum it was cataclysmic. A culture was forced to change much faster than change could be adjusted to. All corruptions of culture produce breakdowns of morale, of communal integrity, and of personality, and this force was as strong as any other in the white man's subjugation of the red man."

I have quoted these sentences from DeVoto because, the obvious differences aside, he is so clearly describing a revolution that did not stop with the subjugation of the Indians, but went on to impose substantially the same catastrophe upon the small farms and the farm communities, upon the shops of small local tradesmen of all sorts, upon the workshops of independent craftsmen, and upon the households of citizens. It is a revolution that is still going on. The economy is still substantially that of the fur trade, still based on the same general kinds of commercial items: technology, weapons, ornaments, novelties, and drugs. The one great difference is that by now the revolution has deprived the mass of consumers of any independent access to the staples of life: clothing, shelter, food, even water. Air remains the only necessity that the average user can still get for himself, and the revolution has imposed a heavy tax on that by way of pollution. Commercial conquest is far more thorough and final than military defeat. The Indian became a redskin, not by loss in battle, but by accepting a dependence on traders that made *necessities* of industrial goods. This is not merely history. It is a parable.

DeVoto makes it clear that the imperial powers, having made themselves willing to impose this exploitive industrial economy upon the Indians, could not then keep it from contaminating their own best intentions: "More than four-fifths of the wealth of New France was furs, the rest was fish, and it had no agricultural wealth. One trouble was that whereas the crown's imperial policy required it to develop the country's agriculture, the crown's economy required the colony's furs, an adverse interest." And La Salle's dream of developing Louisiana (agriculturally and otherwise) was frustrated because "The interest of the court in Louisiana colonization was to secure a bridgehead for an attack on the silver mines of northern Mexico . . . ."

One cannot help but see the similarity between this foreign colonialism and the domestic colonialism that, by policy, converts productive farm, forest, and grazing lands into strip mines. Now, as then, we see the abstract values of an industrial economy preying upon the native productivity of land and people. The fur trade was only the first establishment on this continent of a mentality whose triumph is its catastrophe.

My purposes in beginning with this survey of history are (1) to show how deeply rooted in our past is the mentality of exploitation; (2) to show how fundamentally revolutionary it is; and (3) to show how crucial to our history—hence, to our own minds—is the question of how we will relate to our land. This question, now that the corporate revolution has so determinedly invaded the farmland, returns us to our oldest crisis.

We can understand a great deal of our history—from Cortés' destruction of Tenochtitlán in 1521 to the bulldozer attack on the coalfields four-and-a-half centuries later—by thinking of ourselves as divided into conquerors and victims. In order to understand our own time and predicament and the work that is to be done, we would do well to shift the terms and say that we are divided between exploitation and nurture. The first set of terms is too simple for the purpose because, in any given situation, it proposes to divide people into two mutually exclusive groups; it becomes complicated only when we are dealing with situations in succession—as when a colonist who persecuted the Indians then resisted persecution by the crown. The terms exploitation and nurture, on the other hand, describe a division not only between persons but also within persons. We are all to some extent the products of an exploitive society, and it would be foolish and self-defeating to pretend that we do not bear its stamp.

Let me outline as briefly as I can what seem to me the characteristics of these opposite kinds of mind. I conceive a strip-miner to be a model exploiter, and as a model nurturer I take the old-fashioned idea or ideal of a farmer. The exploiter is a specialist, an expert; the nurturer is not. The standard of the exploiter is efficiency; the standard of the nurturer is care. The exploiter's goal is money, profit; the nurturer's goal is health—his land's health, his own, his family's, his community's, his country's. Whereas the exploiter asks of a piece of land only how much and how quickly it can be made to produce, the nurturer asks a question that is much more complex and difficult: What is its carrying capacity? (That is: How much can be taken from it without diminishing it? What can it produce *dependably* for an indefinite time?) The exploiter wishes to earn as much as possible by as little work as possible; the nurturer expects, certainly, to have a decent living from his work, but his characteristic wish is to work *as well* as possible. The competence of the exploiter is in organization; that of the nurturer is in order—a human order, that is, that accommodates itself both to other order and to mystery. The exploiter typically serves an institution or organization; the nurturer serves land, household, community, place. The exploiter thinks in terms of numbers, quantities, "hard facts"; the nurturer in terms of character, condition, quality, kind.

It seems likely that all the "movements" of recent years have been representing various claims that nurture has to make against exploitation. The women's movement, for example, when its energies are most accurately placed, is arguing the cause of nurture; other times it is arguing the right of women to be exploiters—which men have no *right* to be. The exploiter is clearly the prototype of the "masculine" man—the wheeler-dealer whose "practical" goals require the sacrifice of flesh, feeling, and principle. The nurturer, on the other hand, has always passed with ease across the boundaries of the so-called sexual roles. Of necessity and without apology, the preserver of seed, the planter, becomes midwife and nurse. Breeder is always metamorphosing into brooder and back again. Over and over again, spring after spring, the questing mind, idealist and visionary, must pass through the planting to become nurturer of the real. The farmer, sometimes known as husbandman, is by definition half mother; the only question is how good a mother he or she is. And the land itself is not mother or father only, but both. Depending on crop and season, it is at one time receiver of seed, bearer and nurturer of young; at another, raiser of seed-stalk, bearer and shedder of seed. And in response to these changes, the farmer crosses back and forth from one zone of spousehood to another, first as planter and then as gatherer. Farmer and land are thus involved in a sort of dance in which the partners are always at opposite sexual poles, and the lead keeps changing: the farmer, as seed-bearer, causes growth; the land, as seed-bearer, causes the harvest.

The exploitive always involves the abuse or the perversion of nurture and ultimately its destruction. Thus, we saw how far the exploitive revolution had penetrated the official character when our recent secretary of agriculture remarked that "Food is a weapon." This was given a fearful symmetry indeed when, in discussing the possible use of nuclear weapons, a secretary of defense spoke of "palatable" levels of devastation. Consider the associations that have since ancient times clustered around the idea of food—associations of mutual care, generosity, neighborliness, festivity, communal joy, religious ceremony—and you will see that these two secretaries represent a cultural catastrophe. The concerns of farming and those of war, once thought to be diametrically opposed, have become identical. Here we have an example of men who have been made vicious, not presumably by nature or circumstance, but by their *values*.

Food is *not* a weapon. To use it as such—to foster a mentality willing to use it as such—is to prepare, in the human character and community, the destruction of the sources of food. The first casualties of the exploitive revolution are character and community. When those fundamental integrities are devalued and broken, then perhaps it is inevitable that food will be looked upon as a weapon, just as it is inevitable that the earth will be looked upon as fuel and people as numbers or machines. But character and community—that is, culture in the broadest, richest sense—constitute, just as much as nature, the source of food. Neither nature nor people alone can produce human sustenance, but only the two together, culturally wedded. The poet Edwin Muir said it unforgettably:

> Men are made of what is made,
> The meat, the drink, the life, the corn,
> Laid up by them, in them reborn.
> And self-begotten cycles close
> About our way; indigenous art
> And simple spells make unafraid
> The haunted labyrinths of the heart
> And with our wild succession braid
> The resurrection of the rose.

To think of food as a weapon, or of a weapon as food, may give an illusory security and wealth to a few, but it strikes directly at the life of all.

The concept of food-as-weapon is not surprisingly the doctrine of a Department of Agriculture that is being used as an instrument of foreign political and economic speculation. This militarizing of food is the greatest threat so far raised against the farmland and the farm communities of this country. If present attitudes continue, we may expect government policies that will encourage the destruction, by overuse, of farmland. This, of course, has already begun. To answer the official call for more production—evidently to be used to bait or bribe foreign countries—farmers are plowing their waterways and permanent pastures; lands that ought to remain in grass are being planted in row crops. Contour plowing, crop rotation, and other conservation measures seem to have gone out of favor or fashion in official circles and are practiced less and less on the farm. This exclusive emphasis on production will accelerate the mechanization and chemicalization of farming, increase the price of land, increase overhead and operating costs, and thereby further diminish the farm population. Thus the tendency, if not the intention, of Mr. Butz's confusion of farming and war, is to complete the deliverance of American agriculture into the hands of corporations.

The cost of this corporate totalitarianism in energy, land, and social disruption will be enormous. It will lead to the exhaustion of farmland and farm culture. Husbandry will become an extractive industry; because maintenance will entirely give way to production, the fertility of the soil will become a limited, unrenewable resource like coal or oil.

This may not happen. It *need* not happen. But it is necessary to recognize that it *can* happen. That it can happen is made evident not only by the words of such men as Mr. Butz, but more clearly by the large-scale industrial destruction of farmland already in progress. If it does happen, we are familiar enough with the nature of American salesmanship to know that it will be done in the name of the starving millions, in the name of liberty, justice, democracy, and brotherhood, and to free the world from communism. We must, I think, be prepared to see, and to stand by, the truth: that the land should not be destroyed for *any* reason, not even for any apparently good reason. We must be prepared to say that enough food, year after year, is possible only for a limited number of people, and that this possibility can be preserved only by the steadfast, knowledgeable *care* of those people. Such "crash programs" as apparently have been contemplated by the Department of Agriculture in recent years will, in the long run, cause more starvation than they can remedy.

Meanwhile, the dust clouds rise again over Texas and Oklahoma. "Snirt" is falling in Kansas. Snow drifts in Iowa and the Dakotas are black with blown soil. The fields lose their humus and porosity, become less retentive of water, depend more on pesticides, herbicides, chemical fertilizers. Bigger tractors become necessary because the compacted soils are harder to work—and their greater weight further compacts the soil. More and bigger machines, more chemical and methodological shortcuts are needed because of the shortage of manpower on the farm—and the problems of overcrowding and unemployment increase in the cities. It is estimated that it now costs (by erosion) two bushels of Iowa topsoil to grow one bushel of corn. It is variously estimated that from five to twelve calories of fossil fuel energy are required to produce one calorie of hybrid corn energy. An official of the National Farmers Union says that "a farmer who earns $10,000 to $12,000 a year typically leaves an estate valued at about $320,000"—which means that when that farm is financed again, either by a purchaser or by an heir (to pay the inheritance taxes), it simply cannot support its new owner and pay for itself. And the *Progressive Farmer* predicts the disappearance of 200,000 to 400,000 farms each year during the next twenty years if the present trend continues.

The first principle of the exploitive mind is to divide and conquer. And surely there has never been a people more ominously and painfully divided than we are—both against each other and within ourselves. Once the revolution of exploitation is under way, statesmanship and craftsmanship are gradually replaced by salesmanship.* Its stock in trade in politics is to sell despotism and avarice as freedom and democracy. In business it sells sham and frustration as luxury and satisfaction. The "constantly expanding market" first opened in the New World by the fur traders is still expanding—no longer so much by expansions of territory or population, but by the calculated outdating, outmoding, and degradation of goods and by the hysterical self-dissatisfaction of consumers that is indigenous to an exploitive economy.

*The craft of persuading people to buy what they do not need, and do not want, for more than it is worth.

This gluttonous enterprise of ugliness, waste, and fraud thrives in the disastrous breach it has helped to make between our bodies and our souls. As a people, we have lost sight of the profound communion—even the union—of the inner with the outer life. Confucious said: "If a man have not order within him/He can not spread order about him . . . ." Surrounded as we are by evidence of the disorders of our souls and our world, we feel the strong truth in those words as well as the possibility of healing that is in them. We see the likelihood that our surroundings, from our clothes to our countryside, are the products of our inward life—our spirit, our vision—as much as they are products of nature and work. If this is true, then we cannot live as we do and be as we would like to be. There is nothing more absurd, to give an example that is only apparently trivial, than the millions who wish to live in luxury and idleness and yet be slender and goodlooking. We have millions, too, whose livelihoods, amusements, and comforts are all destructive, who nevertheless wish to live in a healthy environment; they want to run their recreational engines in clean, fresh air. There is now, in fact, no "benefit" that is not associated with disaster. That is because power can be disposed morally or harmlessly only by thoroughly unified characters and communities.

What caused these divisions? There are no doubt many causes, complex both in themselves and in their interaction. But pertinent to all of them, I think, is our attitude toward work. The growth of the exploiters' revolution on this continent has been accompanied by the growth of the idea that work is beneath human dignity, particularly any form of hand work. We have made it our overriding ambition to escape work, and as a consequence have debased work until it is only fit to escape from. We have debased the products of work and have been, in turn, debased by them. Out of this contempt for work arose the idea of a nigger: at first some person, and later some thing, to be used to relieve us of the burden of work. If we began by making niggers of people, we have ended by making a nigger of the world. We have taken the irreplaceable energies and materials of the world and turned them into jimcrack "labor-saving devices." We have made of the rivers and oceans and winds niggers to carry away our refuse, which we think we are too good to dispose of decently ourselves. And in doing this to the world that is our common heritage and bond, we have returned to making niggers of people: we have become each other's niggers.

But is work something that we have a right to escape? And can we escape it with impunity? We are probably the first entire people ever to think so. All the ancient wisdom that has come down to us counsels otherwise. It tells us that work is necessary to us, as much a part of our condition as mortality; that good work is our salvation and our joy; that shoddy or dishonest or self-serving work is our curse and our doom. We have tried to escape the sweat and sorrow promised in Genesis—only to find that, in order to do so, we must forswear love and excellence, health and joy.

Thus we can see growing out of our history a condition that is physically dangerous, morally repugnant, ugly. Contrary to the blandishments of the salesmen, it is not particularly comfortable or happy. It is not even affluent in any meaningful sense, because its abundance is dependent on sources that are being rapidly exhausted by its methods. To see these things is to come up against the question: Then what *is* desirable?

One possibility is just to tag along with the fantasists in government and industry who would have us believe that we can pursue our ideals of affluence, comfort, mobility, and leisure indefinitely. This curious faith is predicated on the notion that we will soon develop unlimited new sources of energy: domestic oil fields, shale oil, gasified coal, nuclear power, solar energy, and so on. This is fantastical because the basic cause of the energy crisis is not scarcity; it is moral ignorance and weakness of character. We don't know *how* to use energy, or what to use it *for*. And we cannot restrain ourselves. Our time is characterized as much by the abuse and waste of human energy as it is by the abuse and waste of fossil fuel energy. Nuclear power, if we are to believe its advocates, is presumably going to be well used by the same mentality that has egregiously devalued and misapplied man- and womanpower. If we had an unlimited supply of solar or wind power, we would use that destructively, too, for the same reasons.

Perhaps all of those sources of energy are going to be developed. Perhaps all of them can sooner or later be developed without threatening our survival. But not all of them together can guarantee our survival, and they cannot define what is desirable. We will not find those answers in Washington, D.C., or in the laboratories of oil companies. In order to find them, we will have to look closer to ourselves.

I believe that the answers are to be found in our history: in its until now subordinate tendency of settlement, of domestic permanence. This was the ambition of thousands of immigrants; it is formulated eloquently in some of the letters of Thomas Jefferson; it was the dream of the freed slaves; it was written into law in the Homestead Act of 1862. There are few of us whose families have not at some time been moved to see its vision and to attempt to enact its possibility. I am talking about the idea that as many as possible should share in the ownership of the land and thus be bound to it by economic interest, by the investment of love and work, by family loyalty, by memory and tradition. How much land this should be is a question, and the answer will vary with geography. The Homestead Act said 160 acres. The freedmen of the 1860s hoped for forty. We know that, particularly in other countries, families have lived decently on far fewer acres than that.

The old idea is still full of promise. It is potent with healing and with health. It has the power to turn each person away from the big-time promising and planning of the government, to confront in himself, in the immediacy of his own circumstances and whereabouts, the question of what methods and ways are best. It proposes an economy of necessities rather than an economy based upon anxiety, fantasy, luxury, and idle wishing. It proposes the independent, free-standing citizenry that Jefferson thought to be the surest safeguard of democratic liberty. And perhaps most important of all, it proposes an agriculture based upon intensive work, local energies, care, and long-living communities—that is, to state the matter from a consumer's point of view: a dependable, long-term food supply.

This is a possibility that is obviously imperiled—by antipathy in high places, by adverse public fashions and attitudes, by the deterioration of our present farm communities and traditions, by the flawed education and the inexperience of our young people. Yet it alone can promise us the continuity of attention and devotion without which the human life of the earth is impossible.

Sixty years ago, in another time of crisis, Thomas Hardy wrote these stanzas:

> Only a man harrowing clods
>   In a slow silent walk
> With an old horse that stumbles and nods
>   Half asleep as they stalk.
>
> Only thin smoke without flame
>   From the heaps of couch-grass;
> Yet this will go onward the same
>   Though Dynasties pass.

Today most of our people are so conditioned that they do not wish to harrow clods either with an old horse or with a new tractor. Yet Hardy's vision has come to be more urgently true than ever. The great difference these sixty years have made is that, though we feel that this work *must* go onward, we are not so certain that it will. But the care of the earth is our most ancient and most worthy and, after all, our most pleasing responsibility. To cherish what remains of it, and to foster its renewal, is our only legitimate hope.

MEANING

1. Can you state Berry's persuasive thesis in a sentence? Does he state it directly anywhere in the essay?
2. On what does Berry base his appeal? To what extent does he weave emotion and ethics together here? Find specific passages to support your answer.

3. What is the "revolution" Berry refers to? What was overthrown and what put in its place?
4. What attitude does Berry decry? What are some of the historical sources of this attitude?
5. Berry sets up a series of polarities or opposites, claiming that the world, or people, can be placed squarely in one camp or the other. Explain Berry's division and the characteristics of those who fall into each category.

METHOD

1. Reread Berry's essay carefully for examples of his persuasive strategies. Cite as many instances as you can of connotative language, metaphor, description and narration, and his persuasive style.
2. A poet as well as an essayist, Berry is not one to mince words. Where is his language the strongest? What effect, for example, does he elicit with such phrases as "we have ended by making a nigger of the world"?
3. If this piece were evaluated as argument, would it be flawed by any logical fallacies (Chapter 11)?

AUDIENCE

1. What evidence can you find that Berry sees himself writing for a general, if educated, audience rather than a specialized one of farmers and agribusinessmen?
2. How do you react to Berry's obviously strong feelings and potent language? Are you convinced that he is correct in his attack on American agricultural practices and values?
3. To what extent does Berry pull you in or push you away in this essay?

WRITING SUGGESTION

"The Unsettling of America" is, among other things, an example of *polemic*—an "aggressive attack on or refutation of . . . opinions or principles." It is also a call to action. Try your hand at writing a polemic, a strong attack on an opinion, attitude, principle, or policy you find seriously flawed. Don't shy away from strong, pointed language—if you can stay in control of it. Examine Berry's method of presenting analysis of a problem in vividly persuasive terms. Ask yourself what you really think about your subject, what you might say about it in intimate company, and try to put this blunt honesty into your essay. Ask yourself how much your audience will accept, how far you may push your persuasive language before it becomes self-defeating.

You may wish to combine the polemic with an explicit call to action, a positive statement that will balance the attack and may help win converts. However, a powerfully negative position can often do much to *imply* the positive choice or solution without stating it directly.

ADDITIONAL WRITING SUGGESTIONS

1. Write a letter to a close friend or relative in which you try to convince him or her to give up a bad habit, silly opinion, obnoxious mannerism, or the like. Do not insult your correspondent.
2. Write an election stump speech for yourself or a fellow student running for office.
3. Write a call to action addressed to your fellow students in which you exhort them to join together to change a specific policy or rule at your school.
4. As in Suggestion 3 above, address your pitch to fellow employees over a needed change in working conditions, pay, benefits, and so forth.
5. Study several recent print advertisements for their use of persuasive strategies. Do the ads have any common characteristics? Then try to imitate ad-copy style in your own advertisement for a product with which you're familiar. Consider what you'll base your appeal on, and whether your ad will promote a product or service you believe to be worthwhile.
6. Write a public-service advertisement, as above, after studying several examples. (A public-service ad does not sell a product as much as a good cause—stamping out forest fires, donating to charity, refusing to let a friend drive drunk.)
7. Design a small-scale ad campaign for a product or service you believe to be worthwhile. Write two or three print ads for different audiences or markets, a TV spot, a radio spot. For print and TV, explain the visual element in your design, and for radio include notes on voices and sound effects.

PART FIVE

Writing to Express or Entertain

WRITING FOR ITS OWN SAKE

As we've seen thus far, a great deal of nonfiction writing is shaped by three essential purposes: informing, analyzing, and convincing. Much of the workaday prose of business, government, journalism, and education addresses one or more of these aims. Another realm of nonfiction exists, however, that has little to do with conveying information, analyzing or explaining problems, or influencing others to think or act in certain ways. The writing we've studied so far is practical; its purposes are concrete. Because life is always more than the sum of our practical endeavors, however, some of the writing we do will have a less practical purpose.

When we write to express ourselves (whether to ourselves or to other people), or when we write to entertain or delight our audience, we do it for its own sake, not necessarily because we hope to accomplish a practical goal. Certainly self-expression and entertainment are worthy aims, but they aren't easy to quantify; their value is less objective than that of other kinds of nonfiction. (A banker's autobiographical reminiscence of his childhood, for example, is quite a different thing than his annual report to shareholders.) As a result, expressive writing is the least systematic, the hardest to teach, and perhaps the most difficult to do well (depending on our talents and interests). Writing expressively means risking the part of ourselves that normally will be more protected in less overtly personal kinds of work.

The risk, however, is well worth taking. We've all told jokes and had them fall flat; we've tried to say something profound and had it come out sounding silly. Still, we've learned much through the attempt, and our jokes usually get better, our profundities less grandiose. To write expressively will mean struggle and failure—trying to make something new, trying to articulate something we can't quite grasp, trying to face deep fears and disturbing ideas. It also will mean success, however, for eventually we'll be rewarded with insight, knowledge, and a depth of satisfaction in the creative process that only this kind of writing can provide.

14

EXPRESSIVE ESSAYS

A FELT NEED

Novelists, poets, dramatists, when asked why they write, often reply, "I *have* to—I don't have any choice in the matter." Such people consider themselves driven to write, sometimes to the point of desperation, when, if they don't or can't write, they suffer terribly. It may be too much to ask all student writers to display this passion for self-expression. After all, each of us has his or her own way of sounding off: writing music, dancing, running cross-country, throwing pots. But it's probably true that although our means of self-expression differ, each of us does, from time to time, feel a need to make a statement—a poem, a journal entry, a photograph, a song.

That sense of need, of some imperative, is the common element in all expressive arts, including writing. Whether he or she is working in fiction or nonfiction, the maker feels impelled to produce something as a way of resolving, or at least bringing out in the open, a thought or emotion of some urgency. The source of the impulse might be intellectual: a sudden idea or flash of insight; it might be emotional: a feeling of anger, dread, loss, or joy; or it might be experiential: based on an incident or event. In any case, it will have some power to move us to the act of writing about it.

The task then will be to choose the most appropriate form for expressing whatever it is we feel. Our first choice might be the diary or journal forms, generally private ways for us to talk to ourselves without worries about audience, content, style, and so forth. (Although diaries and journals are published as nonfiction, their chief purpose for most of us is "writer-based" or self-enclosed.) When we seek a more public form for our expressive impulse, or when we want to *shape* that impulse, even if only for ourselves, we turn again to essays and narratives. In the next chapter, "Expressive Narratives," we will look at autobiography and memoir— expression shaped as story. Here, we consider the personal essay and the expressive-writing process

THE ESSAY FORM

Using the essay form as a vehicle of self-expression means shaping that expression according to its dictates. For instance, we've seen that the essay by nature is controlled by an overriding point, or thesis, which it presents and supports. In an informative essay, the thesis is factual; in an analytical essay, it is explanatory; and in an argumentative or persuasive essay, it asserts a position. In an expressive essay, then, the controlling idea will voice the writer's feeling, and the essay itself will embody, support, and develop it.

Beyond that, the personal essay is open to the writer's inventiveness. Whether in first or third person, it often is informal as it plays loosely with conventions of structure and style. In some cases, for example, the writer may leave the thesis implied or indirectly stated, and instead allow illustrations and examples to evoke the expressive point. Sometimes the writer may state his or her point in a number of different ways, experimenting with the subtleties or variations of a theme, no one of them being the last word. Expressive essays, too, may make greater use of conversational language and sentence rhythms, and may use narration and description extensively even though the overall form is not that of a story. Some expressive essays are very literal, not concerned with figurative language and metaphor, and others are just the opposite in using figurative language as a principal way of making a point. And, of course, personal essays may employ any of the rhetorical methods we discussed in Chapter 8, "Analytical Writing."

The process of writing an expressive essay is no different from that for any other essay purpose. Those stages of exploration, drafting, and revising we've already detailed (see especially Chapters 2, 6, and 9) also apply. What's different is the *focus* of the process and the *content* the writer eventually builds. All essays, we've said, exhibit a writer's personal encounter with a subject, whatever the purpose. In expressive essays, however, the *subject itself* is personal. Therefore, the focus of the process may be the writer's own inmost self—or that self's felt response to something else—and the content he or she builds from the writing process then will be self-revealing. Expressive essays are personal in that they present more than the meeting of writer and subject; they may also present the writer *as* the subject.

OPENNESS AND HONESTY

All good writing relies on openness and honesty—the reader's trust that the writer is telling the truth as he or she sees it, without caginess or insincerity. In expressive writing, however, candor is especially important, since the whole point is to get at what's *really* there in the writer's mind and heart. We must be open and honest not only toward our subject and audience, but toward ourselves as well.

As you follow the steps of the writing process, then, here are some things to remember:

1. Choose a subject you need to write about. Really good expressive writing seems always to emerge from some sense of necessity—a need to think something through, to come to grips with an emotion or circumstance. Since there are few if any moments in our lives when we're completely content, when we're not perturbed or puzzled, we always have available to us a wealth of potential topics. Ask yourself what you are honestly concerned about, and pursue it.

2. Don't be afraid to say what you actually think or feel. In the early stages of the process, especially, when you are the only reader of your words, take the opportunity to be as frank and open as you can. Even if what you write seems outrageous, narrow-minded, or unimaginative, be honest. The process is not the product, and you very likely will need to work *through* early material and to react to your own statements. (As an analogy, when we talk we say things that seem right as we say them, but, having said them, we often immediately refine or revise, responding to our own remarks.) It's important for us to know what we *think* we think, so that we can decide if that truly *is* what we think.

3. Acknowledge *all* your thoughts and feelings, even if they may be inconsistent. Being of two minds about something is often the rule rather than the exception. In fact, the dilemma we're in may be the very source of the expressive impulse. Writing toward some accommodation or resolution must entail our admitting to contradictory ideas and emotions. Expressing doubt, confusion, or uncertainty may be the first step in coming to terms with whatever problem moves us to write.

Openness and honesty of expression in the writing process will ensure that your finished product, too, will have these qualities. The process will have given you time and space to select, sharpen, and arrange—to find a suitable design and emphasis for what you have come to say.

VOICE

All of us use a wide range of "voices" when we speak, depending on who we're talking to, and for what reason. The persuasive voice we use to convince our parents we're mature and responsible is not the one for expressing love to a friend. Similarly, the voices we employ in writing will be influenced by purpose and audience.

For most of us, the question of which voice to use is less complicated than it might seem at first. In general, each of us has one voice that we may modulate to suit specific situations. In large part, that voice is unconscious until we begin to see it emerge on paper, when we can gain some control over it. The voice we use in nonfiction writing is a result of our mastery of writing technique (Chapter 4, "Good Writing") and of those unique features of personality, experience, upbringing, and self-image that we've "internalized" over time. It is, in most cases, our own natural way of saying things—if constrained often by rules and expectations.

We can think of this one voice of ours as having to work in two different types of situations: public and private. In private ones, we are not writing for anyone but ourselves or a few others. Letters, diaries, journals, and so on employ a personal voice that may be totally uninhibited—a voice like the one we use to talk to our closest friends. In public situations, however, even when we are writing with an expressive aim, our voice will be controlled to a fair degree.

All of the writing situations described in this book are public. That is, each assumes the possibility of an audience beyond one composed of close friends. There is a potentially large difference in the voice we use to inform, explain, and argue, however, and the one we use to express ourselves. Because expressive writing is personal, our voice may be closer to the one we use for private purposes.

Thus, a word of caution: Whether we're conscious of it or not, our prose voice helps to carry the meaning of what we write, and it reveals more than what we might like about our attitude toward ourselves and our subject, as well as about our character. In its vocabulary, sentence style and rhythms, and honesty, it tells our reader all kinds of things between the lines. So, when writing expressively and letting the energy and content of our private thoughts and feelings flow into our work, we should take care with the *authenticity* of our voice. The need that drives us to write, and our commitment to candor, may take us on a wild ride. What we finally end up saying will be our reader's only sound of us, so we must try to make that sound true.

When we read back our own voice, does it seem genuine—not affected, faked, posed? Have we given the reader cause to trust our voice? Does it carry the sense and meaning we want it to? Does it imply an attitude we hadn't intended or don't wish to express? Does it reveal our character as we honestly perceive it or hope to alter it? If so, we are probably writing in good faith, and our voice will show it.

QUESTIONS

1. What impulse feeds the expressive arts, including writing?
2. What are some general characteristics of expressive essays?

3. How are expressive essays different from essays written for other purposes?
4. Why are openness and honesty important in expressive writing?
5. What role does voice play in fulfilling an expressive purpose?

EXERCISES

1. Expressive writing, as much as any other kind, uses all the tools and techniques at the writer's disposal. In addition, expressive writing, if it is to truly reflect the writer's honest feelings in a genuine voice, must be as accurate, specific, detailed, and concrete as writing for any other purpose. As a pre-writing exercise, think about the most recent moment in your life when you had very strong feelings about something. Then, writing as freely as you can, try to take down as many particulars about the moment as you can remember. Where were you? What brought on the feeling(s)? What specific thoughts or emotions did you experience? With whom were you? What details of mood, time, place, and so forth stick out in your mind?

2. If you keep a diary or journal (or even random notes on scraps of paper), go over some of your recent entries and analyze them as a critic might. What subjects get the most attention? What kinds of specific details do you seem to notice and remember? To what extent could any of this private prose be transplanted in a public essay? To what degree do you shape your entries with controlling ideas, patterns of organization, or concluding remarks?

Readings

Born in New York in 1924, JAMES BALDWIN is one of America's most prominent and respected black writers, one of the voices who helped bring attention to the plight of blacks in the United States. Baldwin is the author of many books of fiction and essays, and has written plays and film scripts in addition to directing for the stage and screen. He has received numerous awards and honors, including grants from the National Institute of Arts and Letters and the Ford Foundation, and his novel Just above My Head *was nominated for an American Book Award in 1980. Among his other works: novels—*Go Tell It on the Mountain *(1953);* Another Country *(1962);* Tell Me How Long the Train's Been Gone *(1968); and* If Beale Street Could Talk *(1974); essays—*Notes of a Native Son *(1955);* Nobody Knows My Name *(1961); and* The Fire Next Time *(1963). Baldwin has published frequently in such magazines as* Harper's, Nation, Esquire, Partisan Review, *and* The New Yorker. *In the essay below, excepted from* Esquire, *Baldwin expresses complex emotions aroused by a visit to the Harlem neighborhood where he grew up.*

Fifth Avenue, Uptown

by James Baldwin

There is a housing project standing now where the house in which we grew up once stood, and one of those stunted city trees is snarling where our doorway used to be. This is on the rehabilitated side of the avenue. The other side of the avenue—for progress takes time—has not been rehabilitated yet and it looks exactly as it looked in the days when we sat with our noses pressed against the windowpane, longing to be allowed to go "across the street." The grocery store which gave us credit is still there, and there can be no doubt that it is still giving credit. The people in the project certainly need it—far more, indeed, than they ever needed the project. The last time I passed by, the Jewish proprietor was still standing among his shelves, looking sadder and heavier but scarcely any older. Further down the block stands the shoe-repair store in which our shoes were repaired until reparation became impossible and in which, then, we bought all our "new" ones. The Negro proprietor is still in the window, head down, working at the leather.

These two, I imagine, could tell a long tale if they would (perhaps they would be glad to if they could), having watched so many, for so long, struggling in the fishhooks, the barbed wire, of this avenue.

The avenue is elsewhere the renowned and elegant Fifth. The area I am describing, which, in today's gang parlance, would be called "the turf," is bounded by Lenox Avenue on the west, the Harlem River on the east, 135th Street on the north, and 130th Street on the south. We never lived beyond these boundaries; this is where we grew up. Walking along 145th Street—for example—familiar as it is, and similar, does not have the same impact because I do not know any of the people on the block. But when I turn east on 131st Street and Lenox Avenue, there is first a soda-pop joint, then a shoeshine "parlor," then a grocery store, then a dry cleaners', then the houses. All along the street there are people who watched me grow up, people who grew up with me, people I watched grow up along with my brothers and sisters; and, sometimes in my arms, sometimes underfoot, sometimes at my shoulder—or on it—their children, a riot, a forest of children, who include my nieces and nephews.

When we reach the end of this long block, we find ourselves on wide, filthy, hostile Fifth Avenue, facing that project which hangs over the avenue like a monument to the folly, and the cowardice, of good intentions.

James Baldwin, from "Uptown, Fifth Avenue." Reprinted with permission of the author. This article first appeared in *Esquire*, July 1960.

All along the block, for anyone who knows it, are immense human gaps, like craters. These gaps are not created merely by those who have moved away, inevitably into some other ghetto; or by those who have risen, almost always into a greater capacity for self-loathing and self-delusion; or yet by those who, by whatever means—War II, the Korean war, a policeman's gun or billy, a gang war, a brawl, madness, an overdose of heroin, or simply, unnatural exhaustion—are dead. I am talking about those who are left, and I am talking principally about the young. What are they doing? Well, some, a minority, are fanatical churchgoers, members of the more extreme of the Holy Roller sects. Many, many more are "moslems," by affiliation or sympathy, that is to say that they are united by nothing more—and nothing less—than a hatred of the white world and all its works. They are present, for example, at every Buy Black street-corner meeting—meetings in which the speaker urges his hearers to cease trading with white men and establish a separate economy. Neither the speaker nor his hearers can possibly do this, of course, since Negroes do not own General Motors or RCA or the A&P, nor, indeed, do they own more than a wholly insufficient fraction of anything else in Harlem (those who *do* own anything are more interested in their profits than in their fellows). But these meetings nevertheless keep alive in the participators a certain pride of bitterness without which, however futile this bitterness may be, they could scarcely remain alive at all. Many have given up. They stay home and watch the TV screen, living on the earnings of their parents, cousins, brothers, or uncles, and only leave the house to go to the movies or to the nearest bar. "How're you making it?" one may ask, running into them along the block, or in the bar. "Oh, I'm TV-ing it"; with the saddest, sweetest, most shamefaced of smiles, and from a great distance. This distance one is compelled to respect; anyone who has traveled so far will not easily be dragged again into the world. There are further retreats, of course, than the TV screen or the bar. There are those who are simply sitting on their stoops, "stoned," animated for a moment only, and hideously, by the approach of someone who may lend them the money for a "fix." Or by the approach of someone from whom they can purchase it, one of the shrewd ones, on the way to prison or just coming out.

And the others, who have avoided all of these deaths, get up in the morning and go downtown to meet "the man." They work in the white man's world all day and come home in the evening to this fetid block. They struggle to instill in their children some private sense of honor or dignity which will help the child to survive. This means, of course, that they must struggle, stolidly, incessantly, to keep this sense alive in themselves, in spite of the insults, the indifference, and the cruelty they are certain to encounter in their working day. They patiently browbeat the landlord into fixing the heat, the plaster, the plumbing; this demands prodigious patience; nor is patience usually enough. In trying to make their hovels habitable, they are perpetually throwing good money after bad. Such frustration, so long endured, is driving many strong, admirable men and women whose only crime is color to the very gates of paranoia.

One remembers them from another time—playing handball in the playground, going to church, wondering if they were going to be promoted at school. One remembers them going off to war—gladly, to escape this block. One remembers their return. Perhaps one remembers their wedding day. And one sees where the girl is now—vainly looking for salvation from some other embittered, trussed, and struggling boy—and sees the all-but-abandoned children in the streets.

MEANING

1. What feelings or emotions is Baldwin expressing in "Fifth Avenue, Uptown"? Does he state them directly or imply them? Point up specific passages to support your view.
2. What "felt need" seems to underlie Baldwin's essay? Explain.
3. This essay was first published in 1960. What evidence can you find that it predicts what was to become a period of unrest for blacks in the United States?
4. How would you describe Baldwin's voice?

METHOD

1. What structuring device does Baldwin use to organize his essay?
2. Baldwin's eye for detail is particularly acute. Which details are especially effective in capturing the mood, physical appearance, or way of life in Harlem?
3. Where is Baldwin's language strongest or most revealing of his feelings? Does this language share any qualities with the style or diction of persuasion? Why or why not?

AUDIENCE

1. Is Baldwin writing for a mostly black audience, or a mostly white one? How can you tell?
2. Are you affected at all by Baldwin's clearly heartfelt prose? What about this piece hits you hardest? Its tone? Its concrete, observed detail? Its expressive language?

WRITING SUGGESTIONS

1. Think about the times in your life when you've felt real anger or outrage about a place, situation, or person. Can you remember how you felt, the specific circumstances, and your reaction to them? Imagine yourself going back to that moment—as Baldwin visits his old neighborhood—to re-create it in writing. Your focus is not on a story of what happened (although you may need to sketch in background, as Baldwin does) but rather on your response to the situation through an expressive rendering of it.

2. Using Baldwin as a model, write an expressive essay about a current circumstance about which you feel a strong emotion—anger, pity, fear, love, or hate. Try to express your feelings through a careful and precise depiction of the circumstance itself.

GEOFFREY WOLFF was born in 1937 in Los Angeles, California. He is a graduate of Princeton University, and attended Churchill College, Cambridge. He lectured in comparative literature in Istanbul, Turkey in the early sixties, and was chairman of the department of American Civilization at Istanbul University. From 1964 through 1969, Wolff served as book editor for the Washington Post. *He has since been book editor for* Newsweek, *taught at the Corcoran School of Art, Washington, D.C.; Princeton; and Middlebury College, Middlebury, Vermont. He has been a senior fellow, National Endowment of the Humanities, a Woodrow Wilson fellow, and a Fulbright scholar. Wolff has published fiction—*Bad Debts *(1969) and* Inklings *(1977); biography—*The Brief Transit and Violent Eclipse of Harry Crosby *(1976) and numerous essays and reviews for such publications as* American Scholar, The New Republic, *and* Atlantic Monthly. *In the following essay, the opening chapter of Wolff's biography of his father,* The Duke of Deception *(1979), he sketches a portrait of a confidence man who fabricated a life based on lies.*

Duke

by Geoffrey Wolff

I listen for my father and I hear a stammer. This was explosive and unashamed, not a choking on words but a spray of words. His speech was headlong, edgy, breathless: there was neither room in his mouth nor time in the day to contain what he burned to utter. I have a remnant of that stammer, and I wish I did not; I stammer and blush, my father would stammer and grin. He depended on a listener's good will. My father depended excessively upon people's good will.

As he spoke straight at you, so did he look at you. He could stare down anyone, though this was a gift he rarely practiced. To me, everything about him seemed outsized. Doing a school report on the Easter Islanders I found in an encyclopedia pictures of their huge sculptures, and there he was, massive head and nose, nothing subtle or delicate. He was in fact (and how diminishing those words, *in fact,* look to me now) an inch or two above six feet, full bodied, a man who lumbered from here to there with deliberation. When I was a child I noticed that people were respectful of the cubic feet my father occupied; later I understood that I had confused respect with resentment.

I recollect things, a gentleman's accessories, deceptively simple fabrications of silver and burnished nickel, of brushed Swedish stainless, of silk and soft wool and brown leather. I remember his shoes, so meticulously selected and cared for and used, thin-soled, with cracked uppers, older than I was or could ever be, shining dully and from the depths. Just a pair of shoes? No: I knew before I knew any other complicated thing that for my father there was nothing he possessed that was "just" something. His pocket watch was not "just" a timepiece, it was a miraculous instrument with a hinged front and a representation on its back of porcelain ducks rising from a birch-girt porcelain pond. It struck the hour unassertively, musically, like a silver tine touched to a crystal glass, no hurry, you might like to know it's noon.

He despised black leather, said black shoes reminded him of black attaché cases, of bankers, lawyers, look-before-you-leapers anxious not to offend their clients. He owned nothing black except his dinner jacket and his umbrella. His umbrella doubled as a shooting-stick, and one afternoon at a polo match at Brandywine he was sitting on it when a man asked him what he would do if it rained, sit wet or stand dry? I laughed. My father laughed also, but tightly, and he did not reply; nor did he ever again use this quixotic contraption. He took things, *things,* seriously.

My father, called Duke, taught me skills and manners; he taught me to shoot and to drive fast and to read respectfully and to box and to handle a boat and to distinguish between good jazz music and bad jazz music. He was patient with me, led me to understand for myself why Billie Holiday's understatements were more interesting than Ella Fitzgerald's complications. His codes were not novel, but they were rigid, the rules of decorum that Hemingway prescribed. A gentleman kept his word, and favored simplicity of sentiment; a gentleman chose his words with care, as he chose his friends. A gentleman accepted responsibility for his acts, and welcomed the liberty to act unambiguously. A gentleman was a stickler for precision and punctilio; life was no more than an inventory of small choices that together formed a man's character, entire. A gentleman was this, and not that; a *man* did, did not, said, would not say.

My father could, however, be coaxed to reveal his bona fides. He had been schooled at Groton and passed along to Yale. He was just barely prepared to intimate that he had been tapped for "Bones," and I remember his pleasure when Levi Jackson, the black captain of Yale's 1948 football team, was similarly honored by that secret society. He was proud of Skull and Bones for its hospitality toward the exotic. He did sometimes wince, however, when he pronounced Jackson's Semitic Christian name, and I sensed that his tolerance for Jews was not inclusive; but I never heard him indulge express bigotry, and the first of half a dozen times he hit me was for having called a neighbor's kid a guinea.

There was much luxury in my father's affections, and he hated what was narrow, pinched, or mean. He understood exclusion, mind you, and lived his life believing the world to be divided between a few *us's* and many *thems*, but I was to understand that aristocracy was a function of taste, courage, and generosity. About two other virtues—candor and reticence—I was confused, for my father would sometimes proselytize the one, sometimes the other.

If Duke's preoccupation with bloodlines was finite, this did not cause him to be unmindful of his ancestors. He knew whence he had come, and whither he meant me to go. I saw visible evidence of this, a gold signet ring which I wear today, a heavy bit of business inscribed arsy-turvy with lions and flora and a motto, *nulla vestigium retrorsit.* "Don't look back" I was told it meant.

After Yale—class of late nineteen-twenty something, or early nineteen-thirty something—my father batted around the country, living a high life in New York among school and college chums, flying as a test pilot, marrying my mother, the daughter of a rear admiral. I was born a year after the marriage, in 1937, and three years after that my father went to England as a fighter pilot with Eagle Squadron, a group of American volunteers in the Royal Air Force. Later he transferred to the OSS, and was in Yugoslavia with the partisans; just before the Invasion he was parachuted into Normandy, where he served as a sapper with the Resistance, which my father pronounced *ray-zee-staunce.*

His career following the war was for me mysterious in its particulars; in the service of his nation, it was understood, candor was not always possible. This much was clear: my father mattered in the world, and was satisfied that he mattered, whether or not the world understood precisely why he mattered.

A pretty history for an American clubman. Its fault is that it was not true. . . . True, there were many boarding schools, each less pleased with the little Duke than the last, but none of them was Groton. There was no Yale, and by the time he walked from a room at a mention of Skull and Bones I knew this, and he knew that I knew it. No military service would have him; his teeth were bad. So he had his teeth pulled and replaced, but the Air Corps and Navy and Army and Coast Guard still thought he was a bad idea. The ring I wear was made according to his instructions by a jeweler two blocks from Schwab's drugstore in Hollywood, and was never paid for. The motto, engraved backwards so that it would come right on a red wax seal, is dog Latin and means in fact "leave no trace behind," but my father did not believe me when I told him this.

My father was a Jew. This did not seem to him a good idea, and so it was his notion to disassemble his history, begin at zero, and re-create himself. His sustaining line of work till shortly before he died was as a confidence man. If I now find his authentic history more surprising, more interesting, than his counterfeit history, he did not. He would not make peace with his actualities, and so he was the author of his own circumstances, and indifferent to the consequences of this nervy program.

There were some awful consequences, for other people as well as for him. He was lavish with money, with others' money. He preferred to stiff institutions: jewelers, car dealers, banks, fancy hotels. He was, that is, a thoughtful buccaneer, when thoughtfulness was convenient. But people were hurt by him. Much of his mischief was casual enough: I lost a tooth when I was six, and the Tooth Fairy, "financially inconvenienced" or "temporarily out of pocket," whichever was then his locution, left under my pillow an IOU, a sight draft for two bits, or two million.

I wish he hadn't selected from among the world's possible disguises the costume and credentials of a yacht club commodore. Beginning at scratch he might have reached further, tried something a bit more bold and odd, a bit less inexorably conventional, a bit less calculated to please. But it is true, of course, that a confidence man who cannot inspire confidence in his marks is nothing at all, so perhaps this tuneup of his bloodline, educational *vita*, and war record was merely the price of doing business in a culture preoccupied with appearances.

I'm not even now certain what I wish he had made of himself: I once believed that he was most naturally a fictioneer. But for all his preoccupation with make-believe, he never tried seriously to write it. A confidence man learns early in his career that to commit himself to paper is to court trouble. The successful bunco artist does his game, and disappears himself: Who *was* that masked man? No one, no one at all, *nulla vestigium [sic] retrorsit [sic]*,* not a trace left behind.

Well, I'm left behind. One day, writing about my father with no want of astonishment and love, it came to me that I am his creature as well as his get. I cannot now shake this conviction, that I was trained as his instru-

[*Correct form: *nulla vestigia retrorsum.*]

ment of perpetuation, put here to put him into the record. And that my father knew this, calculated it to a degree. How else explain his eruption of rage when I once gave up what he and I called "writing" for journalism? I had taken a job as the book critic of *The Washington Post*, was proud of myself; it seemed then like a wonderful job, honorable and enriching. My father saw it otherwise: "You have failed me," he wrote, "you have sold yourself at discount" he wrote to me, his prison number stamped below his name.

He was wrong then, but he was usually right about me. He would listen to anything I wished to tell him, but would not tell me only what I wished to hear. He retained such solicitude for his clients. With me he was strict and straight, except about himself. And so I want to be strict and straight with him, and with myself. Writing to a friend about this book, I said that I would not now for anything have had my father be other than what he was, except happier, and that most of the time he was happy enough, cheered on by imaginary successes. He gave me a great deal, and not merely life, and I didn't want to bellyache; I wanted, I told my friend, to thumb my nose on his behalf at everyone who had limited him. My friend was shrewd, though, and said that he didn't believe me, that I couldn't mean such a thing, that if I followed out its implications I would be led to a kind of ripe sentimentality, and to mere piety. Perhaps, he wrote me, you would not have wished him to lie to himself, to lie about being a Jew. Perhaps you would have him fool others but not so deeply trick himself. "In writing about a father," my friend wrote me about our fathers, "one clambers up a slippery mountain, carrying the balls of another in a bloody sack, and whether to eat them or worship them or bury them decently is never cleanly decided."

So I will try here to be exact. I wish my father had done more headlong, more elegant inventing. I believe he would respect my wish, be willing to speak with me seriously about it, find some nobility in it. But now he is dead, and he had been dead two weeks when they found him. And in his tiny flat at the edge of the Pacific they found no address book, no batch of letters held with a rubber band, no photograph. Not a thing to suggest that he had ever known another human being.

MEANING

1. Does Wolff's essay have a thesis or controlling idea? What is it?
2. Does the essay provide any clues about why Wolff needs to write about his father?
3. What are some of Duke's qualities, both good and bad?
4. On balance, do you think Wolff is ashamed of his father? What other emotions does the author express in this essay?

METHOD

1. Wolff uses a controlling device in this portrait, his father's signet ring with its "dog latin" inscription. How many times does Wolff mention the ring or what it says? Why does he keep coming back to it?
2. How would you assess Wolff's candor here? Point out sentences or passages that seem particularly, painfully honest.
3. Wolff is especially effective in his use of specific detail. What are some of the most striking or memorable details in this essay?

AUDIENCE

1. Wolff writes about very private matters for a general audience. Why should the general reading public be interested in Wolff's memoir of his con-artist father?
2. How do you react to this portrait? What feelings does the piece stir in you? Do you feel pity for Duke or his son? Embarrassment? Affection? Does Duke remind you of anyone you know?

WRITING SUGGESTION

Using Wolff's essay as a model, characterize the most interesting, remarkable, strange, or irritating person you know—someone you've wanted to get down on paper but never have. Practice your most skillful powers of memory and observation, and render your sense of your subject in particular detail. Remember, too, however, this is not just a static description but an expression of your feelings as well.

ANNIE DILLARD was born in 1945 in Pittsburgh, received her B.A. and M.A. degrees from Hollins College, in Virginia, and has been a college English teacher and bestselling author. Her first book, a poetry collection entitled Tickets for a Prayer Wheel *(1973) was followed by* Pilgrim at Tinker Creek *(1974), which gave her a national reputation and a Pulitzer Prize. In* Tinker Creek, *Dillard writes with striking clarity and vision about nature, and expresses a stunning range of knowledge, perception, and emotion. Among her other books:* Living By Fiction *(1982), a collection of critical essays, and* Teaching a Stone to Talk *(1982), a collection of essays on nature. In "Heaven and Earth in Jest," taken from the opening chapter of* Pilgrim at Tinker Creek, *Dillard expresses one of the central questions every thinking person must eventually face.*

Heaven and Earth in Jest

by Annie Dillard

I used to have a cat, an old fighting tom, who would jump through the open window by my bed in the middle of the night and land on my chest. I'd half-awaken. He'd stick his skull under my nose and purr, stinking of urine and blood. Some nights he kneaded my bare chest with his front paws, powerfully, arching his back, as if sharpening his claws, or pummeling a mother for milk. And some mornings I'd wake in daylight to find my body covered with paw prints in blood; I looked as though I'd been painted with roses.

It was hot, so hot the mirror felt warm. I washed before the mirror in a daze, my twisted summer sleep still hung about me like sea kelp. What blood was this, and what roses? It could have been the rose of union, the blood of murder, or the rose of beauty bare and the blood of some unspeakable sacrifice or birth. The sign on my body could have been an emblem or a stain, the keys to the kingdom or the mark of Cain. I never knew. I never knew as I washed, and the blood streaked, faded, and finally disappeared, whether I'd purified myself or ruined the blood sign of the passover. We wake, if we ever wake at all, to mystery, rumors of death, beauty, violence. . . . "Seem like we're just set down here," a woman said to me recently, "and don't nobody know why."

These are morning matters, pictures you dream as the final wave heaves you up on the sand to the bright light and drying air. You remember pressure, and a curved sleep you rested against, soft, like a scallop in its shell. But the air hardens your skin; you stand; you leave the lighted shore to explore some dim headland, and soon you're lost in the leafy interior, intent, remembering nothing.

I still think of that old tomcat, mornings, when I wake. Things are tamer now; I sleep with the window shut. The cat and our rites are gone and my life is changed, but the memory remains of something powerful playing over me. I wake expectant, hoping to see a new thing. If I'm lucky I might be jogged awake by a strange birdcall. I dress in a hurry, imagining the yard flapping with auks, or flamingos. This morning it was a wood duck, down at the creek. It flew away.

I live by a creek, Tinker Creek, in a valley in Virginia's Blue Ridge. An anchorite's hermitage is called an anchor-hold; some anchor-holds were simple sheds clamped to the side of a church like a barnacle to a rock. I think of this house clamped to the side of Tinker Creek as an anchor-hold. It holds me at anchor to the rock bottom of the creek itself and it keeps me steadied in the current, as a sea anchor does, facing the stream of light pouring down. It's a good place to live; there's a lot to think about. The creeks—Tinker and Carvin's—are an active mystery, fresh every minute. Theirs is the mystery of the continuous creation and all that providence implies: the uncertainty of vision, the horror of the fixed, the dissolution of the present, the intricacy of beauty, the pressure of fecundity, the elusiveness of the free, and the flawed nature of perfection. The mountains— Tinker and Brushy, McAfee's Knob and Dead Man—are a passive mystery, the oldest of all. Theirs is the one simple mystery of creation from nothing, of matter itself, anything at all, the given. Mountains are giant, restful, absorbent. You can heave your spirit into a mountain and the mountain will keep it, folded, and not throw it back as some creeks will. The creeks are the world with all its stimulus and beauty; I live there. But the mountains are home.

The wood duck flew away. I caught only a glimpse of something like a bright torpedo that blasted the leaves where it flew. Back at the house I ate a bowl of oatmeal; much later in the day came the long slant of light that means good walking.

If the day is fine, any walk will do; it all looks good. Water in particular looks its best, reflecting blue sky in the flat, and chopping it into graveled shallows and white chute and foam in the riffles. On a dark day, or a hazy one, everything's washed-out and lackluster but the water. It carries its own lights. I set out for the railroad tracks, for the hill the flocks fly over, for the woods where the white mare lives. But I go to the water.

Today is one of those excellent January partly cloudies in which light chooses an unexpected part of the landscape to trick out in gilt, and then shadow sweeps it away. You know you're alive. You take huge steps, trying to feel the planet's roundness arc between your feet. Kazantzakis says that when he was young he had a canary and a globe. When he freed the canary, it would perch on the globe and sing. All his life, wandering the earth, he felt as though he had a canary on top of his mind, singing.

West of the house, Tinker Creek makes a sharp loop, so that the creek is both in back of the house, south of me, and also on the other side of the road, north of me. I like to go north. There the afternoon sun hits the creek just right, deepening the reflected blue and lighting the sides of trees on the banks. Steers from the pasture across the creek come down to drink; I always flush a rabbit or two there; I sit on a fallen trunk in the shade and watch the squirrels in the sun. There are two separated wooden fences suspended from cables that cross the creek just upstream from my tree-trunk bench. They keep the steers from escaping up or down the creek when they come to drink. Squirrels, the neighborhood children, and I use the downstream fence as a swaying bridge across the creek. But the steers are there today.

I sit on the downed tree and watch the black steers slip on the creek bottom. They are all bred beef: beef heart, beef hide, beef hocks. They're a human product like rayon. They're like a field of shoes. They have cast-iron shanks and tongues like foam insoles. You can't see through to their brains as you can with other animals; they have beef fat behind their eyes, beef stew.

I cross the fence six feet above the water, walking my hands down the rusty cable and tightroping my feet along the narrow edge of the planks. When I hit the other bank and terra firma, some steers are bunched in a knot between me and the barbed-wire fence I want to cross. So I suddenly rush at them in an enthusiastic sprint, flailing my arms and hollering, "Lightning! Copperhead! Swedish meatballs!" They flee, still in a knot, stumbling across the flat pasture. I stand with the wind on my face.

When I slide under a barbed-wire fence, cross a field, and run over a sycamore trunk felled across the water, I'm on a little island shaped like a tear in the middle of Tinker Creek. On one side of the creek is a steep forested bank; the water is swift and deep on that side of the island. On the other side is the level field I walked through next to the steers' pasture; the water between the field and the island is shallow and sluggish. In summer's low water, flags and bulrushes grow along a series of shallow pools cooled by the lazy current. Water striders patrol the surface film, crayfish hump along the silt bottom eating filth, frogs shout and glare, and shiners and small bream hide among roots from the sulky green heron's eye. I come to this island every month of the year. I walk around it, stopping and staring, or I straddle the sycamore log over the creek, curling my legs out of the water in winter, trying to read. Today I sit on dry grass at the end of the island by the slower side of the creek. I'm drawn to this spot. I come to it as to an oracle; I return to it as a man years later will seek out the battlefield where he lost a leg or an arm.

A couple of summers ago I was walking along the edge of the island to see what I could see in the water, and mainly to scare frogs. Frogs have an inelegant way of taking off from invisible positions on the bank just ahead of your feet, in dire panic, emitting a froggy "Yike!" and splashing into the water. Incredibly, this amused me, and, incredibly, it amuses me still. As I walked along the grassy edge of the island, I got better and better at seeing frogs both in and out of the water. I learned to recognize, slowing down, the difference in texture of the light reflected from mudbank, water, grass, or frog. Frogs were flying all around me. At the end of the island I noticed a small green frog. He was exactly half in and half out of the water, looking like a schematic diagram of an amphibian, and he didn't jump.

He didn't jump; I crept closer. At last I knelt on the island's winterkilled grass, lost, dumbstruck, staring at the frog in the creek just four feet away.

He was a very small frog with wide, dull eyes. And just as I looked at him, he slowly crumpled and began to sag. The spirit vanished from his eyes as if snuffed. His skin emptied and drooped; his very skull seemed to collapse and settle like a kicked tent. He was shrinking before my eyes like a deflating football. I watched the taut, glistening skin on his shoulders ruck, and rumple, and fall. Soon, part of his skin, formless as a pricked balloon, lay in floating folds like bright sum on top of the water: it was a monstrous and terrifying thing. I gaped bewildered, appalled. An oval shadow hung in the water behind the drained frog; then the shadow glided away. The frog skin bag started to sink.

I had read about the giant water bug, but never seen one. "Giant water bug" is really the name of the creature, which is an enormous, heavy-bodied brown beetle. It eats insects, tadpoles, fish, and frogs. Its grasping forelegs are mighty and hooked inward. It seizes a victim with these legs, hugs it tight, and paralyzes it with enzymes injected during a vicious bite. That one bite is the only bite it ever takes. Through the puncture shoot the poisons that dissolve the victim's muscles and bones and organs—all but the skin—and through it the giant water bug sucks out the victim's body, reduced to a juice. This event is quite common in warm fresh water. The frog I saw was being sucked by a giant water bug. I had been kneeling on the island grass; when the unrecognizable flap of frog skin settled on the creek bottom, swaying, I stood up and brushed the knees of my pants. I couldn't catch my breath.

Of course, many carnivorous animals devour their prey alive. The usual method seems to be to subdue the victim by downing and grasping it so it can't flee, then eating it whole or in a series of bloody bites. Frogs eat everything whole, stuffing prey into their mouths with their thumbs. People have seen frogs with their wide jaws so full of live dragonflies they couldn't close them. Ants don't even have to catch their prey: in the spring they swarm over newly hatched, featherless birds in the nest and eat them tiny bite by bite.

That it's rough out there and chancy is no surprise. Every live thing is a survivor on a kind of extended emergency bivouac. But at the same time we are also created. In the Koran, Allah asks, "The heaven and the earth and all in between, thinkest thou I made them *in jest?*" It's a good question. What do we think of the created universe, spanning an unthinkable void with an unthinkable profusion of forms? Or what do we think of nothingness, those sickening reaches of time in either direction? If the giant water bug was not made in jest, was it then made in earnest? Pascal uses a nice term to describe the notion of the creator's, once having called forth the universe, turning his back to it: *Deus Absconditus.* Is this what we think happened? Was the sense of it there, and God absconded with it, ate it, like a wolf who disappears round the edge of the house with the Thanksgiving turkey? "God is subtle," Einstein said, "but not malicious." Again, Einstein said that "nature conceals her mystery by means of her essential grandeur, not by her cunning." It could be that God has not absconded but spread, as our vision and understanding of the universe have spread, to a fabric of spirit and sense so grand and subtle, so powerful in a new way, that we can only feel blindly of its hem. In making the thick darkness a swaddling band for the sea, God "set bars and doors" and said, "Hitherto shalt thou come, but no further." But have we come even that far? Have we rowed out to the thick darkness, or are we all playing pinochle in the bottom of the boat?

Cruelty is a mystery, and the waste of pain. But if we describe a world to compass these things, a world that is a long, brute game, then we bump against another mystery: the inrush of power and light, the canary that sings on the skull. Unless all ages and races of men have been deluded by the same mass hypnotist (who?), there seems to be such a thing as beauty, a grace wholly gratuitous. About five years ago I saw a mockingbird make a straight vertical descent from the roof gutter of a four-story building. It was an act as careless and spontaneous as the curl of a stem or the kindling of a star.

The mockingbird took a single step into the air and dropped. His wings were still folded against his sides as though he were singing from a limb and not falling, accelerating thirty-two feet per second per second, through empty air. Just a breath before he would have been dashed to the ground, he unfurled his wings with exact, deliberate care, revealing the broad bars of white, spread his elegant, white-banded tail, and so floated onto the grass. I had just rounded a corner when his insouciant step caught my eye; there was no one else in sight. The fact of his free fall was like the old philosophical conundrum about the tree that falls in the forest. The answer must be, I think, that beauty and grace are performed whether or not we will or sense them. The least we can do is try to be there.

Another time I saw another wonder: sharks off the Atlantic coast of Florida. There is a way a wave rises above the ocean horizon, a triangular wedge against the sky. If you stand where the ocean breaks on a shallow beach, you see the raised water in a wave is translucent, shot with lights. One late afternoon at low tide a hundred big sharks passed the beach near the mouth of a tidal river in a feeding frenzy. As each green wave rose from the churning water, it illuminated within itself the six- or eight-foot-long bodies of twisting sharks. The sharks disappeared as each wave rolled toward me; then a new wave would swell above the horizon, containing in it, like scorpions in amber, sharks that roiled and heaved. The sight held awesome wonders: power and beauty, grace tangled in a rapture with violence.

We don't know what's going on here. If these tremendous events are random combinations of matter run amok, the yield of millions of monkeys at millions of typewriters, then what is it in us, hammered out of those same typewriters, that they ignite? We don't know. Our life is a faint tracing on the surface of mystery, like the idle, curved tunnels of leaf miners on the face of a leaf. We must somehow take a wider view, look at the whole landscape, really see it, and describe what's going on here. Then we can at least wail the right question into the swaddling band of darkness, or, if it comes to that, choir the proper praise.

At the time of Lewis and Clark, setting the prairies on fire was a well-known signal that meant, "Come down to the water." It was an extravagant gesture, but we can't do less. If the landscape reveals one certainty, it is that the extravagant gesture is the very stuff of creation. After the one extravagant gesture of creation in the first place, the universe has continued to deal exclusively in extravagances, flinging intricacies and colossi down aeons of emptiness, heaping profusions on profligacies with ever-fresh vigor. The whole show has been on fire from the word go. I come down to the water to cool my eyes. But everywhere I look I see fire; that which isn't flint is tinder, and the whole world sparks and flames.

MEANING

1. What is the expressive point or thesis of "Heaven and Earth in Jest"? Is the essay controlled by a single idea or perhaps a cluster of related ones?
2. According to Dillard, what is the essential conflict in our understanding of nature? Why do we respond to nature in such a complex way?
3. Does Dillard's essay express her concern with religious themes? If so, what religious ideas or problems does she address?
4. Does the author seem to be at peace with her complex feelings? Why or why not?

METHOD

1. Is this essay formally or informally organized? Is there a pattern or plan to the arrangement of Dillard's details?
2. Are you prepared for the incident of the giant water bug? Why does Dillard plant it as a surprise?
3. Dillard expresses herself through description and poetic language. Point out some passages where her language is particularly vivid, moving, or beautiful.
4. Why do you think Dillard includes shocking or disturbing details in her prose?

AUDIENCE

1. Dillard's book *Pilgrim at Tinker Creek* is written as a journal of a year alone with nature. What gestures or clues does she include in her essay that open this seemingly private writing to a public audience?

2. Does Dillard make you feel as deeply about nature as she clearly feels? Does this essay express any of your own feelings about "heaven and earth"?

WRITING SUGGESTION

Compose an expressive essay in which you confront head-on your honest feelings about the world, nature, the cosmos. Try to avoid cloudy abstraction, however, and focus instead (as Dillard does) on the concreteness of awe or mystery. What specific things in the world provoke mystical or religious stirrings in you? What makes you particularly happy, exhilarated, anxious, or full of dread? Express your feelings through your treatment of these actualities.

ADDITIONAL WRITING SUGGESTIONS

Write an expressive essay on one of the following topics. Don't limit yourself to just a definition or description. Try to give rich, full expression to your thoughts and feelings.

- Love
- Death
- Loneliness
- Longing
- Beauty and ugliness
- Mystery
- God
- Sense of self
- Hope
- Fear

- Family
- Ambition and success
- Failure
- Moral Dilemmas
- Pain or suffering
- A favorite or despised time or place
- A current social issue
- A personal problem
- A philosophy of life

15

EXPRESSIVE NARRATIVES

AUTOBIOGRAPHY AND MEMOIR

The expressive impulse may come from any direction—thought, emotion, or experience. The form we choose to shape the writing that flows from this impulse depends on our subject and what we want to do with it. The personal essay, we've seen, gives voice to feelings and ideas, and is organized around a controlling focus or thesis. However, some subjects fit the essay form less well than do others, and may be better or more naturally expressed as stories. When we want to convey the feeling of experience itself, of time passing—when we want to give shape to a slice of life—we turn to expressive or personal narrative: autobiography and memoir.

The terms *autobiography* and *memoir* (both mean essentially the same thing) connote self-recording and memory, a recollection and re-creation of one's past. A descendant of Christian confessional writing, autobiography wasn't widely practiced until the 18th century. Since then it has become an immensely popular form of nonfiction literature.

In autobiography or memoir, we try to recapture a period of time in our life, sometimes the whole span of that life. We try to recall all the significant or meaningful facts and details that characterize the time and our reactions to it. We attempt to embody our experience in language, to render what may be largely private or subjective into public or objective form: in short, to give readers our experience and make them feel it as their own.

Some autobiographies dwell almost exclusively on the author's public life, citing lists of accomplishments, anecdotes about family and friends, and a detailed chronology of events. Perhaps the most interesting memoirs, however, blend a lively account of outward life with plenty of introspection (more about this later). Depending on the writer's inclination, too, autobiography may be slanted intellectually, concerned with the play of ideas in life, or emotionally, toward mood, feeling, and sensation.

Whatever the focus or slant, though, any writer of self-history must *select* from the massive amount of data that make up one's past. True, some autobiographers have tried to record their lives almost literally minute by minute, and the minutiae thus collected may have limitless fascination for them. For the rest of us, however, a life in time can have meaning only if it's drawn with distinct lines. As readers, we need to understand what the author feels to be important, where he or she places emphasis, why he or she thinks or feels a certain way.

With this in mind, let us look at some of the concerns we face when shaping our own lives as narrative.

THE TEXTURE OF EXPERIENCE

We have already talked at some length in Chapters 7 and 10 about the general process of constructing narrative: getting the facts, assembling a chronology, organizing for interest, and using description, dialog, and scenic construction in telling the story. For the rest of this chapter, we will consider how these elements bear on our present purpose.

When we write about our own lives, we want to express how time and experience feel to us. We want to evoke the *special* nature of what we've lived through—what makes it unique, memorable, exciting, moving—to capture the texture of life. A few basic questions will help point us toward this goal.

What is the felt need, the expressive impulse, behind the story?   Knowing why we want to write about some part of our lives will give us something to focus on, a principle or guide to help the process of selection. Is the impulse a painful emotion, say, embarrassment or shame? If so, then we should select those details and moments that best express it. If the impulse is grounded in an event or sequence of events, then we must select those features that best demonstrate why the impulse feeds the story, why it compels the story to be told. Moreover, if our impulse is *too* private, one that our reader is likely not to care about, this, too, should affect our decisions about what to say, or whether we should say anything at all.

What makes the subject or story unique?   Human life being what it is, many of us have had similar experiences, similar pains and joys. Yet although we share the human condition, each of us lives life as a unique individual. In getting the facts of our own story, then, we must try to be at least somewhat objective, and to ask at times difficult questions about ourselves. What was so special about that time our parents disappointed us, or we broke up with a girl- or boy-friend, or we were fired from a job, or we suffered grief over loss of a loved one, or we traveled to some exotic or dreary place? What *specific* thoughts, feelings, and incidents did we experience, and were these in any way remarkable? What was unusual, unexpected, disturbing, exhilarating, or just different?

What makes the story representative of anything beyond private experience?   Although the uniqueness of a personal story is what makes it most interesting to us, good autobiography usually reveals something more. It evokes a particular time, place, or situation *through* the individual experience. When selecting facts, descriptive detail, the language of dialog or conversation, and so on, we should look for things that reveal the *concreteness* of these specific times, places, and situations: details of fashion in dress and behavior, slang expressions, prevalent values and customs, and significant background information such as current events or issues. In this way, we show our lives to be rooted, connected to and expressive of a distinct moment.

With these questions in mind, we can assemble the materials that will best embody the feelings, thoughts, and experiences we want to convey in our stories to give them a texture all their own.

MOVEMENT AND CONFLICT

All narrative prose tries to capture life in motion, to give us the drama of life unfolding. In fictional stories (novels, movies, plays), readers usually expect the action or plot to revolve around a conflict, even if only a small or subtle one. The typical course of a dramatic story moves from announcement of the conflict through mounting struggle to a climax and resolution of the difficulty. In nonfiction narrative, on the other hand (largely because it *is* nonfiction and not open to the author's total imaginative control), we can't always rely on dramatic formulas. As we've seen in earlier chapters, writers can do much to make true stories as interesting as fiction, but they can't manufacture conflicts or force a nondramatic story into a dramatic mold.

When writing about ourselves, we face the same problem—telling the truth, and at the same time telling a good story. Is there a way to accomplish both goals? We can if we *search for autobiographical subjects that are themselves dramatic.* Like fiction writers, we can look for material in the various conflicts that shape human lives—in this case our own. Here, too, some basic questions will help guide us.

What kinds of inner struggles have influenced our character and actions?   Whether we're looking at the whole span of a life or only a piece of it, we can't fully express experience without acknowledging what motivates us. What self-contradictions have we tried to resolve? What strengths, weaknesses, vices, and virtues rule us?

What external conflicts have shaped our experience?   Likewise, our lives entail struggles with other people, institutions, and unforeseen circumstances. Which of these encounters have taken us in new directions? Has success or failure in one such instance permanently changed life's course? What conditions have we tried to create or escape? What struggles continue to define life now or in the future?

How has experience shaped character, and how has character thus affected experience? Finally, giving narrative expression to our lives means constructing a unified view of self in the world, bringing the inner and outer realms together. Who are we, what have we done, what have we thought or felt about it, how have we changed or tried to, what do we hope to do with ourselves and the world?

It would be wrong to suggest that we experience only conflict in our lives; certainly much affects us that does not call for struggle. Yet it's probably true that many of the really interesting and formative events in our autobiographies—the ones we'd want to stress—do involve some strife. The suggestions above are not limits, then, but just places to start looking at ourselves.

A final point: The nuts and bolts of narrative writing covered in Chapter 7 also should guide us here. Although the material of the story may be intimately known to us, it still pays to map out a chronology (especially of our inner life, the moments of which tend to run together in a blur), to play with various ways of organizing the *telling* of the story (leading with an event out of sequence, starting at the end and retracing, using flashback, withholding information to create suspense, and so on), and to keep the reader's interest always in mind.

When we write about others, such as in biography, we can't know for certain the whole truth of their inner lives, although we may know some of it and can speculate about the rest. While we also may never know the whole truth of our own lives, when we write about ourselves we can come to know much about the internal landscape we move through, and the drama of how it affects, and is affected by, the external one.

MAKING YOUR LIFE COME ALIVE ON THE PAGE

We've already discussed the importance of voice in personal writing (Chapter 14, "Expressive Essays"), and in personal narrative, certainly, the writer's voice carries meaning for the story and tells us much about his or her attitude and character. Although an authentic voice is necessary, however, it alone cannot make the author's experience live for the reader. None of what we've said so far can work without precise and energetic attention to the *stuff* of life, of experience grounded in particulars.

When telling our stories through narration, dialog, and scenes, then, we should keep reminding ourselves of two simple but demanding rules:

Observe closely.   Really close, accurate observation is not easy. It means study, not a quick pass. It means noticing what we see, hear, taste, smell, touch, learning its name, and remembering it. When we observe closely, we learn to *write from the thing itself,* whatever it might be: physical detail, sound, behavior, motion.

Listen carefully.   Listen for the words people use, and the patterns of their speech. Notice their voices, rhythms, vocabularies. Try to develop an *ear* for dialog, for the expressiveness of talk.

Whether the story you wish to tell is simple, with a single, unified action controlling it, or complex, with a number of events linked together or intertwined, tell it with your eyes and ears. Press your memory for specifics of time, place, mood, human character, and behavior. As you write, reimagine the experience in words as if you were reliving it in fact. The closer you get to the feel of the original moment in all its concreteness, the greater will be your reader's involvement and appreciation.

QUESTIONS

1. What kinds of subjects are better suited to the narrative than to the essay form? Why?
2. What guiding questions should we ask when writing stories about ourselves?
3. When choosing an autobiographical subject, why is it a good idea to look for dramatic material?
4. What guidelines will help in locating such material?
5. Why are close listening and observation important for vivid, expressive narrative?

EXERCISES

1.   As a pre-writing exercise, list at least 10 different autobiographical story possibilities. Which moments in your past seem to have been turning points? Which events or circumstances stand out as particularly memorable, moving, hilarious, or significant?

2.   Next, go through your list of story ideas and check the ones that are most attractive to you as subjects for expanded treatment. Which ones have you considered writing about but have yet to try? Which ones still hold your interest and are likely to be just as interesting to readers?

3.   From among this smaller list, now, ask yourself which subjects seem especially unique or revealing of your individual experience? For each, list some of the details you think illustrate this uniqueness. What aspects of the story make it special?

4. Next, jot down any characteristics or details that make these story possibilities representative of other persons' experiences. Which subjects, in other words, seem to be both individual and representative at the same time? (For example, a story about high school graduation might evoke something quite personal about your life yet also speak to others' similar experiences.)

5. Keeping focused on this narrowing field of subjects, ask which ones seem most dramatic. What kinds of conflicts come in to each story? Inner struggles or dilemmas? External battles with other people, situations, or institutions?

6. Finally, ask yourself which of your story ideas best illustrates the play of character and experience. That is, which moments in your life have had the greatest influence on making you who you are? Which ones show how your character has helped to shape your experience?

Note: Use this material, and this process for developing story ideas, as a starting point for the writing suggestions that follow this chapter's readings.

Readings

NORA EPHRON was born in New York in 1941 and grew up in Beverly Hills, California, the daughter of Hollywood screenwriters. She earned her B.A. from Wellesley College in 1962, and went to work for the New York Post *as a reporter in 1963. In 1968 she turned to freelancing, and worked for* Esquire *and* New York *magazines in the 1970s as a writer and contributing editor. Her pieces have been collected in* Wallflower at the Orgy *(1970) and* Crazy Salad *(1975). She is also the author of a novel,* Heartburn *(1983). In the following, Ephron tells the painful but funny story of her physical development and what it meant to her, and in doing so she speaks for a general human experience of growing up with a perceived imperfection.*

A Few Words about Breasts

by Nora Ephron

I have to begin with a few words about androgyny. In grammer school, in the fifth and sixth grades, we were all tyrannized by a rigid set of rules that supposedly determined whether we were boys or girls. The episode in *Huckleberry Finn* where Huck is disguised as a girl and gives himself away by the way he threads a needle and catches a ball—that kind of thing. We learned that the way you sat, crossed your legs, held a cigarette and looked at your nails, your wristwatch, the way you did these things instinctively was absolute proof of your sex. Now obviously most children did not take this literally, but I did. I thought that just one slip, just one incorrect cross of my legs or flick of an imaginary cigarette ash would turn me from whatever I was into the other thing; that would be all it took, really. Even though I was outwardly a girl and had many of the trappings generally associated with the field of girldom—a girl's name, for example, and dresses, my own telephone, an autograph book—I spent the early years of my adolescence absolutely certain that I might at any point gum it up. I did not feel at all like a girl. I was boyish. I was athletic, ambitious, outspoken, competitive, noisy, rambunctious. I had scabs on my knees and my socks slid into my loafers and I could throw a football. I wanted desperately not to be that way, not to be a mixture of both things but instead just one, a girl, a definite indisputable girl. As soft and as pink as a nursery. And nothing would do that for me, I felt, but breasts.

I was about six months younger than everyone in my class, and so for about six months after it began, for six months after my friends had begun to develop—that was the word we used, develop—I was not particularly worried. I would sit in the bathtub and look down at my breasts and know that any day now, any second now, they would start growing like everyone else's. They didn't. "I want to buy a bra," I said to my mother one night. "What for?" she said. My mother was really hateful about bras, and by the time my third sister had gotten to the point where she was ready to want one, my mother had worked the whole business into a comedy routine. "Why not use a Band-Aid instead?" she would say. It was a source of great pride to my mother that she had never even had to wear a brassiere until she had her fourth child, and then only because her gynecologist made her. It was incomprehensible to me that anyone could ever be proud of something like that. It was the 1950's, for God's sake. Jane Russell. Cashmere sweaters. Couldn't my mother see that? *"I am too old to wear an undershirt."* Screaming. Weeping. Shouting. "Then don't wear an undershirt," said my mother. "But I want to buy a bra." "What for?"

I suppose that for most girls, breasts, brassieres, that entire thing, has more trauma, more to do with the coming of adolescence, of becoming a woman, than anything else. Certainly more than getting your period, although that too was traumatic, symbolic. But you could *see* breasts; they were there; they were visible. Whereas a girl could claim to have her period for months before she actually got it and nobody would ever know the difference. Which is exactly what I did. All you had to do was make a great fuss over having enough nickels for the Kotex machine and walk around clutching your stomach and moaning for three to five days a month about The Curse and you could convince anybody. There is a school of thought somewhere in the women's lib/women's mag/gynecology establishment that claims that menstrual cramps are purely psychological, and I lean toward it. Not that I didn't have them finally. Agonizing cramps, heating-pad cramps, go-down-to-the-school-nurse-and-lie-on-the-cot cramps. But unlike any pain I had ever suffered, I adored the pain of cramps, welcomed it, wallowed in it, bragged about it. "I can't go. I have cramps." "I can't do that. I have cramps." And most of all, gigglingly, blushingly: "I can't swim. I have cramps." Nobody every used the hard-core word. Menstruation. God, what an awful word. Never that. "I have cramps."

The morning I first got my period, I went into my mother's bedroom to tell her. And my mother, my utterly-hateful-about-bras mother, burst into tears. It was really a lovely moment, and I remember it so clearly not just because it was one of the two times I ever saw my mother cry on my account (the other was when I was caught being a six-year-old kleptomaniac), but also because the incident did not mean to me what it meant to her. Her little girl, her firstborn, had finally become a woman. That was what she was crying about. My reaction to the event, however, was that I might well be a woman in some scientific, textbook sense (and could at least stop faking every month and stop wasting all those nickels). But in another sense—in a visible sense—I was as androgynous and as liable to tip over into boyhood as ever.

I started with a 28AA bra. I don't think they made them any smaller in those days, although I gather that now you can buy bras for five year olds that don't have any cups whatsoever in them; trainer bras they are called. My first brassiere came from Robinson's Department Store in Beverly Hills. I went there alone, shaking, positive they would look me over and smile and tell me to come back next year. An actual fitter took me into the dressing room and stood over me while I took off my blouse and tried the first one on. The little puffs stood out on my chest. "Lean over," said the fitter (to this day I am not sure what fitters in bra departments do except to tell you to lean over). I leaned over, with the fleeting hope that my breasts would miraculously fall out of my body and into the puffs. Nothing.

"Don't worry about it," said my friend Libby some months later, when things had not improved. "You'll get them after you're married."

"What are you talking about?" I said.

"When you get married," Libby explained, "your husband will touch your breasts and rub them and kiss them and they'll grow."

That was the killer. Necking I could deal with. Intercourse I could deal with. But it had never crossed my mind that a man was going to touch my breasts, that breasts had something to do with all that, petting, my God they never mentioned petting in my little sex manual about the fertilization of the ovum. I became dizzy. For I knew instantly—as naïve as I had been only a moment before—that only part of what she was saying was true: the touching, rubbing, kissing part, not the growing part. And I knew that no one would ever want to marry me. I had no breasts. I would never have breasts.

My best friend in school was Diana Raskob. She lived a block from me in a house full of wonders. English muffins, for instance. The Raskobs were the first people in Beverly Hills to have English muffins for breakfast. They also had an apricot tree in the back, and a badminton court, and a subscription to *Seventeen* magazine, and hundreds of games like Sorry and Parcheesi and Treasure Hunt and Anagrams. Diana and I spent three or four afternoons a week in their den reading and playing and eating. Diana's mother's kitchen was full of the most colossal assortment of junk food I have ever been exposed to. My house was full of apples and peaches and milk and homemade chocolate-chip cookies—which were nice, and good for you, but-not-right-before-dinner-or-you'll-spoil-your-appetite. Diana's house had nothing in it that was good for you, and what's more, you could stuff it in right up until dinner and nobody cared. Bar-B-Q potato chips (they were the first in them, too), giant bottles of ginger ale, fresh popcorn with melted butter, hot fudge sauce on Baskin-Robbins jamoca ice cream, powdered-sugar doughnuts from Van de Kamps. Diana and I had been best friends since we were seven; we were about equally popular in school (which is to say, not particularly), we had about the same success with boys (extremely intermittent) and we looked much the same. Dark. Tall. Gangly.

It is September, just before school begins. I am eleven years old, about to enter the seventh grade, and Diana and I have not seen each other all summer. I have been to camp and she has been somewhere like Banff with her parents. We are meeting, as we often do, on the street midway between our two houses and we will walk back to Diana's and eat junk and talk about what has happened to each of us that summer. I am walking down Walden Drive in my jeans and my father's shirt hanging out and my old red loafers with the socks falling into them and coming toward me is . . . I take a deep breath . . . a young woman. Diana. Her hair is curled and she has a waist and hips and a bust and she is wearing a straight skirt, an article of clothing I have been repeatedly told I will be unable to wear until I have the hips to hold it up. My jaw drops, and suddenly I am crying, crying hysterically, can't catch my breath sobbing. My best friend has betrayed me. She has gone ahead without me and done it. She has shaped up.

Here are some things I did to help: Bought a Mark Eden Bust Developer. Slept on my back for four years. Splashed cold water on them every night because some French actress said in *Life* magazine that that was what *she* did for her perfect bustline.

Ultimately, I resigned myself to a bad toss and began to wear padded bras. I think about them now, think about all those years in high school I went around in them, my three padded bras, every single one of them with different sized breasts. Each time I changed bras I changed sizes: one week nice perky but not too obtrusive breasts, the next medium-sized slightly pointy ones, the next week knockers, true knockers; all the time, whatever size I was, carrying around this rubberized appendage on my chest that occasionally crashed into a wall and was poked inward and had to be poked outward—I think about all that and wonder how anyone kept a straight face through it. My parents, who normally had no restraints about needling me—why did they say nothing as they watched my chest go up and down? My friends, who would periodically inspect my breasts for signs of growth and reassure me—why didn't they at least counsel consistency?

And the bathing suits. I die when I think about the bathing suits. That was the era when you could lay an uninhabited bathing suit on the beach and someone would make a pass at it. I would put one on, an absurd swimsuit with its enormous bust built into it, the bones from the suit stabbing me in the rib cage and leaving little red welts on my body, and there I would be, my chest plunging straight downward absolutely vertically from my collarbone to the top of my suit and then suddenly, wham, out came all that padding and material and wiring absolutely horizontally.

Buster Klepper was the first boy who ever touched them. He was my boyfriend my senior year of high school. There is a picture of him in my high-school yearbook that makes him look quite attractive in a Jewish, horn-rimmed glasses sort of way, but the picture does not show the pimples, which were airbrushed out, or the dumbness. Well, that isn't really fair. He wasn't dumb. He just wasn't terribly bright. His mother refused to accept it, refused to accept the relentlessly average report cards, refused to deal with her son's inevitable destiny in some junior college or other. "He was tested," she would say to me, apropos of nothing, "and it came out 145. That's near-genius." Had the word underachiever been coined, she probably would have lobbed that one at me, too. Anyway, Buster was really very sweet—which is, I know, damning with faint praise, but there it is. I was the editor of the front page of the high-school newspaper and he was editor of the back page; we had to work together, side by side, in the print shop, and that was how it started. On our first date, we went to see *April Love* starring Pat Boone. Then we started going together. Buster had a green coupe, a 1950 Ford with an engine he had hand-chromed until it shone, dazzled, reflected the image of anyone who looked into it, anyone usually being Buster polishing it or the gas-station attendants he constantly asked to check the oil in order for them to be overwhelmed by the sparkle on the valves. The car also had a boot stretched over the back seat for reasons I never understood; hanging from the rearview mirror, as was the custom, was a pair of angora dice. A previous girl friend named Solange who was famous throughout Beverly Hills High School for having no pigment on her right eyebrow had knitted them for him. Buster and I would ride around town, the two of us seated to the left of the steering wheel. I would shift gears. It was nice.

There was necking. Terrific necking. First in the car, overlooking Los Angeles from what is now the Trousdale Estates. Then on the bed of his parent's cabana at Ocean House. Incredibly wonderful, frustrating necking, I loved it, really, but no further than necking, please don't, please, because there I was absolutely terrified of the general implications of going-a-step-further with a near-dummy and also terrified of his finding out there was next to nothing there (which he knew, of course; he wasn't that dumb).

I broke up with him at one point. I think we were apart for about two weeks. At the end of that time I drove down to see a friend at a boarding school in Palos Verdes Estates and a disc jockey played *April Love* on the radio four times during the trip. I took it as a sign. I drove straight back to Griffith Park to a golf tournament Buster was playing in (he was the sixth-seeded teen-age golf player in Southern California) and presented myself back to him on the green of the 18th hole. It was all very dramatic. That night we went to a drive-in and I let him get his hand under my protuberances and onto my breasts. He really didn't seem to mind at all.

Do you want to marry my son?" the woman asked me.
"Yes," I said.
I was nineteen years old, a virgin, going with this woman's son, this big strange woman who was married to a Lutheran minister in New Hampshire and pretended she was Gentile and had this son, by her first husband, this total fool of a son who ran the hero-sandwich concession at Harvard Business School and whom for one moment one December in New Hampshire I said—as much out of politeness as anything else—that I wanted to marry.
"Fine," she said. "Now, here's what you do. Always make sure you're on top of him so you won't seem so small. My bust is very large, you see, so I always lie on my back to make it look smaller, but you'll have to be on top most of the time."
I nodded. "Thank you," I said.
"I have a book for you to read," she went on. "Take it with you when you leave. Keep it." She went to the bookshelf, found it, and gave it to me. It was a book on frigidity.
"Thank you," I said.

That is a true story. Everything in this article is a true story, but I feel I have to point out that that story in particular is true. It happened on December 30, 1960. I think about it often. When it first happened, I naturally assumed that the woman's son, my boyfriend, was responsible. I invented a scenario where he had had a little heart-to-heart with his mother and had confessed that his only objection to me was that my breasts were small; his mother then took it upon herself to help out. Now I think I was wrong about the incident. The mother was acting on her own, I think: that was her way of being cruel and competitive under the guise of being helpful and maternal. You have small breasts, she was saying; therefore you will never make him as happy as I have. Or you have small breasts; therefore you will doubtless have sexual problems. Or you have small breasts; therefore you are less woman than I am. She was, as it happens, only the first of what seems to me to be a never-ending string of women who have made competitive remarks to me about breast size. "I would love to wear a dress like that," my friend Emily says to me, "but my bust is too big." Like that. Why do women say these things to me? Do I attract these remarks the way other women attract married men or alcoholics or homosexuals? This summer, for example. I am at a party in East Hampton and I am introduced to a woman from Washington. She is a minor celebrity, very pretty and Southern and blonde and outspoken and I am flattered because she has read something I have written. We are talking animatedly, we have been talking no more than five minutes, when a man comes up to join us. "Look at the two of us," the woman says to the man, indicating me and her. "The two of us together couldn't fill an A cup." Why does she say that? It isn't even true, dammit, so why? Is she even more addled than I am on this subject? Does she honestly believe there is something wrong with her size breasts, which, it seems to me, now that I look hard at them, are just right. Do I unconsciously bring out competitiveness in women? In that form? What did I do to deserve it?

As for men.

There are men who minded and let me know they minded. There were men who did not mind. In any case, I always minded.

And even now, now that I have been countlessly reassured that my figure is a good one, now that I am grown up enough to understand that most of my feelings have very little to do with the reality of my shape, I am nonetheless obsessed by breasts. I cannot help it. I grew up in the terrible Fifties—with rigid stereotypical sex roles, the insistence that men be men and dress like men and women be women and dress like women, the intolerance of adrogyny—and I cannot shake it, cannot shake my feelings of inadequacy. Well, that time is gone, right? All those exaggerated examples of breast worship are gone, right? Those women were freaks, right? I know all that. And yet, here I am, stuck with the psychological remains of it all, stuck with my own peculiar version of breast worship. You probably think I am crazy to go on like this: here I have set out to write a confession that is meant to hit you with the shock of recognition and instead you are sitting there thinking I am thoroughly warped. Well, what can I tell you? If I had had them, I would have been a completely different person. I honestly believe that.

After I went into therapy, a process that made it possible for me to tell total strangers at cocktail parties that breasts were the hang-up of my life, I was often told that I was insane to have been bothered by my condition. I was also frequently told, by close friends, that I was extremely boring on the subject. And my girl friends, the ones with nice big breasts, would go on endlessly about how their lives had been far more miserable than mine. Their bra straps were snapped in class. The couldn't sleep on their stomachs. They were stared at whenever the word "mountain" cropped up in geography. And *Evangeline*, good God what they went through every time someone had to stand up and recite the Prologue to Longfellow's *Evangeline*: ". . . stand like druids of eld . . . /With beards that rest on their bosoms."* It was much worse for them, they tell me. They had a terrible time of it, they assure me, I don't know how lucky I was, they say.

I have thought about their remarks, tried to put myself in their place, considered their point of view. I think they are full of shit.

MEANING

1. What conclusion has Ephron come to about the role her breasts played in her life? How does the story she tells embody or illustrate that judgment?
2. What about Ephron's story makes it unique? Cite specific details that evoke her individual experience.
3. What about her story makes it representative of others' experience? Can a young man, for example, find anything that speaks to his life in this story? Explain.
4. What sort of conflicts does Ephron detail in her narrative? Are they largely inner conflicts, external ones, or a combination?
5. In what ways did experience shape Ephron's character? Has her character had any subsequent effect on her experience?

METHOD

1. Ephron is a master at looking and listening. Cite some of her most effective descriptions and dialog.
2. How does the author use scenes with her narration? Which scenes are most revealing or expressive of Ephron's story?
3. What principle does Ephron use to guide her selection of detail? What effect does such a focusing principle have on her story?
4. How would you describe the author's voice, tone, and attitude? Point up some examples of where her language is particularly expressive of these qualities.

AUDIENCE

1. Does Ephron aim this story at a mostly female readership? Is there any evidence to suggest she's writing just as much for male readers?
2. What is your response to "A Few Words about Breasts"? Does Ephron draw you into her experience and make you feel it? Do you tend to laugh at her story or find in it a humorous treatment of a serious subject?

WRITING SUGGESTIONS

1. Write an autobiographical narrative in which you focus the story (and your selection of events and detail) on a single concern or theme. Use description, dialog, scenes, and an expressive voice to create a compelling experience for your reader.

2. Write an autobiographical account of a single event that has both serious and funny sides. Experiment with different approaches to telling the story, and emphasize one aspect or the other, until you find the one that best expresses your feelings about what happened.

RUSSELL BAKER was born in 1925 in Virginia. He grew up amid poor surroundings but interesting people, and decided early in life that he wanted to be a writer. He earned his B.A. from Johns Hopkins University in 1947. Joining the Baltimore Sun *as a staff writer that same year, he became London bureau chief in 1953. In 1954 Baker moved to* The New York Times *Washington bureau, and began writing his now widely followed "Observer" column for the* Times *in 1962. His books include* An American in Washington *(1961);* All Things Considered *(1965);* Poor Russell's Almanac *(1972);* So This Is Depravity *(1980); and his autobiography* Growing Up *(1982), for which he won one of his two Pulitzer Prizes. In the following selection, the first chapter of* Growing Up, *Baker tells of a hospital visit to his ailing mother, and evokes a sense of her entire life.*

A Braided Cord

by Russell Baker

At the age of eighty my mother had her last bad fall, and after that her mind wandered free through time. Some days she went to weddings and funerals that had taken place half a century earlier. On others she presided over family dinners cooked on Sunday afternoons for children who were now gray with age. Through all this she lay in bed but moved across time, traveling among the dead decades with a speed and ease beyond the gift of physical science.

"Where's Russell?" she asked one day when I came to visit at the nursing home.

"I'm Russell," I said.

She gazed at this improbably overgrown figure out of an inconceivable future and promptly dismissed it.

"Russell's only this big," she said, holding her hand, palm down, two feet from the floor. That day she was a young country wife with chickens in the backyard and a view of hazy blue Virginia mountains behind the apple orchard, and I was a stranger old enough to be her father.

Early one morning she phoned me in New York. "Are you coming to my funeral today?" she asked.

It was an awkward question with which to be awakened. "What are you talking about, for God's sake?" was the best reply I could manage.

"I'm being buried today," she declared briskly, as though announcing an important social event.

"I'll phone you back," I said and hung up, and when I did phone back she was all right, although she wasn't all right, of course, and we all knew she wasn't.

She had always been a small woman—short, light-boned, delicately structured—but now, under the white hospital sheet, she was becoming tiny. I thought of a doll with huge, fierce eyes. There had always been a fierceness in her. It showed in that angry, challenging thrust of the chin when she issued an opinion, and a great one she had always been for issuing opinions.

"I tell people exactly what's on my mind," she had been fond of boasting. "I tell them what I think, whether they like it or not." Often they had not liked it. She could be sarcastic to people in whom she detected evidence of the ignoramus or the fool.

"It's not always good policy to tell people exactly what's on your mind," I used to caution her.

"If they don't like it, that's too bad," was her customary reply, "because that's the way I am."

And so she was. A formidable woman. Determined to speak her mind, determined to have her way, determined to bend those who opposed her. In that time when I had known her best, my mother had hurled herself at life with chin thrust forward, eyes blazing, and an energy that made her seem always on the run.

She ran after squawking chickens, an axe in her hand, determined on a beheading that would put dinner in the pot. She ran when she made the beds, ran when she set the table. One Thanksgiving she burned herself badly when, running up from the cellar oven with the ceremonial turkey, she tripped on the stairs and tumbled back down, ending at the bottom in the debris of giblets, hot gravy, and battered turkey. Life was combat, and victory was not to the lazy, the timid, the slugabed, the drugstore cowboy, the libertine, the mushmouth afraid to tell people exactly what was on his mind whether people liked it or not. She ran.

But now the running was over. For a time I could not accept the inevitable. As I sat by her bed, my impulse was to argue her back to reality. On my first visit to the hospital in Baltimore, she asked who I was.

"Russell," I said.

"Russell's way out west," she advised me.

"No, I'm right here."

"Guess where I came from today?" was her response.

"Where?"

"All the way from New Jersey."

"When?"

"Tonight."

"No. You've been in the hospital for three days," I insisted.

"I suggest the thing to do is calm down a little bit," she replied. "Go over to the house and shut the door."

Now she was years deep into the past, living in the neighborhood where she had settled forty years earlier, and she had just been talking with Mrs. Hoffman, a neighbor across the street.

"It's like Mrs. Hoffman said today: The children always wander back to where they come from," she remarked.

"Mrs. Hoffman has been dead for fifteen years."

"Russ got married today," she replied.

"I got married in 1950," I said, which was the fact.

"The house is unlocked," she said.

So it went until a doctor came by to give one of those oral quizzes that medical men apply in such cases. She failed catastrophically, giving wrong answers or none at all to "What day is this?" "Do you know where you are?" "How old are you?" and so on. Then, a surprise.

"When is your birthday?" he asked.

"November 5, 1897," she said. Correct. Absolutely correct.

"How do you remember that?" the doctor asked.

"Because I was born on Guy Fawkes Day," she said.

"Guy Fawkes?" asked the doctor. "Who is Guy Fawkes?"

She replied with a rhyme I had heard her recite time and again over the years when the subject of her birth date arose:

> "Please to remember the Fifth of November,
> Gunpowder treason and plot.
> I see no reason why gunpowder treason
> Should ever be forgot."

Then she glared at this young doctor so ill informed about Guy Fawkes' failed scheme to blow King James off his throne with barrels of gunpowder in 1605. She had been a schoolteacher, after all, and knew how to glare at a dolt. "You may know a lot about medicine, but you obviously don't know any history," she said. Having told him exactly what was on her mind, she left us again.

The doctors diagnosed a hopeless senility. Not unusual, they said. "Hardening of the arteries" was the explanation for laymen. I thought it was more complicated than that. For ten years or more the ferocity with which she had once attacked life had been turning to a rage against the weakness, the boredom, and the absence of love that too much age had brought her. Now, after the last bad fall, she seemed to have broken chains that imprisoned her in a life she had come to hate and to return to a time inhabited by people who loved her, a time in which she was needed. Gradually I understood. It was the first time in years I had seen her happy.

She had written a letter three years earlier which explained more than "hardening of the arteries." I had gone down from New York to Baltimore, where she lived, for one of my infrequent visits and, afterwards, had written her with some banal advice to look for the silver lining, to count her blessings instead of burdening others with her miseries. I suppose what it really amounted to was a threat that if she was not more cheerful during my visits I would not come to see her very often. Sons are capable of such letters. This one was written out of a childish faith in the eternal strength of parents, a naïve belief that age and wear could be overcome by an effort of will, that all she needed was a good pep talk to recharge a flagging spirit. It was such a foolish, innocent idea, but one thinks of parents differently from other people. Other people can become frail and break, but not parents.

She wrote back in an unusually cheery vein intended to demonstrate, I suppose, that she was mending her ways. She was never a woman to apologize, but for one moment with the pen in her hand she came very close. Referring to my visit, she wrote: "If I seemed unhappy to you at times—" Here she drew back, reconsidered, and said something quite different:

"If I seemed unhappy to you at times, I am, but there's really nothing anyone can do about it, because I'm just so very tired and lonely that I'll just go to sleep and forget it." She was then seventy-eight.

Now, three years later, after the last bad fall, she had managed to forget the fatigue and loneliness and, in these free-wheeling excursions back through time, to recapture happiness. I soon stopped trying to wrest her back to what I considered the real world and tried to travel along with her on those fantastic swoops into the past. One day when I arrived at her bedside she was radiant.

"Feeling good today," I said.

"Why shouldn't I feel good?" she asked. "Papa's going to take me up to Baltimore on the boat today."

At that moment she was a young girl standing on a wharf at Merry Point, Virginia, waiting for the Chesapeake Bay steamer with her father, who had been dead sixty-one years. William Howard Taft was in the White House, Europe still drowsed in the dusk of the great century of peace, America was a young country, and the future stretched before it in beams of crystal sunlight. "The greatest country on God's green earth," her father might have said, if I had been able to step into my mother's time machine and join him on the wharf with the satchels packed for Baltimore.

I could imagine her there quite clearly. She was wearing a blue dress with big puffy sleeves and long black stockings. There was a ribbon in her hair and a big bow tied on the side of her head. There had been a childhood photograph in her bedroom which showed all this, although the colors of course had been added years later by a restorer who tinted the picture.

About her father, my grandfather, I could only guess, and indeed, about the girl on the wharf with the bow in her hair, I was merely sentimentalizing. Of my mother's childhood and her people, of their time and place, I knew very little. A world had lived and died, and though it was part of my blood and bone I knew little more about it than I knew of the world of the pharaohs. It was useless now to ask for help from my mother. The orbits of her mind rarely touched present interrogators for more than a moment.

Sitting at her bedside, forever out of touch with her, I wondered about my own children, and their children, and children in general, and about the disconnections between children and parents that prevent them from knowing each other. Children rarely want to know who their parents were before they were parents, and when age finally stirs their curiosity there is no parent left to tell them. If a parent does lift the curtain a bit, it is often only to stun the young with some exemplary tale of how much harder life was in the old days.

I had been guilty of this when my children were small in the early 1960s and living the affluent life. It galled me that their childhoods should be, as I thought, so easy when my own had been, as I thought, so hard. I had developed the habit, when they complained about the steak being over-cooked or the television being cut off, of lecturing them on the harshness of life in my day.

"In my day all we got for dinner was macaroni and cheese, and we were glad to get it."

"In my day we didn't have any television."

"In my day . . . "

"In my day . . . "

At dinner one evening a son had offended me with an inadequate report card, and as I leaned back and cleared my throat to lecture, he gazed at me with an expression of unutterable resignation and said, "Tell me how it was in your days, Dad."

I was angry with him for that, but angrier with myself for having become one of those ancient bores whose highly selective memories of the past become transparently dishonest even to small children. I tried to break the habit, but must have failed. A few years later my son was referring to me when I was out of earshot as "the old-timer." Between us there was a dispute about time. He looked upon the time that had been my future in a disturbing way. My future was past, and being young, he was indifferent to the past.

As I hovered over my mother's bed listening for muffled signals from her childhood, I realized that this same dispute had existed between her and me. When she was young, with life ahead of her, I had been her future and resented it. Instinctively, I wanted to break free, cease being a creature defined by her time, consign her future to the past, and create my own. Well, I had finally done that, and then with my own children I had seen my exciting future become their boring past.

These hopeless end-of-the-line visits with my mother made me wish I had not thrown off my own past so carelessly. We all come from the past, and children ought to know what it was that went into their making, to know that life is a braided cord of humanity stretching up from time long gone, and that it cannot be defined by the span of a single journey from diaper to shroud.

MEANING

1. In this brief, compressed story of a woman's life, Baker manages to say much about his mother's character. What sort of person was she? What feelings does her son express about her?
2. List some of the details that help make this story unique. Why is it, at the same time, a story evoking universal human experience?
3. What conflicts has Baker used to help shape and focus this narrative?
4. Why does Baker include a scene with his son in this story?

METHOD

1. Baker's story has a complex structure. Why does he reorder the strict chronology of his mother's life?
2. This story actually has two different narrative lines or actions. One has to do with Baker's mother's biography. What is the other?
3. Where is Baker especially effective in his use of description, dialog, and scenes?
4. What do the author's voice and prose style tell you about his character? Why do you think Baker allows humor to enter his story?

AUDIENCE

1. As a syndicated columnist, Russell Baker had a wide readership established before he published his autobiography. What effect is such an audience likely to have on the way a writer chooses and presents his mate-

rial? What effect would it have on your writing if you knew a group of fans was waiting for your work?

2. If you are not a fan of Baker's, what is your response to this first chapter of his autobiography? Does it make you want to keep reading? Are you engaged by the author's voice, style, humor?

WRITING SUGGESTION

Narrate an autobiographical account of your encounter with a significant person in your life either in a single event or in a series of them. Let a portrait of your subject emerge through the story's scenes and details. Write about those moments that especially reveal important qualities about the person and your feelings about him or her.

MICHAEL J. MILLER was born in Galena, Illinois, in 1964 and grew up in Hanover, Illinois. As a student at Hanover High School, Miller served as president of the freshman class, played varsity baseball, was a national winner in a Marvel Comics essay contest (Miller is a collector and comic-book aficionado), published fiction in the Hanover Hi-Lites, *and was an honors speaker at his graduation. He will be a 1986 graduate of Loras College, Dubuque, Iowa, where he double-majors in English and Writing, works on the yearbook staff, and belongs to the Literary Club. Miller plans to earn his living as a writer. In the following piece, he narrates the story of a high school ritual, and captures it with sharp observation and playful but affectionate style.*

Out of the Frying Pan . . .

by *Michael J. Miller*

Humiliation has never been one of my strong suits. Call me stuffy, but making a complete idiot of myself has always been something I've tried to avoid. I really don't enjoy such activities as showering on my knees, kissing someone else's shoe, being shut in an empty locker for a half hour or burying my face in a giant bowl of whipped cream. However, I performed all these wondrous and amusing tasks (and more!) on that fateful day in May of 1979. Another Slave Day was upon good ol' Hanover High, and this year it was *my* Slave Day.

Slave Day. The name pretty much says it all. Each year freshmen would be herded together in the old gym while upperclassmen glared at them from the bleachers, their mouths salivating as they wrung their hands in anticipation. This was the one day of the year when sadism was encour-

Michael J. Miller, "Out of the Frying Pan . . ." Used by permission.

aged. Freshmen's names would be placed in a hat and drawn at random. The freshmen picked would walk out in the middle of the gym and stand on a large wooden platform while science teacher/auctioneer Lawrence Barber would take "bids" from the upperclassmen. The highest bidder would then "own" that freshman for the whole day. From then on, the upperclassman's wish was the freshman's command.

There was a carnival atmosphere in the old gym that warm May morning. Sophomores, juniors and seniors had padded their wallets with fives, tens, and in some cases twenties in hopes of purchasing their very own human punching bags.

The attendance on the annual Slave Day broke records, with even the most notoriously truant students putting in appearances. I saw faces staring at me from across the floors that I had seen only once or twice all year.

At last, it was time for us to march in, thirty-four pale and expectant fourteen-year-olds. We sat rigidly on the old gym stage, about fifty feet from the bleachers. The girls giggled nervously. Slave Day was usually not nearly as excruciating for girls, since they were either bought by girlfriends or guys who were interested in them. We boys were coldly silent. We knew what was in store for us.

Amid the general chaos expected when 150-or-so teenagers were gathered together, principal Harlon Edwards walked to the center of the gym, cleared his throat, and began reading the "rules" for the day.

"No whips, chains, or other restrictive devices may be used on slaves," Mr. Edwards read aloud from the student handbook. "A master may not strike a slave, and doing so will result in the removal of that slave from that master's ownership."

Great speech, Harlon, I thought as I sat on the stage with accumulating dread.

Mr. Barber had appeared in the middle of the gym. A rapidly balding, chimp-faced man he seemed to take genuine pleasure from being the auctioneer at this event. He drew a name from the hat.

"Tim Melvin," Mr. Barber announced loudly.

As the names began to dwindle in the hat, I wondered vaguely who would try to buy me. No matter who did it was certain humiliation, of course. I was just worried about the *degree* of humiliation.

"Mike Miller," bellowed Mr. Barber, turning ceremoniously toward the stage, his finger pointing in my direction.

I felt myself jump off the stage and walk trancelike to the black wooden platform. I looked anxiously into the swarming crowd, feeling absurdly like Hester Prynne in *The Scarlet Letter*. Lawrence Barber began scurrying back and forth in front of me.

"Do I hear an opening bid?" he barked, gesturing wildly.

As he waited for a bid, I noticed some of my classmates who had been sold before me were already jumping through their master's proverbial hoops. Upperclassmen were pulling out their various instruments of torture: cans of shaving cream, jars of Dippety-Doo, women's undergarments, frogman's flippers. Joe Gelt was busily using his nose to push a penny around the gym floor, while his master nodded approvingly. Cal Martz stood behind Mr. Barber, mocking his every gesture. Mark Norris awkwardly attempted to squeeze his 6'4" frame into a dress that had obviously been owned by someone's grandmother. Cindy Shelton diligently tied my shoelaces together, despite my protests. A boy infamous for his greasy hair was dragged off to the showers, where his master vowed to make him wash his hair each hour.

"You can't make me!" the boy screamed. "You can't make me!"

As I later learned, he *did* make him. Meanwhile, in a distant corner, Johnny Collins was doing the "dying cockroach," which consists of lying on your back, arms and legs stretched skyward.

"Two dollars! I've got two dollars bid, do I hear three?" Mr. Barber boomed.

I tried to find where that bid had come from, craning my neck to see. Harry Hicks grinned maliciously at me from the bleachers.

Oh, no, *Harry Hicks* was bidding on me! Picture a muscular, blond, long-haired Barry Manilow, and you have a good image of Harry Hicks. He had been my personal terror all year. He seemed to exist for no other purpose than to hammer at me in fifth hour gym. The reason was fairly simple: he was big, and I wasn't. That was enough reason for Harry. At that point I wondered why he bothered to bid on me at all. He'd been pounding me for free all year! Harry had a reputation for testing the limits of those "slave–master" rules, and I knew he would like nothing better than to have me as this year's guinea pig.

I felt weak as the blood surged to my head, pounding against my temples. If this guy was going to be my master, I was as good as dead.

"I hear three! Three dollars!" Mr. Barber raved. "Do I hear four dollars?"

Someone had made a counterbid! A quick check of the crowd found Pete Ferris, an upperclassman friend of mine, raising three fingers triumphantly in the air.

My eyes locked on Harry. He was in conference with some of his Cro-Magnon buddies, obviously trying to borrow money. Harry was notoriously cheap. At last they broke the huddle.

"Four!" he shouted, nodding his head at me.

"Four dollars are bid! Do I hear five?"

"Five," I heard Pete say. Good old Pete.

There was a long hesitation. I knew five dollars was not very much for a slave. Over the years I'd heard tales of slaves going for 25 or 30 dollars. The bidding wasn't over yet.

Harry had involved still more of his buddies in this second huddle. His face was animated, his eyes wide, his nostrils flaring. This was a man who desperately wanted me for a slave.

"I hear five dollars, do I hear six? I hear five dollars . . . " Mr. Barber said, looking only at Harry, since no one else had shown much interest, thank God. "Five dollars going once, going twice . . ."

I exhaled heavily. Harry had been defeated. I had been granted a last minute reprieve.

"Ten dollars!" Harry blurted out.

This is it, I thought. The next day's headlines formed in my head. "Slave Day Ends in Tragedy, Freshman Miller Killed in Band Saw 'Accident'." My eyes pleaded with Pete, who was now in a conference of his own. This did not bode well. Pete was my friend and didn't want to see me fall into Harry's clutches, but ten dollars was ten dollars.

Time seemed frozen. Pete continued talking in hushed tones with three or four others. I noticed two of them shaking their heads vigorously, while Pete pointed accusingly at Harry.

Harry had produced his wallet, and so had some of this friends theirs. I tried to envision what dark and unspeakable ordeals I would soon be forced to endure. I glanced forlornly at Pete, who shrugged as if to say, "Well, at least I tried."

". . . going once, going twice," Mr. Barber was saying. "Going once . . . what? Do I hear a bid?"

I hadn't heard anything, but Mr. Barber was looking at Pete. Had he decided to outbid Harry?

"Fiftee . . ." Pete mumbled.

Mr. Barber grinned, smelling a sale and goading Pete on. "Did I hear fifteen?"

"Yes," Pete said weakly. He obviously was none too happy about having to shell out so much money.

I heaved a sigh. Harry sat down slowly, dejected as he replaced his wallet. He continued to stare at me coldly, as if to say, "Consider yourself lucky, punk."

Pete placed three fives in Mr. Barber's eager hands, and motioned for me to come over. At last I was going to get off that damned platform! I took a small, nervous step forward and fell flat on my face. In the excitement of the auction I had forgotten Cindy had tied my shoes together.

Finally I righted myself and waddled over to Pete, still waiting in the bleachers. "Thanks, man, you saved my life!"

He nodded, not looking at me. As I disentangled my shoelaces, I noticed he was digging around in a large shopping bag.

"What's with the bag?" I asked.

Pete turned to face me, holding a long, frilly pink dress. A toothy smile filled his face.

"O.K., Slave," he said. "Put it on."

My legs felt as if they would melt out from under me. My savior had become my tormentor! The whole gym began to swirl as I mentally heard the jeering hoots and hollers of the next eight hours. *Oh, man!* I thought. Why hadn't Harry tried to outbid this jerk?

MEANING

1. How would you describe Miller's attitude toward the "Slave Day" events he recounts in this story? Is he critical of the ritual? Cite specific evidence supporting your interpretation.
2. "Out of the Frying Pan . . . " is built around a specific conflict. What is it? Does the story express any general conflicts or themes of adolescence? If so, what might they be?

METHOD

1. Miller's story has a classic narrative structure. Point out the sections of this piece where he sets the scene, establishes the conflict, develops the struggle, builds toward a climax, and resolves the conflict.
2. Throughout the story, Miller uses a variety of narrative techniques. Find particularly apt or effective examples of description and dialog. What do you think these passages add to this tale?

AUDIENCE

1. To what extent does Miller's account seem slanted toward a specific audience? What qualities of this story might appeal to a more general, especially older, reader? Why?
2. Do you find "Out of the Frying Pan . . . " a convincing or authentic portrayal of high school? Why or why not?

WRITING SUGGESTION

Compose an autobiographical narrative about a single incident in your life that embodies a conflict. Following Miller's lead, structure the story in stages, developing the tension of the conflict, bringing it to a climax, and resolving it. Pay particular attention, as does Miller, to specific detail, and to advance the action of the story, and characterization.

ADDITIONAL WRITING SUGGESTIONS

The following topics may help you develop and focus material for autobiographical narrative.

- A frightening experience
- Breaking away from parents
- First love
- A major loss
- First big success
- Learning reluctantly
- Transitions
- Leaving home

- Failure or humiliation
- Increased awareness
- A near-miss
- The most important day
- Breaking up
- Witness to history
- A heroic deed
- A final decision

16

ENTERTAINMENTS

WRITING TO DELIGHT

We conclude our survey of expressive nonfiction with a kind of prose most of us love to read but find nearly impossible to write: humor. We may admire the likes of Woody Allen, James Thurber, Mark Twain, and any number of other humorous writers, but when moved to express ourselves by writing something funny we may freeze up. We sense the risk (what is more humiliating than a bad joke?) and the difficulty (what to write about?). We know that humorists are gifted people and that without the gift you might as well forget it. But while it's true that great humor does seem to come from a select crew of geniuses, any of us can learn to express this side of ourselves and to shape our ideas and experiences for entertaining effect.

The work we speak of here is not really different from what we've covered in the last two chapters, but it is perhaps a more specialized application. Humorous writing is aimed directly at the audience, and its purpose is to make the audience laugh. It may meet all the qualifications of expressive prose, but it has one extra burden to shoulder: Personal essays and stories need not delight us to be effective—they may speak to any emotion or circumstance; humorous essays and stories, on the other hand, not only express what we need to say, but they must be funny. All expressive writing may *use* humor; entertainments make it their chief aim.

The term *humor* is complex and includes an assortment of types, methods, and media of expression: from sweet, folksy stories to savage satire; from jokes, puns, and gags to complicated dramatic narratives; from filmed food-fights to the cerebral wit of *The New Yorker*. For our purposes, we distinguish between two basic forms of written humor, fiction and nonfiction. The two are sometimes indistinguishable, but we can say at least that humorous nonfiction is built from actual events and references, while humorous fiction goes beyond these limits to construct a separate fanciful world. Two common types of fictional humor, parody and satire, give us ridiculous or scornful imitations of real things, people, and situations. Humorous nonfiction, as essays and narratives, frequently use mockery and sarcasm but must stop short of a full substitution of imagination for the real world. Like fictional humor, however, nonfiction entertainments do employ the full range of verbal and situational wit—humor based on language and ideas, on the one hand, and on character and circumstance, on the other.

Whatever form humor takes (and this includes both fiction and nonfiction), its major element is the unexpected—whether as an association of incongruous or incompatible things or ideas, or as a sudden shock of recognition pleasing in its truthfulness or accuracy. Writing humorous nonfiction means trying to discover and suitably shape such surprises for our reader's, as well as our own, delight.

SOME PROBLEMS

Aside from the sheer agony of *trying* to be funny (which may be the worst way to approach the task), writing humorous essays and nonfiction stories does present a number of special obstacles. In the long run, however, if we allow the writing process the time to work, and if we pay attention to what happens, we should be able to exercise as much control (and thus surmount the obstacles) as we would in any of the writing we've studied.

Probably one of the most intimidating features of humor is its subjectivity. Some scream (and groan) with pleasure at Monty Python movies, while others are outraged by their tastelessness. Some people love puns, the more awful the better, and others hate them. It's the same for every brand of humor, from pie-in-the-face slapstick to Shakespeare. Every time we venture forth with humor, we expose our own subjectivity, and, even more to the point, we expose ourselves to the subjectivity of others. It's not for nothing that stand-up comics, after a poorly received performance, say they "died up there."

Still, any time we write anything for public consumption (even if the audience is no larger than a college class) we take this chance. Potential critics will always await us in the shadows, sometimes in plain sight. We must learn to temper their responses with our own critical self-appraisal. This is especially important for a writer of humor. Our humor is nothing if it is not uniquely our own—not copied, not influenced by others until it's theirs and not ours. We must be true to our own honest sense of what's funny and what isn't, and we must be willing to stand by it, even if the audience has to learn to appreciate us. (How often have you changed your opinion of a comic writer or performer after a weak first impression?) Our goal is to make the audience laugh at what *we* laugh at, not to cater to its expectations. By this we do not mean complete disregard of the reader's tastes and attitudes—it rarely pays to consciously offend people—but a healthy respect for our own comic instincts.

A related problem: How do we *know* when our humor is working? Doesn't its very subjectivity make it difficult to evaluate objectively? It does, so it often helps to get another point of view. When you've reached a stage where you have, say, a solid second draft, something you feel a growing sense of confidence about, let a friend read it. Consider his or her response as one of a number of possible reactions, not the last word. How close was it to what you'd hoped for? Are you being too subtle, or too obvious? Did the reader laugh in the right places? Do suggestions for changes make sense?

Another obstacle that faces the budding humorist is choice of subject. What to write about? But here again the answer is simpler than we might guess. The felt need of the expressive writer applies as much to humor. Much of the wit, sarcasm, parody, and jokes we produce spontaneously in talk is in *reaction* to something, and our humorous response meets a need created by that thing. Humorous writers, likewise, are forever reacting to the world, to people, events, ideas—especially to foolishness, self-importance, greed, and a myriad of human shortcomings. Sometimes subjects fall into our laps like gifts; sometimes we have to work to find them. In either case, we must first trust our own judgment and pick subjects that honestly appeal to us and elicit from us a humorous reaction.

Finally, there is the problem of originality. All of the writing we do calls for some original thinking and creativity, and as the work grows in complexity, so does the need for these qualities. In personal or expressive writing, we expect originality almost by definition. In some quarters, unfortunately, the word has come to mean novelty for its own sake—and the more wild, horrendous, and bizarre, the more "brilliant." Humor, too, may be pushed to such extremes, and in the right hands it can be stunning, breaking new ground. Even the most apparently insane creativity can't work for long, however, without control and intelligence; real originality isn't just novelty, but novelty that *means* something.

The goal of originality takes us back again to the writing process. Certainly we should allow ourselves to write and think as freely as possible as we explore humorous possibilities by following comic lines to absurd conclusions, if that's where they lead. Nonetheless, the process also demands that we stand back and evaluate where we've gone. Does the work honestly express our sense of humor? Does it make sense or interesting *non*-sense? Is the reader likely to "get" it? Is it *heavily* influenced by the tone or style of someone else's humor? Does it seem fresh? Is it funny?

SOME GUIDELINES

Since humor delights us with the unexpected (the *punch*line of a joke), we should keep the element of surprise in our favor. Telegraphing—warning the reader with statements such as "Now, here comes the really funny

370 Writing to Express or Entertain

part" or "This next thing is *hilarious!*"—short-circuits humor and drains its
energy. The opposite strategy, building suspense and anticipation by holding back the surprise, is almost always the better choice. The humorous
payoff may be small (a phrase at the end of a sentence, for example) or
large (the climactic scene of a narrative), but it should be unanticipated.

One major source of humor, we've said, is the association of the incongruous or incompatible—the dignified fellow who gets a bucket of paint
dumped on his head. When two mutually exclusive worlds are brought
together as one, the resulting conflict or tension can produce opportunities
for humor. In the following example, Woody Allen, one of the masters of
this technique, joins the abstruse language of economics and the most
ordinary of concerns in this passage from his parody of a college bulletin:

> *Economic Theory:* A systematic application and critical evaluation of the basic
> analytic concepts of economic theory, with an emphasis on money and why it's
> good. Fixed coefficient production functions, cost and supply curves, and
> nonconvexity comprise the first semester, with the second semester concen-
> trating on spending, making change, and keeping a neat wallet. The Federal
> Reserve System is analyzed, and advanced students are coached in the proper
> method of filling out a deposit slip. Other topics include: Inflation and Depres-
> sion—how to dress for each. Loans, interest, welching.

Notice the shape of each sentence: starting with a straight-faced use of
"official" language and style, each dives suddenly into the unexpectedly
banal—from "systematic application and critical evaluation" to "money
and why it's good," from "fixed coefficient production functions" to
"keeping a neat wallet." We may not have the talent of a professional like
Allen, but we can learn much from his and others' use of such a basic
humorous strategy.

The other major source, the pleasing "shock of recognition," informs all
expressive writing and comes from keen observation. In humor, the unexpected detail, lifelike dialog and characterization, and the telling remark
create truthfulness and believability. The old saying "Truth is stranger than
fiction" might be amended to read "Truth is as funny as fiction—if it's
accurate." Sharp perception gives humor life. For instance, notice how
author Kate White, in just a few words, captures a characteristic behavior
of men she defines as "creeps":

> Creeps have *"boyish charm."* Because creeps are self-absorbed, they don't like
> responsibility and commitment and thus resist becoming full-fledged adults.
> It's not that they're immature exactly. You can certainly dress them up and take
> them anyplace. Instead, they have a propensity for hanging on to many of the
> props of their youth. Be extremely wary of any man who wears a lucky hat;
> calls his car by a name (or, worse, his apartment: One creep I went out with
> asked me if I wanted to go back to his "tree fort"); still orders kegs for parties;

considers getting drunk an accomplishment ("Boy, do I have a hangover!"); and displays a picture in his apartment of himself in a rugby shirt having beer poured over his head or with six guys throwing a girl off a dock.

Although at first glance these details may seem exaggerated, we quickly realize the pointed truth in them, and we laugh.

Still another way writers achieve humorous effect is through *tone*, which may be droll, sarcastic, naïve, whimsical, tongue-in-cheek, deadpan, and so on depending on the writer's attitude and the effect he or she wants. It's usually wise to avoid extremes of tone (extreme sarcasm, for example, can become grating after a short while), keeping more toward understatement. The subtle approach—letting the humor "dawn" on the readers rather than hammering them on the head—may work better on the page. Exaggeration and overstatement ("I was so embarrassed I turned fifteen shades of red!") can work for emphasis, pacing, characterization, but should be used in moderation; too much exaggeration tends to create an hysterical tone, which may be funny only if it's intended.

Along with tone, our *prose style* will affect humorous expression. Some writers have been successful with an ornate, elaborate style that is funny in its very excesses, but such a style is hard to learn and harder to control. Most of us are better off staying with our own unhyped-up voice and by being brief and suggestive instead of gaudy. This does not mean to hold back from making honest, emphatic statements, but to keep language simple, direct, natural—the pain but individual styles we've seen throughout this book.

Finally, as we look for humorous subjects and struggle with the process of writing about them, we should keep the metaphor of play always in mind. While all writing has its playful dimension, humorous writing is play for its own sake, play purely for the fun of it. Play, as we have seen, however, is not mindless frivolity; the fun of play comes from our taking the game seriously. Expressing ourselves through humor, too, is serious. It demands that we be intelligent, sensitive, truthful, and that we exercise our fullest powers of observation. It asks that we take life seriously enough to laugh about it.

QUESTIONS

1. How does humor differ from other forms of expressive writing?
2. What characteristics distinguish humorous nonfiction from humorous fiction? What feature do both nonfiction and fictional humor share?
3. What are four common problems writers face when trying to be funny?
4. What are some of the techniques writers use for humorous effect?

EXERCISES

1.   Think about the people you know who make you laugh. Why are the things they say or do funny? Do they seem to use any humorous techniques consistently or with special skill? Analyze their methods of style, delivery, use of surprise.

2.   Apply the same sort of analysis to your favorite humorous writers or performers. What consistent traits or qualities do you notice about their work?

3.   List every type of humor you can think of and the things you like or dislike about each type (Examples: slapstick or physical humor, situational comedy, verbal humor, and so on). What kinds of comedy or humor are you most attracted to? Why?

4.   As in the exercises for the previous chapter, make a working list of possible subjects for humorous writing—strange or funny experiences, weird situations, odd characters, surprises. Try to briefly develop each topic for its humorous possibilities, and see which ones offer the most potential for writing. Then jot down as many specifics as you can for each—details, funny lines, mishaps, aspects of character—for use in the writing assignments to follow.

Readings

WOODY ALLEN, born Allen Stewart Konigsberg in 1935, grew up in Brooklyn, New York. He attended New York University and City College, but left school to pursue a full-time career in show business. In high school, Allen sold jokes to celebrities, and his material was good enough to land him a staff writing job at NBC in 1952 at age 16, where he wrote for such television comics as Sid Caesar, Art Carney, Buddy Hackett, and Jack Paar. In 1961 Allen began making professional nightclub and TV appearances as a standup comedian, and he won a national following almost immediately. His record albums were bestsellers, and he soon expanded his career to include writing for the stage and screen. Allen is now best known as a director of elegant and original films, many of them comedies. Among his movies: Take the Money and Run *(1969);* Play It Again, Sam *(1972);* Sleeper *(1973);* Annie Hall *(1977);* Manhattan *(1979);* A Midsummer Night's Sex Comedy *(1982);* Zelig *(1983);* Broadway Danny Rose *(1984); and* The Purple Rose of Cairo *(1985). He is also the author of three books of humor:* Getting Even *(1971);* Without Feathers *(1975); and* Side Effects *(1980). In the following satirical essay, Allen addresses a serious subject with typical irreverence.*

A Brief, Yet Helpful, Guide to Civil Disobedience

by Woody Allen

In perpetrating a revolution, there are two requirements: someone or something to revolt against and someone to actually show up and do the revolting. Dress is usually casual and both parties may be flexible about time and place but if either faction fails to attend, the whole enterprise is likely to come off badly. In the Chinese Revolution of 1650 neither party showed up and the deposit on the hall was forfeited.

The people or parties revolted against are called the "oppressors" and are easily recognized as they seem to be the ones having all the fun. The "oppressors" generally get to wear suits, own land, and play their radios late at night without being yelled at. Their job is to maintain the "status quo," a condition where everything remains the same although they may be willing to paint every two years.

When the "oppressors" become too strict, we have what is known as a police state, wherein all dissent is forbidden, as is chuckling, showing up in a bow tie, or referring to the mayor as "Fats." Civil liberties are greatly curtailed in a police state, and freedom of speech is unheard of, although one is allowed to mime to a record. Opinions critical of the government are not tolerated, particularly about their dancing. Freedom of the press is also curtailed and the ruling party "manages" the news, permitting the citizens to hear only acceptable political ideas and ball scores that will not cause unrest.

The groups who revolt are called the "oppressed" and can generally be seen milling about and grumbling or claiming to have headaches. (It should be noted that the oppressors never revolt and attempt to become the oppressed as that would entail a change of underwear.)

Some famous examples of revolutions are:

The French Revolution, in which the peasants seized power by force and quickly changed all locks on the palace doors so the nobles could not get back in. Then they had a large party and gorged themselves. When the nobles finally recaptured the palace they were forced to clean up and found many stains and cigarette burns.

The Russian Revolution, which simmered for years and suddenly erupted when the serfs finally realized that the Czar and the Tsar were the same person.

It should be noted that after a revolution is over, the "oppressed" frequently take over and begin acting like the "oppressors." Of course by then it is very hard to get them on the phone and money lent for cigarettes and gum during the fighting may as well be forgotten about.

Methods of Civil disobedience:

Hunger Strike. Here the oppressed goes without food until his demands are met. Insidious politicians will often leave biscuits within easy reach or perhaps some cheddar cheese, but they must be resisted. If the party in power can get the striker to eat, they usually have little trouble putting down the insurrection. If they can get him to eat and also lift the check, they have won for sure. In Pakistan, a hunger strike was broken when the government produced an exceptionally fine veal cordon bleu which the masses found was too appealing to turn down, but such gourmet dishes are rare.

The problem with the hunger strike is that after several days one can get quite hungry, particularly since sound trucks are paid to go through the street saying, "Um . . . what nice chicken—umm . . . some peas . . . umm . . ."

A modified form of the Hunger Strike for those whose political convictions are not quite so radical is giving up chives. This small gesture, when used properly, can greatly influence a government, and it is well known that Mahatma Gandhi's insistence on eating his salads untossed shamed the British government into many concessions. Other things besides food one can give up are: whist, smiling, and standing on one foot and imitating a crane.

Sit-down Strike. Proceed to a designated spot and then sit down, but sit all the way down. Otherwise you are squatting, a position that makes no political point unless the government is also squatting. (This is rare, although a government will occasionally crouch in cold weather.) The trick is to remain seated until concessions are made, but as in the Hunger Strike, the government will try subtle means of making the striker rise. They may say, "Okay, everybody up, we're closing." Or, "Can you get up for a minute, we'd just like to see how tall you are?"

Demonstration and Marches. The key point about a demonstration is that it must be seen. Hence the term "demonstration." If a person demonstrates privately in his own home, this is not technically a demonstration but merely "acting silly" or "behaving like an ass."

A fine example of a demonstration was the Boston Tea Party, where outraged Americans disguised as Indians dumped British tea into the harbor. Later, Indians disguised as outraged Americans dumped actual British into the harbor. Following that, the British disguised as tea, dumped each other into the harbor. Finally, German mercenaries clad only in costumes from *The Trojan Women* leapt into the harbor for no apparent reason.

When demonstrating, it is good to carry a placard stating one's position.

Some suggested positions are: (1) lower taxes, (2) raise taxes, and (3) stop grinning at Persians.

Miscellaneous methods of Civil Disobedience:

Standing in front of City Hall and chanting the word "pudding" until one's demands are met.

Tying up traffic by leading a flock of sheep into the shopping area.

Phoning members of "the establishment" and singing "Bess, You Is My Woman Now" into the phone.

Dressing as a policeman and then skipping.

Pretending to be an artichoke but punching people as they pass.

MEANING

1. One of America's most original and skillful humorists, Woody Allen rarely makes fun of only one thing at a time. What are some of the targets of Allen's humor in "A Brief, Yet Helpful, Guide"?
2. Does Allen's parody have a single controlling point or idea? If so, what do you think it is?

METHOD

1. Point out examples of Allen's use of surprise. Are most of his surprises incongruous remarks or shocks of recognition? Explain.
2. How would you describe the tone of Allen's essay? What writing style is he imitating?
3. How does Allen use descriptive detail for humorous effect? Cite several examples.

AUDIENCE

1. Like many humorists, Allen has a loyal following—and another group who can't understand why people like him. What about this piece is likely to appeal only to fans? Are there aspects to this humor that might make a nonfan laugh?
2. In which group are you? Do you think "Guide" is funny? If so, what do you like about it? If not, try to be specific in your criticism.

WRITING SUGGESTION

Write a satirical essay that pokes fun at a subject that amuses, irritates, or otherwise interests you. What makes the subject worthy of ridicule? What about it seems silly, inconsistent, or just funny? Some targets: advertising, politics, romance, education, status-seeking, parents, popular culture.

JAMES THURBER (1894–1961) was one of the United States' most admired and widely read humorists for several decades, and many of his books are still in print a quarter century after his death. Thurber was born in Columbus, Ohio, and graduated from Ohio State University in 1919. He worked as a newspaper reporter for the Columbus Dispatch, the Chicago Tribune, and the New York Evening Post before joining the staff of The New Yorker in 1927. The magazine became Thurber's home base for the rest of his career, and over the years he contributed scores of drawings, essays, short stories, and fables to its pages. Among his most famous books: Is Sex Necessary? (co-authored with E. B. White, 1929); My Life and Hard Times (1933/1968); Fables for Our Time (1940); The Thurber Carnival (later the source for a Broadway review, 1945); The Years with Ross (1959). In the following chapter from My Life and Hard Times, Thurber tells the unlikely story of a single evening of chaos at his childhood home in Columbus.

The Night the Bed Fell

by James Thurber

I suppose that the high-water mark of my youth in Columbus, Ohio, was the night the bed fell on my father. It makes a better recitation (unless, as some friends of mine have said, one has heard it five or six times) than it does a piece of writing, for it is almost necessary to throw furniture around, shake doors, and bark like a dog, to lend the proper atmosphere and verisimilitude to what is admittedly a somewhat incredible tale. Still, it did take place.

It happened, then, that my father had decided to sleep in the attic one night, to be away where he could think. My mother opposed the notion strongly because, she said, the old wooden bed up there was unsafe: it was wobbly and the heavy headboard would crash down on father's head in case the bed fell, and kill him. There was no dissuading him, however, and at a quarter past ten he closed the attic door behind him and went up the narrow twisting stairs. We later heard ominous creakings as he crawled into bed. Grandfather, who usually slept in the attic bed when he was with us, had disappeared some days before. (On these occasions he was usually gone six or eight days and returned growling and out of temper, with the news that the federal Union was run by a passel of blockheads and that the Army of the Potomac didn't have any more chance than a fiddler's bitch.)

We had visiting us at this time a nervous first cousin of mine named Briggs Beall, who believed that he was likely to cease breathing when he was asleep. It was his feeling that if he were not awakened every hour during the night, he might die of suffocation. He had been accustomed to setting an alarm clock to ring at intervals until morning, but I persuaded him to abandon this. He slept in my room and I told him that I was such a light sleeper that if anybody quit breathing in the same room with me, I would wake instantly. He tested me the first night—which I had suspected he would—by holding his breath after my regular breathing had convinced him I was asleep. I was not asleep, however, and called to him. This seemed to allay his fears a little, but he took the precaution of putting a glass of spirits of camphor on a little table at the head of his bed. In case I didn't arouse him until he was almost gone, he said, he would sniff the camphor, a powerful reviver. Briggs was not the only member of his family who had his crotchets. Old Aunt Melissa Beall (who could whistle like a man, with two fingers in her mouth) suffered under the premonition that she was destined to die on South High Street, because she had been born on South High Street and married on South High Street. Then there was Aunt Sarah Shoaf, who never went to bed at night without the fear that a burglar was going to get in and blow chloroform under her door through a tube. To avert this calamity—for she was in greater dread of anesthetics than of losing her household goods—she always piled her money, silverware, and other valuables in a neat stack just outside her bedroom, with a note reading: "This is all I have. Please take it and do not use your chloroform, as this is all I have." Aunt Gracie Shoaf also had a burglar phobia, but she met it with more fortitude. She was confident that burglars had been getting into her house every night for forty years. The fact that she never missed anything was to her no proof to the contrary. She always claimed that she scared them off before they could take anything, by throwing shoes down the hallway. When she went to bed she piled, where she could get at them handily, all the shoes there were about her house. Five minutes after she had turned off the light, she would sit up in bed and say "Hark!" Her husband, who had learned to ignore the whole situation as long ago as 1903, would either be sound asleep or pretend to be sound asleep. In either case he would not respond to her tugging and pulling, so that presently she would arise, tiptoe to the door, open it slightly and heave a shoe down the hall in one direction, and its mate down the hall in the other direction. Some nights she threw them all, some nights only a couple of pair.

But I am straying from the remarkable incidents that took place during the night that the bed fell on father. By midnight we were all in bed. The layout of the rooms and the disposition of their occupants is important to an understanding of what later occurred. In the front room upstairs (just under father's attic bedroom) were my mother and my brother Herman, who sometimes sang in his sleep, usually "Marching Through Georgia" or "Onward, Christian Soldiers." Briggs Beall and myself were in a room adjoining this one. My brother Roy was in a room across the hall from ours. Our bull terrier, Rex, slept in the hall.

My bed was an army cot, one of those affairs which are made wide enough to sleep on comfortably only by putting up, flat with the middle section, the two sides which ordinarily hang down like the sideboards of a drop-leaf table. When these sides are up, it is perilous to roll too far toward the edge, for then the cot is likely to tip completely over, bringing the whole bed down on top of one, with a tremendous banging crash. This, in fact, is precisely what happened, about two o'clock in the morning. (It was my mother who, in recalling the scene later, first referred to it as "the night the bed fell on your father.")

Always a deep sleeper, slow to arouse (I had lied to Briggs), I was at first unconscious of what had happened when the iron cot rolled me onto the floor and toppled over on me. It left me still warmly bundled up and un-hurt, for the bed rested above me like a canopy. Hence I did not wake up, only reached the edge of consciousness and went back. The racket, how-ever, instantly awakened my mother, in the next room, who came to the immediate conclusion that her worst dread was realized: the big wooden bed upstairs had fallen on father. She therefore screamed, "Let's go to your poor father!" It was this shout, rather than the noise of my cot falling, that awakened Herman, in the same room with her. He thought that mother had become, for no apparent reason, hysterical. "You're all right, Mamma!" he shouted, trying to calm her. They exchanged shout for shout for perhaps ten seconds: "Let's go to your poor father!" and "You're all right!" That woke up Briggs. By this time I was conscious of what was going on, in a vague way, but did not yet realize that I was under my bed instead of on it. Briggs, awakening in the midst of loud shouts of fear and apprehension, came to the quick conclusion that he was suffocating and that we were all trying to "bring him out." With a low moan, he grasped the glass of camphor at the head of his bed and instead of sniffing it poured it over himself. The room reeked of camphor. "Ugf, ahfg," choked Briggs, like a drowning man, for he had almost succeeded in stopping his breath under the deluge of pungent spirits. He leaped out of bed and groped toward the open window, but he came up against one that was closed. With his hand, he beat out the glass, and I could hear it crash and tinkle on the alleyway below. It was at this juncture that I, in trying to get up, had the uncanny sensation of feeling my bed above me! Foggy with sleep, I now suspected, in my turn, that the whole uproar was being made in a frantic endeavor to extricate me from what must be an unheard-of and perilous situation. "Get me out of this!" I bawled. "Get me out!" I think I had the nightmarish belief that I was entombed in a mine. "Gugh," gasped Briggs, floundering in his camphor.

By this time my mother, still shouting, pursued by Herman, still shout-ing, was trying to open the door to the attic, in order to go up and get my father's body out of the wreckage. The door was stuck, however, and wouldn't yield. Her frantic pulls on it only added to the general banging and confusion. Roy and the dog were now up, the one shouting questions, the other barking.

Father, farthest away and soundest sleeper of all, had by this time been awakened by the battering on the attic door. He decided that the house was on fire. "I'm coming, I'm coming!" he wailed in a slow, sleepy voice— it took him many minutes to regain full consciousness. My mother, still believing he was caught under the bed, detected in his "I'm coming!" the mournful, resigned note of one who is preparing to meet his Maker. "He's dying!" she shouted.

"I'm all right!" Briggs yelled to reassure her. "I'm all right!" He still believed that it was his own closeness to death that was worrying mother. I found at last the light switch in my room, unlocked the door, and Briggs and I joined the others at the attic door. The dog, who never did like Briggs, jumped for him—assuming that he was the culprit in whatever was going on—and Roy had to throw Rex and hold him. We could hear father crawling out of bed upstairs. Roy pulled the attic door open, with a mighty jerk, and father came down the stairs, sleepy and irritable but safe and sound. My mother began to weep when she saw him. Rex began to howl. "What in the name of God is going on here?" asked father.

The situation was finally put together like a gigantic jigsaw puzzle. Father caught a cold from prowling around in his bare feet but there were no other bad results. "I'm glad," said mother, who always looked on the bright side of things, "that your grandfather wasn't here."

MEANING

1. Is Thurber telling this "somewhat incredible tale" strictly for entertainment, or does the story embody any themes or ideas beyond the merely bizarre?
2. How believable are Thurber's characters—Roy, Briggs, Aunt Gracie Shoaf, Herman? Do you think Thurber is telling the whole truth and nothing but the truth? Why?

METHOD

1. Thurber plants any number of surprises in this story, some having to do with character, others with the situation. What are some of these surprises? How would you describe them?
2. To what extent do Thurber's voice and prose style contribute to the humor in "The Night the Bed Fell"? Point out several sentences you think funny and analyze why they make you laugh.
3. Much of the humor here relies on characterization. Cite some examples of especially effective or striking description and detail.
4. What narrative writing strategies does Thurber use in his story?

AUDIENCE

1. Is there anything about Thurber's subject or brand of humor likely to limit his audience? If so, why?
2. How do you respond to "The Night the Bed Fell"? What are its humorous strengths and weaknesses for you?

WRITING SUGGESTION

Using Thurber as a model, write a "comedy of errors" story about an actual event you experienced or know of second hand. Study Thurber's techniques of setting up the story, developing character, pacing the action, building to a climax, and maintaining a light, humorous tone.

Born in Washington, DC in 1938, JUDITH MARTIN (Miss Manners) earned her B.A. at Wellesley College. She joined the Washington Post *as a reporter in 1960 and later became a film and drama critic for that newspaper. She is the author of* The Name on the White House Floor *(1973), a collection of columns on Washington social life. She began writing a regular column as Miss Manners in 1978, and her exhaustive* Miss Manners' Guide to Excruciatingly Correct Behavior *was published in 1982. Martin's latest book is called* Miss Manners' Guide to Rearing Perfect Children *(1984). In the following essay, an excerpt from the Introduction to her first Miss Manners book, Martin speaks with humor about the need for manners in social behavior.*

Some Thoughts on the Impulse Rude and the Mannerly Way of Life

by Judith Martin

"Assertiveness," "Looking out for number one," and other systems for the dissemination of rudeness are abhorrent to Miss Manners. That people should spend hours studying vile little books and then disciplining themselves so as best to add to the general unpleasantness in the world is shocking.

Why, they could be spending that time learning to behave like Miss Manners.

Miss Manners is unfailingly polite. When Miss Manners is treated badly, she responds courteously. This is known as Not Stooping, or Shaming Them, or Setting a Good Example. It generally works. In any case, Miss Manners believes that two wrongs make a blight.

Miss Manners also believes that, if one always does the right thing, one does not have to read nasty little books about how to deal with guilt. One never has any.

Nevertheless—and this is the interesting part—Miss Manners does not suffer from the indignities that "assertiveness" asserts it can correct. No one ever takes advantage of Miss Manners without her consent. (What happens when she consents is also interesting, but another story.)

It is true that Miss Manners occasionally says "Yes" when she means "No" and, on special occasions, "No" when she means "Yes." Some ambiguity is desirable in social relations, of only to keep us all paying attention. What Miss Manners usually says when pressed to do something she does not wish to is "Oh, I would *so* love to, but I can't possibly," or "How delightful—*do* let me call you when I see my way clear."

As for the rudeness of others, Miss Manners finds that is conquered by politeness. For example, a gentleman of Miss Manners' acquaintance dislikes being honked at by impatient drivers for not starting his automobile quickly enough when a traffic signal turns to green. Instead of honking back, however, he puts on his emergency brake, emerges from his car, presents himself to the honker in the vehicle behind, and inquires gently, "Did you summon me?"

It is not, however, that Miss Manners has never felt the Impulse Rude. You wouldn't trust a preacher who never experienced the temptations of sin, would you?

The rudeness of others arouses that bestial desire in Miss Manners: the hotel clerk who shrugs when you ask what "Guaranteed reservation" means if having one doesn't entitle you to a room; the waiter who snaps "Can't you see I'm busy?" when you want to get a check and leave, believing your business to be as important as his; the secretary who demands your name, puts you on hold, and then comes back minutes later and demands your name again; the taxi driver who asks your destination and then drives away while you are telling it.

How one longs to strike back. But if rudeness begets rudeness, which begets more rudeness, where will it all end? (And when did Miss Manners turn into a preacher? The verb "to beget" was never in her vocabulary before, surely.) There are now many believers in the art of getting back, and many books, classes, and discussions on techniques for doing so. Miss Manners often receives letters from people who assume that she is such a believer and can supply a method for "putting down" this person or that.

Alas. At the risk of sounding unbearably saintly, Miss Manners will not subscribe to such behavior. She does not allow rude people to spoil her life, but she does not seek satisfaction in spoiling theirs.

For one thing, they outnumber her. One can easily encounter a dozen provoking rudenesses on the way to work in the morning, and a matching set on the way home. A lunch hour spent shopping, or, for that matter, trying to buy lunch, can increase the total tenfold. For another thing, counterrudenesses are escalating, sometimes beyond rudeness itself into violence. Even the lexicon of rudeness one hears these days is explicitly violent, although the specific words are usually sexual. (Does anyone know why such a nice practice as sex should have to supply the words for uncontrolled hostility? Miss Manners needs that explained to her, because she has never understood. On second thought, she would prefer that it not be explained to her.)

What, then, does one do with one's justified anger? Miss Manners, who makes a distinction between people and things, will sometimes look the other way if you wish to take out your anger on objects, within the limits of legality. Yet that can be dangerous. A gentleman of Miss Manners' acquaintance who recently kicked a large inanimate object—a Buick—that had offended him, found a large animate object emerging from it to continue the fight.

Miss Manners' meager arsenal consists only of the withering look, the insistent and repeated request, the cold voice, the report up the chain of command, and the tilted nose. Also the ability to dismiss inferior behavior from her mind as coming from inferior people.

You will perhaps point out that she will never know the joy of delivering a well-deserved sock in the chops. True—but she will never inspire one, either. . . .

On Correcting Others

It would be futile for Miss Manners to pretend to know nothing of the wicked joy of correcting others.

There is that pleasant bubble in the throat, a suppressed giggle at another person's ignorance; that flush of generosity accompanying the resolve to set the poor soul straight; that fever of human kindness when one proclaims, for the benefit of others, one's superior knowledge. Isn't that, after all, the great reward of the trade that Miss Manners practices? Can Miss Manners, whose vocation, whose calling, is correcting people for their own good, condemn the practice?

Certainly.

Miss Manners corrects only upon request. Then she does it from a distance, with no names attached, and no personal relationship, however distant, between the corrector and the correctee. She does not search out errors, like a policeman leaping out of a speed trap. When Miss Manners observes people behaving rudely, she never steps in to correct them. She behaves politely to them, and then goes home and snickers about them afterward. That is what the well-bred person does. The only way to enjoy the fun of catching people behaving disgustingly is to have children. One has to keep having them, however, because it is incorrect to correct grown people, even if you have grown them yourself. This is the mistake that many people make when they give helpful criticism to their children-in-law, who arrive on the scene already grown.

Miss Manners is constantly besieged by people who want to know the tactful manner of pointing out their friends' and relatives' inferiorities. These people, their loved ones report to Miss Manners, chew with their mouth open, mispronounce words, talk too loudly, crack their knuckles, spit, belch, and hum tunelessly to themselves. They have bad breath and runs in their stockings. They are too fat, dress badly, and do their hair all wrong.

How can those who love these people dearly, for reasons that are not clear, and who wish to help them, for reasons that unfortunately are clear, politely let them have it?

The answer is that they cannot, certainly not politely. There are times, in certain trusting relationships, when one can accomplish this impolitely. One can sometimes say, "Cracking your knuckles drives me up the wall and if you do it one more time I'll scream," or "Have a mint—there's something wrong with your breath," or "What's that thing on your left front tooth?" No reasonable person should take offense at these remarks. Because they are so frank, they do not seem to carry a history of repulsion long predating the offense. Also they deal with matters that are more or less easily correctable (although Miss Manners knows some determined knuckle crackers she suspects aren't half trying to stop), and which it is plausible to assume the offenders hadn't noticed.

What is unacceptable is to criticize things a person cannot easily remedy or may not want to. People who you think are too fat either disagree about what too fat is, are trying to do something about it, or are not trying to do something about it. In no case is it helpful for them to know that other people consider them too fat.

It is admittedly difficult to arrest the pleasure of correcting and advising long enough to ask oneself who will feel better after the correction is delivered—the person issuing it, or the one who gets it full in the face? But it is well worth the effort, not only for kindness' sake, but because it is a law of nature that he who corrects others will soon do something perfectly awful himself.

Even if it be proven that the mistakes of others come from gross ignorance or from maliciousness, it is not the place of anyone except God, their mothers, or Miss Manners to bring this to their attention. As dear Erasmus said, "It is part of the highest civility if, while never erring yourself, you ignore the errors of others."

Miss Manners prefers to believe that everyone means well, and that if anyone seems to be doing something wrong, it is probably not from intent but from forgetfulness, busyness, absence of mind, or illness. Miss Manners may be mistaken in this now and again, but she leads a happier life for believing it. . . .

On Embarrassment

While guilt is an emotion Miss Manners does without, having taken the simple precaution of always doing everything right the first time, embarrassment interests her. Miss Manners cannot be expected to experience embarrassment firsthand, but it is something for which she has a moderate amount of sympathy. The proper use of embarrassment is as a conscience of manners. As your conscience might trouble you if you do anything immoral, your sense of embarrassment should be activated if you do anything unmannerly. As conscience should come from within, so should embarrassment. Hot tingles and flushes are quite proper when they arise from your own sense of having violated your own standards, inadvertently or advertently, but Miss Manners hereby absolves everyone from feeling any embarrassment deliberately imposed by others.

The less scrupulous of those who sell funeral services try to embarrass people with the suggestion that anyone who cares about the recently deceased will "spare no expense" in the burial, an emotional non sequitur if ever there was one. The same tactic has been adopted by other professions. The whole posture of being what is termed, in the vernacular, "snooty" is cultivated by some headwaiters, real estate salespeople, boutique clerks, and others who hope to embarrass honest customers into spending more than they wish to spend.

This should be seen as a commercial ploy, not a challenge of manners. It is perfectly good manners to check over one's bill and ask for an explanation if it seems to be wrong; it is good manners to spend what one wishes to spend and not what one doesn't want to or cannot afford; and it is good manners to ask for what is coming to one if it does not seem to be forthcoming. What is dreadful manners is to attempt to embarrass anyone into spending money. That is a matter that ought to make those who practice it feel horribly guilty.

Then there are the people who keep trying to entice Miss Manners to play Gotcha! It is a nasty game, and Miss Manners wants nothing to do with it.

Gotcha! has a particularly sneaky opening move. The player sidles up to Miss Manners, or to a surrogate Miss Manners among his acquaintance, and says innocently, "Tell me, my dear Miss Manners, what do you think of such and such a behavior? Is that considered impolite? Would you even say it was rude?" There follows an example of the most horrendously bad behavior, with no possible ambiguity. Poor Miss Manners is forced to agree, and the questioner smiles quietly and says only, "I thought it might be, but I'm glad to have your opinion."

Miss Manners has now learned to recognize that sly smile and knows when she sees it that she has been trapped, once again, in a game of Gotcha! The game continues when the questioner goes running back to the wrongdoer, armed with the awesome authority of Miss Manners, and endeavors to carry out his true purpose, which was to make someone feel just terrible.

Therefore, the purpose of Gotcha! is to create unproductive discomfort in others. Miss Manners' unwitting aid in this unpleasant procedure is obtained fraudulently. The story told to Miss Manners always turns out to have been deliberately constructed so as to leave out all mitigating circumstances that might have swung the case to the other side.

Gotcha! creates gratuitous discomfort because it concerns itself with a situation that is already past. If the wedding was planned wrong, it is of no use now to tell the bride's parents. They are not going to do it all over again right.

Miss Manners hereby declares the entire game of Gotcha! to be rude.

MEANING

1. According to Miss Manners, what basic rules should govern civilized behavior among adults? Is there one overriding principle that can guide us toward the mannerly way of life? What is it?
2. Is Miss Manners serious? Is she making fun of rude people? If so, why does she adopt a tone that seems to mock the very kind of "proper" persons she would like them to become? Is she both serious and self-mocking at the same time? What is going on here?

METHOD

1. Much of Judith Martin's humor comes from close observation of ordinary behavior. Cite some of the pleasantly surprising details of life you recognize in this essay.
2. How would you describe Martin's tone and prose style? What about these features works for humorous effect? Why?

AUDIENCE

1. For whom is Martin writing? Are the rude sorts she describes likely to take her advice? If the boors among us are not her audience, who is? How do you know?
2. How does Miss Manners strike you? Do you like her lightly satiric tone? What characteristics of her essay appeal most, or least, to you? Why? Do you agree with her?

WRITING SUGGESTION

The behavior of human beings is an endlessly fascinating subject for most of us. Write a humorous essay or story in which you observe as closely as possible the details of ordinary behavior you find most amusing, obnoxious, revealing, or in need of change. Take time to observe actual people doing things—in restaurants, classrooms, living quarters, sports arenas, offices, factories. Use your reporting experience to gather material, but look at it from a humorous perspective. You might, like Miss Manners, wish to present your own code of desirable behavior (or its opposite) in certain specific situations.

ADDITIONAL WRITING SUGGESTIONS

1. Write a humorous essay or story on one of the following topics. Be as creative and experimental as you can in your early drafts; don't hold anything back. Then, as you develop material, try to select and shape it according to the strategies you've been studying all along, but with particular attention to surprise, unexpected recognition, tone of voice, and prose style.
    *   The funniest true story you know
    *   Your most embarrassing moment
    *   The thing you find most ridiculous in the world
    *   Social customs, manners, fashions
    *   Parent–child relationships
    *   The strangest or funniest experience you've had
    *   The biggest mistake you've ever made
    *   How to lose money
    *   Human folly
    *   Leaders who should get out of public life
    *   Silly sports
    *   People who deserve to be made fun of
    *   A humorous treatment of any topic listed at the end of Chapters 14 and 15

2. Try writing a humorous essay or narrative which, while funny, also raises a serious or important contemporary issue. Don't shy away from the big topics of the day; almost anything—the nuclear arms race, political corruption, social reform, love and marriage, the world of work—can be a subject for satire. Think about the satirical writers and performers you admire, and ask yourself how they approach serious subjects through humor. To what extent do they use irony, incongruity, and ridicule to unmask social ills?

PART SIX

The Research Paper

17

THE RESEARCH PAPER: INFORMING, EXPLAINING, ARGUING

WHY RESEARCH?

Of all the methods for gathering information—research, observation, interviewing, experiment (see Chapter 5)—research is the most universal and broad-based. That is, researching occurs in every field and discipline, even though it may share the fact-gathering weight with other methods. It would be difficult to think of a subject about which at least some information couldn't be acquired through research. For that reason, the research paper has become one of the staples of college writing—not only in composition classes but in all disciplines and at all levels of study. In fact, the freshman English research paper is frequently seen as a sort of threshold over which each student must pass in order to graduate to the increasingly higher, harder, more complex writing tasks of a college education.

But why? What is it about research that makes it so central to writing, education, continued learning? Research is the link between us and all the other people who have thought and acted before us. It is the process by which we maintain the continuity of knowledge between ourselves and others, with both the past and the future. The work we do rests on that of others, and itself becomes a potential source for others' use.

The research paper, as a college writing assignment, teaches a number of vital, interrelated skills: accurate fact gathering and reporting; organizing both research material and our own explanations and interpretations of it; planning and sticking to a schedule; managing an extended writing task that may take weeks or months to complete; being ethically responsible in our use of others' words and ideas.

Finally, the research paper offers students a superb opportunity to use writing as a way of learning. Through the research-writing process, we become familiar with a body of knowledge, studying it and shaping it, giving it a new written form. In this chapter we will consider how the purposes of nonfiction writing discussed in this book apply to the research assignment, and how the process of writing a research paper can fulfill those purposes.

TYPES AND PURPOSES OF RESEARCH PAPERS

Although the research project is often viewed as a single, specific assignment, it takes a variety of shapes depending on subjects and purposes. Research papers range from short reports to book-length theses and dissertations. Let's look at some common types of research assignments and the purposes for which they are written.

Research projects can be divided into two broad categories: report papers and thesis papers. Within the second group, we find a subdivision into research with an analytical emphasis, and research with an argumentative (or critical) emphasis.

Report Papers

Research report papers, in any academic subject, present information usually without comment or interpretation. Although the format of such reports will vary according to discipline, the report paper is essentially the same as any report—a collection of important or useful data organized in a logical, understandable pattern. (See Chapter 5, "Reports.")

The purpose of a report paper is *informative*—to be clear, complete, accurate, objective.

Thesis Papers

Research thesis papers differ from report papers in a fundamental way. While reports remain largely uninterpreted, thesis papers present the writer's analysis, explanation, or argument about the information he or she has gathered. The thesis paper is a *research essay*—one writer's extended, research-based encounter with a subject.

Analytical emphasis.   Like any analytical essay, a thesis paper may present and explain information; its thesis is the essential point of the writer's analysis. (See Chapter 9, "Analytical Essays.") In a thesis paper with an analytical or explanatory emphasis, the writer seeks to clarify a subject, draw important distinctions, and evaluate the topic to improve the reader's understanding as well as his or her own.

Argumentative (or critical) emphasis.   Similarly, a thesis paper may take analysis a further step, toward argument—an attempt to convince readers to change their opinions or actions. In this case the thesis of the paper, like the thesis of any argumentative or critical essay, is the point the writer hopes to convince his readers to accept. (See Chapter 11, "Argument," and Chapter 12, "Criticism.") When research thesis papers have a critical slant— usually in arts, literature, or humanities courses—they attempt to argue convincingly for a particular evaluation or judgment of the merits of a painting, novel, musical piece, or other created work. (See sample student research paper 1, "Arthur Miller's *Death of a Salesman,*" at the end of this chapter.)

Whatever its emphasis, a thesis research paper is solidly within the essay form, its content based both on research itself and the writer's reaction to it.

In summary, each type of research paper fulfills a specific purpose. Report papers are informative; thesis papers with an analytical emphasis are both informative and explanatory; thesis papers with an argumentative or critical emphasis combine three basic purposes—informing, analyzing, and convincing.

THE RESEARCH-WRITING PROCESS

Because most research projects assigned in college are thesis papers with either an analytical or argumentative emphasis, we will look at the research-writing process in terms of the research essay.

The process may be divided into the following basic steps:

1. *The topic stage:* Problems, questions, first narrowing
2. *Preliminary research:* Reading for a working bibliography
3. *Focused research:* Using sources, taking notes
4. *Forming a tentative thesis and working outline:* Project starting to take shape
5. *Writing the first draft:* Integrating information, analysis (and argument)
6. *Appraising the first draft:* What's missing?
7. *Second full draft:* Additional research and writing
8. *Final draft:* Composing the finished version—revising, editing, proofreading

The Topic Stage: Problems, Questions, First Narrowing

The research-writing process begins with selection of a topic, assuming one has not been assigned. In many research projects, students are free to choose a topic, while in others the paper will be aimed at specific course material (a critical argument about a short story or poem, for instance). In either case, the only way to make research rewarding is to find a point of genuine *interest* about which we really want to know more. As we've said all along, worthwhile writing always begins with curiosity, and this is especially true with research.

If we already know where our interest lies, narrowing the topic comes next; otherwise, brainstorming and free writing can help uncover potential subjects. As in analytical writing, we begin with a problem or question, a motive for our work. Because problems and questions may be general, however, we must narrow or focus the topic as sharply as possible even at this early stage. A 10- or 15-page paper, although it seems long, is really a small space for any detailed research.

Say, for example, that you are interested in movies and would like to write about them—an enormous subject, impossible to cover in a few thousand words. What specific interests do movies hold for you? You might break the subject down into smaller, more manageable pieces:

Film-making techniques
Types of popular movies
How scripts are made into films
How movies are marketed
Famous directors

Each of these subjects is still quite broad, but at least the topic has begun to narrow. From this list (or a longer one) you should choose the most inviting topics and continue the narrowing process. Say you decide to go further with "Types of popular movies." You might break this subject into even smaller parts:

Horror pictures
Comedies
Detective thrillers
Romantic stories

Now the question becomes, what about each of these makes it interesting? This should lead you to ask further, increasingly specific questions:

What are some typical subjects for horror pictures? How have horror pictures changed?
Do comedies have certain common themes? How do different comedies treat the same theme?
What kinds of characters usually show up in detective movies? Is the detective–hero always the same character?
What plot patterns are common to love stories? Do they always have a happy ending?

You've narrowed the subject from "movies" to something much more pointed and clear. When you research one of these questions, now, you'll know whether or not you're coming up with any answers. You could research "movies" for years and never exhaust such a broadly stated topic.

Finally, research papers are library assignments, and we must be able to locate most of the information there. As you select and narrow topics, ask yourself if you're likely to find out about them in libraries. Subjects that are too recent, too technical, or are limited to a few sources are not good choices for research papers. Instead, we should look for topics that have had time to be treated in books and periodicals, that appeal to a general audience, and that a number of writers have covered. Unfortunately, we can't always know for certain until we start looking.

Preliminary Research: Reading for a Working Bibliography

The Search Strategy

The first stage of research requires that we survey available, potentially useful sources. Our goal here is to assemble a working bibliography—a list of sources that contain information on our topic. Because libraries house an enormous amount of data, we need a *search strategy*, a systematic, logical way to proceed.

Any search strategy begins with a simple question: *What* am I looking for, and *where* do I find it? We already saw that narrowing the subject of our research helps clarify the first part of this question. To answer the second part, we must know what kinds of library sources can give us specific kinds of information. (See "Types of Sources," below.) The search strategy, then, is defined by the topic and carried out by using the best, most appropriate sources.

When reading for a working bibliography, keep these points in mind: Consult both *general* and *specialized* (subject) sources, and look for breadth as well as depth of information; read *primary* as well as *secondary* sources (see below); keep alert for and take note of recurrent facts and ideas in good quality sources.

Types of Sources

Libraries contain a vast array of information sources—everything from general encyclopedias to highly specialized scholarship, from today's newspaper to works written decades or centuries ago. Despite the variety, however, most library sources fall into one of three basic categories: books, periodicals, and reference books. Let's look at each of these.

BOOKS.   When we need information that is comprehensive, in-depth, or that offers an overview of a subject, we look for books. Most of the books in a library's collection are kept in the stacks and can be checked out for extended use.

To find books, we use the *card catalog*, which lists the library's materials according to author, title, and subject. Before consulting the card catalog for books on a particular topic, however, be sure to check the *Library of*

Congress Subject Headings—a two-volume thesaurus or key to the terms used on the catalog cards. The *LCSH* will give you a list of all the related headings under which books may be listed in the card catalog. Too often a search may stop short, because the searcher has failed to look for the appropriate subject heading. Using the *LCSH* should ensure that you find all the potentially valuable books on your topic.

In addition to the card catalog, there is another way to find books: *browsing*. If your library has open stacks, where patrons are allowed access to the books, you should scan the shelves where your search has led for books of related interest. Libraries are arranged so books on the same or similar subjects are grouped together. Browsing may uncover sources you hadn't thought to look up and will broaden your research base.

PERIODICALS (NEWSPAPERS, MAGAZINES, JOURNALS). When our search strategy leads us toward current or recent general information, or shorter, more narrow or specialized treatment of specific subjects, we look for *articles* in periodicals. Most libraries keep very recent periodicals accessible in a designated room or area; those more than a few months old are usually found in bound volumes in the stacks, or on *microfilm*. (Most college libraries, for instance, will have *The New York Times* from 1851 to the present on microfilm. In addition, certain government publications, such as census materials and ERIC [Education Resources Information Center] documents, may be available in your library on *microfiche*. Ask your reference librarian.)

Periodicals are divided into three general categories: newspapers, magazines, and journals. Newspapers and magazines tend to address a general or mass audience, and are published frequently (daily, in the case of most newspapers; weekly or monthly, in the case of most magazines). Journals, by contrast, usually address a professional or specialized audience and, as a rule, are published less frequently.

Just as the card catalog is the primary source for books, periodical *indexes* are the source for articles. Some of the most useful indexes (bound volumes found in your library's reference room) are listed below:

Newspapers:
New York Times Index
Wall Street Journal Index
Newspaper Index (Chicago Tribune, Los Angeles Times, Washington Post, and others)

Magazines (general periodicals):
Reader's Guide to Periodical Literature
Magazine Index (on microfilm)

Journals (according to subject):
Humanities: *Humanities Index*
Art:

        Art Index
    History (also considered a social science):
        Historical Abstracts
        America: History and Life
    Literature and English:
        MLA Bibliography
        Abstracts of English Studies
        Essay and General Literature Index
    Music:
        Music Index
    Philosophy and Religion:
        Philosopher's Index
        Religion Index One: Periodicals

Social Sciences: *Social Sciences Index*
    Education:
        Current Index to Journals in Education
        Education Index
    Political Science:
        A. B. C. Pol. Sci.
        Public Affairs Information Service
    Psychology (sometimes considered a science):
        Psychology Abstracts
    Sociology and Social Work:
        Social Work Research Abstracts

Economics and Business: *Business Periodicals Index*

Natural Science: *General Science Index*
    Biology:
        Biological and Agricultural Index
        Biological Abstracts
        Biological Digest
    Chemistry:
        Chemical Abstracts
    Medical Science and Nursing:
        Abridged Index Medicus
        Cumulative Index to Nursing and Allied Health Literature
    Physics and Engineering:
        Applied Science and Technology Index
        Engineering Index

REFERENCE BOOKS.   Finally, when we need to find background information, specific facts, or detailed information on specific subjects, we consult reference books. These books, also in the library's reference room, are classified in two groups: general and subject references.

  General Reference Books:
    Encyclopedias:
        Academic American Encyclopedia (21 volumes)

Encyclopedia Americana (30 volumes)
Encyclopedia Britannica (30 volumes)
Dictionaries (unabridged):
The Oxford American Dictionary
The Oxford English Dictionary (13 volumes)
Webster's Third New International Dictionary
Biographical Sources:
Biographical Index
Dictionary of American Biography
The McGraw-Hill Encyclopedia of World Biography
Who's Who in America
Yearbooks and Almanacs:
Britannica Book of the Year (1938–)
Facts on File (1940–)
Information Please Almanac (1947–)
Statistical Abstracts of the United States (1878–)
World Almanac and Book of Facts (1868–)
Atlases and Gazetteers:
Columbia Lippincott Gazetteer of the World
National Geographic Atlas of the World
Government Documents:
Index to Publications of the U.S. Congress
Monthly Catalog of U.S. Government Publications

Subject Reference Books:
Humanities:
Art:
Encyclopedia of World Art
The Oxford Companion to Art
History:
Dictionary of American History
Encyclopedia of American History
An Encyclopedia of World History
Literature and English:
Bartlett's Familiar Quotations
Book Review Digest (excerpts of reviews)
Book Review Index (index to review articles)
Contemporary Authors
Contemporary Literary Criticism
Oxford Companion to American Literature
Oxford Companion to English Literature
Short Story Index (index to published stories)
Music:
The Concise Oxford Dictionary of Music
The Harvard Dictionary of Music
The New Grove Dictionary of Music and Musicians
Philosophy and Religion:
The Encyclopedia of Philosophy

The Interpreter's Dictionary of the Bible
A Dictionary of Non-Christian Religions
Theater, Film, Media:
Encyclopedia of World Theatre
A History of Broadcasting in the United States
International Encyclopedia of Film
International Television Almanac
Oxford Companion to Film
Play Index

Social Sciences:
Dictionary of the Social Sciences
International Encyclopedia of the Social Sciences
Education:
Dictionary of Education
Encyclopedia of Education
Political Science:
Almanac of American Politics
American Political Dictionary
The Literature of Political Science
Psychology:
A Dictionary of Psychology and Related Fields
Encyclopedia of Psychology
Sociology and Social Work:
Encyclopedia of Social Work

Economics and Business:
Business Information Sources
Dictionary of Business and Economics
McGraw-Hill Dictionary of Modern Economics
Moody's Manuals

Natural Sciences:
McGraw-Hill Encyclopedia of Science and Technology
Van Nostrand's Scientific Encyclopedia
Biology:
Encyclopedia of the Biological Sciences
Chemistry:
Encyclopedia of Chemistry
Handbook of Chemistry and Physics
Medical Science and Nursing:
Encyclopedia and Dictionary of Medicine, Nursing, and Allied Health
The Nurse's Almanac
Stedman's Medical Dictionary
Physics and Engineering:
The Encyclopedia of Physics
Engineering Encyclopedia

Primary and Secondary Sources

Much of the information we find in libraries is in secondary sources—books and periodicals which are themselves based on research. Whenever possible, however, we should try to supplement this base of information with primary source material, original works by people who are part of the subject we're studying. For instance, an appraisal of presidential rhetoric would rely not only on the works of historians and other writers on the subject but on original speeches, letters, books by presidents themselves. The former sources are secondary—coming after the fact; the latter are primary—part of the subject itself, not *about* it.

Major Points and Good Quality Sources

When reading for a working bibliography, it's important that we get a sense of what others have emphasized about our topic. Look for facts and ideas that your sources point out as significant; this will help greatly in selecting from a huge amount of research data.

Moreover, make sure that your sources are appropriate, and that they provide high-quality information. Ask your reference librarian which sources are best or most reliable. Many common secondary sources, such as popular newspapers and magazines, are not authorities in every field they cover. A research paper on nutrition, for instance, shouldn't rely on articles in *Time* and *Newsweek* (although some valuable facts may be found there); it would be better to base such a paper on material from subject sources and scholarly publications, and to supplement the data with more general information.

When evaluating sources, remember that the object of college research is to go *beyond* the general, secondary information we find in popular books and magazines. With a sufficiently narrowed topic, and an awareness of the variety of specific sources available in most libraries, you will be able to delve deeply into your subject to really discover something interesting and detailed. You'll also learn how to unlock and use the knowledge your library contains.

Documentation

As we track down and evaluate potential sources, we record them in writing for future reference. The working bibliography is a list of sources, and it's usually best to record each item on a separate bibliography card. Later, when we decide which sources we'll actually use, our selected bibliography will be in correct form for the "Works Cited" page at the end of the paper.

Bibliographic formats vary, depending on the discipline. Whichever one you choose or are assigned to use, employ it consistently. Accurate bibliographic form keeps source information precise and lets your reader find your sources for further reference. For papers in language and literature courses, use the Modern Language Association (MLA) format, detailed examples of which follow. At the end of this section, there are examples of the American Psychological Association (APA) form, for papers in the social and most of the natural sciences, and in business.

MLA Bibliographic Form

Books

One author

Herr, Michael. Dispatches. New York: Knopf, 1978.

Several authors

Mirkin, Gabe, M.D., and Marshall Hoffman. The Sportsmedicine Book. Boston: Little, Brown, 1978.

Poppeliers, John C., S. Allen Chambers, Jr., and Nancy B. Schwartz. What Style Is It? Washington, D.C.: The Preservation Press, 1983.

Lauer, Janice M., et al. Four Worlds of Writing. 2nd ed. New York: Harper & Row, 1985.

Corporate author

American Institute of History and Art. Hudson Valley Painting, 1700–1750. Albany, N.Y.: Albany Institute of History and Art, 1959.

Later edition

Graves, Robert, and Alan Hodge. The Reader Over Your Shoulder. 2nd. ed., revised and abridged. New York: Random House, 1979.

Reprint

Hofstadter, Richard. The American Political Tradition. 1973. New York: Vintage Books, 1974. [Reprint issued year following original edition.]

Edited work

Katz, Steven T., ed. Mysticism and Philosophical Analysis. New York: Oxford University Press, 1978.

Selection from an anthology

Johnson, Diane. "Rape." The Contemporary Essay. Ed. Donald Hall. New York: St. Martin's Press, 1984. 338–348. [Note page numbers of article or story following publication date.]

Book in more than one volume

Durant, Will. The Story of Civilization. 11 vols. New York: Simon and Schuster, 1957. Vol. 6: The Reformation. [Only one volume cited; if all are cited, omit last item.]

Book in a series

Sahakian, William S. History of Philosophy. Barnes & Noble College Outline Series 2. New York: Barnes & Noble, 1968.

Translated edition

Tolstoy, Leo. Anna Karenina. Trans. Rosemary Edmonds. Baltimore, Maryland: Penguin, 1954.

Periodicals

Unsigned newspaper article

"Talks Agenda Stirs Interest of Soviets." Chicago Tribune 10 Nov. 1984, sec. 1:1 [Note absence of punctuation between publication source and date; also, section and page number are sufficient.]

Signed newspaper article

Williams, Winston. "Cashing in on Fitness Foods." New York Times 4 Nov. 1984, National Ed., sec. 3:1, 8-9. [If citing a particular edition of a newspaper, identify after date; note also page numbers indicate article begins on page 1, continues on pages 8 and 9.]

Magazine article

Rossi, Alice S. "The Biosocial Side of Parenthood." Human Nature June 1978: 72–79.

"The Church and Capitalism." Businessweek 12 Nov. 1984: 104–112. [Note difference in dates of monthly and weekly publications.]

Journal with continuous pagination

"The Changing Role of Libraries in Higher Education." College &

<u>Research Libraries News</u> 45.10 (1984): 541–542. [*Note:* unsigned article; also, if issue number is included, it follows volume number after period: above, volume 45, issue 10.]

Journal with separate pagination

Sexson, Lynda. "Craftsman of Chaos." <u>Parabola</u> 4.1 (1979): 24–33.

Editorial

"The Reagan 45." Editorial. <u>The New Republic</u> 16 April 1984: 5–7.

Book review

Brustein, Robert. "Ciao! Manhattan." Rev. of <u>A Margin of Hope: An Intellectual Biography</u>, by Irving Howe. <u>New York Review of Books</u> 3 Feb. 1983: 5–6.

Encyclopedias

Unsigned article

"Music in the Modern World." <u>The Larousse Encyclopedia of Music</u>. 1971 ed.

Signed or initialed article

W[estermann], C[laus]. "Sacred Kingship." <u>Encyclopedia Britannica: Macropaedia</u>. 1978 ed. [*Note:* Consult list of contributors in index volume for full name; omit brackets if name appears in full on title page of article.]

Other sources

Pamphlets, bulletins, government publications

<u>Keep Your Child from Choking</u>. American Lung Association, 1978.

<u>U.S. Government Manual</u>. Washington, D.C.: GPO, 1980.

United States. Bureau of the Census. <u>Historical Statistics of the United States</u>. 2 vols. Washington, D.C.: GPO, 1975. [Use this form when government bureau is identified.]

Unpublished dissertation

Pfitsch, John Hollis. "Whitehead and Propositions." Diss. U. of Georgia, 1973.

Films, television programs

<u>Ghostbusters</u>. Columbia Pictures, 1984.

"CBS Evening News with Dan Rather." CBS. WBBM-TV, Chicago. 29 Oct. 1984.

Theatrical performance

<u>Death of a Salesman</u>. Broadhurst Theatre, New York. 12 June 1984.

Recording

Goodman, Steve, and John Prine. "The Twentieth Century Is Almost Over." <u>Say It in Private</u>. Asylum Records, 7E 1118, 1977.

Interview

Bellow, Saul. Personal interview. 15 May 1982.

APA Bibliographic Form*

Books

One author

Mack, J. E. (1974). <u>Nightmares and human conflict</u>. Boston: Houghton Mifflin. [Publication date in parenthesis after author's name—surname and initials only.]

Several authors

Bykov, K. M. & Gantt, W. H. (1957). <u>The cerebral cortex and the internal organs</u>. New York: Chemical Publishing.

Corporate author

American Psychiatric Association. (1980). <u>Diagnostic and statistical manual of mental disorders</u> (3rd ed.). Washington, DC: Author. [Note later edition in parenthesis after title; use "Author" when corporate author is also publisher.]

Selection from an anthology

Gastaut, H., & Broughton, R. (1965). A clinical and polygraphic study of episodic phenomena during sleep. In J. Wortis (Ed.), <u>Recent advances in biological psychiatry</u> (pp. 197–221). New York: Plenum Press.

---

*In American Psychological Association style, the list of cited sources at the end of the paper is entitled "References."

Periodicals (journal articles)

One author

Cohen, W. (1957). Spatial and textural characteristics of the
  Ganzfeld. American Journal of Psychology, 70, 403–410.

Several authors

Foulkes, D., Pivik, T., Steadman, H., Spear, P. & Symonds, J. (1967).
  Dreams of the male child: an EEG study. Journal of Abnormal
  Psychology, 72, 457–467. [If article has six or more authors, use
  abbreviated form for citations in text, as in (Foulkes et al., 1967)].

Periodicals (magazine articles)

One author

McLaughlin, B. (1978, December). Second look: The mother tongue.
  Human Nature, p. 89.

Periodicals (newspaper articles)

Unsigned article

New abuse study released; shows widespread increase. (1982,
  August 4). New York Times, p. 7.

Signed article

Murray, W. (1984, November 14). Back pain—Bad habits and
  stress: The last straws. Chicago Tribune, sec. 2, pp.1, 8.

Focused Research: Using Sources, Taking Notes

Once we have a sense of potentially useful sources, it's time to start taking notes and recording specific information pertinent to our topic. The goal now is to build a solid informational base and to develop our analysis or argument about it.

As you collect information, ask yourself how it may be useful. Where is it likely to go in the paper? Is it general or introductory material? Does it help sketch in a background or context for the topic? Does it pertain directly to the main question or problem you're addressing? Think about the overall shape and content of the paper as you research. Sketch a rough outline or list of general categories of information, and stay alert about how your ongoing research may affect or alter these ideas. As you accumulate notes and develop a stronger sense of your subject, you will move toward a more formal, detailed outline controlled by your thesis (see "Forming a Tentative Thesis and Working Outline," below).

The notes we take from sources are the raw material for the text of the paper we'll eventually write, so it is vital that they be accurate, clear, concise, and fair. Sharp, specific notes should produce a paper with similar qualities; vague, general, or inaccurate notes will give us a paper without focus or substance.

When taking notes from our bibliography of sources, we translate research data into several basic forms: summaries, paraphrases, direct quotations, and explanatory and evaluative comments of our own. Well-written, balanced research papers incorporate all these forms. Each has a purpose, and a paper that skirts or overuses any one will seem lopsided or incomplete.

Summaries

When we summarize information, we condense it in our own words. Summaries allow us to use a large quantity of data economically, much more than if we tried to use it in its original form. A good summary briefly captures the essential meaning of a longer passage and omits unimportant or secondary facts. Our aim in writing a summary is to give a clear, objective (undistorted) interpretation of the original.

Paraphrases

When working with smaller amounts of information where there is no need to condense or abstract, we use the paraphrase. Many statements and facts we uncover in research will be useful, but we can't quote all of them directly or our paper will be a jumble of unconnected remarks. When we paraphrase, we translate other's words and ideas into our own style, keeping the content of the original but restating it wholly in our own language. As in writing a summary, the aim here is to maintain objectivity and to give a fair sense of the original.

Direct Quotations

Although summaries and paraphrases are essential components of research papers, to rely exclusively on them is to drain the blood from research work. It is also necessary that our reader sense the human voice behind our information—especially when it is the voice of authority or memorable expression. When we come across the words of experts, witnesses, and first-hand participants, we should consider letting their words stand as originally written or spoken. Quoting sources directly lends the support of other voices to our work, and helps to substantiate our case and convince our audience.

Beware, however, of overusing quotations. They can easily become too much of a good thing and drown out your own voice. Use quoted remarks sparingly—for accent and emphasis. It's common to limit the total volume of quoted material to about 10 or 15 percent of the whole text. You will find, too, that if you avoid long quotations and instead use brief ones, quoting only key words, phrases, and sentences, you'll be able to quote more sources and to much greater effect. Last, be careful to quote with perfect accuracy, changing nothing in the original. (You may delete words only if this does not alter the meaning of the passage. Indicate such deletions with an ellipsis [. . .].) Identify the speaker or writer of the quotation, or otherwise introduce it so the reader knows why it's there.

One way to use quoted remarks effectively is to combine them with paraphrases. That is, rather than quote an entire passage word for word, paraphrase it but include brief quotations of important phrases or sentences. Combining brief quotation with the paraphrase allows you to retain some flavor of the original passage without excessive quotation.

Note: It is very important to remember that all forms of noted information—summary, paraphrase, quotation—*must be acknowledged in the text of the paper,* not just in the "Works Cited" list. (See "Writing the First Draft," below.)

Explanatory and Evaluative Comments

While the forms discussed above are essential to research writing, they are not enough. We also must include our own reactions, questions, interpretations, and judgments. When we research, we do more than take down facts; we analyze and evaluate what we find. Thus, any of the writing we do in response to the research should become part of our notes, and these notes—just as our summaries, paraphrases, and direct quotations—will feed into the text of our paper to provide a platform for revision and expansion, a big step toward the first draft.

A Word About Plagiarism

Because research papers rely heavily on the words and ideas of others, we must be especially careful to use sources ethically. That is, we cannot borrow information from a source but fail to give proper credit for it. To do so is to commit an act of plagiarism—intellectual theft. Few writers (student or otherwise) plagiarize on purpose; it's usually a result of haste, ignorance, or lack of concern for accuracy and detail. Yet such unintentional theft is as deadly as if you had set out to do it. The result is the same in either case. Plagiarism usually takes one of three basic forms:

Incomplete summary or paraphrase. In incomplete summary or paraphrase, the writer fails to translate a passage into his or her own words, and instead retains much or most of the original language. Even though the source is acknowledged, it is essentially unchanged.

Uncited quotation.   Sometimes, usually while taking notes, the writer will copy a passage word for word but fail to treat it as a direct quotation. Later, the sentence or paragraph turns up in the paper looking like a summary or paraphrase (and the source may be acknowledged), when in fact it's neither one.

Uncited source.   In the case of the uncited source, the writer uses information—in whatever form—without any acknowledgment and thereby steals it outright.

If you take careful, accurate notes and document them properly, plagiarism should be easy to avoid. Does this mean, therefore, that every sentence in a research paper must be acknowledged? (In other words, for what can you the writer take credit?) The answer is simpler than it seems. Acknowledge what you take from sources, and everything else is yours: all the creative decisions you make in the process of writing your essay—the concept of your paper; its structure and focus; your explanations, judgments, and other comments. It is, after all, your essay—supported by research, but still yours.

As you continue to look for and record useful information, you build the groundwork for your paper. And as you do so, you move gradually toward the next stage of the research process, where your material takes shape as an organized structure with a central point.

Forming a Tentative Thesis and Working Outline

If our research is energetic, accurate, and comprehensive, sooner or later certain propositions and patterns will emerge from it. It will begin to tell us something. It will then be possible to draft a potential thesis or controlling statement and construct a detailed outline that organizes our material in support of that thesis.

When you think you are ready for this stage, review your notes and arrange them according to the subjects they cover. Experiment with various thesis statements that explain (or make your argumentative case about) what you've found. Then draft an outline according to your thesis to reflect the content and direction the thesis takes. (See Chapters 6 and 9 on the essay-writing process.) The thesis and outline work together—they should say the same thing—so you may find that the outline implies revision of the thesis, or that the thesis doesn't correspond to your outline. Work on both at once and try to arrive at an overall structure and point that best presents your understanding of the subject.

Remember, too, that essays have a basic structure—introduction, body, conclusion—and that this structure can't be avoided in an assignment as formal as a research paper. Use the structure to your advantage. Put together an introduction that makes a gesture of interest to the reader and states your controlling point. Construct the body logically: Start with any background the reader may need to know before the subject will make sense; then present your analysis or argument in specific stages, each one paving the way for the following. Conclude with your assessment of the significance of what you've learned, a judgment about the likely future of your subject, or an emphatic final statement.

If you can see the shape and content of your paper in outline form, and if it looks sound and sensible to you, then you're prepared for the next step.

Writing the First Draft

We have said much in this book about the process of composing first drafts, and we won't repeat that material here. There are few clear-cut directions for such a complicated undertaking. The essay writing process for research papers does make some extra demands, however.

Since research papers rely on specific, documented information, drafting the paper means weaving our data *and* our explanation of (or argument from) that material into a single thread. Drafting the paper is a process of integrating the research with the essay it supports.

Working from our thesis and outline on the one hand, and our notes on the other, we write each section of the paper as we would the parts of any essay, but use the notes for each section to support what we say. We

- *introduce* the research (not only in the paper's introductory section but in the topic sentences of our paragraphs);
- *present* it (as summary, paraphrase, direct quotation);
- *document* it (in parenthetical references to our list of "Works Cited" [see below]);
- *explain* it (in our own analyses, evaluations, interpretations); and
- *argue* from it (by building a logical, convincing case from evidence and valid reasoning).

As we work our notes into a first draft, *we build toward a synthesis of purposes*—informing, explaining, convincing—just as the essay itself is a synthesis or combination of materials.

Incorporating Notes into a First Draft: Parenthetical Documentation

Forms of documentation change. The traditional method of giving credit (citations) has been the numbered footnote or endnote. A new, revised system has been recommended by the Modern Language Association: to place all references to sources within the text of the paper. The new method uses numbered notes only for additional comments (textual notes), and references to more than a single source, should any be necessary. When incorporating noted material into your paper, then, follow these two basic rules: (1) Instead of using footnotes or endnotes, cite references in parentheses in your paper; (2) place a list of "Works Cited" at the end (a bibliography of sources actually used in the paper, alphabetized by author).

The revised system still demands complete acknowledgment of all information taken from sources, of course, but it makes it easier for your reader to see how specific sources have been employed.

Here are some guidelines for parenthetical documentation:

1. Be concise, but include all *necessary* information, enough to point the reader to the appropriate source. (See examples below.)

2. The first time you use a source, introduce the person by his or her full name, and include an identifying phrase to define the source's relevance:

> Stith Thompson, in his comprehensive study of folklore,
> writes that "the telling of tales is a constant activity
> everywhere" (13).

In this example, only the page reference is in parenthesis.

3. For subsequent references to a source already introduced and identified, use only the last name and page number:

> In his discussion, Thompson also points out the presence of
> magic in a large proportion of folktales (67).
>
> Folktales, it has been noted, frequently contain magical
> elements (Thompson 67).

4. When referring to more than one work by a single author, include the title or a shortened version of it:

> Thompson goes on to discuss the role of folktales in ancient
> Egypt (The Folktale 273–276), claiming that . . .

If you include either the author's name or the title of the work in the text of your sentence, omit it from the parenthetical reference.

5. To cite an unsigned or anonymous work, include the title or a shortened form of it:

> One recent editorial ("Why Not Democracy?") gives the
> impression that . . .

Sample Citations—MLA Form

One work by a given author identified in the text

> In her discussion of adolescence, Winn describes "the myth
> of the teenage werewolf"—the parents' fear that their child

will become an "uncontrollable monster" (14). [Note that the parenthetical reference is inside the period, immediately following the combined paraphrase/quotation.]

One work by a given author not identified in the text

Many writers have addressed parents' fears about their child's teen years, what one author has termed "the myth of the teenage werewolf" (Winn 14).

One of two or more works by an author identified in the text

In her discussion of adolescence, Winn describes "the myth of the teenage werewolf" (Children Without Childhood 14). [A short version of the title (*Children* 14) would be possible as long as it could not be confused with another source.]

One of two or more works by an author not identified in the text

Many writers have addressed parents' fears about their child's teen years, what one author has termed "the myth of the teenage werewolf" (Winn, Children 14).

Both author and title identified in the text

A prominent writer on family life, Marie Winn, in Children Without Childhood, describes the fears of parents about their adolescent children—what she calls "the myth of the teenage werewolf" (14).

Works by authors with the same last name

Today's children, one writer claims, have been robbed of their childhood (Marie Winn). [Note that reference is to entire source, not a specific page.]

Still, the case isn't closed on this issue; another study shows that adolescents today are just as innocent of adult concerns as were earlier generations (Kenneth Winn 56). [Here only one work by the author is used in the paper.]

Multiple authors of a single work

One important study confirms Winn's thesis (Smith, Jones, and Harris), while another contradicts it (Hoffman et al.). [For two or three authors, include all names; for more than three, use the first name followed by *et al.* ("and others").]

Note: When citing longer quotations—ones set off from the text of your paper—place the parenthetical reference at the end, after the closing punctuation.

Sample Citations—APA Form

APA citations substitute the date of the work for its title. The same general rules for parenthetical documentation apply, however. If you identify the author in your text, give only the date (when citing the entire source) or the date and page (when citing a specific passage).

Author not identified in text

> One study of nightmares (Mack, 1974) indicates that . . .

> Separation from the parents during sleep is a prime cause of children's nightmares (Mack, 1974, p. 59). [Abbreviation *p.* included.]

Author identified in text

> In his discussion, Mack (1974) claims that . . .

> Mack (1974) attributes childhood nightmares to "the separation from the parents . . . that occurs with sleep" (p. 59). [For subsequent references to the same works within a paragraph, omit the year if no other works by that author are cited. E.g., "Mack goes on to say . . ."]

Special cases.   For references with two or more authors, cite all names each time. When a work has six or more authors, however, cite the surname of the first, followed by *et al.* each time.

For corporate authors, abbreviate only if the name is long and the abbreviation is clear. Give the full name for the first citation (National Association for the Advancement of Colored People [NAACP], 1984) and the included abbreviation for subsequent citations (NAACP, 1984).

For citations of works without an author, give the first two or three words of the title as identification. For example, an article or chapter ("Researchers Discover," 1983); a book (*Encyclopedia of Psychology*, 1984).

Appraising the First Draft

As we've seen in earlier chapters, the creative work of writing always encompasses the critical—we become judges of our work as part of the creative process. When you have a first draft of your research essay, it's time to stand back and read it as a critic. What's missing? Is the base of information complete? Does it make sense? Does it support your interpretation of it? Is the explanation or argument clear, logical, without gaps? Would you want this paper to be graded?

When you evaluate your first draft, apply to it all the standards you would to any essay draft, and note every strength and weakness you can find. (See Chapter 4 for a basic checklist.) You may find that further research is necessary to plug obvious holes. Perhaps certain sections of the paper are underdeveloped but not under-researched and require a rewrite for expanded explanation. Some parts may be too detailed and could be cut down without damage. Perhaps the structure of the paper needs to be altered, some parts or paragraphs rearranged. Whatever you find, be hard-nosed in your critical appraisal. Most of the really difficult work is behind you.

Second Full Draft

Based on your honest evaluation of your work, and after you've done the necessary patching, cutting, expanding, clarifying, go through the paper again from start to finish. Type a fresh copy, testing every sentence and paragraph against your best sense of what you want to say. You should find your second draft richer, clearer, more precise, more pointed, smoother. The first draft was only an experiment, really. The second draft will come much closer to your final presentation, made possible only because you had a first draft to which you could react.

Final Draft

Some students will see to it that their second draft is the final one, no matter what. But in the best of all possible worlds, the second draft should play a role similar to that of the first, although this time you hope to have far fewer things to fix. With any luck, the second version of your paper should leave you to concentrate on the much finer points of style, grammar, mechanics, and documentation.

The final copy of your paper will usually contain certain specific parts, depending on the assignment. Most long research papers include a title page, a thesis and outline page (your final, revised thesis and outline), and a "Works Cited" page (your final list of sources used in the paper) at the end of the paper's main text. Type and proofread your work with extreme care and a sense of craft.

In a composition course, your paper may be the culmination of a semester's (or an entire year's) work. Chances are it will be graded heavily. Your final draft then becomes even more than a final version of a single assignment; it may be your chance to show what you've learned on every level of writing—that threshold we mentioned at the start. In this last, long essay, you combine your mastery of *purpose, form, content,* and *style,* all of these woven about a body of research. Having successfully executed such a project is no small matter, and the knowledge of how to do it again should stay with you forever.

SAMPLE RESEARCH PAPERS

The following essays are examples of two common research-writing assignments. The first, a short critical paper, uses the work of several literary critics to support the author's interpretation of Arthur Miller's play *Death of a Salesman* as a modern tragedy. Here, the essay combines analysis and argument, with an argumentative thesis. In the second example, a longer "term paper" assignment, the author combines the informative and analytical purposes to explain the effect of birth order on personality. Ultimately, however, the paper acts as an argument for the theory of birth order, supported by evidence gathered through research.

ARTHUR MILLER'S <u>DEATH OF A SALESMAN</u>:
A MODERN TRAGEDY

Joan Hall
Critical Writing
November 5, 1984

OUTLINE

Thesis: In <u>Death of a Salesman</u>, Arthur Miller has written a legitimate, modern tragedy.

   I.   Modern tragic temperament vs. ancient tradition
        A.   Aristotle's definition and today's
        B.   The question of whether tragedy is possible today
        C.   Miller's view of "tragedy and the common man"
  II.   Willy as a tragic character
        A.   Represents our society's values—wants to gain his "rightful" position
        B.   His downfall
        C.   His struggle for dignity
 III.   <u>Death of a Salesman</u> as a tragedy
        A.   Sympathy for character
        B.   Arouses pity and fear in us
  IV.   Conclusion

Joan Hall, "Death of a Salesman: A Modern Tragedy." Used by permission.

ARTHUR MILLER'S DEATH OF A SALESMAN:
A MODERN TRAGEDY

Over twenty-five hundred years ago, the philosopher Aristotle set down his interpretation of what constitutes a tragedy. His concept has been held in high regard throughout the world for centuries, but today there is a great deal of controversy over the elements that define and justify tragedy. The "ancient tragic concept" has evolved and needs to be examined in a new light. I believe that tragedies do exist in modern dramatic literature, contrary to the opinions of some critics. In Death of a Salesman, Arthur Miller has written a legitimate, modern tragedy.

According to Aristotle's first and most influential definition, sketched out in his Poetics, tragedy is a unified action; it is serious, complete, plausible; it has action of substantial extent; it concerns the fall of a man of great reputation (nobility) whose character is good but not perfect and whose misfortune is brought about not by vice or depravity but by some error or fault—the tragic fault or flaw; its incidents arouse pity and fear, and in doing so accomplish the "purgation or catharsis" of these emotions in the audience (Mandel).

Today, tragedy is still held to be a serious work arousing the audience's deepest emotions. The audience must sense and feel a basic sympathy for the protagonist, whose downfall must grip the audience as significant. The tragic hero's decline must not result from chance events, but must come inevitably from some influential decision or enterprise.

While traditionally tragedy has attached a terrifying importance to the destiny of humanity, now it is asked whether in a "debunking and unheroic" age such a vision of human stature can be maintained. Some critics suggest that there are too many sociological and ideological factors working against the tragic temperament. One such critic, sociologist Orrin E. Klapp, writes in "Tragedy and the American Climate of Opinion":

> The objective mediocrity of the modern hero . . . make[s]
> it very unlikely that an impression of grandeur will be
> produced when a man goes to pieces or blows his brains
> out before an American audience. (36)

Klapp feels that in our perceptions of the modern hero we find that
he often reflects themes of our culture. But he is a mystery to us—
even possibly a fool in our eyes (36).

It is evident that society in varying and subtle ways is working
against the tragic sense. Can modern society and modern thought
about the nature of man and his universe allow us to interpret life
in tragic terms? Arthur Miller seems to have answered this
question in Death of a Salesman, in which he claims, along with
many critics, to constitute a tragedy in both form and vision.

Through the character of Willy Loman, Miller attacks the
Aristotelian conception of tragedy as something fit only for kings.
Willy is a reflection of Miller's views of tragedy "and the common
man":

> I think the tragic feeling is evoked in us when we are in
> the presence of a character who is ready to lay down his
> life, if need be, to secure one thing—his sense of personal
> dignity. From Orestes to Hamlet, Medea to Macbeth, the
> underlying struggle is that of the individual attempting to
> gain his "rightful" position in his society. ("Tragedy"
> 1341)

Miller goes on to redefine the concept of the tragic flaw, seeing it
not as a weakness but a strength, the protagonist's "inherent
unwillingness to remain passive in the face of what he conceives to
be a challenge to his dignity, his image of his rightful status"
(1341). According to Miller, this struggle to achieve a place in
society and to preserve one's human dignity is at its greatest in the
common man, and thus he is a natural figure for tragedy.

Willy Loman, a common man, represents a type of living and
thinking which we all share. His values are those of our society—
the pursuit of the American Dream of "making it." Throughout Act
I, Willy brags to his sons that he has the secret of success: "Be

liked and you will never want" (1274). And he claims that he has
achieved it, that he is known "up and down New England" and that
when he parks his car on the street there "the cops protect it like
their own" (1273). But from the opening of the play, when Willy's
"exhaustion is apparent" (1263), it becomes increasingly obvious
that Willy is not the success he had hoped to be. He tells Linda, his
wife: "I am tired to the death. . . . I couldn't make it. I just couldn't
make it, Linda" (1263).

Although Miller gives us a painfully brief moment of hope toward
the end of Act I ("Everything'll be all right," Willy says), we know
that Willy is headed for disaster. When we see his hypocrisy
revealed in Act II in Biff's discovery of the prostitute (the truth
that has poisoned Biff and Willy's relationship), we understand that
Willy's downfall results from his failure to see himself and his
values for what they really are. And when we realize that Willy's
suicide is a final attempt to redeem his failure by selling the only
thing he has left—his own life—for the insurance money, we see
his struggle for dignity, and his tragedy.

Even though Willy fails, however, his struggle elevates him. Critic
John Gassner feels that the audience must sympathize with Willy,
whose struggle is heroic: "Willy is passionately unwilling to resign
himself to failure and the cheat of days. His very agony gives him
tragic stature within the recognizable world of middle class
realities" (26).

Willy Loman is a character capable of arousing our interest,
sympathy, and sense of identification. In him we see a good man
driven to suicide, and in Miller's play a family in despair—a
portrayal of American life that invites us to indulge in a tragic
vision of man's fate. Willy Loman never learns of or acknowledges
the errors of his ways. To the grim end he is a strong believer in
the very ideology that destroys him. And his entire family are
victims, for they have lived in the false dream which he has
created. In the play's concluding "Requiem," Biff expresses Willy's
tragedy, saying, "He had the wrong dreams. All, all, wrong" (1327).

But Charley, Willy's one friend, speaks for his heroism: "A salesman is got to dream, boy. It comes with the territory" (1328).

Although some critics argue that Willy Loman is not a character worthy of tragedy—only a pathetic character who arouses our pity but not our terror—I think that Willy does strike us with a fear: a fear of ourselves, our society, and our own destiny. Willy embodies a certain danger, the menace of failure in our lives. We may think of Willy as a fool, but can we be sure we ourselves aren't headed for the same fate?

Death of a Salesman, when viewed in terms of an "evolved" or modern theory of tragedy, does constitute a contemporary tragic drama. Arthur Miller has successfully created a character who embodies a downfall of significant value to today's audience. In Willy we see and hear a common man lifting his small but notable voice against the hurricane of society. We see in Willy's fate one which we all fear—the shattering of our beliefs and hopes, the shattering of our dreams.

WORKS CITED

Gassner, John. "Tragic Perspectives: A Sequence of Queries." Two Modern American Tragedies. Ed. John D. Hurrell. New York: Scribner's, 1961. 16–27.

Klapp, Orrin E. "Tragedy and the American Climate of Opinion." Two Modern American Tragedies. 28–36.

Mandel, Oscar. "Tragedy." Academic American Encyclopedia. 1981 ed.

Miller, Arthur. Death of a Salesman. Literature: An Introduction. 3rd ed. Ed. X. J. Kennedy. Boston: Little, Brown, 1983. 1262–1328.

———. "Tragedy and the Common Man." Literature: An Introduction. 1340–43.

THE EFFECT OF BIRTH ORDER ON PERSONALITY

Janet Kiefer

English 5

November 14, 1983

OUTLINE

Thesis: Within the family, the different birth order of each child results in a unique environment, which in turn helps produce a different or characteristic personality for each birth order position.

I. The issue of birth order and personality
II. Theoretical background
    A. Alfred Adler
    B. Forer and Very
    C. Ongoing research
III. Major birth orders
    A. First-borns (oldest and only children)
        1. Parents' expectations
        2. Overachievement
        3. Attitude toward authority
        4. Conformity
        5. Educational achievement
    B. Middle- and later-borns
        1. Status of middles
        2. Need to catch up
        3. Popularity
        4. Ability to get along with others
    C. Youngest
        1. Motor skills
        2. Youngest status and treatment
        3. Sense of humor
IV. The use of birth order theory
    A. Attitude toward birth order position
    B. Awareness and changed behavior

Janet Kiefer, "The Effect of Birth Order on Personality." Used by permission.

THE EFFECT OF BIRTH ORDER ON PERSONALITY

What causes personality? It is probably impossible to pinpoint a lone cause, since many different factors have an influence. Heredity, personal experience, and environment all play an important role in the development of personality.

In their attempts to understand how individual personalities are formed, psychologists have tried to isolate and study these various influences. One of the most interesting environmental factors is birth order—the child's position in his family. Students of birth order have theorized that each child grows up in a unique situation, a different one for each birth order position. Although all researchers in this field do not agree on the effect of birth order (Adams 430), and there is still no general or comprehensive theory of birth order (Driscoll and Eckstein 154), childhood environment is acknowledged as a contributing factor in personality development. Within the family, the different birth order of each child results in a unique environment, which in turn helps produce a different or characteristic personality for each birth order position.

Theoretical Background

Alfred Adler, a psychiatrist, personality theorist and colleague of Sigmund Freud in the early years of the century, was the first to fully develop a theory that birth order is related to personality (Bierer 52). Adler believed that many different personality traits resulted from feelings of inferiority or superiority, and that man, in seeking to perfect himself, may strive for superiority or overcompensate for inferiority ("Alfred Adler"). Each birth order position presents situations which lead to the development of these feelings. A person who feels inferior, for instance, will compensate by seeking power, and the degree to which someone seeks or holds power influences his personality (Harris 71). Adler believed that experiences "associated with birth order" influenced the type of personality the child would develop (Driscoll and Eckstein 154).

Since Adler's time there has been a great deal of research into the effect of birth order, not all of it consistent. Psychologists Lucille Forer and Philip S. Very, for example, disagree on the personality characteristics assumed by later children in families of more than three siblings. Forer believes that in four-child families, the second and third children will have middle-child characteristics, while the oldest has those of the first-born, and the youngest those of the last-born. In contrast, Very sees a three-person cycle: the first three children develop traits as though they were the only children in the family (oldest, middle, and youngest); when a fourth is born, he develops the characteristics of a first-born; the fifth develops those of a second-born; the sixth, those of a last-born. After the sixth child, the cycle begins again (Rowley 63). Very claims that spacing causes this, that children associate with their siblings who are closest in age (Bierer 54).

Other researchers question the role of birth order in light of complicating factors such as social class and the methodology of research (Adams 430). However, even though the effect of birth order may be more general than in Adler's theory, it continues to be studied in more strictly controlled experiments, with recent findings pointing up the importance of the child's perception of his birth order over the "mere biological birth position" (Driscoll and Eckstein 154).

Major Birth Orders

Birth orders are usually classified under the following categories: first-born, middle- or later-born, youngest, and only children. First-born and only children have much in common (the oldest was an only child for a while) and so will be discussed together.

Both oldest and only children come first in the family, and parents, because of their excitement and inexperience, tend to expect more from the first child. When he or she reaches one goal, the parents can't wait for the next. (With later children, the parents are not as excited by the child's achievements.) First-borns are often expected to become what their parents are, or are not (Wilson and Edington 13).

This parental pressure often leads to one of the main characteristics of this category: overachievement. According to Driscoll and Eckstein, first-borns "are more likely to score at the upper extremes on intelligence tests, be highly motivated, achieve eminence, and have a high need for achievement." They dominate as winners of National Merit Scholarships and in Who's Who (155). While both the oldest and the only child are achievement oriented, the oldest is even more so because he is trying to regain the attention he had as an only (Bierer 52). Psychologist Irving Harris, in his book The Promised Seed, explains the inferiority feeling of the first-born, which "resides in the fact that he was displaced from parental affection by the next sibling" and so feels "unworthy and envious of the younger" (71).

As an only child, a first-born sees relationships like the one between him and his parents with himself in the lower position. When he becomes an older sibling, however, he sees himself in the authority position of the relationship (Scotland, Sherman, and Shaver 49–50). Because the parents expect the eldest to set examples for the younger children, the oldest often becomes "bossy" in order to make the younger children behave. This attitude then may be carried over to the oldest child's peers, who dislike it (Forer and Still 139).

Another characteristic of first-borns is that they are included in adult activities more than are most other birth orders. (It is easier to include one child; with more than one, parents may be more likely to leave the children with a sitter.) Having become accustomed to being included, first-borns (and especially only children) hate to feel left out (Wilson and Edington 52). In their book <u>Empathy and Birth Order</u>, for instance, Scotland, Sherman, and Shaver report that studies "found that FOs [onlies and oldests grouped together] tended to conform more when they felt moderate acceptance from others, as if they could win more acceptance by conforming" (51).

The first-born's desire for acceptance and his need to achieve may explain one of the most interesting findings of birth order research: that first-born and onlies attain greater educational position and are more likely to attend college (Adams 418). But there is an underside to the first-born and only's success. Both may be more "anxious and fearful" in tense situations, and also more dependent on others for comfort (Adams 421). And it has been found that only children tend to be more prone to psychological disorders (even though they also make the best teachers) (Driscoll and Eckstein 155).

The next major birth order category is the middle- or later-born. Among middle children, two writers, Forer and Still, have distinguished between middles and "later middles" (xvi). The difference between them is that the middle child is often only thought of as the second of three children, and the later middles are between the second and the last-born in a family of four or more. Sometimes, however, middles refers to all children but the eldest and youngest.

Many people think that middle children have things worse in life, and to some extent they're right. Middles often feel out of place, lost in the crowd. To compensate, they may develop interests that are different from those of other family members. But by distinguishing themselves, they can also alienate themselves from the family (Wilson and Edington 94–95).

Later-borns in general feel a need to catch up to their older siblings. They often find themselves being compared to their elders, and unable to compete. Avoiding comparison is thus another reason for developing different interests (Bierer 52). Sometimes, however, they can't avoid the competition, and they become good at it. According to Forer, the practice of competing in childhood helps middles when they become adults and enter the business world (57–58).

It would seem that middle children, who may become competitive, would be unpopular, but in fact they are more likely to be popular, perhaps because they know how to deal with the competition. Later-borns don't feel they are in authority positions, and so learn to cooperate with others better than do first-borns (Markus 36). Loretta Bierer explains that "later-born children tend to be more friendly and less demanding than first-borns. This is especially true of the middle child who—because of his experience in dealing with an older, more powerful sibling and a demanding younger one—develops extraordinary skills in handling others" (52). While middles may be outsiders in their families, in other words, they usually are not among their peers.

Besides their experience with others, later middles have the quality of friendliness because of their parents. After the first few children, the parents begin to calm down. Parents' actions (affection and punishment, for example) are divided among the children rather than being directed only at one child. The younger ones are under less pressure than their older brothers and sisters. They are more used to relationships with peers and can better handle them (Forer and Still 142–43).

Like the first-born, the youngest child has a more clearly defined place (Driscoll and Eckstein 155). Since he has more role models than his older siblings, he tends to develop motor skills earlier (Bierer 53). Especially during his first year, this may make him look like the achiever in the family, even though that role is generally filled by the first-born.

The baby of the family is usually either treated kindly (sometimes pampered), or he is ridiculed. The treatment he receives affects the way he treats others. If he's treated well, he will respond to others similarly. On the other hand, if he is teased by others, he may become distrustful, easily angered, and shy (Forer and Still 62–63, 144–45). If the youngest child finds himself unable to compete with his older siblings, he may lose his self-confidence (Bierer 53). Older brothers and sisters are able to see younger siblings holding ideas and feelings that <u>they</u> felt at that age, and they feel better knowing they weren't alone. But the youngest child doesn't see others with these feelings, and he begins to feel abnormal. As a result, he may doubt his judgment (Wilson and Edington 113).

However, the youngest also receives certain benefits. He is more likely to have a sense of humor. The youngest child grows up making jokes about authority figures (Wilson and Edington 116). He learns to enjoy watching his elders squirm because of his actions, which help him feel superior to them.

The Use of Birth Order Theory

No one should assume that his life will automatically follow a direct pattern as explained by birth order. However, the way a child feels about his position in the family can influence his behavior and the development of his personality. According to Driscoll and Eckstein:

> The oldest child, who is given much attention until the second is born, may become so discouraged by the fall from power (dethronement) as to develop hostility toward others and insecurity. The second child may walk in the shadow of the older sibling, whom he or she—a "striver"—seeks to overtake. The youngest child tends to be spoiled and may shrink from competition with others. . . . The only (lonely) child tends to be spoiled by parents and may devote the rest of his or her life trying to regain the favored position. (155)

By the same token, a person might be able to use his knowledge of birth order and personality to change his negative attitudes or actions (Forer and Still 251). For example, one might be less bothered by another's overbearing personality when he realizes the other is a first-born. Similarly, the first-born may try to be less dominant over another who resists it.

A person isn't doomed to failure or promised success because of his birth order. But still, it does appear to be a significant influence. Dr. Philip Very (quoted by Gordon Rowley):

> Anybody can be anything he wants. It's all relative. I know a second-born who is a full professor at an Ivy League college. Not bad . . . for a second-born. But his first-born brother, also a scholar, is a Nobel Prize winner! You see, it's all relative. (118)

WORKS CITED

Adams, Bert N. "Birth Order: A Critical Review." Sociometry 35.3 (1972): 411–439.

"Adler, Alfred." Encyclopedia Britannica: Micropaedia. 1978 ed.

Bierer, Loretta M. "Firstborn, Lastborn." Parents March 1980: 52–55.

Driscoll, R. E., and D. G. Eckstein. "Birth Order and Personality." Encyclopedia of Psychology. 1984 ed.

Forer, Lucille, and Henry Still. The Birth Order Factor: How Your Personality Is Influenced by Your Place in the Family. New York: McKay, 1976.

Harris, Irving D. The Promised Seed: A Comparative Study of Eminent First and Later Sons. London: Free Press of Glencoe, 1964.

Markus, Hazel. "Sibling Personalities: The Luck of the Draw." Psychology Today June 1981: 35–37.

Rowley, Gordon E. "How Birth Order Affects Your Personality." Saturday Evening Post Nov. 1980: 62–63, 118.

Scotland, Ezra, Stanley E. Sherman, and Kelly G. Shaver. <u>Empathy and Birth Order: Some Experimental Explorations</u>. Lincoln: University of Nebraska Press, 1971.

Wilson, Bradford, and George Edington. <u>First Child, Second Child: Your Birth Order Profile</u>. New York: McGraw-Hill, 1981.

INDEX